Will Grohmann   **Wassily Kandinsky**   **Life and Work**

Will Grohmann

Wassily Kandinsky

Life and Work

Harry N. Abrams, Inc., New York

Library of Congress Catalog Card Number: 58-13479

All rights reserved. No part of the contents of this book

may be reproduced without the written permission

of Harry N. Abrams, Incorporated.

Milton S. Fox, Editor

Translated from the German by Norbert Guterman

Printed and bound in Japan

Contents

The reproductions in this book, including color plates, gravure plates, halftones, and line drawings, are referred to by page number; the CC-numbers refer to the Classified Catalogue.

Preface

This book is a biography of Wassily Kandinsky, painter and thinker. It is not an analysis of abstract painting, as this founder of superobjective art illustrated it. We have used as our source material, not only his paintings, watercolors, drawings, and prints, but also his books, essays, and notes, as well as his letters (in so far as they were available), particularly those addressed to Gabriele Münter for the early part of his career, and those addressed to this writer for the period following his return from Moscow in 1921. The existing artistic and literary documentation was greatly enriched in 1957, thanks to the Gabriele Münter Foundation (Städtische Galerie, Munich).

The author has primarily been concerned with the paintings; the catalogue of Kandinsky's works, added to the biography, is based on the painter's own records, but the data concerning ownership have been brought up to date. Only some of the exhibitions have been listed, for reasons of space. Preference has been given to those watercolors which served as preliminary studies for paintings; Kandinsky kept a record of them from 1922 on. He listed some of the oil studies and tempera pictures separately: this list is appended, with a supplementary one of paintings and studies discovered later.

The author has refrained from listing or reproducing all the early studies—among others, those included in the Gabriele Münter Foundation—in order to avoid overemphasis on the early periods. However, sufficient place has been given to the works prior to Murnau, 1908. Details will be found in the prefaces to the catalogues and in the Bibliography.

The Catalogue of Works includes: first, the works Kandinsky himself kept a record of, arranged chronologically; and then, also in chronological order, the works discovered later. As the reader will often find the paintings treated in groups, all the more care was taken to preserve chronological order in the Catalogue.

The author feels indebted, first and most deeply, to Mrs. Nina Kandinsky, the painter's widow, for her helpful collaboration, for making available the materials in her possession, as well as for her permission to reproduce them. In the years since Kandinsky's death, Nina Kandinsky has taken exemplary care of the works in her collection, and, in

7

conjunction with her associates, the Galerie Aimé Maeght in Paris, has done everything possible to make the works accessible to the public. The author also wishes to express his thanks to the Solomon R. Guggenheim Museum in New York, which houses the largest and most important Kandinsky collection in the world, and to its director, James Johnson Sweeney, for permission to study the works in its possession, with the aid of more than a hundred photos, and for permission to reproduce them. Thanks are due also to the Museum of Modern Art, New York, for permission to use its archives and library, and to Mr. Bernard Karpel, Librarian of the Museum, who prepared a comprehensive bibliography, and was helpful in many other ways. It would take too much space to thank individually all the co-operating museums and private collectors; mention of their names should be taken to imply gratitude for their assistance. Special thanks are due to Mr. G. David Thompson of Pittsburgh, for his personal help; to Mr. Karl Gutbrod for his efforts in behalf of this book, and to Mr. Müller-Kraus of Stockholm, for his co-operation. Mr. Kenneth C. Lindsay was so kind as to let me see his very valuable dissertation on microfilm as well as his catalogue of the Kandinsky exhibitions. My work owes a great deal to his friendliness and his research. The Bibliography contains additional notice of works I found helpful.

May I, finally, thank the Verlag DuMont Schauberg in Cologne, as well as the publishing houses associated with it: Harry N. Abrams, Inc., New York; Flammarion, Paris; and Il Saggiatore di Alberto Mondadori Editore, Milan, for their intelligent co-operation and their efforts to give this book its present form.   W.G.

I The Man and the Artist

Fourteen years after his death, and almost fifty years after he had created his first abstract painting, Kandinsky's name is universally known. The Italian artist Prampolini calls him "the Giotto of our time," the painter who brought painting back to life. His closest friends, Paul Klee and Franz Marc, were already on record that during the crucial years of the rebirth of European art, Kandinsky was far in the vanguard and supplied them with courage to go on. His uncompromising attitude to life and art, his faith in the unconquerability of the human spirit, came with him from Russia. He remained Russian to the last, although both by blood and spirit he was related to western Europe as well as to Asia. However, from his thirtieth year on, from 1896 to his death in 1944, he lived in Germany and in Paris, except for a seven-year stay in Moscow between 1914 and 1921.

Kandinsky the man has remained for most people as great a mystery as Kandinsky the artist. Although he was in contact with a very large number of his contemporaries, with prominent personalities, and during his Bauhaus period, with hundreds of students, and was frank and informal in manner, most people know little about him beyond the fact that he was aristocratic in appearance, and possessed both integrity and amiability. He struck his contemporaries as more like a diplomat or a widely traveled scholar than as an artist. Only his closest friends and pupils knew how kind he was, let alone the full range of his spiritual and creative gifts. Even they sensed a solitary greatness in this man who remained a foreigner despite all the attraction he felt toward Europe, its problems and achievements, and regardless of the friendship and respect it showed to him. He clung to the Greek Orthodox Church and to a faith in his native land. He read the Russian classics, loved Russian music, and was happy whenever he could speak Russian. His marriage with a Russian woman kept alive his sense of being a Russian, especially in his own home. If Kandinsky, for all his cheerfulness, struck many of his friends as cold and aloof, it was because he had remained different. Moreover, he wanted to keep the secret of his inner being, as well as that of his work. "To express mystery in terms of mystery" is one of his characteristic utterances. Here lies the solution, perhaps, to many riddles presented by his life, including his separation

from the very Germanic Gabriele Münter, and his happy marriage later to a far younger woman who respected his secret.

The more Kandinsky became aware of his psychic constitution, the more he developed a capacity to control himself, or, as an Oriental would say, to save face. He always dressed with meticulous care, spoke quietly and attentively, and was never wounding. He behaved impeccably even in painful situations, such as the nature of his profession and teaching activities did not fail to bring about. He always treated others with consideration. He sought to reduce the tensions around him, and in the Bauhaus conflicts was a prudent negotiator, genuinely in search of a solution. He never gave up, until the voice of reason was overwhelmed by brute force.

Few men can boast of having been close to Kandinsky. During the Blaue Reiter years, Franz Marc's courage protected his older friend, and it was his intelligence and worldly wisdom that helped bring their common plans to fruition. After the First World War, when Kandinsky came back from Russia, he found a friend in Paul Klee, who had in the meantime developed from an unassuming draftsman into an artist of his own stature. Together at the Bauhaus, they became intimate, and no cloud ever troubled their relationship. In the catalogue of the exhibition held on the occasion of Kandinsky's sixtieth birthday, Klee wrote these words: "I might have been his pupil and perhaps I was, for on many occasions things he said have given me encouragement and illumination ... Our feelings for each other have never changed ... And today I am waving to him from the West. I see him taking a step toward me." Klee said "from the West," for the moment forgetting his own non-European blood. But Kandinsky's remoteness from Europe was greater. This became clear in Paris, when he lived among Mediterranean men, to whom the East—Moscow, Byzantium, Eastern Asia—was alien. His new friendships were not close; as for his fellow countrymen there, most had become French. Kandinsky was always most comfortable in his own home and when traveling. He preferred chance acquaintances to half-friendships, and changes of scenery made it easier for him, once he had quitted his homeland, to be a citizen of the world. Such a status suited him better, as it also suited many of his friends. He felt closer to them than to his neighbors in Paris.

His faith in the spirit was also a faith in the future. He never ceased hoping that the nightmare which poisoned the last years of his life would one day end, and that he would be free to continue his work unhindered and successful. He was denied the fulfillment of this hope in his lifetime, but his work rose to new heights during the Paris years, comparable to the Blaue Reiter period.

Kandinsky demanded more of himself than did his contemporaries. He was unable to stop and rest at any phase of his development, and let the public catch up with him. The storm and stress of the Munich years produced, first, mythical landscapes in which he achieved color tones of an unprecedented intensity and freedom. Then he went on to the romantic *Improvisations* and *Compositions,* the first seven of which, painted before 1914, are symphonies possessing a life of their own. The fact that they are nonobjective seems to us today less important than their inner music and their direct power of persuasion. His writings of this period are as musical as they are religious, suggesting an artistic gospel. Today it seems incomprehensible that his

early works should have been so little understood, even arousing a hatred such as has seldom occurred in the history of art. But next came the cold paintings of the Bauhaus period, in which intuition and knowledge have attained a Neo-Classical balance. "The hidden," the "mysterious," which was always a part of Kandinsky's nature, retreated behind the logos. This was the period of circles, architectonic order, and essays on the theory of art. But Kandinsky did not abandon his enduring theme—"the Absolute in the seriousness of its world-creating play." Later works in Paris abound in new forms and unreal colors. After Romanticism and Neo-Classicism appears a kind of Baroque of great inventiveness, which derived from his creative intuition like his previous works, but at the same time concretized the spiritual in a mysterious way. Now the inner melody became the image, beauty "the end beyond the end." The wheel comes full circle: the paintings of the Paris period become myth, like those of the Blaue Reiter period before them. If the earlier works make us think of Moscow and the early Stravinsky, while the later "cold" ones make us think of Schönberg's twelve-tone scale, we can find no analogy for the works of the last period with their evocation of the Far East. Severity of form is combined with previously unheard sounds and images yet unseen, which oblige us to recall the Mongolian components in Kandinsky's ancestry. The "multidimensional simultaneity" referred to by Klee is here contributed by a world-historical force.

Kandinsky's influence on young artists is today greater than it was during his lifetime. Imitators apart, his influence is clearly discernible in Abstract Expressionism, and in the application of mathematical concepts to painting. When the young French painter Manessier writes: "We have to discover a language or a system of signs which will preserve as one both the sensory world as stimulus and the spiritual world as ultimate revelation," he comes close to the early Kandinsky, albeit with a thoroughly modern awareness. The same is true of Jean Bazaine, Afro, Winter, Nay, and many other painters. On the other hand, when Max Bill speaks of paintings as "thoughts become form," he, like many others of his contemporaries and juniors (Richard Mortensen, for example), echoes the master of the Bauhaus period. Between these extremes lie conceptions unrelated to Kandinsky's achievement, for all that his achievement paved the way for the later developments. If a poll of painters were taken, asking which modern master has exerted the greatest influence, it is quite certain that Kandinsky would win. "What is training?" Kandinsky wrote to the author on November 1, 1934. "It is decadent to appropriate outer forms, but in fact training looks to the future...It means inner fecundation."

Only in Russia has Kandinsky's art left no trace. Situated as it is between Europe and Asia, it might have normally given direction to the forces he unleashed. Presumably the works of his last period would especially have appealed to his land. Wanderer between two worlds, Kandinsky was denied this satisfaction in his lifetime, but the day may yet come, when his influence both in Russia and the rest of the world will become effective, for the interpenetration of East and West, begun with Goethe's *Westöstlicher Divan*, is irresistibly marching on.

Cover of Catalogue of an Exhibition at the Izdebsky
gallery, Odessa. Woodcut, 1911

II The Years in Russia

Youth, Academic Career and Early Impressions of Art

1866-1896

Kandinsky was born in Moscow, on December 4, 1866, at a time when Russia was going through a phase of political and cultural progress. Under the regime of Czar Alexander II serfdom was abolished (in 1861), the educational system was improved by reorganization on the German pattern, restrictions on foreign travel were lifted, and many exiles were permitted to come back from Siberia. Among those who came back were Kandinsky's parents, who had spent several decades in Kyakhta, a Siberian city on the border of Mongolia, a center of the tea trade, the eastern section of which belonged to China. Kandinsky's father had been born in Kyakhta. There was Mongolian blood in his family: one of the painter's great-grandmothers was a Mongolian princess. His mother, Lydia Tikheeva, came of a Moscow family. Wassily Kandinsky grew up in this ancient capital of the Czars; its cathedrals and palaces, chiming bells, and rich colors were to haunt him to the end of his life. In 1871 the family moved to Odessa, and during his stay there Kandinsky often longed to be back in the sacred city on the Moskva River. "Every city has one face, but Moscow has ten faces," he would say. Later, when he spoke of Moscow, his early childhood impressions fused with those of his student years into a single symphony of colors and sounds, in which history and landscape, the Kremlin and the hills by the river, man and his environment form an indissoluble unity, transcending individual motives and themes. For Kandinsky, Moscow was the epitome of Russia. He regarded it as the source of his artistic aspirations, as his pictorial tuning fork. "I have the feeling that it has always been so," he wrote, "and that at bottom I have always painted this single 'model' merely strengthening the expression and perfecting the form over the years." Like Nietzsche, he saw in Russia, down to the First World War, Europe's great opportunity. At the same time Moscow was for him the symbol of the Orthodox religion, the true faith of the Eastern Church with all its saints. After he moved to western Europe, he never failed to attend Easter services in a Russian church. During his Bauhaus period he went every Easter to Dresden, where there was a Russian church.

The 1860s marked a high point in Russian culture. Tolstoy's *War and Peace* was published serially between 1864 and 1869; Dostoevsky's *Crime and Punishment* appeared in 1869, and Goncharov's *Ravine* in 1870. Pushkin, Lermontov, and Gogol were read by all the educated. The leading composers were Borodin, Mussorgsky (*Boris Godunov*, 1868–1871), and Rimsky-Korsakov (whose first Russian symphony was performed publicly in 1865). Creative writing and music were now Russian through and through, and for that very reason aroused the interest of the elite of western Europe, for the first time enjoying a glimpse into the nature of Russia and its peoples.

The fine arts, however, did not share in this flowering. It cannot be said that Russia was without traditions in this field. Such a statement would be truer of literature and music. But the great achievements represented by the cathedrals of Novgorod, Vladimir-Suzdal, and Moscow, and the fame of the classical painted icons went very far back into the past, and modern Russians were no longer aware of this past as their own. In contrast, they welcomed the influence of Europe with open arms. As early as the fifteenth century, Italian architects had worked in Moscow, though they kept strictly to ancient Russian models (Uspensky Cathedral, Granevitaia Palata). From the eighteenth century on, Italian, French, and German artists were active in Russia, executing orders for the court and the nobility. Only around 1800, in the pseudo-classical period, did native Russian architects and painters appear.

In the 1880s the fine arts had sunk to a low level, not unlike the situation in Russia today. Painting was naturalistic in style, and subordinated to political and social theories. An organization, formed in 1870 to send exhibitions of paintings all over Russia, sought to propagate the tendentious art of the period in the provinces. This art remained dominant until the turn of the century. Only after Serge Diaghilev, who later organized the Russian Ballet, had founded the periodical *Mir Iskustva* ("The World of Art") in 1898 (publication continued until 1904), gathering around him such talented innovators as V. Serov, M. A. Vrubel, Bakst, and K. A. Somov, did a change take place. By then Kandinsky had left Moscow. But it is probable that before leaving Moscow in 1896, he had been acquainted with the works in the Petersburg Rococo style by Somov, and those of some other artists, who reflected the prevalent Victorian tendencies.

The circumstances, both personal and environmental, of Kandinsky's childhood and youth, he has described himself in *Backward Glances*, an autobiography written in 1913, and in conversations. He speaks with great reverence of his father (p. 18) who, he says, was very patient with him, displaying great understanding for his childish dreams and moodiness. Kandinsky's father had studied in Moscow, and later was manager of a Russian tea firm. He must have recognized his son's artistic inclinations at an early date, for he engaged a private drawing teacher for him. Kandinsky was ten when his father explained to him the difference between the *gymnasium* with its curriculum emphasizing humanistic studies and the *realgymnasium* which stressed science, and left it up to him to choose between the two. The boy chose the *gymnasium*. As was common in Russian upper class families, his father took the position that children had a right to their own lives, and that their relations with their parents should be based on confidence and friendship. He had "a deeply human and loving soul," Kandinsky says. He understood the spirit of Moscow, and it was a pleasure to listen to his stories about the city, its history, landmarks, and churches. At the age of twenty Kandinsky drew one of these churches (p. 15) with great accuracy.

Church in Moscow. Drawing. 1886

·As we have said, the family moved to Odessa in 1871; the reason for this was the father's health. Every summer he went back to Moscow for a few weeks, and from his thirteenth year Kandinsky went with him on these trips. At the age of nineteen, when he began his university studies, he moved to Moscow. In Odessa the family felt somewhat out of their element, and Kandinsky kept few memories of this city. However, later on he was to mention it occasionally, for example, in the notes on exhibitions from 1903 to 1914, which Kandinsky recorded in his private catalogue, and later during the Bauhaus period, when his father died at Odessa in 1926. The friendly relations between father and son remained undisturbed throughout. His father came to stay with Kandinsky while he was living at Munich, Rapallo, and Sèvres.

Kandinsky's mother was a native of Moscow (p. 18), and the ideal image he kept of her in his heart coincides, according his notes, with that of "golden-haired Mother Moscow." She was characterized by inexhaustible energy and marked nervousness, but also by a strikingly austere beauty, majestic calm, and self-control—the same duality that is to be noted in the external appearance of Moscow, yet all of a piece. There are no somber spots in his recollections of these years; probably the fact that he had been so far away, and for so long, from both Moscow and his parents at the time he wrote about them, helped him to put his early years in such a clear light, although he must have gone through severe ordeals. Because of their difference in temperament, the parents were divorced while Kandinsky was still a child, but mother and son remained close, and the latter transferred his love for her to his two stepsisters (p. 19).

His mother's older sister, Elizabeta Tikheeva (p. 19) played an important role in the artist's life. Kandinsky speaks of her inner purity and her great influence on his development. She supervised his games, and he kept a pleasant memory of the racing game, recalling particularly a certain ocher-colored horse. He liked it so much that he suddenly felt he was home again when he happened to see a similar horse one day in the streets of Munich. "It was one of my earliest impressions, and the strongest single one," he wrote in 1913. "It brought back to life the little lead horse, and it associated Munich with my childhood years ... My love for such horses has not left me to this day." Horses and riders emerge time and again in Kandinsky's early pictures, and the device of the review founded by Kandinsky and Franz Marc in 1911 was a Blue Rider. Kandinsky also mentions another game, which he calls "riding," and for which the family coachman would peel off strips of bark from green birches. The color of the wood was white, the bark was green inside and brown-yellow outside; white, green, and yellow brown were colors that always retained an emotional significance for him. This game is the source of the theme of the *troika*, the Russian three-horse team, which he painted many times.

With his grandmother, Kandinsky read fairytales, the Russian ones, but especially German ones, for his maternal grandmother was a Balt and spoke German. "I grew up half-German; my first language, my first books were German," he wrote to Gabriele Münter on November 16, 1904. A month earlier he had emphasized the fact that he was "Russian and yet un-Russian." He recalled these German fairytales later in Munich, when he saw the old quarters near the Promenadeplatz, Maximilianplatz, and in Schwabing and the Au. The blue tramcars and the yellow mailboxes brought back memories of the fairytales; he associated the yellow of the mailbox with "the song of the canary." It is noteworthy how Kandinsky responded to words and ideas. The "medieval" pictures painted during his Munich years after his graduation from the Academy were based on such recollections and impressions.

The connection between fairytales and reality was cemented by a trip to Rothenburg, which Kandinsky referred to as an "unreal" trip. "I felt as though a magic power contrary to all natural laws had transported me, back over the centuries, ever deeper into the past." On his return to Munich Kandinsky painted *Old City* (1902, CC 3) from memory. "In this painting, too, I actually tried to express a certain hour, which always was and still is the most beautiful time of day in Moscow. The sun is quite low ...

1 Wassily Kandinsky, Paris, 1935

2

3

4

18

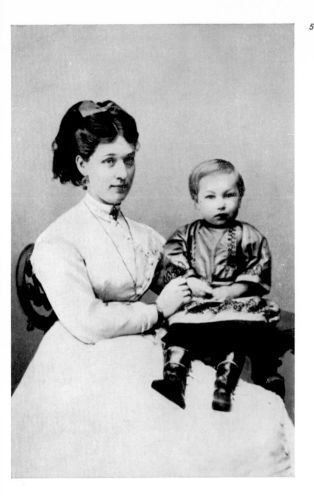

5

6

7

2 Wassily and Nina Kandinsky, Berlin 1933
  Wassily und Nina Kandinsky
  Wassily et Nina Kandinsky.   Wassily e Nina Kandinsky

3 Kandinsky's mother. Portrait painted by an Italian painter
  in Rome
  Kandinskys Mutter, von einem italienischen Maler in Rom
  gemalt
  La mère de Kandinsky. Portrait peint par un artiste italien,
  à Rome
  La madre di Kandinsky. Ritratto eseguito a Roma da un
  pittore italiano

4 Kandinsky's father   Kandinskys Vater
  Le père de Kandinsky   Il padre di Kandinsky

5 Kandinsky (aged two) with his mother in Moscow
  Der zweijährige Kandinsky mit seiner Mutter in Moskau
  Kandinsky (âgé de deux ans) avec sa mère à Moscou
  Kandinsky (all'età di due anni) con sua madre a Mosca

6 Elisabeta Tikheeva, Kandinsky's aunt and governess
  Elisabeth Ticheeva, Kandinskys Tante und Erzieherin
  Elisabeth Ticheeva, tante et gouvernante de Kandinsky
  Elisabeth Ticheeva, zia ed educatrice di Kandinsky

7 Kandinsky as schoolboy with his stepbrother and stepsister,
  Odessa, 1876
  Kandinsky als Gymnasiast mit seinen Stiefgeschwistern
  Kandinsky, collégien, avec son demi-frère et sa demi-soeur
  Kandinsky studente coi suoi fratellastri

19

8

10

8 *Kandinsky's diary with a drawing made during his trip to Vologda, 1889*
Kandinskys Notizbuch mit Eintragungen von der Wologda-Reise, 1889
Carnet de Kandinsky avec des notes du voyage à Vologda, 1889
Agenda di Kandinsky con note sul viaggio a Vologda, 1889

9 *Two pages from Kandinsky's catalogue*
Zwei Seiten aus dem Werkverzeichnis Kandinskys
Deux pages du catalogue de l'oeuvre de Kandinsky
Due pagine del catalogo di Kandinsky

10 *Kandinsky in Munich, 1913*
Kandinsky in München
Kandinsky à Munich   Kandinsky a Monaco

11 *Kandinsky in Paris   Kandinsky in Paris, 1934*
Kandinsky à Paris   Kandinsky a Parigi

12

13

12 Nina Kandinsky, Dessau, 1927

13 Kandinsky in his Dessau Studio, 1932
   Kandinsky in seinem Dessauer Atelier
   Kandinsky dans son atelier à Dessau
   Kandinsky nel suo atelier a Dessau

14 Kandinsky in Munich, 1908
   Kandinsky in München
   Kandinsky à Munich
   Kandinsky a Monaco

15

17
18

20

15 Kandinsky, seated; standing from left to
right: Maria Marc, Franz Marc, Bernhard
Köhler, Campendonk, Thomas von
Hartmann (photo dating from the Blaue
Reiter period)

Kandinsky sitzend; dahinter stehend von
links nach rechts: Maria Marc, Franz
Marc, Bernhard Köhler, Campendonk,
Thomas von Hartmann (Gruppenbild aus
der Zeit des Blauen Reiter)

Kandinsky assis; derrière lui, de gauche à
droite: Maria Marc, Franz Marc, Bernhard
Köhler, Campendonk, Thomas von
Hartmann (Photo de la période du
‹Cavalier Bleu›)

Kandinsky seduto; in piedi da sinistra a
destra: Maria Marc, Franz Marc, Bernhard
Köhler, Campendonk, Thomas von
Hartmann (Gruppo fotografico del periodo
del ‹Cavaliere Azzurro›)

16 Franz Marc. Portrait by August Macke, 1910
Porträtiert von August Macke
Portrait par August Macke
Ritratto dipinto da August Macke

17 Alexej von Jawlensky. Self-Portrait, 1905
Selbstbildnis
Portrait par lui-même
Autoritratto

18 August Macke. Self-Portrait Selbstbildnis, 1909
   Portrait par lui-même Autoritratto

19 Arnold Schönberg. Self-Portrait Selbstbildnis, 1912
   Portrait par lui-même Autoritratto

20 Paul Klee. Painted by Gabriele Münter, 1913
   Gemalt von Gabriele Münter
   Peint par Gabriele Münter
   Dipinto da Gabriele Münter

21 Kandinsky's dining room. Dessau, Burgkühnauer Allee 6, 1926
   Kandinskys Speisezimmer
   Salle à manger de Kandinsky
   Sala da pranzo di Kandinsky

22 Kandinsky's Studio. Neuilly-sur-Seine, 1934
   Kandinskys Atelier
   L'atelier de Kandinsky
   L'atelier di Kandinsky

23

25

27

23 *Kandinsky and Klee in their garden, Dessau, 1929*
   Kandinsky und Klee in ihrem Garten
   Kandinsky et Klee dans leur jardin
   Kandinsky e Klee nel loro giardino

24 *Wassily and Nina Kandinsky. Berlin-Südende, 1933*

25 *Kandinsky and Stokowski, Dessau, 1930*

26 *Wassily and Nina Kandinsky, Mrs. Schönberg, Arnold*
   Schönberg, Wörther See, 1927
   Die Ehepaare Kandinsky und Schönberg, Wörther See, 1927
   Wassily et Nina Kandinsky, Mme Schoenberg, Arnold
   Schoenberg, Wörther See, 1927
   Wassily e Nina Kandinsky, la signora Schoenberg,
   Arnold Schoenberg, Wörther See, 1927

27 *Kandinsky and Grohmann, Berlin, 1933*

*28 Kandinsky, Walter Gropius, **J. J. P. Oud**, Weimar, 1923*

29

30

32

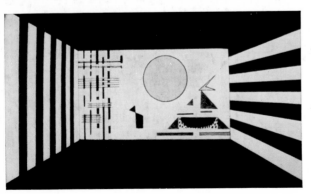

28

another few minutes and it will have turned red from its exertions . . . It melts down the whole of Moscow into a single puddle, which, like a mad bass tuba sets all one's inwardness, one's soul, vibrating. But no, it is not this red uniformity that is the most beautiful hour! This is merely the final chord of the symphony, which brings each color to supreme life, which makes all Moscow vibrate, like the fortissimo of a gigantic orchestra. Pink, lavender, yellow, white, blue, pistachio green, the flaming red houses, the churches—each an independent song—the frantically green lawns, the deeper tones of the trees . . . the red, rigid, silent ring of the Kremlin walls, and above them, towering above everything else, like a cry of triumph, like a delirious hallelujah, the white, long, daintily serious line of the Ivan Veliky spire. And on its high neck . . . the golden head of the dome, which is the sun of Moscow among the golden and many-colored stars of the other domes. To paint these times of day, I thought, was the most impossible, the supreme happiness an artist could ever know." As the years went by, the German fairytales and legends became inseparable from the Russian ones, so that we cannot tell which stories are referred to in Kandinsky's pictures, all the less so because their basic themes are related. However, in the costumes of the figures, the German Middle Ages predominate.

Among Kandinsky's childhood memories there emerge moments of unconscious inner tension, of "inward trembling" during the waking hours, and of dreams full of terror or joy during the night. He composed poems, but only drawing took him "beyond space and time," out of himself. His color memories go back as far as his third year. Sap green, carmine red, ocher yellow, black and white made the greatest impression on him, but the objects were forgotten. He clearly remembered a wall clock in his grandparents' apartment—namely, the white of the dial, and the carmine red of the rose painted on it.

At the age of three he went to Italy with his parents and Russian governess, and he was later able to recall the forest of columns at St. Peter's, the black carriage in which he crossed a bridge in Florence with his mother, black water and a long black boat with a black box in the middle (Venice), and he re-experienced his fears on that occasion. Black always signified fear for him. As a very small child he once painted a dappled horse in watercolor. He put in everything except the hoofs, which he planned to paint after his helpful aunt returned. But he could not wait so long; he put as much black as possible on his brush, and suddenly four spots were stuck on the horse's legs, which struck him as "repulsive." This misfortune had lasting effects; later it was quite a torment for him to put pure black on canvas. While staying in Florence, Kandinsky was sent to a nursery school and had to communicate with Italian children. This does not seem to have been difficult for him; from the outset he had a gift for languages.

Little is known about the nine years he attended the *gymnasium* at Odessa. Kandinsky learned easily, but had no special interest in any subject. He drew and painted and took piano and cello lessons. During the vacation months he went with his family to summer resorts in the Caucasus and the Crimean peninsula; on one occasion he took a boat trip with his father to the Kazan province, where he was struck by the diversity of the nationalities in that part of Russia.

Kandinsky-Exhibition. Moscow, 1920

Kandinsky's design for Cup: Leningrad Porcelain Manufacture, 1919

-33 Three designs for Mussorgsky's 'Pictures at an Exhibition' Dessau, 1928

At the age of thirteen or fourteen, in Odessa, he bought himself a paintbox and oil paints. To see the paint coming out of the tubes was a great experience, which he recalled in detail much later. "Jubilant, solemn, meditative, dreamy, self-absorbed, serious or roguish, sighing with relief or deeply aggrieved, defiant and resistant, soft and yielding, stubborn, self-controlled, sensitive, precariously balanced, those peculiar things called "colors" emerged one after another—living creatures, independent, endowed with all the properties necessary for a life of their own, ready to submit to new combinations, to mix with each other, and to create infinite series of new worlds... It often seemed to me that when the brush tore into these living colors with its inflexible will, the sound of its tearing made music." Even though in retrospect Kandinsky may have exaggerated the rich complexity of the experience, he must even then possessed a great sensitivity to color, and a feeling for the relationships between color and musical sound. These youthful experiences lead in a straight line to later experiences described in his account of his Munich years.

It might be supposed that after Kandinsky obtained his bachelor's degree, he would have chosen the career of artist. The fact that he did not become a painter at that time, that at the age of nineteen he entered the University of Moscow to study law and economics may perhaps be accounted for by the circumstance that the vocation of artist was looked upon as unusual in his family, and that he was deterred by the risks involved in such a venture. "I found my capacities too weak to justify abandoning my other duties." Art was for him something so far beyond ordinary affairs as to be almost inaccessible. His only confidence was in his intelligence.

Kandinsky took his studies seriously, and painted only in his infrequent spare time; still, he painted. In the Russian edition of *Backward Glances* (1918) he reports that as a student he painted many church interiors in Moscow, in strong colors, copying the ornaments on the church walls. He studied economics, his special subject, under Professor A. J. Chuprov; Roman law, the refined "structure" of which fascinated him, though he was repelled by its inflexible logic; and criminal law, which he judged very much in the spirit of Lombroso. He was particularly interested in the history of Russian law, and the old peasant code, which he liked because it is not a *ius strictum,* but flexible, and adjusted to the requirements of human nature. Its guiding principle is, "According to each man"; not the action itself (reality), but the root or origin of the action (abstraction) is good or evil. Inner precision lies in the depths, form is exclusively determined by inwardness. One is reminded a little of his concept of "inner necessity," which he was to define in the Blaue Reiter period. What he chiefly gained from his studies, he thought, was the capacity for abstract thinking.

During his university years Kandinsky participated to some extent in student affairs, and in the All-Russian student organization which was directed against the reactionary university statute of 1885, and against bureaucratic abuses. The 1880s were a very agitated time; Russia, whose expansionist policies were resisted everywhere, sought to preserve autocratic rule at home against both reformists and nihilists. Sharing the students' aspirations for self rule, Kandinsky became involved in politics, but his scientific and artistic interests kept him out of trouble.

In 1889 the Society for Natural Science, Ethnography, and Anthropology sent him to the northern province of Vologda to report on the peasant laws and survivals of paganism among the local Syryenian tribes. During this trip he executed drawings, some of them in a small diary (p. 20, 8), and made a study of peasant architecture and decoration. The results were printed in the publication of the Society, which elected him member shortly before he was admitted to the university's Juridical Society. In 1892 Kandinsky passed his law examination; in 1893, on the basis of a paper on the law governing workers' wages, he was appointed instructor. In 1896 he was offered a professorship at the University of Dorpat, but by then his interest in art had become so overpowering that he rejected the offer, giving up his academic career. At the age of thirty he went to Munich to devote himself to painting.

During his scientific expedition to the Vologda province Kandinsky had discovered folk art in its original form. Traveling by train, small steamer, and cart through villages, woods, marshes, and sandy deserts, he had the feeling of being on another planet. People in their local costumes moved about like pictures come to life; their houses were decorated with colorful carvings, and inside on the walls were hung popular prints and icons; furniture and other household objects were painted with large ornamental designs that almost dissolved them into color. Kandinsky had the impression of moving about inside of pictures, of living inside pictures—an experience of which he later became quite conscious when he invited the beholder to "take a walk" in his pictures, and tried "to compel him to forget himself, to dissolve himself in the picture." Thus, seven years before Munich he had fairly clear ideas of his own as to the possibilities of art. Also, his sense for the concealed, the hidden, the indirect was already present; he became aware of it during his Vologda trip, and felt that it preserved him from confusing genuine with spurious folk art. In Kandinsky's further development the concept of "the hidden" played an increasingly important part, and his abandonment of objective painting may be connected with his reluctance to disclose his inner world: "I hate it that people should see what I really feel," he had written to Gabriele Münter. At all events, Vologda marks a stage in his artistic career.

In the same year, 1889, Kandinsky visited the Hermitage in St. Petersburg. There he was deeply impressed by Rembrandt, whose chiaroscuro he describes as a reciprocal resonance of light and dark that dissolves color differentiations into color "energies" and contrasts independent of natural forms. He observed "the slow penetration of the pictures" into the beholder who understands the meaning of this "resonance" only gradually; years later Kandinsky interpreted this phenomenon in terms of the time factor. In referring to this "reciprocal resonance" he had in mind Richard Wagner's trumpets. If this surprises, it becomes more understandable when we are told of the great impression which *Lohengrin* made on him at this time. In its score, he saw with his own eyes all the colors he had thought of, he saw and heard that Moscow twilight which he so much desired to paint, and sensed that "painting can develop the same energies as music." In other words, he was impressed by Wagner's colorism, "the color" of the instruments and its direct expression, as well as the allegorical element of the leitmotives, which the listener interprets symbolically. Did Kandinsky, here too, feel something like a reciprocal resonance?

About a year before leaving Russia he saw an exhibition of French Impressionists in Moscow, and for the first time became aware of the characteristics of modern painting. Before one of Claude Monet's *Haystacks,* he did not recognize the object, missed it, but at the same time he noticed that the picture moved him deeply, becoming engraved in his memory with all its special character. He was not yet able to draw inferences from this experience; he only understood the power of the palette, which was far greater than he had imagined. "Painting acquired a fabulous power and splendor. But, unconsciously, the object as an indispensable element of the picture became discredited. On the whole I had the impression that, after all, a small particle of my Moscow dream already existed on canvas." What if the object were to be altogether eliminated? Kandinsky did not raise this question at once, but when he did, he recalled his encounter with Monet.

It seems that this encounter was of crucial importance, and strengthened him in his resolve to become a painter. At that time Kandinsky was not active as a lawyer; he was manager of a printing shop that specialized in reproductions. He was very much interested in color prints because they brought him into contact with the painters whose works were reproduced in his shop. The fact that he engaged in such an activity is surprising, and can be accounted for only as an expression of the great attraction he felt for art.

On the other hand, his short trips to Paris in 1889 and 1892 seem to have had little significance for him. He mentions them nowhere, although at that time there was much talk about Van Gogh and Gauguin, their unhappy meeting at Arles, Pont Aven and its painters, and Gauguin's journey to Tahiti. In 1889 Kandinsky was still a law student, and in 1892 he had just passed his examinations before he left for Paris. Presumably his trips abroad were motivated by purely academic or personal reasons.

III The Munich Years

Toward Maturity

A Studies, Travels, and Early Works

1896-1907

Late in 1896, Kandinsky arrived in Munich with his young wife. In 1892 he had married Ania Chimiakin, a cousin, but the marriage was an unhappy one, and they were divorced in Munich in 1911. Kandinsky remained on friendly terms with Ania and her married sister; as late as 1916 he painted a landscape in three panels for the estate of the Abrikosovs, relatives of his cousin and her sister.

At the beginning of 1897 he enrolled at the Azbé School, and stayed there two years, for the most part producing drawings only. The teaching at Anton Azbé's was little to his taste, although he remembered his teacher as "a talented artist and a man of rare kindness." There was the usual painting from the nude, with pupils of both sexes from various nations thronging around the bored models, and drawing them as true to life as possible. Kandinsky was engaged in a continual defensive battle; completely disillusioned, he felt alone, and often worked at home or out of doors instead of going to class. He was somewhat more interested in the anatomy class, particularly the second one under Professor Molliet; he was, however, taken aback when he was told that there was a direct relationship between anatomy and art. His visits to the Pinakothek, to his relief, taught him that nature and art followed very different paths.

At the Azbé School Kandinsky became acquainted with a fellow countryman, Alexej von Jawlensky, who was two years older than Kandinsky, and who had come to Munich at about the same time, in company with Marianne von Werefkin, a young artist, and two friends who, like Kandinsky, had studied law. Jawlensky had given up his post as a captain of cavalry in St. Petersburg; before going abroad he had studied at the Petersburg academy, and was well acquainted with leading Russian artists, such as Repin. He had also heard about Van Gogh and Cézanne, and was at that time better informed about artistic problems than Kandinsky. The two did not become close until much later, in the summer of 1908, when Jawlensky visited Kandinsky at Murnau.

Outside of school Kandinsky painted studies and compositions. His coloring was exaggerated, and his fellow students labeled him a "colorist." This annoyed him although he could not deny that he felt at home in the realm of color. "I was very much intoxicated by nature," he wrote in 1925 in a biographical note addressed to the Dessau

Municipal Council, "and I tried time and again to express the main things, and later everything, through color." Curiously enough, he goes on to say: "At that time non-objective drawing seemed to me particularly difficult and enigmatic. I sought my salvation in the wrong way, and I was punished for it: I took a test in the drawing class of the Munich academy, and failed." In *Backward Glances* he gives a slightly different version of the incident: he says that unfortunately he submitted only his school studies to Stuck, and on the latter's advice took the entrance examination for the drawing class, but without success.

For one year Kandinsky continued to work on his own, and in the end went back to Stuck, this time with sketches for paintings and landscape studies, and was happy when he was admitted to the painting class. Although the master found fault with the pupil's extravagant colors and advised him to paint in one color in order to be able to study form more effectively, he had a good opinion of Kandinsky. Kandinsky's opinion of his teacher was also good; he found his advice useful, particularly regarding how to complete a picture—that one must not work nervously, that one must not hurriedly execute the interesting part, but do only what must be done at each given moment. "But for many more years I was like a monkey in a net." Nevertheless, he had taken the first steps. After another year, Kandinsky was on his own.

Incidentally, he was with Stuck at the same time as Paul Klee, who spoke of the teacher with praise, like Kandinsky; but he did not become personally acquainted with Kandinsky until 1911. Franz Marc, later their mutual friend, studied under G. Hackl and Wilhelm Diez, who were influenced by Piloty, while Stuck was influenced by the allegorical painting of Arnold Böcklin.

The artistic atmosphere in Munich at the time of Kandinsky's debut as an artist was anything but encouraging. Impressionism had not yet supplanted historical and genre painting in the naturalistic style, and in the portrait, Lenbach's "old master" manner was predominant. The cultivated painting of the Leibl group of around 1870 was forgotten; the German Impressionists—Liebermann, Corinth, and Slevogt—had no success, being eclipsed by the painters of the Scholle group founded in 1899, with Erler, Putz, Münzer, and Feldbauer; and before 1900 no French Impressionists were to be seen in Munich. The *Stimmungslandschaften* ("mood" landscapes) of Adolf Hölzel and Ludwig Dill of the Dachau group (Munich *Sezession*) were the most original works at that time: at least they were lyrical, though lacking a new definition of reality, and more Romantic than contemporary in character. These painters might be described as a belated Barbizon school, and their use of the decorative line brings to mind the Jugendstil.

Shortly before 1900, the Jugendstil produced something like a revolution in Munich, and its influence is evident in all those interested in transcending the traditional styles and mixtures of styles. Munich was the German center of this movement which had started in England (Mackintosh) and Belgium (Van der Velde).

Beginning with an attempt to transform the environment, especially architecture, the Jugendstil very soon extended to illustration and book design, and finally to painting and sculpture (H. Christ). The relationship between the Jugendstil and the painting of the 1890s is well known (Gauguin, Valloton, Hodler, Munch), as well as the ideological

34

connection with the Nabis and the *Revue blanche*. The many periodicals that were founded just before the turn of the century (*The Studio*, 1893; *Pan*, 1895; *Jugend* and *Simplicissimus* in Munich, 1896; *Die Insel*, 1897; *Ver sacrum*, 1898) rapidly spread the new ideas. In 1897 two rooms of the Glaspalast in Munich were given to the Jugendstil; in 1900 Mackintosh and G. Klimt were invited to the exhibition of the Secession, and Klimt exhibited at the Glaspalast.

O. Eckmann in Munich represented the floral style, H. van der Velde in Brussels the style of abstract lines and surfaces. But even the floral style is far removed from nature, and the spiritual leaders of the two directions skirted the problem of the abstract in art. "The line is a force, which like all elementary forces is active; forces connected by opposing lines have the same effect as several elementary forces in opposition to each other," wrote Van der Velde in his *Lay Sermons* (1902); he also spoke of "complementary lines," and of the absurdity of trying to introduce real things into the network of lines, and judged the borrowing of motives to be arbitrary. At that early date he also emphasized "the effective brain activity" of the artist. A. Endell, who in 1897 had built the Elvira Studio in Munich and had decorated it grandiosely, with a dragon motive, noted in 1898: "If we want to understand and enjoy formal beauty, we must learn to think of seeing as a distinct action ... not skim over the forms, but follow them with our eyes, so as to perceive every bend, every intersection, every extension, every reduction, in short, every expression of the form."

We have no documentary evidence as to how much Kandinsky was interested in such matters. He lived amid these new stirrings, and they must have touched him more closely than the mass production of the Munich painters. He was very responsive to everything that was in the air, especially if it had spiritual aspects, and here were active artists whose interests were not purely materialistic, and whose orientation was international. Two of them, Christ and Van der Velde, he encountered personally in Munich. They may have suggested to Peter Behrens that Kandinsky should be offered the class in decorative painting at the Düsseldorf Academy.

Kandinsky paid his tribute to the Jugendstil when, in 1901, he composed the poster for the first exhibition of the Phalanx group, which he founded (color wood engraving, p. 37, 1). This poster reflects the illustrative style of the period. In the center, between Doric columns, two Roman warriors are shown about to attack with their lances; at the left there is a castle being stormed by the phalanx; at the right a battle scene of rather fairytale character. The picture is probably intended to symbolize the phalanx of artists storming the bastions of tradition. The forms are emphatically flat and linear; the horizontals, verticals, and curves in parallel, the colors (blue, blue-gray, and green-gray) all repeated. The flowing printed characters at the top and bottom, and the mosaic-like borders enhance the decorative character of the poster. While we cannot speak here of abstract or floral arabesques, the general rhythmic impression and symbolism are unmistakably related to the borders and illustrations to be found in magazines and books of the period. The elements drawn from antiquity, the German Middle Ages, and fairytales have nothing in common with historical painting, the contrasting subject matters having found a formal common denominator in the Jugendstil. The poster is obviously the result of intensive critical study. Elements of the Jugendstil are also to be found in Kandinsky's early woodcut illustrations, and in oils and temperas painted before 1906. Among the twenty-seven diaries and sketchbooks in the Kandinsky Foundation at Munich some, which must be assigned to the early 1900s, contain, in addition to studies of all kinds, copies of Jugendstil ornaments. Some of these drawings were made as late as 1904.

The sketchbooks also afford a glimpse into Kandinsky's studies of the nude and of anatomy; the drawings are sober and industrious, and their level is not above the average. Next to them are landscape sketches done from nature, perhaps at Rothenburg or Kallmünz, preliminary studies for woodcuts such as *Trysting Place,* stylized female figures, which in their exaggeration have the effect of parodies on the line drawings of the Munich *Jugend,* and many costume studies done from reproductions in specialized works on the subject. Kandinsky studied these things thoroughly, and even noted the titles of the books—Leitner, *Waffensammlung des Österreichischen Kaiserhauses* (Arms Collection of the Austrian Imperial House); Isselburg,*Nürnberger Geschlechter* (Nuremberg Families); Charles Diehl, *Justinien et la civilization byzantine du 6ième siècle* (Justinian and the Byzantine Civilization of the Sixth Century), and others. He also drew in museums and in the Munich Kupferstichkabinett and on visits to old cities. Up until 1906 he eagerly made use of what he learned. But he was not given to slavish imitation. The *Russian Scenes* of 1904 and 1906 were, to be sure, Russian in their general effect, but copies of European costumes can often be found in details of armor, weapons, headgear, and other garments. In a lecture (which was prepared but never given) we also read that he dealt very freely with the auxiliary material he had thus acquired, and that in his Russian pictures he worked from memory and imagination. However, when Kandinsky drew from nature, for instance in Moscow or at Venice (in a notebook of 1903), his line is more intense and more alive.

The sketchbooks are instructive also for their biographical information and glimpses into Kandinsky's character. Kandinsky records meetings, appointments, financial transactions, occasionally in Russian. We find names such as Hans Purrmann, Karl Caspar, Erich Mühsam, Edouard Schuré, addresses of travel agencies, the hours for visiting museums, and deadlines for sending works to exhibitions, dates of delivery and opening, for instance, for the Dresden International Art Exhibition of 1904. The entries suggest a highly developed habit of orderliness.

In 1901 Kandinsky founded the Phalanx, becoming president of the group the following year, and in 1904 he dissolved it, its success with the public having been negligible. The painter H. Schlittgen, one of the members, reports in his *Recollections* that there were almost no visitors, and that Kandinsky had to cancel a Pissarro exhibition which had been planned. Schlittgen does not mention the Phalanx's showing of Monet. The Munich critic H. Wolf writes that in 1904 the Phalanx, unlike the other galleries, exhibited the Neo-Impressionists Signac, Rysselberghe, and others, and this is confirmed in one of the above-mentioned diaries. In reference to a meeting scheduled for February 3, we find the names of Signac, Rysselberghe, Luce, Angrand, and Valloton. We also find a reference to the eleventh and last Phalanx exhibition.

This group unquestionably attempted to stimulate the artistic life of Munich, which was extremely conservative. When foreign painters were exhibited, they were almost

1 *Kandinsky's Poster for 'First Phalanx Exhibition'. Munich, 1901*

Kandinskys Plakat für die erste Ausstellung der Künstlergruppe ›Phalanx‹. München

Affiche par Kandinsky pour la première exposition du groupe d'artistes «Phalanx». Munich

Cartellone di Kandinsky per la prima esposizione ‹Phalanx›. Monaco

2 *Night   Nacht   Nuit   Notte, 1903*

3 *Singer   Sängerin, 1903*
Chanteuse   Cantante

4 On the Beach, 1902
 Am Strand
 Sur la plage
 Sulla spiaggia

5 Farewell II, 1903
 Abschied II
 Adieu II
 Addio II

6 Moonrise, 1903
 Mondaufgang
 Lever de lune
 Luna che sorge

7 Summer, 1903
 Sommer
 Eté
 Estate

8 Poster for 'Neue Künstlervereinigung – München',
 1909

 *Plakat für ›Neue Künstler-
 vereinigung – München‹*
 *Affiche pour «Association
 nouvelle des artistes –
 Munich»*
 *Cartellone per la ‹Nuova
 associazione degli artisti –
 Monaco›*

9 Color woodcuts from
 'Klänge', (1913)
 *Farbholzschnitte aus
 ›Klänge‹*
 *Bois gravés en couleur
 tirés de «Sonorités»*
 *Incisione a colori su legno
 da ‹Suoni›*

8

9

10 Oars (Study for
'Improvisation 26'),
1912
Ruder (Studie zu
›Improvisation 26‹)
Rames (Etude pour
«Improvisation 26»)
Remi (Studio per
‹Improvvisazione 26›)

11 Improvisation, 1911
Improvvisazione

invariably the wrong ones. In 1904 Heinemann exhibited the French painters of the Salon; and while the Munich Kunstverein also exhibited a few Gauguins, Van Goghs, and Cézannes, and the Secession in 1905 exhibited Blanche, Carrière, Toorop, Hodler, and Amiet, there was nowhere as little interest in the moderns, Wolf writes, as in the Bavarian capital. Glancing through the German art periodicals of those years and reading the accounts of the exhibitions and government art acquisitions in Munich, we encounter dozens of names that have long been forgotten.

The Phalanx was connected with a school in which Kandinsky taught painting and drawing from the nude, but it had few pupils, and after a year was closed. Kandinsky kept his classes going, but stopped teaching even before he left Munich for good, probably in the fall of 1903, for the classes took too much of his time. He must have been a very gifted teacher, for he was highly praised by his pupils of both sexes. For his educational excursions and other trips in Bavaria he used a bicycle, and summoned his troop together for criticism after a session by blowing a police whistle. One of his pupils from 1902 on was Gabriele Münter, who remained his companion until his departure from Germany at the outbreak of the First World War.

One of his first pupils was Mrs. M. Strakosch-Giesler; some of the works by Kandinsky, which she purchased in this period came on the art market in 1956. She was a theosophist, and after Rudolf Steiner left the theosophist movement, an anthroposophist. She acquainted Kandinsky with the new doctrine. He himself attended some of Steiner's lectures: he was interested in the occult. His English translator, Michael Sadler, who visited him at Murnau in 1911, speaks at length of this preoccupation in his recollections of Kandinsky. His *Ariel Scene* of 1908 (CC 594) was painted after he attended a lecture by Steiner in Berlin on March 26, 1908 (note by C. Weiler). In the early 1920s Kandinsky still spoke about these matters, mentioning Annie Besant's and E. W. Leadbeater's *Gedankenformen* a copy of which he owned (first edition, Leipzig 1908), although at this later date he was far removed from Steiner's ideas. But in the years before 1914 the influence of Steiner may occasionally be noted, all the more so because Steiner comes close to the mystical, religious, and theosophical ideas of the Russian philosopher Vladimir Soloviev (d. 1900). There are also connections with Steiner in the field of the psychology of color.

From 1901 to 1903, in addition to paintings and graphic works Kandinsky was engaged in research into technical problems: he tested various paints and glues, he painted with oil, tempera, combinations of tempera and other media, made his own grounds, using plaster, casein, clay, and ground egg shells. These things were at first more important to him than problems of expression and idiom, and only some time later did he display concern for style. Kandinsky did not know in what direction he was moving, having as yet seen too little, and found no standards of comparison in Munich. He wanted to experience art, he wanted to learn, and he made a number of trips accompanied (except on trips to Russia) by Gabriele Münter. He was no less fond of travel than his fellow countryman Stravinsky. In 1903 he spent ten days at Venice (September 2 to 11), and a short time later went to Odessa and Moscow for a few weeks (October 22 to November 18). Before this trip, on September 30, he gave up his apartment in Munich. From Christmas 1904 to April 1905 he was in Tunis; that summer he was in Dresden

(June 1–August 15), and in the fall in Odessa (October 4–November 8), from the end of December 1905 to April 30, 1906 in Rapallo (Italy), and from June 1906 to June 1, 1907 —that is, for about a year—he lived at Sèvres near Paris (spending only the first five weeks in Paris itself). In August 1907 he went to Switzerland for three weeks, and from September 4, 1907 to April 25, 1908—eight months—stayed in Berlin. After a short visit to the southern Tyrol, and a six-week stay at Murnau, he finally went back to Munich.

His purpose on those trips was to become acquainted with the Western world and to see what it had achieved in art. But it is noteworthy that he spent so much time in the country, at the seaside, and in places like Sèvres rather than in the large cities. His trips were partly connected with exhibitions of his work. In the catalogue he kept, he

Arrival of the Merchants. Woodcut, 1905

carefully listed the cities to which he sent his paintings. As early as 1902 we find Odessa and St. Petersburg, Berlin (Secession), Wiesbaden, and Krefeld; in 1903, he mentions Odessa, Moscow, Budapest, Prague, Berlin, Wiesbaden; in 1904, Moscow, St. Petersburg, Warsaw, Cracow, Paris (Salon d'Automne), Rome, and Hamburg; in 1905, Moscow, Dresden, Berlin (Cassirer), Hamburg, Düsseldorf, and Cologne; in 1906, 1907, Paris and others. As we can see, his relations with Russia were by no means broken off. Kandinsky also recorded sales: "sold at Stettin," "sold to the Grand Duke Vladimir," and gifts: "gift to my brother [stepbrother]" or "to Mrs. Abrikosov [his cousin]," and a few times he wrote "destroyed."

It must be assumed that on his travels Kandinsky made the acquaintance of art dealers and organizers of exhibitions, and especially of fellow painters, but no records about this exist or are available. In his biographical note of 1925 he wrote that he had been three times rejected by the Munich Secession, but was elected member of the Berlin Secession, and soon afterward by the German Union of Artists, and the Salon d'Automne in Paris. This must have occurred between 1903 and 1906. In 1904 and 1905 he was awarded medals in Paris; in 1905 he was elected member of the jury of the

Salon d'Automne, and in 1906 he was awarded the Grand Prix. Thus he had some success during the early years.

Kandinsky enters history as a distinct personality only after his return to Munich, when he was almost thirty-four years old. He had become an independent artist not much earlier. It cannot be said that his works in the years immediately following 1900 were already very original; he took his time, he made a laborious study of techniques, but he also tried to discover the potentialities of pictorial expression, and studied the old masters in the Munich Pinakothek, as well as the works of painters in dealers' galleries. It is noteworthy that as president of the Phalanx he brought in paintings by Claude Monet and planned to show those of Pissarro. But it is not possible, on the basis of his early works, to point out specific influences or a guiding pattern.

His work between 1900 and his return to Munich may be divided into four groups—the woodcuts, the so-called "color drawings," which are actually paintings in tempera, the oil studies, and the paintings proper. He recorded everything, noting the titles, usually also the medium and the dimensions, where exhibited, and occasionally even prices. In a general way it may be said that in those years from 1901 to 1907 Kandinsky wavered between the East and the West, between Russia and Europe, and that his works, both thematically and formally, are either Russian or European, even when they date from the same period.

Kandinsky's graphic work prior to his return to Munich was fairly extensive. Among the works now in Paris and in the Kandinsky Foundation in Munich, there are about forty woodcuts he printed himself by hand, for the most part in two versions, one black-and-white and one in color. He sent them to exhibitions in Russia, Germany (Berlin Secession from 1906 to 1908) and Paris (Salon d'Automne, 1904 to 1908, Salon des Indépendants 1908), and six to the Brücke exhibition in Dresden (1907). The chronology is not quite certain. Presumably he executed *Promenade, Evening, Winter, Singer* (p.37,3), *On the Beach* (p.38,4), *Night* (p.37,2), *Farewell* (p.38,5), *Summer* (p.38,7), *Solitary Voyage* (or *The Golden Sail*), *Tamer of Beasts, Winter Day*, and *Moonrise* (p.38,6) in 1902 and 1903. *Twilight, Bouquet, Hilly Landscape* (or *Church in Bavaria*) and *Conversation* date from 1904. The rest date from 1905–1907, including *Park of St.Cloud, Governesses, Arrival of the Merchants* (p.42), *The Black Cat* (p.47), *People of Dresden*, and *Arab Riders*.

A clue to dates may be noted in the two portfolios of prints. In 1904 the Stroganov publishing house in Moscow issued Kandinsky's *Poems Without Words* (p.44) consisting of twelve black-and-white woodcuts, one vignette, and one woodcut on the cover, and in 1906, during his one-year stay at Sèvres, *Tendances nouvelles* in Paris published a portfolio, *Xylographies*, consisting of five black-and-white woodcuts, three vignettes, and one vignette on the binding. In the periodical *Tendances nouvelles* (Nos. 26, 27, and 28, 1906 and 1907) there also appeared twenty-three woodcuts, about half of which date from 1906 and 1907, while the rest comprise reprints of earlier works. Kandinsky produced other black-and-white woodcuts and a few linoleum cuts; not all are represented in the Paris collection and in the Kandinsky Foundation. In his records he mentioned the following color linoleum cuts (1907): *With the Ravens, Two Girls, With Green Women, Woman and Child, Lyre, Hunter, Monk*, and *Mirror*.

*Title page for
Poems Without Words
Woodcut, 1904*

The woodcuts of the *Poems Without Words* include, in addition to new prints *(The Rhine, Mountain Lake, Old Town),* a few older ones, namely, *Evening, Farewell,* and *The Night.* Those of the *Xylographies* are entirely new, the most Russian of all his woodcuts. The figures in *Femmes au bois* (p. 45) with their national costumes make us think of Russian folk art and fairytales; this is also true of *Les Bouleaux, Les Cavaliers* and *L'Eglise.* The most advanced in style of the series is *Les Oiseaux,* the subject being entirely dissolved in lines of force and arabesques. In *Xylographies* Kandinsky came close in feeling to the *Scènes russes* he painted the same year in tempera, in which the original magic quality of old Russian folksongs and legends asserts itself. In their emotional quality, these prints are closely related to the poems by Konstantin Balmont, a Russian poet who was about the same age as Kandinsky.

The thematic range is much the same as in the paintings of that period. Some titles are repeated: for instance, *Promenade, Farewell, Evening, Winter Day, Knights. The Spectators* exist in both a tempera version and a woodcut in *Poems Without Words; Sunday* is the title both of an oil painting (1904) and a woodcut; *Night* is an oil study (p.37, 2) and a color woodcut. The romantic element is as strong in the graphic works as in the paintings. We have the rising of the moon, women in woods, knights errant, archers, Russian birch woods, drifting clouds, crows flying on the horizon. The costumes change: there are medieval, Rococo, Victorian, contemporary, and national costumes. The woodcuts dating from before 1904 make a more Western impression, and in color show many similarities to the works of the Nabis in Paris, but Kandinsky had not yet seen them. The color harmonies—faded pink and graduated blues and violets—are repeated, and amid them, without transitions, a shrill vermilion or a harsh white. A color woodcut such as *Summer* (p. 38, 7) is just as refined in its color composition as the early color lithographs by Vuillard or Bonnard. The various greens and blues, the modulations from pink over blue-pink to carmine are remarkably sensitive. *Farewell* (p. 38, 5) exists in several versions, which reveal Kandinsky's effort to achieve color expression. The white horse galloping through a moonlit landscape in *Evening Twilight* has a ghostly effect. In *Golden Sail* Kandinsky used bronze gilt, just as in one of his later glass paintings he used silver paper to enhance the color tone. Alongside these, we have woodcuts sober in line and tone, such as the black-and-white version of the *Singer* (p. 37, 3). This work reminds one of Gordon Craig's subsequent designs for *Hamlet* at the Moscow Art Theater. The style reveals, in addition to Jugendstil influences, echoes of traditional influences, such as the Rococo, Biedermeier, and even pre-Raphaelitism. These echoes are also to be found in Russian works of the period, in Benois, Somov, and particularly in the newer theatrical art of Bakst. Kandinsky may have become acquainted with these works during his frequent visits to his native land.

Woodcut from Xylographies (1906)

The later woodcuts and linoleum cuts, like those in *Xylographies,* are very Russian with respect both to narrative elements and treatment. *With Green Women* is a legend with figures, which are difficult to interpret, set in a Russian village under a deep blue sky. Similarly, *With the Ravens* shows a scene with three women, above whom black birds are soaring like phantoms. As late as 1900, Russian painters and poets were still inventing and recording their own fairytales, and Kandinsky too relied on his own fantasy or re-created existing fairytales. The woodcuts dating from 1905 to 1907 are closely related to the popular prints and Russian book designs of those years. The title page Kandinsky made for the printed score of Glinka's *Life for the Czar* (libretto by N. Bilibin, 1906, CC 761) shows how Russian Kandinsky had remained and how little he had lost contact with what was going on in Moscow.

His graphic works met with success: *Xylographies* contains an enthusiastic foreword by Jérôme Maesse, referring to "Basile Kandinsky," a highly original and extraordinary painter. We would not today ascribe such importance to Kandinsky's graphic works, but we must observe that Kandinsky himself valued them fairly highly. He had to produce them, he says, in order to liberate himself, and for the sake of the music that he heard within him. Unquestionably there is much of his sense of isolation and his melancholy in these prints, and some of them bring to mind a sentence in a letter of 1903 (to Gabriele Münter): "I am sadly happy." There are also cheerful themes, for, as he said in another passage of this letter, his heart always felt diverse emotions at the same time. Moreover, it was a satisfaction for Kandinsky to have "concealed" so many feelings, fantastic ideas, and Russian memories in his woodcuts; he knew that it would be difficult to decipher them.

Kandinsky's most important painting of that period is a life-size portrait of a Russian lady, Maria Krushchov, signed and dated 1900 (p. 257). It marks his farewell to the academy, and shows the painter in a surprising light. It is executed with bravura, it is representative and elegant. Little in it is indebted to his teacher F. Stuck; it is rather in the tradition of Van Dyck, Gainsborough, and Lenbach. There is a large black hat, a long gray coat with its blue lining showing; we see also part of the carmine red blouse, and a white cat on the black-gloved right arm; in the background there is a sketchy landscape in the manner of the Dachau painters, with brown trees at the right, rusty red foliage at the left, and a light green meadow below. It is amazing how quickly Kandinsky assimilated European painting and how much he learned during his four years at Munich. He had what it took to become a good realist.

But the portrait is an isolated case; the other early studies and paintings are different, and a few of them, we know from his own notes, were executed in the spirit of that impression of Rembrandt in St. Petersburg—"the resonance" of his complex chiaroscuro, in which Kandinsky later saw "a time factor." But he made no progress on this arduous path, and began, "chiefly in old Schwabing," to paint one or two oil studies from nature every day. With the palette knife he applied color in flat bands or in spots to the canvas, and made them "sing" as loudly as he could. The color-saturated scale of the Munich light inspired him, but in his studio the sketches seemed to him "un-

The Black Cat. Woodcut, 1907

successful attempts to capture the energy of nature." At the same time he often painted "from memory." but he was still far removed from "composition." The very word
made him shudder. "This word affected me like a prayer." What he meant by pictures
"painted from memory" is presumably illustrated by such romantic works as *Trysting
Place* (1901) and *Bright Air* (1902), as well as by his "color drawings" (tempera paintings), *Nocturnal Riders* (1901) and *Promenade* (1902). In an autobiographical sketch
written in French he listed for the year 1902 *"paysages et compositions romantiques."*
Among the landscapes executed before 1907 there are oil studies, a number of paintings in tempera, and about forty of the oils listed in the catalogue. There were certainly
more, for time and again landscapes that cannot be identified from this list turn up in
the most various places. At first Kandinsky seems to have attached less importance
to his landscapes than to his "romantic" and more "compositional" works. In 1913
when *Der Sturm* issued *Backward Glances* (Kandinsky supervised the printing from
Munich), he reproduced only the *Sluice* (dated 1901 on Kandinsky's list, but actually
1902), one out of about 200. On the other hand, he reproduced twenty-seven "romantic"
works, painted on the basis of poetic and musical experiences and from memory.
Park of Akhtyrka (CC 535) was one of the first landscape studies (1901); in it
Kandinsky boldly translated the essentials of his impression into a very few colors
applied in broad impasto bands. Similar to it is the *Sluice* (CC 5), a motive from
the park on his sister-in-law's estate. He painted it twice, first quite small and without
the tiny accessory figure. These works bring to mind the phrase coined by Kirchner to
designate Schmidt-Rottluff's early landscapes—"monumental Impressionism." Here
Kandinsky is fairly independent; the painters of the Munich "Scholle" also used impasto and applied paint with the palette knife, but in a more decorative arrangement.
Also similar to the *Park of Akhtyrka* are the oil studies and paintings of Schwabing
(*Winter in Schwabing*, 1902, CC 545), of Kochel (CC 541), of Kallmünz (*On the Nab near
Regensburg*, CC 536), and of the environs of Dresden and Berlin. They range from 1901
to 1907; the early ones are not signed, and only a few are dated. Among the pictures at
the Galerie Maeght exhibition in 1950 were a number of works previously unknown;

47

other such posthumous discoveries turned up when the Kandinsky Foundation in Munich became public property in February 18, 1957. Among these were studies of the Staffelsee, of the lake of Starnberg, of the valley of the Isar, and a number of sketches of Rapallo and St. Cloud which belong to a later period. Some of the earlier ones can be dated. *Bridge at Kochel* (CC 543) is from 1902, and the open *View of the Riverbank at Kallmünz* is from 1903. In this latter study, Kandinsky's method of working with the palette knife produced a luminosity of color already far removed from nature. The manner in which a sharp emerald green, a bright pink or a luminous violet suddenly emerge from among the duller local colors, can be accounted for only by an attempt to move away from reality.

Kandinsky's method of raising the horizon, and thus weakening the illusionistic sense of space, points in the same direction. He attaches no value to depth, and moves his subjects to the upper edge of the picture. In *Spring* (CC 540) and *Mountain Landscape in the Upper Palatinate* (1904, CC 539) they cover the entire surface: the pink flowers, the fences, and the walls reach to the very top.

In May 1906 Kandinsky went to Paris for a year; since 1892 he had visited it only once for five days, in 1904. He lived at Sèvres, and exhibited at the Salon d'Automne and the Indépendants. In the Salon d'Automne of 1906 there was a special Gauguin exhibit, and a section devoted to the modern Russians, which had been assembled by Diaghilev; the Indépendants in 1907 showed Matisse's *Bonheur de vivre,* which aroused violent protests. Kandinsky must have seen these exhibitions, and it would be natural to suppose that in his groping frame of mind at that time, he would have borrowed from the French avant-garde. But this is not the case. In the St. Cloud landscapes (CC 557–560) Kandinsky continues to apply his color patches with the palette knife; the golden ochers and pinks of the sun-drenched landscape are set against the deep green and blue of the shadows, but Kandinsky now adds broken and supplementary tones to the main colors. This does not make the paintings more airy, but more solid, and the arrangement of the color tones results in no great effect of depth; there is no succession of picture planes, but rather an overlapping. At all events, the St. Cloud landscapes show that the accidental and sketchy elements have become less prominent, and that a distinct progress in the direction of pictorial form has been made. As compared with the contemporaneous works of Matisse, Picasso, and Braque they must have struck Kandinsky's artist friends in Paris as backward, and we are told that a visit by Gertrude Stein to his studio was disappointing to both of them.

Kandinsky could paint from memory thanks to his excellent visual memory, which served him well at school and university, as he reports in *Backward Glances*. With its help he could visualize whole poems or entire pages of numbers and recite them back. Even as a boy he kept so clear a memory of pictures he had seen only once that he could copy them at home, as exactly as his skill permitted. He registered optical impressions even without trying, being able, for instance, to list and describe all the shop windows he had passed along in the street. This gift troubled him, and he was glad to discover one day that it was diminishing at the expense of other capacities indispensable to his artistic development.

(top) Market Place 1901 ▶

(bottom) Festive ▶
Procession 1903

Kandinsky's visual memory served him well in his imaginary and romantic pictures. The former continue thematically the color woodcuts of 1902 and 1903. *Bright Air* (1902, CC 4) shows Biedermeier ladies dressed in white crinolines in a park, with a horse and rider in the background. The subject recalls the color woodcuts *Evening* and *Roses*. Here, too, the landscape continues up to the edge of the picture, so that the scene seems to take place on a stage with little depth. Biedermeier costumes occur again later, in *Skaters* (1906, CC 653), and finally in the large canvas, *Group in Crinolines* (1909, CC 30).

In addition to Biedermeier scenes, Kandinsky painted medieval ones, for example, the first version of *Promenade* (CC 1), executed in impastos, *Bridal Procession* (CC 646), and *Festive Procession* (color plate, p. 49) which probably date from 1902 or 1903. The riders and the costumes in *Bridal Procession* resemble those on other paintings and woodcuts of those years in their representation of old German motives. This painting is in tempera on a black ground, and possibly it was the graphic character of such works that induced Kandinsky to catalogue them as "color drawings" rather than as tempera paintings. He allowed parts of the black ground to stand so as to bring out the red and blue accents of the other colors. The horses have been captured both at rest and movement expertly, and it is possible that Kandinsky saw some such panoplied scene in one or another South-German town, during a holiday celebration. It has a slightly theatrical effect. Such works may have been inspired by opera performances. This may also be the case with the Russian pictures—*Sunday* (*Old Russia*) (CC 8) and *Russian Scene* (1904, CC 648). Thematically and technically they are related to *Motifs russes* of 1906, *Troika* (CC 12), *Riding Couple* (CC 658), *Volga Song* with its gorgeous Viking ships (CC 651), and *Panic* (1907, CC 13). Most of them were painted at Sèvres. Kandinsky must have encountered his homeland in Paris, in the flesh or spiritually; at that time the Russians, the Russian ballet, the Russian opera, and the Stanislavsky company were popular in the French capital. Or had Kandinsky, in the course of his frequent trips to Moscow, attended performances of Glinka's and Rimsky-Korsakov's fairytale operas? After 1900, the productions in Moscow were symbolist rather than naturalistic in style, and the mixture of melancholy and folksong, dramatic gravity and decorative gestures is present both in these operas and in Kandinsky.

Stravinsky, too, loved Russian folksongs *(Souvenirs de mon enfance)* and the contrast between fairylike beings and demons. He loved the pagan emphasis upon the forces of nature, together with the exorcising of these powers. In Kandinsky's *Night* (1906, CC 659) and *Storm Bell* (1907, CC 14) the same contrasts emerge, between the good spirits and the evil magicians, but we cannot say from what source the painter drew. *Russian Beauty in a Landscape* (1906, p. CC 656) looks like a fairytale character of the opera stage, waiting for her cue.

Like *Festive Procession*, all these canvases are painted in tempera on black grounds, and occasionally the ground shows through the mosaic of spots of color. In certain of them, for instance, *Sunday* and *Russian Scene*, the paint is put on irregularly; in others, as in *Russian Beauty*, it is like a structure of pink and green ovoid pebbles. *Riding Couple* is a scintillation of specks and spots of color, and in this not unlike the works of Klimt. Kandinsky himself describes his painting as an outlet for homesickness. "At that time, I tried, by lines and by distribution of mottled points of color, to express the musical spirit of Russia. Other pictures of that period reflected the contradictions, and later the eccentricities of Russia" (letter to the author, October 12, 1924). This technique is at its boldest in *Troika, Panic,* and *Storm Bell.* The manner in which Kandinsky fits together brick-like forms, both large and small, in *Troika* brings him close to the contemporaneous *Nocturne with Cab* by Delaunay (1906, CC 760). The pattern of spots that runs across the entire surface blurs contours, modeling, and space, so that resemblances to nature are largely hidden. Here Kandinsky reached a turning point leading him on to a more severe sense of form.

A final group of works painted "from memory" is preceded by a number of lyrical works, which one might call a continuation of the *compositions romantiques,* referred to by Kandinsky in the above-mentioned autobiographical note. Among them are *Trysting Place* (1902, CC 6), *Riding Couple* (1903, CC 658), and *The Blue Rider* (1903, p. 258) —his first version of the subject—whose title was to provide a name for the group of Kandinsky and his friends a little later. (A second, lost version was executed by Kandinsky in 1909.) The first two of these works are outspokenly illustrative, pre-Raphaelite in structure and mood, and neutral as regards color (tempera), while the *Blue Rider* (oil), which shows a horseman galloping across an open meadow in front of a cluster of birch trees, suggests restlessness both in treatement and in the color. The technique is like that of Monet's *Duckpond* (1873), not like that of the *Haystacks* which Kandinsky had seen in Moscow in 1895. One might also be reminded of K. Roussel's technique in painting mythological scenes. This was the Nabi who had been influenced by Monet, but who interpreted him much more decoratively than Kandinsky. *Blue Rider* stands somewhat apart in the sequence of Kandinsky's works; prior to 1907, the painter's development was scarcely in a straight line.

For these seven years, Kandinsky was continually coming to grips with the differences between Russia and Europe. He was neither a Panslavist like Dostoevsky, nor a partisan of the West like Turgenev. He was extraordinarily receptive to all the stimulations afforded by the West, but he was not overwhelmed by them, and the Russian element remained in evidence. He had not yet reached the point of trusting in his own originality, nor yet of choosing to follow one of the leading artists of the beginning of the century. His landscapes were more nearly related to those being painted at the time by the Brücke artists than to those painted by the Fauves, and were sometimes closer to Liebermann than to the Expressionists. On the other hand, there were the romantic compositions painted "from memory," and these, with their legendary subjects, and their expression and form, are not unlike Russian folk art and the decorative works of his fellows countrymen, including stage design. With his St. Cloud landscapes of 1907, Kandinsky attained the level of western European painting; his *Motifs russes* (1904 to 1907) mark a successful personal attempt to get away from objective art. His resemblance to Delaunay is accidental, and the design of *Troika* was created before he knew the work of the French painter. In 1907, when he left Paris to go back to Munich, his instinct was sound. In Paris he might have been swamped by the proliferation of an art alien to him; not so in Munich, where the new movements had not yet reached. Here an atmosphere prevailed with which he was familiar and from which he expected to profit. But possibly considerations of health were the primary factor in his decision. In Paris he had come close to a severe nervous breakdown. The first thing he did on his return was to go for a rest cure to Reichenhall, where he recovered.

Kandinsky himself interpreted and evaluated his early development somewhat differently. In notes for a lecture in 1914, he spoke of two periods prior to Murnau, "the dilettante period of his childhood with vague, predominantly painful stirrings, impregnated with a nostalgia incomprehensible to him," and "the period after having finished school, when these stirrings gradually acquired more definite form, becoming clearer to him." It was this he sought to express, in all kinds of external forms and objects, and he spent a great deal of time struggling against tradition, only very gradually defeating one prejudice after another.

Kandinsky saw more in his woodcuts than we are inclined to see, when, for instance, he speaks of "the hidden," a term that recurs time and again as a leitmotiv, and announces his eventual concealment of the naturalistic element. In retrospect it seemed to him that he had always known many things, but became aware of them only after years of labor. Gabriele Münter reports that Kandinsky in his Tunis period (1905) once said that he had planned a painting without objects when he was still a student in Moscow. If we accept as true the opening words of his projected lecture, that the artist in advance "possesses a tuning fork resounding in the depths of his soul, which he cannot tune to another pitch," it would not be surprising if he had thought of painting a nonobjective picture years earlier. Although Kandinsky was thirty when he began to study art, it took him a long time—twelve years—before he produced significant works. This was during the Murnau period. Nor should we be surprised that it took him so long. The jump into the abstract, which he ventured in 1910, was so bold and momentous that without long preparation it could scarcely have been successful.

B The Murnau Period and Blaue Reiter

1908-1914

In the summer of 1907 Kandinsky was back in Munich but his restlessness did not subside. He seems to have been torn by psychological and intellectual conflicts. His personal situation was complicated as a result of his still undissolved marriage with his cousin and his association with Gabriele Münter. Perhaps he also sensed that he faced great artistic decisions. For a while he took to traveling again. In 1907 he went for a short time to Switzerland, then for a longer period to Berlin. In 1908 he visited the southern Tyrol and Murnau, and on October 1 he moved with Gabriele Münter to an apartment at No. 36 Ainmillerstrasse in Munich. Paul Klee, who was later to become one of his close friends, lived at No. 32. The lease, which survives among Kandinsky's papers in Paris, shows that the apartment consisted of four rooms, plus a kitchen, two closets, and a bathroom; the rent was 1,400 marks a year, a considerable sum for that time. The layout can be found in one of the sketchbooks, which also contains drawings of chairs and a dressing table, suggesting that Kandinsky helped in planning the furnishings. He lived in Munich most of the year, spending summers at Murnau where he bought a house in 1909. The house was later occupied by Gabriele Münter, but except for a stereotype frieze with horsemen and flowers on the wooden staircase nothing in it recalls that period. In 1909 this little town in Upper Bavaria looked less urban than it does today; situated between Staffelsee and Moos, with a view on the mountains, it has still a good deal of charm.

In this Alpine landscape Kandinsky and Gabriele Münter began to paint works quite different from those they had painted in Sèvres and Berlin. Alexej von Jawlensky and Marianne von Werefkin came to visit them, and there were lively discussions about art. Jawlensky had painted in Brittany and in Provence in 1905, he had exhibited at the Salon d'Automne, and was acquainted with Matisse. In Munich he was acquainted with W. Verkade, who was a painter as well as a member of a religious order; he had also known Gauguin and the Nabi P. Sérusier, and in 1908 he had often seen the dancer A. Sacharoff. Jawlensky was a painter of some reputation, a discriminating judge of art, and had the ability to stimulate others. Kandinsky liked to listen to his fellow countryman, but followed a path of his own, whereas Jawlensky's brilliantly colored areas with black edges, in the style of so-called "Synthetism," point to the influence of Gauguin and the school of Pont Aven.

The new start Kandinsky made at Murnau can be accounted for only by a combination of reasons. It is likely that he was no longer satisfied with his late-Impressionist landscapes, any more than with the stylistically more advanced *Scènes russes,* which seemed more abstract to him, however, than to us. In 1912 he included them in his first one-man show at the Sturm gallery in Berlin, and at Goltz's in Munich, along with his later "Improvisations" and "Compositions." During the weeks he spent at Murnau in 1908 he seems to have achieved the peace of mind he had long been deprived of, and this peace of mind stayed with him after his return to Munich. His restless traveling ceased; until the outbreak of the war, except for annual visits to his relatives in Moscow and Odessa, he almost never left his place. He worked both in Munich and in his country house, and in 1909, with the foundation of the Neue Künstlervereinigung, he began increasingly to move in the society of painters, his equals, who were of more significance to him than the casual encounters of his trips.

The passionate character of the landscapes he painted in the Bavarian Alps comes as a surprise after the earlier work, which strikes us as rather cold. The same may be said of the somewhat decorative Russian scenes. He never went back to them. In *On the Spiritual in Art,* which he wrote in 1910, he mentions only Cézanne, Matisse, and Picasso as painters who stimulated him, although he had seen a number of others, including exhibitions of both Henri Rousseau and Georges Rouault in Paris. Presumably he had also seen the works of Van Gogh, Gauguin, the Nabis, and the Fauves, even though, for reasons of health, he went out little. During his stay in Berlin he saw an exhibition of Cézanne, Matisse, and Munch at Cassirer's gallery. By that time works of the Brücke group were on show at the Berlin Secession, and in 1908 there had been two simultaneous exhibitions of Van Gogh in Munich. Everywhere prejudices against the modernists were weakening, and they were being more and more discussed. Kandinsky did not look for models to imitate, but he was open to stimulation, and ready to incorporate new insights into his own conceptions. He was to some extent influenced by Russian folk art and icons, as well as by another type of folk art that he and Gabriele Münter had first become acquainted with at Murnau in 1909, namely the southern Bavarian paintings on glass. He was particularly impressed by the extreme simplicity and religious purity of these works.

The painting of his great contemporaries at all events strengthened his determination to turn his back on the past. He may also have been influenced by Rudolf Steiner's "spiritual vision," with which he had come into contact in Berlin: in his sketchbooks we find the name of Edouard Schuré, a friend of Steiner, whose *Persephone* had been performed in Munich in 1907, and whose *Great Initiates* had been published in German in 1909. Kandinsky must have been assailed by strong doubts regarding the scientific view of the world, doubts which were confirmed to him by science itself. "The disintegration of the atom was to me like the disintegration of the whole world," he writes in *Backward Glances.* In that period he had another shattering experience. One day, at twilight, he came to his studio and suddenly saw "an indescribably beautiful painting, permeated by an inner glow." He saw in it nothing but forms, no subject matter at all.

54

It was a picture he seemed to have made. The next day the spell was gone, and he recognized the objects represented in it with painful distinctness. "Now I knew with certainty that the object harms my paintings." He had regarded the object as indispensable, but now he realized that "the ends (and hence also the means) of nature and art differ essentially, organically, and by virtue of a universal law."

Kandinsky had not yet arrived at the nonobjective painting, but in the works he created at Murnau the object had lost its obtrusiveness. Even in the domain of linguistic expression, the factual element now became irrelevant. In 1909 Kandinsky wrote *Yellow*

Sound, an almost abstract "composition for the stage," which at the time was also called *The Giants.* His directions accompanying the play are in keeping with the style of the landscapes dating from the same period, and the five light-yellow giants with blurred faces are not unlike figures in his paintings. His directions for the human voices, the orchestra, and the staging, and the use of colored lights are all anti-naturalistic, and the ending, with the giant growing taller and taller, and finally becoming a cross, is symbolic. It is a work synthesizing all the arts, a mystery play of the kind that Scriabin, the composer who was Kandinsky's age, dreamed of. The composer Thomas von Hartmann, a friend of Kandinsky's, was to have provided a musical score, but the project remained a beautiful dream, like the play itself. Not until 1956 was it prepared for production by Jacques Polieri, the stage director, and Jean Barraque, the composer. Some of the poems that Kandinsky published in the volume *Klänge* ("Sounds") in 1913 were probably written at Murnau in 1909.

The years 1908 and 1909 were transitional: they mark a stage preliminary to the period that extended until the outbreak of the war in 1914. As early as 1909, however, Kandinsky occasionally produced forms that suggest the nonobjective works to come, and the impetus of his Murnau period continued unabated until he left Munich.

He was overflowing with energy, as if he had been forced to hold himself back for a long time. His landscapes of this period vary a great deal in structure, technique, color, and expression, and the other works differ greatly from his landscapes. The landscapes are commonly referred to as Fauvist, but Kandinsky's expressive painterly style, which was also Jawlensky's and Münter's, is quite as independent of the Fauves as of the Brücke. In twentieth-century painting, just as in science, related tendencies and insights make their appearance simultaneously in various countries. This is also true of music and poetry. The disintegration of the Impressionist style, which in music ended with Debussy and Scriabin, was followed by a reaction which took on similar forms in all countries. This reaction was characterized by force, by emphasis on the elemental, and by archaism. It accounts for Stravinsky's, Bartok's and Pratella's use of folk motives. In poetry, too, we may observe everywhere the prominence of imaginative, unreal elements, and of an impersonal self. The "hidden" assumes forms that compel the reader, as they compelled Kandinsky in Vologda, to get inside the work of art itself, rather than to view it from outside.

Kandinsky's Murnau paintings differ from those of the Fauves and of the Brücke group, as Murnau differs from Collioure and from the Dresden countryside. Expressiveness and primitivism are stylistic concepts dominant in both, but whereas in the Fauves expression almost coincides with harmony, and in the Brücke group with drama, a naive inwardness is preponderant in Kandinsky. He has a rural quality, just as the Brücke painters have an urban quality, and the Fauves sophistication. The term "rural" denotes here Kandinsky's affinity with Russian folk art and the religious paintings on glass. Folklore meant to Kandinsky much the same thing that the folk art of Brittany meant to Gauguin, and Polynesian art to Kirchner. But we would characterize only one feature of the Murnau paintings in this way. Another resides in the richness of the color tones.

56

Street in Murnau. 1908 ▶

As Gauguin had prophesied, painting was now entering a musical phase. Van Gogh had written that it should be more musical and less plastic. The harmony of color tones in Kandinsky corresponds to that of musical sounds, and the psychological effect of color invests the object with a symbolic character, or at least divests it of its solidity and naturalistic meaning. The specific features of a house or a cloud become unspecific. It is because he has turned to self-expression that Kandinsky is now less interested in a rich variety of motives and themes than in variations on one and the same theme. Jawlensky, who did not follow Kandinsky into abstraction, did not go beyond variations, but starting from the principle of melodic variations on the theme of the head, explored very thoroughly its human, religious, and formal potentialities.

Kandinsky's variations are harmonic and rhythmic rather than melodic, and his paintings are for the most part built on a primary chord of blue, red, and yellow, in various gradations and shades, and have been given a diagonal rhythm (street, road, woods). For two years he painted landscapes on this basis, without repeating himself. His paintings are often preceded by a more or less elaborate oil study, not too different from the final version. The more important landscapes, such as *Street in Murnau* (1908, color plate, p. 57), *Autumn Landscape with Road* (1908, CC 16), *Bavarian Mountains* (1908, CC 573), and *Landscape with Tower* (1908–1909, color plate, p. 59) all exist in at least two versions.

In *Street in Murnau*, with the green wall, the colors reflect delight in bold contrasts; on the other hand, the structure of the houses and the perspective are so clear that a certain dissonance is created, customarily the opposite of harmony. This is a foreign world, southern Bavarian in details, but as a whole Russian; the mask-like two women and the child are also foreign. Kandinsky places the carmine reds in various degrees of brilliance against intense violet and a blue-green mixed with chalk, shifts from pink to yellow in the street, and continues the yellow in the gray-green of the sky, revealing an extraordinary sense of color. The chords result in a complicated harmony. The musical treatment of such unreal colors carries the naturalistic theme to a fantastic conclusion. The depth of the painting is limited as in Cézanne, the street for the most part being relegated to the plane of the foreground.

The conventional element has not yet entirely disappeared, as can be seen in other paintings (*Before the City*, 1908, CC 592; *Houses*, 1908, CC 591), but ist is increasingly rare, and in the more casual studies of the Lake of Starnberg (CC 585, 588, 589), of the Staffelsee (1908, CC 584, 586, 587), and the Bavarian plateau (1908, CC 574), the structure and tonality, the restrained drawing and the simplified brushwork are voluntary rather than spontaneous. The manner in which the pink of the jetty in *Lake of Starnberg* advances into the green of the water, while the beach is modulated from yellow through pink to violet, shows that Kandinsky now thinks in terms of color even when recording nature.

The tendency to eliminate static elements is occasionally discernible as early as 1908, for instance, in *Autumn Landscape with Road* (CC 16), which shows the Murnau church in the distance. In 1909 this tendency asserted itself more strongly (*Bavarian Mountains*, CC 573), and is most apparent in a view of houses grouped in a half-circle (*Houses at Murnau*, CC 596). There are exceptions: *Bavarian Mountains* (1909, color plate,

58

Landscape with Tower. ▶
1909, 72

p. 63) is purely static; in *Landscape with Tree* (*Murnau*, 1909, CC 20) only the church is slightly off the axis, and the railroad seems animated only because direction is so strongly emphasized. The toylike *Railroad near Murnau* (1909, CC 600) seems less static than it is because of the unrealistic colors, while *Landscape with Locomotive* (1909, CC 599) has quite a different character, thanks to projecting outlines of clouds and trees.

Kandinsky's evolution from 1908 to 1910 can be most easily followed in the treatment of a single motive, the church of Murnau. In 1908 the unity of the work is still maintained by rhythmic, parallel brush strokes, by the balance of the color chords, and by emphasis upon the flat plane (*Church of Murnau*, CC 568, and *Village Church*, CC 571). In 1909 appeared the great poetic developments of the theme, which are represented in the Paris collection, in the Salomon R. Guggenheim Museum, and the Museum of Modern Art, New York (p. 59, and CC 597 and 598). The colors are more conspicuous than the construction, however correct; they glow like illuminated windows at night, while outlines are merely approximate accompaniments to the objects. These latter appear to be internally related, and their volumes are reduced to a minimum. The hill near the church has no more body and weight than the conglomerations of white clouds. Kandinsky has used contrasts of light and dark, and of colors, putting pink and violet in the tower, and accents of carmine, violet, and black on the wooded hill. At some points of the canvas nothing is to be seen but a tapestry of color tones. The definitive version (in Paris) displays a surer pictorial instinct than the study, while the third painting is built on the contrast between the severity of the architecture and the softness of the landscape, between cold and passionately warm chords of color.

In the views of the Murnau church executed in 1910, both the architecture and the landscape have been set in motion. The tower has become a column, leaning now to the right, now to the left; the perspective has loosened, and distortions have made their appearance. In *Winter in Murnau with Church* (CC 611), the leftward movement is counterbalanced by the diagonals and the clouds, and the resulting triangle restrains the restlessness of the patches of white and other light colors. The Eindhofen version (study, 1910, CC 613) moves the recognizably naturalistic elements upward; the church tower, the houses, and the mountain have grown taller, and the clouds have already assumed forms that are also to be found in nonnaturalistic paintings of the same period. In general, the formal canon is freer. The gables are now merely triangles, and the trees and mountains are in process of assimilation to the triangle. In the dramatic version in the Munich Foundation (CC 614) forms that could denote more than one possible natural element have already appeared. The still recognizable elements look like line drawings, and the unrealistic colors conceal the logical unity. In *Garden* (CC 615) the subject "Murnau with Church" recedes again, the haystack at the left being thrust into the fairytale plant life, which has become the chief element, a kind of Noah's ark; the church is no bigger than the sunflower in the foreground. The subject disappears entirely in *Mountain Landscape* with Church (CC 616), which can scarcely be analyzed into its parts. The initiative has passed to the colors and the color planes, upon which the painter has set down his signs to suggest his meaning.

Color becomes increasingly crucial. The wintry *Murnau* goes far in that direction: the pink and light violet, the deep blue and green, the white and the black have emancipated themselves from the things and create tonalities by themselves. In the Munich canvas the colorful white, the carmine, the light blue and blue-green transport the subject to the sphere of dream and legend. This was the direction of development. The painter distributes and links the colors, combines them and differentiates them, treating them as if they were beings of a specific character and specific significance. As in music, the materials now come to the fore, and in this respect Kandinsky stands between Mussorgsky and Scriabin. The language of color—just as in those composers—calls for depth, for fantasy; and Kandinsky's art will henceforward depend increasingly on its own resources. The sulphurous blue of *Village Street,* for instance, contrasting with deep blue and blue-green, and the violet-pink combined with vermilion, are dissonances behind which stand irrational energies, possibly memories of his youth in Russia.

In addition to the Murnau landscapes, Kandinsky executed a few other paintings. In 1908 he painted the *Ludwigskirche in Munich* (CC 590), with a crowd of people in front of the great doors, rendered entirely in tiny dots and spots of color—a momentary affinity with Monticelli. In 1909 he painted *Arab Cemetery* (p. 264) in his Murnau colors, but with arabesquelike forms—a memory of Tunis. There are a few interiors dating from 1910, the living room in the Ainmillerstrasse (CC 618), and a conversation between Gabriele Münter and Marianne von Werefkin (CC 42). One figure, in pink, violet and blue-green, comes very close to a Bonnard of the same period, the other being closer to the hurriedly sketched landscape studies of the same year. Kandinsky later gave this picture to Klee as a memento. He also painted further Biedermeier scenes (1909, CC 18 and 30), but this time they have nothing in common with the Jugendstil, and are done in violent, though naturalistic colors. Once again inspiration seems to have come from theatrical impressions of Moscow: this is suggested by the first version, with its pseudo-classical stage architecture.

Although Kandinsky, from 1908 on, was aiming at nonobjective works, he continued his attempts to achieve pictorial effects with the help of landscape elements. It must not be assumed that the naturalistic ingredient in his works decreased continuously or gradually. On this principle, if *Murnau Winter Landscape* (1911, p. 271) were not dated, we would have to assign it to 1909, and *Waterfall* (CC 606) to 1911, although it is dated 1909. Recalling his "rain" landscapes, which he was still painting as late as 1913, we must conclude that Kandinsky for a long time preserved an open mind with regard to an "objective" approach, and from 1910 on naturalistic an "absolute" tendencies run parallel, influencing each other and contrasting with each other in the most various ways.

The landscapes he painted between 1911 and 1913 come close to the Improvisations and Compositions, the former falling between the years 1909 and 1910. *Winter II* (1911, CC 55) —the study probably dates from 1910 (CC 624)—reduces a village, perhaps Murnau, to a few crystalline bodies; *Autumn I* of 1911 (color plate, p. 117) is more like an Improvisation with the suggestion of a village on a hillside. The naturalism of the preliminary study (1910, CC 617) has yielded in the painting to a sign language of suggestion, the relatively distinct village to a structure of black triangles and straight lines. Blue-pink and blue-green, next to yellow, ocher, and brown, produce the autumnal tonality; the relation to nature is here comparable to that of Haydn's oratorio *The Seasons. Autumn II* of 1912 (CC 79) with its transposed proportions, its purplish red and dark blue, is on the same level, while *Landscape with Two Poplars* (study 1911; color plate, p. 129; painting, 1912, CC 78) showing a village street with peasant houses, is almost pure play of color, in which the carmine-red at the left contrasts sharply with the cold ice-blue houses at the right. The tension between the inner and the outer world has decreased: "if the artist has outer and inner eyes for nature," Kandinsky says, "nature rewards him by giving him inspiration," i.e., the interpretation of nature becomes more poetic, and the object is now there purely by sufferance of the painter, as it were. The same is true of the last landscape, *Landscape with Rain,* of 1913 (CC 85). The study for it, which ante- dates it by three years (CC 38), is still in the Murnau style, with its diagonal cross, the contrast between buildings and nature, and strident colors. In the definitive version the epic horizontal shape has been replaced by a square, subdivided into several triangles; the village on the mountain slope has become a Cubist interlacement of cylinders and cones, and contrasts between lights and shadows, texture and atmosphere have been eliminated. The chimneys are transformed into vertical supports, and the contrasting colors (violet, blue, and blue-green) are stressed as much as the complementaries red and green. The same principles prevail in the whole and in the details.

Landscape with Rain marks one of the high points of Kandinsky's development in the field of "absolute" art. In 1910 Kandinsky begins his epoch-making breakthrough to the abstract, the innovation for which he is best known. For three years he will paint in three styles concurrently—one of expressive landscapes, the second, an intermediate style, with the dimensions of memory cutting across free elements, and the third of his Improvisations and Compositions. During these crucial years Kandinsky witnessed and participated in developments that reflected a spiritual and artistic revolution, the consequences of which are still being felt today.

One of these developments was the founding of a new association of artists in Munich. Preliminary discussions with a view to forming such a group were held by Jawlensky and his friends in January 1909. The artists were motivated not only by the hostility which the official galleries displayed toward the new painting, but also by the feeling that they were different, and the need to be closer to each other. Kandinsky assumed the chairmanship of the new group which called itself *Neue Künstlervereinigung München,* after Jawlensky and H. Schlittgen, a former member of the Phalanx, had declined to serve in that capacity. In addition to Kandinsky, the founding members were Alexej von Jawlensky, Marianne von Werefkin, Adolf Erbslöh, Alexander Kanoldt, Alfred Kubin, Gabriele Münter, and two art patrons. In the course of 1909 the group was joined by the Neo-Impressionists Paul Baum and Karl Hofer (these two stayed only for a short time), the Russian artist Wladimir von Bechtejeff, Erna Rossi, Moissey Kogan, and the dancer Alexander Sacharoff; and in 1910, by the Frenchmen Pierre Girieud and Le Fauconnier. The group held its first exhibition (December 1–15, 1909) at H. Thannhauser's Moderne Galerie, Theatinerstrasse 7 (poster by Kandinsky, p. 39,8). A second exhibition was held at the same gallery from September 1 to 14. The two exhibitions were shown in several other German cities as well. For the second show

Bavarian Mountains ▶
with Village. 1909

a number of Russian, French, and German artists were represented as guest exhibitors—the brothers David and Vladimir Burliuk, Vasily Denizov, and Alexander Mogilevsky; Braque, Picasso, Rouault, Derain, Vlaminck, and Van Dongen from Paris; in addition, E. Kahler, the sculptors E. Scharff, B. Hoetger, H. Haller, and two less known artists, A. Nieder and S. Soudbinine. Franz Marc, who lived at Sindelsdorf near Munich, saw the second exhibition. Deeply impressed, he called on Jawlensky and Kandinsky in their studios, and joined the association. As a result conservative Munich was suddenly confronted with an avant-garde whose leaders were local residents—a fact that made them all the more objectionable to many.

Only a few of the new ideas were made public. The prospectus merely says that the group is striving for an art expressing the interpenetration of external impressions and inner experiences, seeking forms that will say only the necessary, aiming at an artistic synthesis of the arts (Eichner). The term "the necessary" is obviously Kandinsky's; "synthesis," Jawlensky's. In the catalogue of the second exhibition the artists were less reticent. In the preface, dated Murnau, August 1910, Kandinsky writes:
"The work comes into the world at an undetermined hour, from a source still unknown, but it comes inevitably.
"Cold calculation, random spots of color, mathematically exact construction (clearly shown or concealed), drawing that is now silent and now strident, painstaking thoroughness, colors like a flourish of trumpets or a pianissimo on the violin, great, calm, oscillating, splintered surfaces.
"Is this not form?
"Is this not *the means?*
"Suffering, searching, tormented souls, deeply sundered by the conflict between spirit and matter. Discovery! The part that is living in both animate and inanimate nature. Solace in the phenomena—the outer, the inner. Anticipation of joy. The call. To speak of mystery in terms of mystery.
"Is this not content?
"Is this not the conscious and unconscious *goal* of the compelling urge to create?
"We feel sorry for those who have the power to speak for art, and do not.
'We feel sorry for those whose souls are deaf to the voice of art.
"Man speaks to man of the superhuman—the *language* of art."
The essential ideas are those of *On Spiritual in Art,* which Kandinsky wrote during these same months, and to which we shall return. He was about to commit his theories to writing, having had some practice as a writer—since 1901 he had been noting down his ideas on art from time to time.
The catalogue of the second exhibition contains contributions by Odilon Redon, Le Fauconnier, and the brothers Burliuk. The latter protest vigorously against the idea that they are mere imitators of the French; rather, they say, one should speak of their affinities with each other. At this early date they also mention the archaic and synthesis, and refer to old Russian icons, folk art, and Scythian sculpture. This contribution is interesting as a profession of faith by the Russian avant-garde in their native land as well as in Europe, and is entirely in line with Kandinsky's ideas. The

Burliuks sent their article from the Tavrida province in southern Russia. Their views were soon to be much discussed in St. Petersburg, too.

Both the exhibition and the catalogue caused an uproar in Munich, where most artists were anything but avant-garde. Kandinsky's view of them may be learned from five letters on art he sent to the Russian periodical *Apollo* (1909–1917), between October 1909 and October 1910 (*Zwiebelturm*, 5, 1950). In these letters he complains about the lack of understanding in Munich of Cézanne, Gauguin, Van Gogh, and Matisse, and about the great respect in which Fritz Erler and other inferior painters were held. He kept going back to the Manet exhibition at Thannhauser's (1910), feeling that this French painter had a quality of inner necessity and abstraction. He was struck by Matisse's sense for color and form; the other Fauves, he thought, were interested only in the Expressionist use of color and, despite the lesson of Cézanne, neglected form. He also mentions the new group's two exhibitions, and the reactions of the public, which greeted the works with laughter and abuse, and even spat at them.

Kandinsky did not exaggerate. Press and public were outraged. The *Münchner Neuesten Nachrichten* said: "Either the majority of the members and guests of the Association are incurably insane, or they are shameless bluffers who are not unfamiliar with the age's demand for sensation, and who are capitalizing on it." Franz Marc, always ready to take up the cudgels for the right cause, wrote in reply: "Has the imagination become so philistinized today, so constipated, as to have broken down completely?" (Reprint, 1910). He was planning even then to publish a magazine championing the new artistic tendencies. He already had a title—*Blaue Blätter,* an anticipation of the Blaue Reiter of 1912.

Kandinsky had hesitated for some time before joining the new group: except for Jawlensky, its members seemed to him uninteresting, not because their work was too "objective" for his taste, but because he felt that it was, on the one hand, too "decorative," and, on the other, not independent enough. He had nothing against "objective" art as such: Thomas Hartmann, the composer, in an unpublished lecture he gave in New York in 1950, noted that at this time his friend Kandinsky was extraordinarily patient with fellow painters whose ideas differed from his own. It was the latter who viewed Kandinsky with increasing suspicion, and who had it against *him* that his works were becoming more and more abstract. There were two factions—a group around Kandinsky, another around Erbslöh and Kanoldt. Jawlensky was between them, and would have gladly served as a mediator. By the end of 1910 this situation became critical. Alfred Kubin called Kandinsky's attention to the existing disagreements, and on January 10, 1911, Kandinsky wrote a letter to Jawlensky, in which he resigned from his chairmanship. "Last year showed me with particular clarity that my opinions on the group's aims and activities are not shared by the other leaders or by a majority of the rank and file." (Eichner). He was succeeded by Erbslöh. But disagreement continued, and on August 10, 1911, Franz Marc wrote to Macke: "With Kandinsky, we foresee clearly that the next jury (late in autumn) will lead to nasty quarreling, and that sooner or later there will be a hopeless division of opinion, with one or the other party seceding. The question will be, who is to stay. We do not want to abandon the association, but the untalented members will have to go."

The inevitable split finally occurred when the jury for the third exhibition rejected Kandinsky's *Composition V* on the grounds that it exceeded the prescribed dimensions. This was a pretext, the real reason being the character of the painting. Kandinsky left the group, and he was followed by Franz Marc, Alfred Kubin, and Gabriele Münter; Delaunay declared himself in sympathy with the painters who left. Jawlensky and Marianne von Werefkin remained, but they felt that the group had lost its purpose, and their resignation in 1912 spelled its end.

Upon resigning Kandinsky and Franz Marc decided to organize an exhibition of their own and their friends' works. They approached the dealer Thannhauser, who promised them two rooms. Hugo von Tschudi, who had come to Munich in 1909 to be general director of the state museums, used his influence with Thannhauser in behalf of the artists who wanted to exhibit. On December 18 the first exhibition of the Blaue Reiter group was held, simultaneously with an exhibition of the Neue Künstlervereinigung. The show kept open until January 1st. In the meantime the idea of a periodical exclusively reserved to artists had taken shape, and the Blaue Reiter almanac was readied for publication, as well as the text of Kandinsky's long since completed book, *On the Spiritual in Art*. The two manifestoes which appeared in 1912 were the most important published in prewar Germany.

Meanwhile, the opposition was not silent. It found its hero and interpreter in Otto Fischer, later director of the Basel Kunstsammlung. At the request of the Neue Künstlervereinigung, he published *Das neue Bild*, a beautifully printed book illustrated with color plates, somewhat academic in design. The text reflected the level of the more talented members of the group: "The power of color is a sign of the new conception ... Color is a means of representation ... of expression ... of composition." Fischer elucidated the nature of line and of plane in a manner not unlike Kandinsky's. "The painting is like a world arising out of chaos." But he rejected abstraction, and polemicized against Kandinsky: "The painting is not only expression, but also representation. It does not express the soul directly, but the soul in the object. A painting without an object is meaningless. Half object and half soul is simple delusion. Such are the errors of empty visionaries and deceivers. The muddleheaded may speak of the 'spiritual,' but the spirit does not muddle, it makes things clear." Obviously Fischer was also putting in question Kandinsky's greatest paintings of that period, in this agreeing with the artists of the Künstlervereinigung from which Jawlensky had withdrawn.

The first Blaue Reiter exhibition was epoch-making, although it consisted of no more than forty-three works, by Albert Bloch, David Burliuk, Vladimir Burliuk, Heinrich Campendonk, Eugen Kahler, Wassily Kandinsky, August Macke, Franz Marc, Gabriele Münter, Jean Bloé Niestlé, the composer Arnold Schönberg, Henri Rousseau, Robert Delaunay, and Elisabeth Epstein. Named as the organizers were "The editors of the *Blaue Reiter*, Kandinsky and Franz Marc." The works shown were a small but by no means one-sided selection. Kandinsky exhibited *Composition V, Improvisation 22,* and *Impression Moscow* (which was destroyed late in the Second World War). Marc exhibited, among other works, *Blue Horses* and *Yellow Cow;* Macke, the abstract *Storm;* Delaunay, *St.Sèverin* (1909), and one of his Eiffel Towers (*Tower,* 1911); Gabriele Münter, still life compositions and landscapes; V.Burliuk, a Cubist head; Bloch, a dancelike *Harlequinade;* Schönberg, a self-portrait (p. 24, 19), and two *Visions,* and Rousseau, two small landscapes that Kandinsky had purchased two years earlier. In other words, it was a heterogeneous group, and not all the works were at the same level. The exhibition was taken on tour to other cities, and on March 12, 1912, opened in Berlin as the first show at the Sturm gallery. Works by Klee, Kubin, Jawlensky, and Werefkin had been added by Walden.

The first page of the catalogue includes a sentence that looks very much like a pro-grammatic statement: "In this small exhibition we are not trying to propagate *one* precise and specific form, but we do hope to illustrate, by the variety of the forms represented, how the artist's *inner wish* may be variously embodied." Even before the first exhibition, Franz Marc had said: "Keep away from programs!"

cut for cover of the catalogue
first Blaue Reiter exhibition.
1911

The small catalogue was supplemented with an advance announcement of the Blaue Reiter almanac: "Next spring there will appear . . ." and on the facing page was a kind of statement which could refer to the exhibition as well as to the book: "A great rev-olution, the displacement of the center of gravity in art, literature, and music. Diversity of forms; the constructive, compositional character of these forms; an intensive turn to inner nature, and, linked with it, a refusal to embellish outer nature. These are, in general terms, symptoms of a new spiritual Renaissance. To show the features and manifestations of this change, to emphasize its inner connection with the past, to reveal the expression of inner aspirations in every form suggestive of inwardness—this is the goal that the *Blaue Reiter* is striving to attain." Unquestionably, Kandinsky was the author of this text: it is written in his style and reflects his way of thinking.

The second exhibition was held at Hans Goltz's, Briennerstrasse 8, in Munich, and opened February 12, 1912. It included only prints, drawings, and watercolors, 313 items in all. Among them were works by Hans Arp, Albert Bloch, Georges Braque, Robert Delaunay, André Derain, Maria Franck-Marc, R. de la Fresnaye, Wilhelm Gimmi, Natalie Goncharova, Erich Heckel, Walter Helbig, Wassily Kandinsky (twelve watercolors), E. L. Kirchner, Paul Klee (seventeen prints), Alfred Kubin, Michael Larionov, Robert Lotiron, Oscar Luthy, August Macke, Casimir Malevich, Franz Marc, Moriz Melzer, Wilhelm Morgner, Otto Mueller, Gabriele Münter, Emil Nolde, Max Pechstein, Pablo Picasso, Georg Tappert, Paul Vera, Maurice Vlaminck, and eight Russian popular engravings (newly printed from old woodblocks).

Once again the exhibition was noteworthy in that it brought together artists of several nationalities (German, French, Russian, Swiss, and one American), and of several movements—Expressionists, Fauves, Cubists, and Abstractionists. Not everyone was of the first rank, but all were regarded as such at the time. "We were not trying to create an exclusive movement with specific aims, but simply to juxtapose various mani-festations of the new art on an international basis," Kandinsky wrote retrospectively in *Kunstblatt,* in 1930. In the preface to the catalogue he had referred to the boundless wealth of natural forms, and the adjustment of form to necessity. "Nature creates her forms for her own purposes. Art creates its forms for its own purposes . . . Our de-voutest wish is to arouse joy through giving examples of the inexhaustible wealth of forms, which the world of art creates indefatigably, in accordance with its laws." There is no trace of propaganda in his words; on the contrary, they appeal to the public's goodwill, and reflect an attempt to convince it with indisputable facts. And so far as the artists themselves were concerned, there was not effort to found a party.

The second exhibition did not go on tour, and when Herwarth Walden in October 1913 held the First German Salon d'Automne at the Sturm gallery in Berlin—a large international exhibition consisting of 366 items—he included works of the Blaue Reiter not as a group, but individually, hanging them in different rooms. Kandinsky was represented by seven major works including *Composition VI, Painting with White Border*, and *Improvisation 31*. In 1914 Walden organized a few exhibitions under the banner of the Blaue Reiter, outside Germany.

Russian print, from Blaue Reiter (1912)

In 1912, Kandinsky held a one-man show at the Sturm gallery. He exhibited sixty-four works dated from 1902 to 1912, including early paintings such as *Bright Air* (1902) and *Old Town* (1902), some of the Murnau landscapes, a number of his "legendary" paintings, and purely abstract ones such as *Improvisation 25*. It opened on October 2, 1912, and later was repeated at the Goltz gallery in Munich, with the addition of nine paintings, and certain substitutions among the others. The catalogues to the two exhibitions contained a preface by Kandinsky. In the first printing of 1,000 copies, it consisted merely of a lengthy biographical note; for the second thousand, Kandinsky added an essay in which he replied to critics. Since it is dated January 1, 1913, the catalogue must have remained on sale at the Sturm gallery after the exhibition. Goltz reprinted the new text unchanged. On January 1, the exhibition must still have been open. We will come back to this essay when we discuss Kandinsky's *On the Spiritual in Art*.

Kandinsky replied to the critics of the new movement because he had been the chief target of their attacks. He had been abused in the crudest terms; on the occasion of a small exhibition at the Bock gallery in Hamburg in January 1913, the *Hamburger Fremdenblatt* described his painting as "imbecile" (in the issue of February 15, 1913, reprinted in *Der Sturm*, No. 150/151, 1913). A protest against such brutal criticism appeared in *Der Sturm* (nos. 150/151 and 154/155), and was signed with noteworthy unanimity by artists, museum directors, art historians, and writers, both German and non-German. Among the signatories were Osthaus, Swarzensky, Steenhoff, Hausenstein, Grisebach, Burger, Behne, Döblin, Ehrenstein, Basler, Apollinaire, Delaunay, Léger, Gleizes, Jawlensky, Klee, Arp, Campendonk, Werefkin, and Bechtejeff—in other words, the signatories included former adversaries. This protest caused general amazement, all the more so because some of the signatories expressed their sympathy for the insulted artist in some detail. Guillaume Apollinaire wrote: "I have often spoken of Kandinsky's works when they have been exhibited in Paris. I wish to use this opportunity to express my high regard for an artist whose work I consider both serious and significant." W. Hausenstein wrote that Kandinsky was a gentleman and representative of a new idealism.

For Kandinsky these public declarations were all the more important because he had sold few pictures since 1910. The public had turned its back on him. Even old friends and supporters in Germany and in Russia began to have their doubts, among others Izdebsky, who owned an art gallery in Odessa, and who had previously exhibited Kandinsky's work several times with success. It is astonishing that, despite such violent attacks, Kandinsky managed to get his works exhibited as often as he did, both in Germany and abroad. He continued to keep a careful record, even of exhibitions in which he was represented by only a few works. In 1910, he participated in the Sonderbund exhibition at Düsseldorf, which issued a beautiful catalogue on that occasion; in 1911 he exhibited at the Indépendants in Paris, and in the Berlin Secession; in 1921 at the Sonderbund exhibition in Cologne and at the Neue Bund in Zürich (which Klee reviewed in detail in *Die Alpen*, VI, mentioning Kandinsky by name), and in 1913 at the Armory show in New York. He had one-man shows in Odessa in 1910 and at the Goldschmidt gallery in Frankfurt, in addition to those mentioned above at the Sturm and the Goltz galleries in 1912. There was another at the Bock gallery in Hamburg in 1913. Unquestionably, he attracted more attention than his friends Franz Marc and Paul Klee.

Far from begrudging him this success, these two friends recognized and respected his talent as an artist and his human qualities. Klee repeatedly referred to him in the most flattering terms: "He has an exceptionally fine, clear head," he wrote in his Diaries in 1911, and elsewhere he calls him "the boldest" artist of the group. "Intellectual rigor in him takes productive forms quite naturally . . . The museums do not illumine him, he illumines them, and the greatest works there cannot diminish for him the value of his own spiritual world" (*Die Alpen*, VI, 1912).

Marc shared Klee's admiration for Kandinsky. After Marc's death, his widow wrote that Kandinsky had been his greatest single influence, that he had enriched and confirmed Marc's ideas, and that it had been thanks to Kandinsky that Marc found the courage to be himself. In 1915 Marc wrote in *Der Sturm*: "Whenever I think of him, I always see him in a broad street, thronged with grotesque shouting figures; there is one wise man among them, and this is he ... On the other hand, I always think of Kandinsky's paintings differently—far away from the street, imbedded in the blue wall of the sky ... shortly to fade away in the dark silence of time, only to come back with the radiance of comets ... And there is something else I feel when I think of Kandinsky's pictures: inexpressible gratitude, that there should just once have appeared such a man, capable of moving mountains. And with what nobility has he done so!"

The only artist who, despite friendship for Marc, remained aloof from the Blaue Reiter and from Kandinsky, was August Macke. He had more faith in Matisse and Picasso. Nevertheless, after he visited the first Blaue Reiter exhibition in Cologne, he wrote to Bernard Köhler: "Kandinsky is unquestionably a magnificent artist" (January 22, 1912). A few months earlier he had written to Marc: "He is also a romantic, a dreamer, a visionary and teller of fairytales ... There is boundless vitality in him ... It surges up not only in the form of rocks, castles, and seas, but also in his infinitely tender, pastoral element." This native of the Rhineland, however, was basically as far removed from abstract art as from the literary style of its champion, and he must occasionally have addressed harsh words to Franz Marc.

In memories of this period, Kandinsky repeatedly emerges as the leading figure in Munich. Hugo Ball regarded him as one of "the prophets of the rebirth," and wrote that Kandinsky, "by his sheer presence" set Munich in the vanguard of modernism. His words, his colors, and his tones, he says, were alive in a rare harmony, and according to him, Kandinsky's ultimate purpose was to represent art as such, not merely to create works of art. (*Flucht aus der Zeit, fuga saeculi,* 1927.)

There was a good deal of playing politics in the art world between 1910 and 1912. The steady strengthening of the new movement aroused militant opposition from those who are eternally enamored of yesterday. The Worpswede painter Vinnen published an attack against French art early in 1911, criticizing the German museums for purchasing it. This gave the Munich artists a pretext "to sound the battle cry" (Marc). They replied to Vinnen in a pamphlet called *German and French Art,* under the imprint of Reinhard Piper, publisher of the Blaue Reiter almanac. The pamphlet testified to the high level of artists, gallery directors, and critics, and to their magnificent solidarity. Pauli, Osthaus, Lichtwark, Liebermann, Slevogt, Rohlfs, Worringer, Hausenstein, and Wilhelm Uhde defended French artists and modern art as a whole. Kandinsky, too, took part, but, as is so often the case with creative people, more in his own behalf than in reply to Vinnen's pamphlet. He spoke of the inner and the outer man, of the inner and the outer world, and their inevitable unity, defining the harmony of the work of art as the highest equilibrium between inner and outer, i.e., between content and form. He discussed individual style and the school, and the need to construct: "Next to music, painting will be the second art inconceivable save in terms of construction, and already inconceivable otherwise today." Since the outer [form] must be subordinated to the inner, with-

Improvisation on ▶
Mahogany. 1910, 93a

out compromise, he calls this "renunciation of the natural element." Marc went a bit further into the questions raised, being fond of polemic, but he, too, rose above banal attack. "A strong wind is today carrying the germs of a new art all over Europe . . . The irritation of a few artists on German soil at the fact that the wind is blowing from the west . . . Nor do they like the east wind, for the same seeds are coming from Russia . . . The wind bloweth where it listeth."

Another skirmish was fought in the little magazine *Der Pan* (published in Berlin by W. Herzog), in which Marc wrote about "the new painting" and "the idea of construction in the new painting" (March 7 and 21, 1912). It was Max Beckmann, of all people, at this time under the influence of the Liebermann Secession, who undertook to reply to Marc, insisting that "artistic sensibility is linked with naturalism in art," and spoke of "Siberian-Bavarian memorials to disaster." He was clearly aiming at Kandinsky. Marc took up the challenge, and set "the inner greatness of the work" against Beckmann's ideas.

The time was ripe for the programmatic publication that had been ready for months. In 1912 the *Blaue Reiter Almanac* appeared, shortly after the second edition of *On the Spiritual in Art* (a third edition was announced in *Der Sturm* for October 1912). Kandinsky and Marc were the editors, and contributors included August Macke, David Burliuk, Arnold Schönberg. R. Allard, Thomas von Hartmann, E. v. Busse, L. Subeneieff, and N. Kulbin. The Almanac contained essays on contemporary art, music, and the theater. The reproductions ranged from the art of the primitives, folk art, and children's drawings, to the Orient and ancient Egypt, and from medieval woodcuts and sculpture, to Cézanne, Rousseau, Delaunay, and the group around Kandinsky. The musical supplement was written by Arnold Schönberg, Alban Berg, and Anton von Webern. The composition for the stage was by Kandinsky. Besides the trade edition, there was a de luxe edition of fifty copies, with two added woodcuts, and a "museum" edition of ten copies, each containing an original work by one of the two editors. The cover was designed by Kandinsky who made no fewer than ten preliminary watercolor sketches for it (CC 672-681). Since Piper held up the printing despite Hugo von Tschudi's intercession, the collector Bernard Köhler of Berlin, whose niece was married to Macke, underwrote the sale of a certain number of copies; he also financed *On the Spiritual in Art* and later the Salon d'Automne catalogue for the Sturm gallery. Unfortunately only one volume of the Almanac appeared; we know that further volumes were planned, because certain articles which had been commissioned did not appear in the first volume, and because announcements described a series of volumes to be published at irregular intervals. But the Almanac sold very slowly; moreover, both Kandinsky and Marc became increasingly absorbed in their own work.

The idea for the book goes back to 1910. Toward the end of that year Kandinsky suggested to the Neue Künstlervereinigung that artists should have an opportunity to write about art, and that works of art should be shown In their full range from the archaic epochs to the latest developments. On April 19, 1911 he wrote to Marc that he was considering a kind of yearly almanac, to be published by Piper, and edited by him and Marc; all the contributions were to be written by artists. He was planning to include the past and, if possible, the future, and mentioned some comparative examples. "The

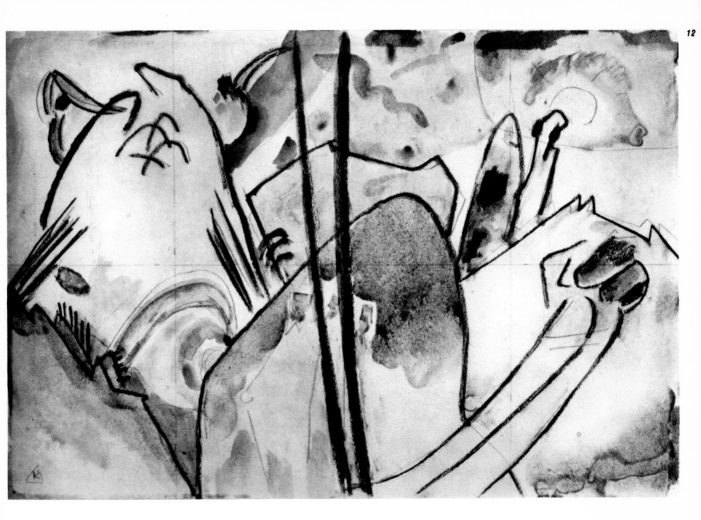

12 *Sketch for 'Composition IV', 1911*
  Entwurf zu ›Komposition IV‹
  Projet pour «Composition IV»
  Abbozzo per ‹Composizione IV›

13 *Study for 'All Saints', 1911*
  Studie zu ›Allerheiligen‹
  Etude pour «Toussaint»
  Studio per ‹Ognissanti›

14 Watercolor, 1911
   Aquarell
   Aquarelle
   Acquerello

15 Lyrical, 1911
   Lyrisches
   Lyrique
   Lirica

16 Study for 'Improvisation 25', 1912
   Studie zu ›Improvisation 25‹
   Etude pour «Improvisation 25»
   Studio per ‹Improvvisazione 25›

17

17 Study for one of the representations of
the 'Last Judgment', 1912
Studie zu einem ›Jüngsten Gericht‹
Etude pour un
«Jugement Dernier»
Studio per un ‹Giudizio Universale›

18 Rain Landscape, 1911
Regenlandschaft
Paysage de pluie
Paesaggio con pioggia

18

book might be called *The Chain* or by some other name." In the summer of 1911, encouraged by Marc, he worked intensively on this project, and began to collect contributions. On September 8, Marc wrote to Macke: "We want to start an almanac, as an organ for all the really new ideas of our day. Painting, music, drama, etc. . . . The emphasis would be on comparative material . . . We expect it to be so useful and stimulating, both for its bearing on our own work and for the clarification of ideas, that this almanac has become the focus of all our hopes." Most of the work for it was accomplished in October. Macke's letters to his wife, those of his wife to the two Marcs, and Mrs. Macke's memoirs afford us a glimpse into those exciting weeks when the Almanac was taking definitive shape. "Every day seems like a holiday!" "An unforgettable period for us all . . . being present at the birth of the Blaue Reiter or, at the very least, its baptism." "Those were unforgettable times, when all the men were working on their manuscripts, polishing and revising . . . then the contributions began to come in from elsewhere, as requested, together with suggestions for works to be reproduced . . . Kandinsky himself was a very unusual, original type, uncommonly stimulating to every artist who came in contact with him. There was something uniquely mystical, highly imaginative about him, linked with rare pathos and dogmatism." Kandinsky did the greater part of the work. He not only wrote for the Almanac (almost half of the text is by him), he also revised, translated the Russian contributions and produced the illustrative material for them, and collected comparative examples, never losing sight of the "spiritual" as the main idea, the common root of the arts and the key to their common affinities. Marc was responsible for the reproductions of works by the Brücke group in Berlin, and Macke concentrated on ethnographic material.

The volume opened with Marc's essay on "Spiritual Values." The first sentences left a deep impression on readers: "It is noteworthy that our attitude toward spiritual values is completely different from our attitude toward material values. For instance, when someone conquers a new colony for his country, the whole nation hails him enthusiastically . . . But if it occurs to someone to present his country with a purely spiritual good, it is almost always rejected angrily and indignantly. The gift is looked upon with suspicion, and every effort is made to obliterate it. Were it still allowed, the giver would be burned at the stake, even today." Marc also wrote Hugo von Tschudi, who died just before the Almanac, which is dedicated to his memory, came out. In another essay he dealt with the problem of making comparisons between works of art. "How do we recognize a genuine work? In the same way as we recognize anything else that is genuine: by its possession of an inner life guaranteeing its truth."
Macke, in an essay entitled "Masks," said that form is a mystery to us, because it expresses mysterious forces. "To create forms is to live . . . The life of man is manifested in forms. Every artistic form is the outward manifestation of man's inner life." Behind these masks, he goes on to say, lie the joys and sorrows of the nations; where these are absent, there is no art.
Schönberg, writing on the relations between music and text, concluded that in listening to Schubert's songs nothing is gained by knowing the texts. He was hardly aware, he wrote, of the poetic content of his own songs. He was in revolt against content,

against the idea that music is not a universal language that "composes and thinks for everyone."

Thomas von Hartmann, a Russian, was close in spirit to Kandinsky when he wrote that "in all art, and in music in particular, every means that derives from inner necessity is correct."

Kandinsky's essays "On the Question of Form," and "On Composition for the Stage" are the most important in the Almanac, but since they are really supplements to his books, we shall discuss them with the latter.

The same sure instinct that chose the contributing artists was exercised in the choice of illustrations. These include Picasso's *Woman with Mandolin*, Delaunay's *Eiffel Tower*, which Bernhard Köhler had bought at the first Blaue Reiter exhibition, Matisse's *La Musique*, and *La Danse* from the Shchukin collection in Moscow, Henri Rousseau's self-portrait, Kokoschka's *Else Kupfer*, Marc's *Bull*, Macke's *Storm*, painted at Sindelsdorf in 1911 under Kandinsky's influence, and Kandinsky's *Lyrical* representing a leaping horse, a design of which the painter was very fond and which also figures as a color woodcut in *Klänge* (1913). Just as felicitous was the selection of works by primitives, examples of Bavarian paintings on glass, paintings by the post-Impressionists Van Gogh and Cézanne, and by the Brücke group. The Almanac is unique in European art literature; no other country produced a single volume that so fully captures the excitement and tensions of the years preceding the First World War.

As for the origin of the title, Kandinsky gave his account much later, in the *Kunstblatt* of 1930: "We thought up the name [*Der Blaue Reiter*] while sitting at a café table in a rose arbor at Sindelsdorf. Both of us were fond of blue things, Marc of blue horses, and I of blue riders. So the title suggested itself." He added that the second volume would have dealt with the relations between art and science. Actually, the choice of title had been somewhat less impromptu. We know that blue was both Kandinsky's and Marc's favorite color, and that Marc was fond of horses and Kandinsky of riders. The motive of the rider goes back to Kandinsky's beginnings as an artist, to his earliest woodcuts; there are riders in *Bright Air* (1902) and *Festive Procession* (1902/1903), and in 1903 he even painted a *Blue Rider*, of which he spoke later. Whether this was a self-portrait, as has been conjectured, seems doubtful; rather, it is an allegory of romantic yearnings. Perhaps there was a trace of the Blue Flower of the German Romantics, who were coming back into fashion at this time. There had been horses and riders in Kandinsky's childhood works; they reappeared later in his romantic paintings, and then again after 1909, in his woodblock design for the membership cards of the Neue Künstlervereinigung. In 1909 there were also riders in *Blue Mountain*, *Improvisation* 2, and *Improvisation* 3; in 1910, we find them in *St. George*, *Improvisation* 9 and *Improvisation* 12, and the rider is in all these appearances a noble figure. For Kandinsky, blue was the typically "celestial color" that summons man to the infinite and arouses his yearning for the pure and the transcendental. He made this statement in *On the Spiritual in Art*. The color blue and the rider are definitely related. Kandinsky would have been quite capable of thinking up the title even without Marc, but Marc's thinking ran along the same lines, and he had just painted his *Blue Horses*.

78

Improvisation 6 ▶
(African). 1910, 96

The title *Blaue Reiter* became a rallying call, symbolizing a renewal of art like the terms "Brücke" and "Fauves." The fact that it was launched by artists of international origins did not make its success any easier in Germany. In other countries, there was as yet no demand for German art. The aims and accomplishments of the Blaue Reiter became clear to the Germans only in the 1920s, and in certain other countries not until 1945.

Membership card, *Neue Künstlervereinigung, Munich.* Woodcut 1903

C On the Spiritual in Art

Discoveries and Experiments

1910-1914

In 1910 Kandinsky wrote *On the Spiritual in Art,* and painted his first abstract work, a watercolor. Both these works were ahead of their time, although by no means outside the international development. The time was ripe for Kandinsky's experiments: in other countries, too, artists were coming to look upon art as a spiritual activity, and to dissolve or eliminate the object.

Thus there are notable parallels to Kandinsky's innovations, but it would be misleading to speak of influences. Kandinsky's absolute painting came into being as independently as Cubism and Delaunay's Orphism in France or Futurism in Italy. The new stirrings in Russia, too, were only in part responses to French stimuli. Kandinsky could have been only slightly familiar with these new conceptions at the time he took his most radical step: Cubism proper did not make its appearance until 1920, and Delaunay's Orphism not before 1912; the first Futurist exhibition was held in Paris in 1912. But Kandinsky had not then been in Paris since 1907, and he did not go back to Russia, after a long absence, until 1910.

Like every other artist Kandinsky was well aware that a great change was in the air, and that the naturalistic vision was giving ground to a more subjective one. Cubism certainly interested him as a kind of statement which, without dispensing with the object, dispensed with all comparison to the object. Within the Blaue Reiter group, Marc and Macke displayed greater interest in the Cubist organization of the picture plane than Kandinsky did, just as they were also more receptive to Futurist ideas, then becoming known. The representation of successive psychic states as simultaneous in paintings, and as visible expressions of the invisible (i.e., of dynamic elements)—Marc and Macke were interested in these discoveries, making use of them and modifying them. At the same time, the concept of placing the viewer inside the painting (*Manifesto of the Futurist Painters* of 1910) was more in line with Kandinsky's ideas.

Delaunay could not have influenced the Blaue Reiter artists in 1910; they did not see his paintings until late in 1911. *St. Séverin* and *Eiffel Tower,* which were shown at the first Blaue Reiter exhibition, were examples of a Cubism made expressive and dynamic through rhythm and color; they were in accord with Marc's and Macke's poetic ideas, but not with Kandinsky's. On the other hand, Delaunay's conviction that "color alone is form and object" was shared by all, as was his declaration that "so long as art does not rid itself of the object, it remains description, literature"—implying that the artist was no longer interested in still life compositions or Eiffel towers, but in "the heartbeat of man." Bur in 1912 Kandinsky had already attained his goal, whereas Marc, Macke, and Klee were all still to learn from Delaunay and called on him in Paris that same year. In the fall of 1912 Klee translated Delaunay's essay on color and light for *Der Sturm,* and in 1914 he applied this new knowledge in his Kairouan watercolors. Marc felt that Delaunay was spiritually akin to him and his "mystical inner constructions," and Macke looked upon Delaunay as his guide in the realm of color.

The Germans did not play a merely passive role, however. They had to their credit several accomplishments that might have been of interest to Delaunay; in any case, inborn dispositions and personal objectives are more important here than questions of chronology. At bottom, each of these artists followed his own path, the ideas of each being less influenced than confirmed by those of the others. What they had in common reflected the common predicament. This is also true of such painters as Kupka, who began to paint abstractly in 1912, in a very personal manner, and produced works whose significance has nothing to do with chronology.

On his visits to Moscow in 1910, Kandinsky could not have seen anything of the new discoveries there. While it is difficult to assign a precise date to M. Larionov's "Rayonism," his first Rayonist work, *The Glass,* was painted in 1909 and exhibited in 1912, and his statement of artistic program did not appear until 1913. It is unlikely that Kandinsky saw *The Glass* before it was exhibited. But even if he had seen the painting with its rays or lines of force emanating—as in Futurist works—from the object, and forming fern-like patterns resembling those to be observed on frosty windowpanes, he would scarcely have regarded it as related to his own ideas. The same is even truer of the works of Natalie Goncharova, who was later, like Larionov, to follow an entirely different line of development. Malevich's Suprematism began around 1913; V.Tatlin's first Constructivist relief dates from the same year. The war and the ensuing political upheavals in Russia stopped such artistic experiments, and the artists in question were able to resume their development after 1921 only outside Russia. The question of whether Kandinsky's subsequent development in Moscow (1914–1921) was influenced by Russian painters, will be discussed later.

As for the prewar situation, a document of some significance has turned up among Kandinsky's papers in Paris—the program of a congress held by an organization of Russian artists, dated December 10, 1912. We learn from it that at the first meeting Kurnibovsky presented a report on Kandinsky's theory of art expounded in *On the Spiritual in Art,* and that at the second meeting David Burliuk discussed contemporary painters. Burliuk covered a great deal of ground, including Cubism, Futurism, and the contemporary French and Russian painters, but nowhere did he mention Larionov or Rayonism. Even within the inner circle Larionov seems to have been unknown at that time. Kandinsky did not attend the congress; on December 13 he left Moscow for Germany. According to Lindsay, he had sent his book to the Congress of 1911, and they republished it in their archives. However, according to Nina Kandinsky, only the sixth chapter was actually translated and printed. Thus, in 1911 and 1912, Kandinsky's name must already have been known and repeated by persons interested in art.

Recently, we have been hearing about a Lithuanian painter, K. Ciurlionis (1875–1911) who painted in the abstract manner as early as 1905, and who has been described as a precursor of Kandinsky. So far as we can judge from reproductions of his works, Ciurlionis has nothing in common either with abstract painting or with Kandinsky. Originally a musician, he switched to painting at the age of thirty. His variations on musical themes and his cosmic visions are decorative; they remind us of the works of Obrist and of the artistic productions of other, more recent musicians who have practised painting. They are "painted music," and are at the same time reminiscent of works by schizophrenics. If Kandinsky ever saw these pictures, either the originals or reproductions of them (in the review *Apollo,* 1911), they are more likely to have given him pause than to have encouraged him.

It is possible that Kandinsky was acquainted with A. Hölzel's search for pure expressive means, as described in a lecture published in *Kunst für Alle* (1904). In this lecture the artist quoted A. Beyersdorf's statement about "the autochthonous force of the artistic means, which carry the psychological law of their effectiveness within themselves." In 1905 Hölzel had come very close to abstraction *(Composition in Red).* But, according to Hölzel, he did not meet Kandinsky, and Kandinsky does not seem to have seen any of his paintings. Nor had he as yet heard of Piet Mondrian, who having gone through a Cubist phase began to paint abstractly in 1913.

The fact that Kandinsky's book went through three printings in one year, between Christmas 1911 and the fall of 1912, permits the inference that his analyses touched upon ideas that were not regarded as absurd in art or elsewhere. At the turn of the century a change had taken place in the arts and sciences, which was transforming the intellectual climate, though its implications were not fully realized until later.

ut for title page of On the Spiritual in Art (1912).

Kandinsky absorbed those of the new ideas that he had need of and that were in line with his own aspirations. As a Russian and a Christian of the Greek Orthodox faith, he was inclined to identify himself with the new movement against materialism. He condemned the prevailing cultural canon, at first alone and anonymously, but more and more deliberately as time went on, and in the end he formulated his views in general terms, going beyond his own personal concerns.

Kandinsky had much in common with Leo Tolstoy. The writer's soul which, according to Tolstoy, justifies the work of art, also justifies it to Kandinsky. The affinity which has often been suggested between Kandinsky's paintings and Russian icons is accounted for by his origins; it is noteworthy that in the period of his breakthrough to abstract art, he conceived of painting as a spiritual or religious act. But his secret principle of construction, based on primary forms such as the triangle, the rectangle, and the circle (trinity, our life here below, and eternity) can be used for purposes of comparison only in relation to his later works; this is also true of the specifically Russian, irrational order of colors—pink, light violet, carmine, yellow, light green, and blue. Kandinsky's frequent visits to Moscow cathedrals suggest that he studied ancient religious art in detail, and in the predominantly religious paintings on glass he did between 1909 and 1914 we find echoes of both the subjects and the forms of icon painting, not only of the

83

early ones in Novgorod but also of the later ones, which are narrative in character. It was probably the mysticism inherent in the Orthodox faith, as well as legends of the saints dear to writers like Leskov, that made Kandinsky susceptible to Eastern supernaturalist influences, such as were represented by the Anglo-Russian H. Blavatsky and Annie Besant in England, and by Rudolf Steiner and the Anthroposophical Society in Germany. We know that prior to 1914 Kandinsky was seriously interested in questions of parapsychology, and that he willingly discussed religious problems and occultism with like-minded individuals (M. E. Sadler, *A Memoir*, 1949). Kandinsky shared Steiner's feeling that the world was headed for disaster, that science had failed, and that there was need for a spiritual rebirth. But he was more interested in the struggle against positivism and the demand for "higher sensory tools" than in spiritual exercises. Many sentences at the end of *Backward Glances* have a Steinerian echo, as when

Woodcut from The Spiritual In Art (1912)

Kandinsky speaks of "the threshold of the third revelation." His interest in such matters subsided as he became clearer in his own mind about the role of rational elements in art. In this he is like Piet Mondrian, who was adept of theosophy from 1899 to 1917, but then was drawn to the doctrine of Neo-Plasticism in which "matter becomes spirit by being internalized," transcending individuation by its specific "equilibrium," and anticipating the society of the future. To Mondrian, the difference between matter and spirit seemed to grow ever smaller, and he anticipated the "inward" man of Zen.
Kandinsky's opposition to materialism brought him close to writers such as Maeterlinck *(L'Intrus)* and philosophers such as Bergson, whose concepts of intuition as organ of knowledge, of time as *durée réelle,* and of consciousness as memory were being widely discussed. Several of his ideas were derived from the German Romantic philosophers, from Fichte's *Wissenschaftslehre* (I=non–I, the world as Idea) and Schelling. Schelling's theories were well known in Russia, and we find echoes of them among Kandinsky's friends, particularly Franz Marc *(Aphorisms)*. Significantly, Hugo von Tschudi, who sponsored the Blaue Reiter, was the man who in 1906 organized a centennial exhibition of the German Romantic painters who had fallen into oblivion. Also the works of the Romantic writers were being reissued at that time.
Kandinsky did not exploit the new spiritual situation, he helped to bring it about. According to all who knew him, his was a complex mind, given to violent contrasts,

and his deep-rooted mistrust of rationalism drove him in the direction of the irrational, that which is not logically graspable. We know that he suffered from periodic states of depression, imagining that he was the victim of persecution, and that he had to run away. He felt that part of his being was closely tied to the invisible; life here and now and in the hereafter, the outer world and the inner soul, did not seem to him opposed, and even spiritism struck him as plausible. We are told that he accepted the doctrine of the materialization of thought, an idea Charcot had defended, and that he believed that one day painters would be able to do without paints or brushes.

The disintegration of the atom confirmed Kandinsky in his belief that science was unreliable. "I should not have been surprised if a stone had melted in the air and become invisible before my very eyes." Curiously enough, Kandinsky interpreted the new discoveries as marking the bankruptcy of scientific research, and at the same time the end of materialism and naturalism. They deeply shook him, and at the same time encouraged him to push forward with his new conception of art. After 1900, the concept of matter lost much of its former "reality" even in physics. Kandinsky drew his own inferences from this fact, though not explicitly nor in intellectual terms, but emotionally. Thus he came to speak of an all-comprehensive totality, transcending both spirit and matter.

The new vision asserted itself in all domains of intellectual and artistic life: in psychology thanks to Freud and Jung; in the history of art thanks to Worringer. It revolutionized poetry and music as well.

It was inevitable that the theory of art should have to revise its basic ideas. Object and form were no longer two distinct entities, form being no longer tied to substance, while the creative process itself became a theme of art, and the idea of "multidimensional simultaneity" began to loom on the horizon. Goethe, Fiedler, and Wölfflin, all of whom had opposed the work of art to nature as a distinct autonomous reality, were now read more attentively. Art became the creation of reality. Necessity and inwardness are recurrent concepts in these writers, and Wölfflin had already dwelt upon the expressive meaning of form as such. With respect to morphology, H. Friedmann's *Welt der Formen* was to become a keystone of the new doctrine, just as Goethe's *Morphologie* had been its foundation.

The Blaue Reiter painters often referred to Worringer's *Abstraktion und Einfühlung* (Abstraction and Empathy). Published in 1907, this book came closest to their own ideas on art. They were also enthusiastic about the ideas of Fiedler who had described the work of art as an independent organism, and advanced the thesis that art did not merely reflect the instinct of imitation but gratified a real psychic need. They were also impressed by the assertion that the essence of art is abstraction, a striving to isolate the object, to make it absolute, unchangeable, necessary. According to this theory, the conflict between the I and the world takes place within the I, and opposes instinct to logic and reason. The tendency toward abstraction was furthered by the growing realization that contemporary man, no longer secure on the proud pedestal of certain knowledge, confronts the world as helplessly and with as much bafflement as the primitive. Not only Kandinsky, but all artists were being affected by such ideas. "Painting shall free me from my fears," Marc wrote at about this time.

In short, Kandinsky's book did not appear in a vacuum. The judgments of contemporary critics quoted in the *Blaue Reiter* include references to "the serious inwardness of his artistic purpose" (the words were Riegl's and Worringer's), and "his attempt to raise art above the domain of nature and its imitation." "Just as there are daemonic people, so there are daemonic books, which deeply affect our minds and force us repeatedly to question old prejudices. Some of the chapters, by virtue of their originality and the force of their ideas, read like the decalogue of a new art."

The reader of *On the Spiritual in Art* had been prepared for Kandinsky's ideas and style by several previously published prefaces to catalogues. As early as December 1909, on the occasion of the first Neue Künstlervereinigung exhibition, there had been talk of "necessary" forms and of synthesis, but the preface to the catalogue of the second exhibition was more explicit (September 1910). Probably Kandinsky had just finished writing *On the Spiritual in Art*, and he summed up his ideas in aphorisms, very much in the prophetic style of Friedrich Nietzsche (cf. p. 64). In this preface he clearly distinguished form from content, the means of art from the end, and stressed the antitheses between calculation and passion, between construction and intuition, as well as their ultimate harmony in the work of art. He defined the purpose of art as "the expression of mystery in terms of mystery."

Kandinsky expressed the same ideas on the occasion of the first *Blaue Reiter* exhibition when he spoke of the artist's "inner wish," of "a shift in the center of gravity . . . the intensive turn toward the inwardness of nature . . . the link with past epochs." By then *On the Spiritual in Art* had appeared and was being read by a number of people. In February 1912, when the second exhibition opened, a second printing of the book was in preparation. The preface to the catalogue is almost more specific than the book (cf. p. 67), and certain pages remind us of Schelling. In the preface to the catalogue for the Sturm exhibition (October 1912) Kandinsky referred to his book ("*Theosophische Programmschrift*," in *Kunst für Alle*, XXVII) and protested against certain misunderstandings of it, denying that his purpose was to paint music or to represent psychic states. No art can be transposed into another art, he said, and while it is true that no work can come into being without an antecedent psychic state, a truly living work may originate from any cause. He says that his purpose is to create, by pictorial means, works that have a life of their own as "purely pictorial beings." The sole reason for limiting the role of external elements is to emphasize inner life.

The first part ("General") of *On the Spiritual in Art* deals with the spiritual foundations of art, and the second ("Painting") with the formal conditions of artistic creation. The first is inspired by absolute faith in the onset of a new era, in which the spirit will move mountains, painting will help overcome the remnants of materialism by asserting the primacy of inner values, and by directly appealing to what is good in man. In collaboration with the other arts painting will advance to the total work of art. Terms such as "spirit," "soul," "life," "world," "sound" occur very frequently. Kandinsky is proclaiming a new gospel and does not hesitate to refer to the Old and the New Testament. "Invisible, Moses comes down from the mountain and watches the dance around the golden calf. Nonetheless, it is he who has brought mankind the solace of wisdom." He speaks apocalyptically of a "spiritual triangle," the lower segment of which is occupied by atheists: "Heaven has become uninhabited, God is dead," and the loftier segments by positivists, naturalists, men of science, and art students; they are dominated by fear, for the inexplicable lies within the realm of possibility, and as a result the confusion is at its greatest at the top. "The abandoned churchyard quakes, the forgotten graves yawn open . . . All the artificially contrived suns have exploded into so many specks of dust . . . Higher up still there is no fear at all . . . there is no impregnable fortress."

Woodcut from Klänge (1913)

The names Kandinsky cites in this chapter are significant. He mentions Kubin and Maeterlinck as "seers" and "prophets" ("his people are directly souls . . . his word is an inner sound"); Robert Schumann ("To send light into the depths of the human heart is the artist's vocation"); Richard Wagner, whose leitmotives constitute a spiritual atmosphere; Debussy, who has refined natural impressions into spiritual images; Mussorgsky and Scriabin, and Arnold Schönberg, who "on the road to inner necessity has already discovered treasures of new beauty . . . with him the music of the future begins." Among painters, he mentions the Neo-Impressionists, and calls Rossetti, Böcklin, and Segantini "searchers for the inner life of the external"; next he speaks of Cézanne as the man who discovered a new law of form and realized it by purely pictorial means; Matisse, who seeks to render "the divine" in his pictures (Kandinsky had read his article in *Kunst und Künstler*, 1909), and finally Picasso, who has never succumbed to external beauty, and who arrives at constructive proportion by way of the mathematical. But he also mentions Rudolf Steiner and Mrs. H. P. Blavatsky, who approach "the problem of the spirit by way of inner enlightenment." He does not mention his friends Marc and Klee, probably because the manuscript had been completed before he met them. Nor does he mention Jawlensky and Gabriele Münter, probably because of his reluctance to discuss personal matters.

Kandinsky observes that in a period of spiritual rebirth the arts move closer to each other, by their common disposition to abstraction, their common concern for the fundamentals, and their common pursuit of inner nature. Like Klee, he believed that music is the most comprehensive art, and thanks to a theory elaborated over the centuries can serve as a model for other arts. Nevertheless, the boundaries of each art must be respected. "One art can learn from another how to use its common principle and how to apply it to the fundamentals of its own medium," and "Every art has its own strength, which cannot be replaced by another." The frequent use of musical analogies is also to be found in Klee, and may be explained by the absence of a canon in painting.

According to Kandinsky the present artistic epoch is similar to certain artistic epochs that go way back in time. While each work of art is a child of its period, analogous inner tendencies result in outward similarities, for instance, the similarity between the moderns and primitives. Worringer had already pointed out that there was a connection between modern man's restlessness, despair, and fear on the one hand, and the tendency to abstraction on the other, and Klee wrote in his diary: "The more horrible the world (as it happens to be in our day), the more abstract art becomes, while a happy world produces a secular art." However, art is not merely an echo, it also points to the future, it has a prophetic power; its movement is an upward one, "that of knowledge," and modern art cannot continue to be like primitive art for very long.

The second part of the book contains a kind of theory of harmony, and opens with considerations on the effects of color, Kandinsky's favorite theme at that time. On the nature of form he wrote extensively only in the book *Punkt und Linie zu Fläche* (Point and Line to Plane), published by the Bauhaus in 1926.

The physiological effect of color is sensory and short-lived; warm colors, like vermilion, attract the eye, and the bright yellow of a lemon is painful. A psychological resonance is produced when the sensory impression causes an emotional vibration, directly or by association (red-flame-blood). The optical, auditive, tactile, or olfactory realms overlap (violet-bassoon; rose madder-velvet; yellow-acidity). Kandinsky refers to contemporary experiments in synesthesia, and to Scriabin's table of equivalent musical and color tones. The problem had been raised by the French Symbolists: Rimbaud identified vowels with colors, *a* with black, *i* with red, and so on.

According to Kandinsky the direct effect of color is greater than the associative effect. "Color is the keyboard. The eye is the hammer, while the soul is a piano of many strings." Harmony rests "on the principle of the corresponding vibration of the human soul," i.e., "the principle of innermost necessity." This crucial phrase now appears for the first time. "The artist does nothing that others regard as beautiful, but only what is necessary for him," Schönberg wrote, in his *Theory of Harmony*.

The longest chapter of the second part is entitled "The Language of Form and Color." Here Kandinsky can draw on the rich experience of his years of transition to show by abundant examples what goal he had pursued in his painting. To create a pictorial composition, the painter has two means at his disposal—color and form. Of these, form can exist for itself, but not so color, which must be limited. While form and color also exist absolutely, in painting they condition each other. A triangle filled with green is different from one filled with yellow; color modifies form, and form color. Deep colors are intensified by round forms (blue in a circle), but inharmonious combinations also afford expressive possibilities and lead to new harmonies.

Form, seen externally, is a boundary line; seen internally, it is also content, and formal harmony, like color harmony, rests on the principle of inner necessity, regardless of whether the form is the outline of an object, is abstract, or is something between the two. "Today the artist cannot progress solely through use of purely abstract forms, as these forms are not sufficiently precise [he means they lack gradation]". "To limit oneself to the imprecise is to deprive oneself of many possibilities, to exclude the purely human, and, therefore, to weaken the power of expression." As can be seen, when he wrote this book, Kandinsky had not yet taken the final step.

In later editions he would be less reticent, but the rapid succession of printings in 1912 gave him no opportunity to insert changes. They were included only after his death in the English and French versions of the book. Among the additions we read: "Today, very few artists can work with purely abstract means. These forms are often too imprecise for the artist. It seems to him that to confine himself exclusively to the imprecise . . . is to weaken his expressive means. But at the same time, even today abstract form has been experienced in purely precise terms and has been used as the sole ingredient of pictorial works. External impoverishment is thereby transformed into inner enrichment." He planned further revisions of later passages in the book. For instance, he meant to add that only a few "hours" separate us from pure composition, that the correct path lies between the abstract, geometric use of color (which might lead to superficial, ornamental art), and the material use of color (which might lead to shallow fantasy). At one point he replaced the term "abstract" with "purely abstract." But he hesitated, and set aside the corrections, planning to use them later for a theory of harmony (Paris papers).

According to Kandinsky, pure artistic composition involves two tasks: (1) the composition of the whole painting, and (2) the modification of the various individual forms and their subordination to the whole. "The composition of the whole picture is followed as a definite aim." Material objects are not wholly rejected, provided that their choice follows the principle of inner necessity. One should not deprive oneself of any possible vibration, thus diminishing one's arsenal of expressive media. "That, at any rate, is the case today." This is one of many reservations. Composition depends on the modifiability of the forms, both individually and as a whole. "Every form is as sensitive as a cloud of smoke," its inner tone depends on imponderables, as well as on "veiled and openly expressed appeals," on the use of rhythmical or unrhythmical treatment, on "counterpoint." Here too the principle of inner necessity is valid, and it rests upon three elements: (1) the artist's personality and his epoch; (2) the eternal, objective nature of art, and (3) the "spring that constantly drives onward," i.e., the mystical something thanks to which we feel an affinity between genuine works of art separated by thousands of years.

To attain the goal, exercises are necessary, in the realm of color as well as elsewhere. And Kandinsky proceeds to develop a theory of primary colors with their modalities of warmth and cold, and their values of light and dark. Warmth in color is an inclination toward yellow, and cold an inclination toward blue: "the warm colors move toward the spectator, the cold ones retreat from him." Light and dark, the mixture of white and black, considerably intensifies the effect of eccentric yellow or concentric blue, bringing it close to white in the one case and to black in the other. Intense yellow is aggressive, and suggests the sound of a trumpet; while blue is the typical heavenly color. Blue develops an element of repose, and, according to its degree of lightness or darkness, suggests the sounds of a flute, a cello, a double bass, or an organ. In green, which is a mixture of yellow and blue, the movements cancel each other: green is passive, smug, it is to the realm of color what the bourgeoisie is to the world of man. White and black are colors. White is a symbol of a world far above us, of silence—not a dead silence, but one full of potentialities. "It is a blank that emphasizes the beginning, as yet unborn. Thus, probably, did the earth resound during the white period of the Ice Age." We are reminded of Mallarmé who said: "The ideal poem would be silence . . . the poem made of nothing but white." By contrast, black is silence without future or hope; in terms of music it is the sign that marks the end of a piece.

Red is purposeful power. It has many shades and just as many psychological effects and symbolic meanings. For instance, vermilion is like an active glowing passion, it "sounds" like a tuba; while a musical equivalent to rose madder may be found in the high notes of a violin (the small bells worn by horses in Russia are said to strike a "raspberry" note); the appeal of orange is like the sound of a church bell, of violet like

Woodcut from
On the Spiritual in Art
(1912)

that of an English horn (the Chinese used violet as the color of mourning). Red and green, and orange and violet, the third and fourth pairs of contrasts, Kandinsky refers to as complementary colors. Thus we have six primary colors, and "to the right and left stand the two great possibilities of silence: birth and death." According to Kandinsky, the essence of color cannot be expressed in words or musical analogies, but colors can produce the same effects as those other arts produce with different means, and thus contribute to intensifying the spiritual atmosphere.

With the help of colors and forms, a harmonious whole is created, which is the painting. When it is abstract, modeling and the third dimension are excluded, but not space. Space can be achieved by color (advancing or retreating) as well as by form (overlapping), so that the painting becomes a being that "hovers in the air."

Needless to say, Kandinsky was acquainted with Goethe's *Farbenlehre*. He undertakes to construct a different system probably because, unlike Goethe, his starting point was not nature, the spectrum, and organic color, but certain strong and physiologically determined contrasts. Blue and yellow are his main antitheses, just as green and red are Goethe's: they are to each other what mind is to nature or distance to proximity. Kandinsky emphasizes the emotional character of color more strongly than Goethe, and he relates it to the emotional character of musical sounds. What he has in mind is analogies with sounds on the basis of emotional associations, not the identification of musical and pictorial quantities. "For my part, I have not tried to paint music, for I consider such painting basically impossible and unattainable," and the same goes for psychic states (Sturm catalogue, 1912).

The last two sections of the book, "Theory," and "Art and Artists," formulate conclusions based on practical experiments, and, like the first section, touch upon general questions. A propos of movement, Kandinsky digresses into dance and drama as a form of monumental art (combining music, painting, and movement).

Drawing. 1912, 6

Time and again Kandinsky tries to circumscribe the part played by nature, until finally he discovers a clear demarcation line, and he discusses the possibilities of pure abstraction and pure realism. He distinguishes between "pure abstraction" (i. e., "further than any geometric form") and "pure realism" (i. e., "fantasy in its sharpest materialistic sense"). Since art is above nature (here Kandinsky quotes Goethe and Delacroix), the question is decided in favor of pure abstraction. Natural forms create boundaries, but the abstract forms are open to the influence of the object, and somewhat hastily Kandinsky shifts from objective forms to "construction" as the preliminary stage of composition, a construction whose richest variety is not in geometric, but in "hidden" resources.

The work of art that has come into being in accordance with the laws of inner necessity is an entity, "a spiritually breathing subject." It lives, it has its own power, and it actively modifies the spiritual atmosphere. Painting is not a pointless activity, but a power that helps to refine the soul: it is the soul's daily bread. However, "the artist should have a message to convey," a message which is revealed to him by his inner voice, and which also accounts for the "beauty" of his work, for only that is beautiful "which results from an inner spiritual need."

In his essay "*Über die Formfrage*" (On the Question of Form) printed in the *Blaue Reiter Almanac* (1912), as well as in *Backward Glances* (1913) and in his contribution to *Der Sturm*, "*Über Kunstverstehen*" (On Comprehension of Art), Kandinsky came back to certain problems that seemed to him important, and in an unprinted lecture of January 1914 he formulated his ideas for the last time before leaving Germany.

"*Über die Formfrage*" was written with poetic élan, during the months when he worked most intensively with Franz Marc, then his closest friend: it is Kandinsky's most mature contribution to the theory of art. This time his point of departure was the creative spirit, which seeks its realization along a path that leads through the soul.

The abstract and the realistic elements, according to Kandinsky, have always existed in art; but, while they were formerly blended, today they have become distinct. Great realistic art expresses the inner "sound" of things; in it the "artistic" element, though reduced to a minimum, is perceived as the most powerfully abstract element (here Kandinsky has Henri Rousseau in mind). Great abstract art expresses the inner "sound" of the painting on the basis of abstract elements. This art skirts reality; in it the "objective" element, though reduced to a minimum, is perceived as the most powerful reality (Kandinsky has his own work in mind). The greatest external diversity (external forms) becomes the greatest internal identity (inner "sound"). Thus realism is equal to abstraction, and abstraction to realism. Kandinsky thinks that true art can be achieved by both methods; we find it in Rousseau, for his "hard" objects have an inner resonance that excludes conventional beauty and emancipates the purely artistic element, and we find it in abstract painters as well. Quantitative decrease results in qualitative increase, outer and inner effects are not identical. The two forms are of equal value; there is no theoretical problem of form.

A general canon will some day be formulated, but it will contain no prescription; it will merely show, as in music, what is possible. Like music, painting will have a theory of harmony based on the principle: "The world vibrates; it is a cosmos of spiritually active beings. Thus dead matter is living spirit." Here we are reminded of Novalis' "life of the universe as an eternal thousand-voiced conversation" (fragment "*Die Natur*"), and of Paul Valéry, to whom music often appeared as a "universal adventure," a number of "abstract combinations," so that he was "no longer conscious of the sensible intermediary, sound" *(Eupalinos)*. An inner affinity between art and the cosmos is also indicated, according to Kandinsky, by the fact that a painting can be represented as a mathematical formula or a number. But there are numbers of all kinds, and "why should we narrow the range of artistic expression by the exclusive use of triangles and similar geometric forms and bodies?" This is a crucial sentence, as we shall see when discussing his works of the Blaue Reiter period.

In his essay "*Malerei als reine Kunst*" (Painting as a Pure Art, *Der Sturm*, 1913), Kandinsky defines content somewhat more clearly, namely, as an inner element, as "the emotion in the artist's soul." The process of producing the work from its conception until it finally reaches the beholder, is described as "emotion-sensation-work-sensation-emotion." Sensation serves as a bridge between the nonmaterial and the material in the artist, and between the material and nonmaterial in the beholder. Kandinsky is also more precise in *Backward Glances,* both in the first edition of 1913,

Woodcut from *The Spiritual in Art (1912)*

and even more in the second, which appeared in Russian in Moscow, in 1918. This autobiographical work, which includes recollections, philosophical observations, critical remarks, and prophecies, is composed like a piece of music. Taking up one subject, continuing with another, interrupting his train of thought, moving backward and forward in time, Kandinsky achieves a deliberately intended confusion and at the same time secures the reader's inner participation.

With seeming effortlessness he describes how he arrived at his understanding of the essential differences between nature and art, thus gaining genuine insight into reality. Everything suddenly revealed its face to him, whether a trouser button lying in the mud or a pure line. He foresaw what would one day separate Dadaism (later Surrealism) from abstract art. He had long been worried by the function of the object, by the question. What is to take the place of the object? His answer to it is a dramatic definition of painting as "a violent clash between different worlds, which, in and through their struggle with each other, are destined to create the new world. Technically speaking, each work of art comes into being as the cosmos did—out of catastrophe. "Out of a chaotic blaring of the instruments a symphony finally emerges, called the music of the spheres. The creation of a work is the creation of a world."

Five years later, in the Russian edition, Kandinsky revised some passages and added others; these changes have been included in the American and French editions. The rational element is more strongly emphasized, and the sentence that nothing can imperil the confirmed artist, not even the much feared brain work, is now followed by the words: "not even if its role outweighs that of intuition in the creative work; in the end inspiration will perhaps be completely eliminated." We can understand only the laws govering the art of the present day, he says, but later it may be possible to produce a work of art by calculation, and the unconscious will then assume a new aspect. Thus Kandinsky anticipated his own further evolution.

The lecture that Kandinsky was invited to give in Cologne in 1914 (cf. p. 36) never took place; it has recently been published from manuscript (Eichner). It contains a casual survey of his evolution in the direction of abstract art. From this summary of his thinking down to 1914, dating from one of his most fruitful periods, one might expect a clear statement on the nature and method of abstract art; but here, too, a good deal is left vague, and use is made of ambiguous concepts. He speaks very graphically about the method of abstract art, but seems to be taking its nature for granted.

On some points, however, he expresses himself somewhat more clearly than before. "The genesis of the work is cosmic in character. The originator of the work is thus the spirit. The work exists abstractly even before it has been embodied, before it has become accessible to human senses." And suddenly Kandinsky introduces a concept which he had not used before—that of tragedy. He had never wanted, he says, to carry harmony "to the extreme, and to treat all pictorial energies in such a way that all equally serve the purest tragic element." In *Composition II,* he goes on to say, he softened the tragic effect by neutral colors, and in other paintings balanced the tragic character of the colors by the "sublimity of the drawn forms." (We see that the nature of abstract art and its method have points of contact.) Painting austere, cold canvases in which white was the dominant color had taught him that the most intense coldness

19 Study for one of the
representations of the
'Last Judgment', 1913
Studie zu einem
›Jüngsten Gericht‹
Etude pour un
«Jugement Dernier»
Studio per un
‹Giudizio Universale›

20 Sketch for 'Bright Painting', 1913
Entwurf zu ›Helles Bild‹
Projet pour «Tableau clair»
Abbozzo per ‹Quadro chiaro›

21 Sketch for 'Painting with White Forms', 1913
   Entwurf zu ›Bild mit weißen Formen‹
   Projet pour «Tableau avec formes blanches»
   Abbozzo per ‹Quadro con forme bianche›

22 Sketch for 'Small Pleasures', 1913
   Entwurf zu ›Kleine Freuden‹
   Projet pour «Petites Joies»
   Abbozzo per ‹Piccole gioie›

23 Study for 'Small Pleasures', 1913
   Studie zu ›Kleine Freuden‹
   Etude pour «Petites Joies»
   Studio per ‹Piccole gioie›

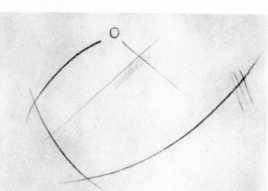

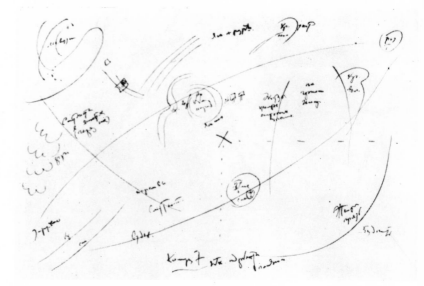

24 Outlines of 'Composition VI', 1913
   Hauptlinien der ›Komposition VI‹
   Lignes principales de la «Composition VI»
   Linee principali per ‹Composizione VI›

25 Watercolor for 'Composition VII', 1913
   Aquarell zu ›Komposition VII‹
   Aquarelle pour «Composition VII»
   Acquerello per ‹Composizione VII›

26 Drawing for 'Composition VII', 1913
   Zeichnung zu ›Komposition VII‹
   Dessin pour «Composition VII»
   Disegno per ‹Composizione VII›

27 Watercolor for 'Composition VII', 1913
   Aquarell zu ›Komposition VII‹
   Aquarelle pour «Composition VII»
   Acquerello per ‹Composizione VII›

is the highest tragedy. "And this is the cosmic tragedy, in which the human element is only one vibration, one of the contributing voices, and in which the center is shifted to a sphere that approaches the divine."

In *Backward Glances,* Kandinsky notes almost apologetically that *On the Spiritual in Art* wrote itself more than he wrote it, that over the years he had recorded individual experiences and only later realized that there were organic connections between them. In another passage, he defends himself against the charge that he set out to create a program or a theory. Nothing was further from his mind, he says, than to appeal to the brain: it was still much too early for that.

Woodcut from Klänge (1913)

The text, like all Kandinsky's texts, is not easy to read; the style is not always clear, nor free from contradictions. To hold this against him, and to list all the inconsistencies in detail would be unfair; we must not forget that Kandinsky was a Russian writing in German, and he was a painter, not a theoretician. Moreover, the established terms of aesthetics and psychology could scarcely serve his purposes; he had to invent concepts, words, and a method for describing psychological and artistic processes.

For instance, nowhere does he explicitly define "content"; his thinking on this score is formulated only in terms of analogy. Among these we find "the inner wish," "feeling" which is nameless, the complex of purposefully organized effects, the expression of mystery in terms of mystery, the superhuman, the abstract, the absolute, the tragic quality as the clash of worlds, or the clash of elements—in the latter case the epithet "tragic" is also applied to the composition. At all events, "content" is something psychic, which in Kandinsky also stands for a cosmic and spiritual element, and often it merely designates the objectively artistic element.

In comparison with "content," the notion of "the object" plays a lesser role: Kandinsky was troubled by the fact that he had eliminated it, but he points out that pure abstraction also uses "things," and that a line, for instance, is just as much a thing as a table. Thus he is able to avoid certain difficulties, and we may conjecture that the object, which he employed in his art before 1908, was for him merely a temporary expedient. Kandinsky never regarded the object as the content of the picture, but merely as a means, and even in his woodcuts and tempera paintings the essential thing is "the hidden," that is to say, something that shines through the painting, but for the realization of which he had not yet discovered the means.

In *On the Spiritual in Art,* Kandinsky is still a dualist, recognizing a polarity between matter and spirit, body and soul; he has as yet come to think of them as aspects of the same unity or whole. However, he transcends this polarity between spirit and non-spirit to the extent that he shifts the center of gravity from the object to form, which often takes the place of the object in his analyses. Here may be noted resemblances to Gestalt philosophy (H. Friedmann), which views the world as a cosmos of forms, and emancipates the experience of form from its ties with the object and with substance. In the same sense, Henry Moore asks us "to feel shape simply as shape." In physics, too, the ultimate material elements are no longer conceived as substances, but as pure form (E. Schrödinger). One might speak of "objects of a higher degree."

Kandinsky's interchangeable usage of the terms "spirit" and "soul" leads to a measure of uncertainty. Now the spirit is the originator of the work, now the psychological experience is the primal ground of its conception and creation, while in other places Kandinsky says that the creation of a work of art is the creation of a world. In his mind, the various formulations are not essentially different, since for him the cosmos is permeated with the spirit, and the soul is of divine and spiritual origin (the religious component). But Kandinsky also speaks of a "creative spirit," which controls logic and intuition, and elsewhere of the obscurity in which the inner necessity of artistic creation is enveloped; the affinity between the spirit and the soul becomes progressively closer, and in the end Kandinsky reminds us of Jung, for whom the spirit is no longer opposed to the soul, and who conceives of a region in which the individual human element merges with the cosmos.

There is a like ambiguity with regard to Kandinsky's oppositions between construction and intuition, logic and feeling. But here, too, some of the contradiction is resolved if we recall that all art is an integration of the conscious and the unconscious, of "intuition and compositional technique," as Hindemith puts it. When Hindemith says that intuition accounts for five per cent, and compositional technique for ninety-five per cent of the work, we realize how great the role of intellect can be even in music; but we also understand why form occupies so large a place in Kandinsky's theory.

Possibly, thinking was for Kandinsky a less abstract function that we assume it to be. Thinking is a sense, like other senses. There is an intellectual sense, just as there are senses of sight, sound, and so on. Its highest goal would be the spirit, wisdom; and this spiritual element would no longer be subjected to space, time, and causality. It would even be outside consciousness, it would be the meditative state of the soul (H. Kayser, *Lehrbuch der Harmonik,* 1950). Subordinated to such a spirit, logic and intuition would no longer be opposites, and the activity of the intellect, in so far as Kandinsky refers to it, would be in accord with the activity of the soul. It would be unfair to criticize Kandinsky for such theoretical efforts: he was entitled to reflect on his art as much as the Cubists, Schönberg, and the French poets—Guillaume Apollinaire, for instance, whose *L'Esprit nouveau et les poètes* (1917) is a kind of poetics.

Kandinsky's abandonment of the object in favor of abstraction must be accounted for by his personal temperament, as well as by his meditations on the philosophy of art. Of introvert tendencies, he was also a master of self-observation. He used "the hidden" in art as he used camouflage in life—"to express mystery in terms of mystery." His sensitivity was almost abnormal, and he fenced himself off from the environment, even from his own family (on his visits to Moscow). He once wrote of himself that he "dissolves in his wishes" *(geht in seinen Wünschen auf),* and he coped with all his problems very much on his own.

Woodcut from Klänge (1913

A number of questions raised by Kandinsky's life and work, such as the role of space and time, and the symbolism of his colors and forms, can be answered more effectively by study of his painting dating from the period 1910–1914, than from his writings. It is surprising how often Kandinsky's ideas come close to, or coincide with, contemporary scientific discoveries, although the painter was completely unacquainted with the methodology and conclusions of modern science at the time he wrote.

During the period of his essays on the theory of art, Kandinsky also wrote a number of poems, which were published in 1912 and 1913. The *Blaue Reiter Almanac* contained

Woodcut from Klänge (1913)

his composition for the stage entitled *Der gelbe Klang* (Yellow Sound); his poems are contained in *Klänge* (Sounds).

Der gelbe Klang was written in German, in 1909; two other stage compositions dating from the same year, *Schwarz und Weiß* (Black and White) and *Grüner Klang* (Green Sound) exist only in Russian versions, later translated into French. A fourth composition for the stage, *Violett* (Violet), in German, should probably be dated 1911; an excerpt, dated 1914, was published in the *Bauhaus Zeitschrift* in 1927. Three stage designs (watercolors) are among the Paris papers. With the exception of *Violett,* which might be called realistic to some extent, his compositions for the stage are nonnaturalistic, operatic, and intended as librettos for musical compositions. But music was actually composed only for *Der gelbe Klang;* Kandinsky asked his friend Thomas von Hartmann, a Russian composer, to write it for him. Hartmann, in the lecture mentioned above, refers to an earlier stage composition based on a fairytale by Andersen, and a version of *Daphnis and Chloe* with the dancer A. Sacharoff.

In the Almanac the text of *Der gelbe Klang* is preceded by an explanatory essay entitled "On Stage Composition," which was written in 1911. Here, too, practice preceded theory. Kandinsky used this opportunity to repeat that while each art is a realm of its own and uses its own means, these means are in the last analysis identical, since all serve the purpose of moving and refining the human soul, and that consequently cooperation among the various arts is possible.

He gave a few hints as to how we are to understand his play. Sound, color, and movement remain outwardly independent, but are all subordinated to the inner purpose.

Words serve merely to record a certain mood, occasionally appearing only as sounds without conceptual meaning. Thus Kandinsky anticipated a poetic form that the Dadaists later used in their "sound poems."

Vague chords serve as prelude to *Der gelbe Klang*. On stage is deep blue twilight, which grows gradually darker. After some time, a small light appears center. A chorus is heard off stage, the bass voices gradually becoming distinct. A deep voice: "Stone-hard dreams ... and speaking rocks ... Earth with riddles of fulfilling questions ... The sky's motion ..." Five shrilly yellow giants, with birdlike creatures flying around them; a man walking as in a dream downstage; small figures crossing over a hill—everything as unreal as in Kandinsky's paintings at this time. An alogical poem, an unreal dream play, archaic, dark, pointing to the unknown. The sensory and the sonorous resources of the theater are emphasized, with the action, however, remaining unfathomable. The motives that are sketchily introduced force the spectator's co-operation by the very fact that they leave everything open. Kandinsky was experimenting, testing various effects with a view to "synthesis" and "monumentality," and contrasting rational ideas with occult notions. The so-called "human" element, which is usually confused with the banal, is completely absent, contact with the world remaining under the threshold of consciousness.

Woodcut from Klänge (1913)

The spectator will presumably react to the whole as to a musical scenario, which he will largely fill in from his own mind, continuing and developing it in his own way. In performance, the main effect will derive from the visual elements, which, harmonizing with the words, the sounds, and the motions, radiate a mysterious magic. After all, Kandinsky is a painter. Much the same may be said of the other plays, except for *Violett*, which is more in the spirit of the few representationel paintings Kandinsky still produced in the year it was written.

The plays were never performed; Hugo Ball, one of the original founders of Dada, who was a stage director in Munich, and who admired Kandinsky, tried in vain to get *Der gelbe Klang* produced. Later he kept in touch with Kandinsky, and after the foundation of the Dada gallery in Zurich (1917) asked him to sign one of the Dada manifestoes; earlier, in 1916, he had had Kandinsky's poems read at the Cabaret Voltaire. The play was to be produced by the Berliner Volksbühne in 1922, but the plan fell through because Thomas von Hartmann was in Russia. Nor were Kandinsky's plays produced at the Bauhaus, despite the fact that it had its own theater.

Klänge was published under the imprint of Piper, who also published the Almanac and *On the Spiritual in Art*. The Piper catalogue of 1904–1954 wrongly lists 1912 as the year of publication. It is a beautifully printed volume on Holland rag paper, with thirty-eight prose poems, twelve woodcuts in color, and forty-three in black-and-white, which will be discussed later in this book. The poems were written between 1908 and 1913, out of the same creative impulses that produced the pictures. In 1938, Kandinsky wrote that he merely changed his instrument when he composed poetry. The prose poems reveal the same tension between inner and outer vibration, abstraction and reality, archaism and consciousness, alogicality and meaning, the music and the meaning of the words.

The words and sentences often result in sound images, but more often in pictorial signs and images, such as are suggested by sensations, recollections, and associa-

First abstract ▶
watercolor (1910)

tions, both rational and irrational. An emotional order prevails, deeply moving the reader, which can however be easily discounted. Repetition of words has the effect Kandinsky describes in *On the Spiritual in Art:* they lose their usual connotations. They are not in the style of Dada, but they are signposts on the road to Dada.

Hans (Jean) Arp, a poet as well as a sculptor, felt that the synthesis of words, sounds, and colors was an unprecedented message from a fabulous world. "There is the breath of the eternally unfathomable in these poems. Shadows spring up, tremendous as speaking mountains. Stars of sulphur and wild poppies bloom on the lips of heaven. Human creatures are disembodied and transformed into rascally mists. Earthly burdens put on ethereal shoes. The sequences of words and sentences in these poems remind the reader of the constant flux of things, they are not didactic and often somber in humor ... Kandinsky's poems disclose the nothingness of the world of appearance and of reason."

One poem begins with the words: "Face. Distance. Cloud ... A man stands with a long sword ..." This recalls Chinese poems: "Cloud, dress, and flower, her face ..." There are affinities with the Far East also in language. Ezra Pound says somewhere that when a European is asked what is red, he will say a color, a vibration of light, a form of energy, a modality of Being, and so on, ad absurdum, whereas a Chinese will say: a rose, rust, a cherry, a flamingo. Kandinsky's poems are something like this.

In his unpublished essay "Over the Wall" (January 1914), commenting on a few lines of poetry, Kandinsky spoke of men who are "exclusively moved by things that concern them," and men "who are moved by things that do not concern them personally," the subjectivists and objectivists. Only the latter, he says, are capable of climbing "over the wall," of hearing more in a single syllable than others in a whole line of poetry.

Woodcut from On the Spiritual in Art (1912)

D Genius in Full Swing

1910-1914

Woodcut from Klänge (1913)

More clearly than in his writings, Kandinsky's artistic intentions are expressed in his paintings of the Munich period (1910–1914). The impetus of this period continued into the war years in Moscow. Only during the Russian revolution and after his return to Germany late in 1921 did his style begin to change, gradually becoming more austere.

Kandinsky embarked on his transvaluation of painting with an enthusiasm that is scarcely paralleled in the history of art. He was inspired by ideas that in their breadth and pathos remind us of Nietzsche. The soul and the spirit as instruments of life, consciousness as mirror of total Being, the spiritual as a sign language, the underlying unity of all phenomena—all this is expressed in Kandinsky's paintings as it is in Nietzsche's poetic writings.

As late as 1913, Kandinsky was still painting the recognizable forms of objects (cf. p. 62). But alongside these canvases appear three other types of work: Impressions, Improvisations, and Compositions. In *On the Spiritual in Art* he defined "Impressions" as those paintings in which the direct impression of outer nature remains recognizable; "Improvisations," as those produced out of an inner impulse, sudden and unconscious; and as "Compositions," those works which had crystallized slowly on the basis of preliminary studies and sketches, and in whose structure the conscious mind played a considerable part. Further, he spoke of these three types of painting as "symphonic," and to him "symphonic" was opposed to "melodic." The "melodic" composition is based upon a single form, the "symphonic" on several forms subordinated to an over-all form. He was at this time interested only in "symphonic" composition.

Kandinsky painted six Impressions, all of them in 1911; the series of Improvisations began in 1909, and by 1914 he had produced thirty-five, which he numbered; in addition, there are three with A-numbers, and five that are not listed as Improvisations. As for Compositions, Kandinsky painted seven of them between 1910 and 1914—three in 1910, two in 1911, and two in 1914. The remaining works dating from these years have the traditional sort of titles, but it is not always clear why he did not call some of these,

103

which suggest natural objects, "Impressions," or others, less suggestive of natural appearance, "Improvisations." In this book the numbering of these works follows Kandinsky's own catalogue (=KK). Works that have been discovered later, a great many of which might well be described as Impressions or Improvisations, and some of which have been so titled by their owners, will be treated separately. The dates and the titles given by Kandinsky cannot be established in every case. The Catalogue of Works gives particulars. We do not know why he failed to include many of his paintings in his own catalogue. Possibly some works were not adjudged finished or failed to come up to his standards; more likely, he did not regard his own catalogue as definitive. For instance, he inserted the number 128-a after KK 171, and began the series of six Impressions with his own No. 2, concluding it with his own No. 5.

It might seem logical to discuss the Impressions, Improvisations, and Compositions separately and in chronological order, but this would compel us to go back several times over a given year in discussing each category. Needless to say, Kandinsky's classification is valid, but it does not mean that works such as *Paradise* (1909) or *Painting with Troika* (1911) are less important than others. We shall therefore discuss together the works that are related chronologically and artistically, and we shall subdivide those dating from 1910, 1911, and 1912 according to their degree of naturalism. It will be necessary at some points to anticipate Kandinsky's later conceptions and to go back to earlier ones. The more naturalistic works of 1908 have already been discussed. There were fifteen of these in 1909, but only four in 1910; there were seven in 1911, five in 1912, two in 1913, and none in 1914.

The year 1909 was a transitional one, during which Kandinsky, in addition to naturalistic landscapes, sketched his first Improvisations. The year before he had produced two works of transitional character, namely *White Sound* (CC 15) and *Elephant* (CC 593) the former an idyllic scene showing people resting in a birch woods, painted in part pointillistically, and predominantly oval in design and white in color, which accounts for the bright, cheerful sonority and for the title. The latter represents a fairytale elephant in front of a tent with banners waving, the armed colored riders just setting out on a lion hunt. The fairylike element in the scenery depicted is also found in the paintings of Murnau gardens; the colors, too, are the same.

This fairylike element is further emphasized in some of the paintings executed between 1909 and 1911, which are still based on a simple, clearly recognizable motive. Paintings such as *On the Beach* (1909, CC 605), *Impression IV (Policeman)* (CC 64), *Horses* (1909, CC 607) and *The Cow* (CC 59) still suggest objects, but are essentially paraphases. The contours have been partly retained, but the colors are purely expressive and independent of the motive. These studies, which Kandinsky kept in Murnau while he was outside Germany, are quite large (approximately one square yard each). Without being masterworks, they mark bold advances into regions where the role of the conscious or the predetermined elements has already diminished.

Sunday (1910, CC 62) and *Concert* (1911, CC 49) have an Impressionist character, with their rapid brush strokes and thin layers of color. Kandinsky himself called *Concert* an "Impression." The strong color harmony varies from painting to painting: in

Woodcut from Klänge. 191

Concert it is black, white, and yellow, and in *Sunday,* green, blue, and white. Distortions and ornamentation have been avoided, and the figures are analogical in character rather than deformations. *Oriental* (1909, CC 608; color woodcut in *Klänge*) and *Improvisation 6* (1909, color plate, p. 79), recollections of Tunis, go a little further. They are architectonic, with severe outlines and a chromatic progression from yellow through orange, vermilion, carmine, and violet, to the blues.

Drawing for Improvisation 14. 1910

Some of the paintings skirt the legendary. *Domes,* subtitled *Red Walls* (1909, CC 19) is a bit of the Kremlin projected into a Bavarian setting; *Mountain* (1909, CC 604), a grandiose apotheosis of all mountains. The two active figures in the painting may have derived from the stage work *Der gelbe Klang.* They have been placed against a white form suggesting a giant—it may be recalled that the original title of the stage work was *The Giants.* The overpowering colors of the mountain range from white through green and blue to carmine; at the lower left there are three black zigzag lines, almost geometrically exact. Black and white now begin to look like colors: they are the most abstract elements in the paintings of this period. The poster for the Neue Künstlervereinigung (1909, p. 39) falls in this category both for its design and its use of color.

In this period Kandinsky was greatly interested in the mountain as motive. In the same year he painted *Blue Mountain* (p. 263) showing a troop of riders on the side of a hill, framed between two tremendous trees, which look down on them like two ghostly masks. *Improvisation 9* (1910, p. 267) is one of Kandinsky's most exciting paintings, showing steep mountains, a rider on one peak, a church on another, at the lower left a compact group of people, and at the right a sleeping giant. The work is still in the possession of Professor Stadler in Zurich, to whom Kandinsky gave it in 1912, referring to it as a "Russian fairytale," although in his book, *On the Spiritual in Art,* he rejects the interpretation of his paintings as fairytales. In this case, as in many others, the theme probably justifies the title, for the painting obviously represents an event similar to the one treated in the stage composition of the same period. The figures in the lower part might be thought of as a chorus to a pictorial poem; if this interpretation is correct, we have here a poetic idea transposed into a picture. For Kandinsky poetry was one of the basic elements of all art, and he once stated that all his ideas were pictorial (Plaut, *Enquête,* 1929).

Mountains and high cliffs recur again and again in Kandinsky's paintings down to 1913, among others, in the first four Compositions and in many Improvisations, in *Pastoral,* in *Park* (1911), in the *Allerheiligen* (All Saints) pictures, in *Landscape with Red Spot,* and *Small Pleasures* (1913), and, as a sign language evoking the past, even in entirely nonobjective works. The subject is to an ever-increasing extent transformed into a theme, and in the end is reduced to the status of one element among many, constituting the complex pictorial material. The same will happen with others of Kandinsky's motives, for example, the horse and rider, and later, in the Bauhaus period, the circle.

Among the paintings in which mountains are still to be found, there is *Impression V (Park)* of 1911 (CC 68) and *Landscape with Church I* of 1913 (p. 277). In *Park* the vermilion red pointed triangle in the center completely dominates the construction, and the irregular colored planes (green, blue, carmine) have the effect of vegetation. The black lines suggest roads or buildings, although the treatment is very free, and in part consist merely of linear effects. In *Landscape with Red Spot* (CC 86), a second version of *Landscape with Church,* a rainbow arches over a silhouette of mountain peaks, broken by the vertical of a church tower. At the lower left we find the same village as in *Winter II;* in the foreground there are small hills, and above them an angular gate of beams over Menhir-like stones that may represent a graveyard. This painting with its slanting tower is a last echo of the Murnau landscapes, a phantasmagoria like Franz Marc's painting of the same period, *Das arme Land Tirol.*

Kandinsky was still feeling his away along different experimental lines, recording his visual and poetic experiences in works of an increasingly purer pictorial content.

From mid-October till the end of December 1910, Kandinsky was in Moscow, Petersburg, and Odessa, and on New Year's day he painted Moscow (*Impression 2,* p. 269). He thus realized his long-cherished wish to celebrate his native city, the splendor of its colors and the sounds of its bells, its double character of placid sensuousness and nervous spirituality. Moscow was his "pictorial tuning fork." This painting, in the collection of Bernhard Köhler in Berlin, was destroyed toward the end of the Second World War. It actually had something about it of the "hymn" Kandinsky composed in praise of Moscow in *Backward Glances;* the big tower seems to be the Ivan Veliky spire; "the golden and mottled stars" are the churches he so often visited for their icons, and the house at the left is either a palace or, perhaps, his family residence. Childhood memories play a significant part in this work, as can be seen from the little horse-drawn carriage in the upper right corner, with the driver who once peeled the bark from branches for a child's game.

The long stay in Moscow inspired another painting, *Troika* (1911, CC 53), which the collector Arthur Jerome Eddy of Chicago acquired prior to the First World War. Under a high cliff crowned by domes a troika flashes by on the way to a hill, below which

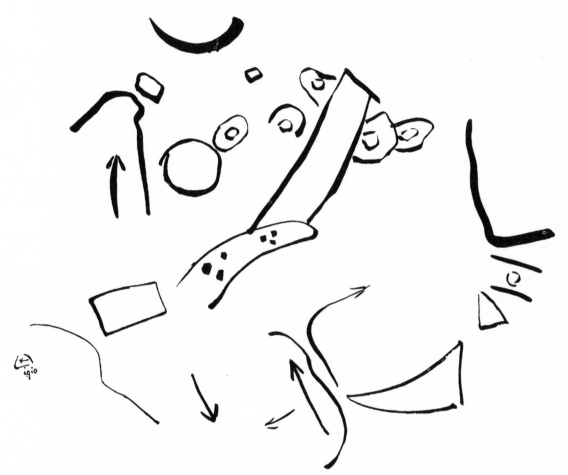

Drawing for Composition II. 1910, 1.

three enormously large Russian soldiers have made their camp. The Troika theme often recurs later, in abridged form, as a combination of three curved lines, for instance, in the watercolor *With Three Riders* (1912, CC 687) and in one woodcut for *Klänge* (1912, p. 104).

Another reminiscence of Russia is *Moscow Lady* (1912, CC 76), which exists as both a painting on glass and on canvas. The paradoxical combination of motives brings Chagall to mind, but the atmosphere here is of the big city, not the village. This is a Moscow street scene with naively painted rows of houses and a carriage going down the street; quite in the foreground, a fashionably dressed lady, surrounded by a halo or Mandala, a magic circle. To her left, a little table with a lap dog, to the right a nebulous form in lavender pink, which must surely be connected with Kandinsky's theosophic ideas, with the ethereal creative forces, perhaps also with Annie Besant's "thought forms." Over it hovers a black torso resembling the male figure. It is a psychoanalytic or parapsychological painting, quite unlike Kandinsky's other works.

107

A separate small group is constituted by the paintings Kandinsky left in Russia, *Lake (Boat Ride)* (CC 41) and *Improvisation 11* (1910, CC. 36). The former, which depicts a rowing regatta on a mountain lake, is reproduced in *Klänge* as a color woodcut. The other is a dramatically dynamic representation of a sailboat being launched on a storm-tossed lake, while bearded old men stand and watch. It tells a story in the manner of certain old Russian legends, such as may be found in *Prince Vladimir's Round Table,* a collection of legends about the Swedish Variags in Kiev c.1000 A.D. In mood it suggests Tristan, while its style is that of a medieval tapestry.

Unlike the agitated views of lakes, *Painting with Boat* (1909, CC 21) is rigidly structured and placidly calm. It could be a voyage to some isle of the dead, like that by Böcklin (whose art was much admired in Munich, and because of whom De Chirico went to study there), but translated into the Blaue Reiter manner. Scylla- and Charybdis-like rocks cut off the boat from the outside world as it comes in, and the emphasized horizontal divides the horizontal canvas into the proportion known as the golden section. Similar in expression is *Improvisation 2, Funeral March* (1909, CC 23)—rocks and water, with a horse and rider at the left. The blue and green at the left are complementary to the orange and red at the right. Black outlines isolate the individual forms, so that they look like stage props. That was no doubt how Kandinsky imagined the setting of Wagner's *Götterdämmerung*. In the definitive version in the Stockholm museum Kandinsky eliminated all the elements of the study (CC 609) that had seemed to him too uncertain in terms of color or drawing.

The desire to penetrate the inner core of nature and the sources of life occasionally induced Kandinsky to choose religious themes for the works of these transitional years. St. George, the Resurrection of the Dead, the Last Judgment, the Feast of All Saints, the Archangel, exist in several versions, as oil paintings, paintings on glass, and woodcuts, and show us how much Kandinsky was attached to the religious teachings he received as a child and how he translated them into art.

Improvisation 8 (p. 266) and the preliminary study for it (CC 33) which, as usual, is executed more clearly than the painting, date from 1910. At the left we see an archangel with a bared sword and beside him a figure whispering something to him; at the right, waiting or dejected figures, and on top, as though suspended in a cloud, a Russian town with churches and domes, the Kremlin or the New Jerusalem. The orange cloud may also be a wall surrounding the town. The colors are separated by strong outlines, which give the painting, or at least the upper part of it, the appearance of a leaded window.

Kandinsky represented St. George in three canvases (color plate, p. 125), and on glass (1911, CC 668). The mounted saint plays an important role in the liturgy of the Eastern church, and the legend of his battle with the dragon made the saint and martyr of Cappadocia a popular figure in all countries. The version that Kandinsky left behind him when he quitted Russia must have been similar to the third canvas (CC 63), in which all that remains of the horse is a line indicating the whip; the rider, a naively painted figure, is shown sticking the threatening dragon with his lance. But the effect of the painting is not one of terror: the colors are springlike, there is much pink, red,

Study for ▶
Composition II.
1910, 98

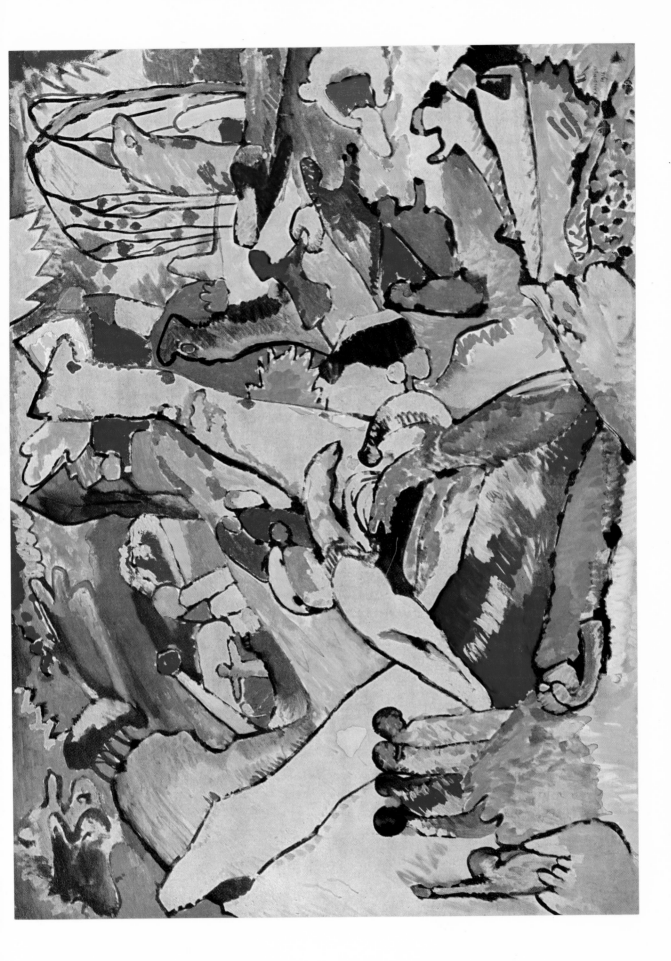

bright green, blue, and white, and the forms suggest that the action depicted is beyond human comprehension. The first version, executed early in 1911, is entirely different. In a vast snowy-white landscape with black-contoured red mountains and rocks, the saint on a rearing horse thrusts his lance into an antediluvian monster, red as blood and with a tail rising to cliff-like proportions. The green forms in the background are coats-of-arms or, perhaps, trees. In this picture, it is only parts of the rider which suggest natural objects; everything else in it may be what you will. The large amounts of white have a luminous effect, suggesting the supernatural light given off by the Christian warrior's feat.

Among the works with a religious theme, the All Saints pictures are the most numerous—two canvases of 1910, two paintings on glass, and two watercolors of 1911, and in addition eight representations of the Last Judgment or of the Resurrection of the Dead, in oil, watercolor, on glass, and woodcuts (1910 and 1911). The All Saints pictures, as Kandinsky had found them in Bavaria, derive from the idea of the *communio sanctorum* representations of the Apocalypse. With them might be grouped—to be sure, in an improper sense—representations of the end of the world, as well as a few representations of paradise.

Kandinsky treats the subject with great freedom; in his All Saints pictures we see mountains both with and without domed churches, angels with trumpets (Doomsday), saints hard to identify, saints on horseback, and in some of the works (p. 73, 13) even a troika, the dead rising from their graves, animals, plants, stars, and in CC 623, a peacock and a salamander, which, properly speaking, are symbols of Eden. One of the canvases (CC 610) shows a peasant-like figure in conversation with a boy, and this motive is repeated in one of the paintings on glass (CC 667) and in a watercolor. Compositionally the works are for the most part held together by arabesquelike lines, within which the figures are set as inside a shell.

Woodcut from Klänge.
(1913)

The essential character of the All Saints pictures is the same as that of the pictures titled *Last Judgment* or *Resurrection of the Dead*. One glass painting (1911, CC 666; repeated in a woodcut in Klänge, CC 757) shows an angel with a trumpet, a resurrected man holding his head in his hands, perhaps St. Dionysius, the suggestion of a mountain with domes, and a horse and rider, the whole divided between a heavenly sphere and an earthly sphere. This schema is repeated quite freely in a painting on glass (1911, CC 663), in a watercolor in the Museum of Modern Art, New York (p. 93, 19), and in a woodcut in *Klänge* (p. 100), in all of which the details can be identified if we trace them back to the more naturalistic works. Then one recognizes the trumpet, the mountain, domes, the horse and rider, and the troika, as well as some purely geometric forms—a triangle, a sickle. Incidentally, the triangle is to be found as early as 1910 (CC 44), but there it still could be a tree. The world of natural appearance is dwindling away, and free curved lines swallow up the world of objects. There is an oil study done in this open manner, presumably dating from 1911 (p. 272), in which we recognize only an angel with a trumpet, a mountain with domes, a triangle, and nothing else, and only the arrangement suggests inferences as to the meaning of the lines and colored forms. There are remote echoes of *Composition V* (1911, p. 270), but the oil study is far more closely related to *Improvisation 21-a* (1911, CC 69), a preliminary stage of *Small Pleasures*

110

(1913, color plate, p. 137). To the same group as *Improvisation 21-a* belong the painting on glass with sun, dated 1910 by Kandinsky (on a photograph, CC 661), and a watercolor in The Hague with somewhat freer forms, which must date from 1911 (p. 95).

Thus the basic conception of *Small Pleasures*, of which more later, goes back a full three years, and, as we can see, Kandinsky kept some of his projects unrealized for long periods of time. In the glass painting with sun, mountain, towered city, and another mountain behind it, these elements are more clearly discernible than in the All Saints pictures, and also the three horsemen galloping up the hills are more clearly recognizable; what is new is the reclining couple, a preliminary stage of the couple in *Composition IV* (1911, color plate, p. 123). All this can also be seen in *Improvisation 21-a*, but largely divested of the objective element; the forms can be identified only with the help of works belonging to the same group. Kandinsky attached little if any importance to this difficulty, for he had his own good reasons for moving on to pure forms.

The group treating the theme of the end of the world includes one more painting (the last of 1910) which looks like a fragment (CC 47), a watercolor (p. 76,17), and two paintings on glass of 1911 (CC 663, 664). The angel with the trumpet, a resurrected man holding his head in his hands, a rock with a domed church at the upper edge; one of the towers leans and looks like the forepart of the hand of a horseman of the Apocalypse. The angel's yellow tuba has a provocative effect within the dark blue and violet, and the vehemence of the colors reminds us of Nolde's religious paintings. These are apocalyptic visions, and in 1911 Kandinsky executed a painting on glass, *Apocalyptic Horsemen* (CC 665). The picture is in line with earlier treatments of the subject. The red horseman on the blue horse is shown holding a bow, the second a sword, the blue one in front on the green horse holds a scales. The vehemence of the movement elongates all the forms, the viewer is made more aware of the speed of the event than of the event itself. Later Kandinsky again painted on glass a group of horses (1914, CC 669) sweeping across a mountain village, with medallions of animals in the four corners; it goes under the title *Apocalyptic Horsemen*, which is not quite correct, even though the strident fantastic elements do suggest the Revelation of St. John.

One degree further from naturalistic appearance is *Deluge I* (p. 274), which Kandinsky finished on March 22, 1912, and also another version (CC 75) dating from the same year, which has no title and is known erroneously as *Transition*. Here, too, we see a mountain, but with a tree instead of domes, and a serpent (Original Sin), a horseman carrying a tuba, other figures, some recognizable and some schematic, the form of a boat (the Ark), foaming water; a strong diagonal movement from the upper right to the lower left in the form of a flash of lightning—an ordered chaos. In the copy all details have been eliminated, the horse and rider have been reduced to a few curves, and only two of the other figures are recognizable as such. In comparison with the All Saints pictures, *Deluge,* particularly the copy, is a concentration of broad, simple forms, and at the same time it is more dynamic.

In the period when he wrote *On the Spiritual in Art,* Kandinsky, as we have just seen, painted a large number of religious works. The reasons for this lie in the painter's personal religious bent, which occasionally manifested itself also later in a "hidden"

Woodcut from Klänge. 1913

way, and in his tense psychological state between 1910 and 1912: his preoccupation with the unknown, with the absolute, naturally reawakened his religious feelings. We also know that Franz Marc planned to illustrate the Bible with his friend.

Throughout his life, Kandinsky was a practising member of the Greek Orthodox Church, and there were always several icons in the places where he lived, but the All Saints pictures have no discernible stylistic relation with icons. Rather, they seem to have been influenced by the Bavarian paintings on glass. Since the eighteenth century Murnau had been one of the principal homes of this art, in which the pictorial, intensely colored type of glass painting was cultivated, rather than the linear style. Though only in rare instances, this popular craft had achieved the high level of the so-called "Primitive painters" who won recognition in the twentieth century. In the church of Froschhausen, which Kandinsky represented (CC 580), he could study a large collection of the best Bavarian glass paintings. In his own paintings on glass he took over the peasant delight in color and the naïve mode of expression, and adapted them to his own artistic sensibility; but he was unquestionably also influenced by reminiscences of Russian prints. He also took over the techniques: he uses silver or quicksilver coatings, and occasionally even his composition is similar to that of Murnau glass paintings, for instance, in *Sancta Francisca* (CC 662) which Kandinsky in 1911 gave his janitor in Munich for Christmas. Most of the paintings on glass are apocalyptic in spirit, but there is also a *Last Supper* (1910), a *Saint Vladimir*, and a *Birds of Paradise with Hound of Hell* (1911). The repertory is fairly extensive. There are twenty-three glass paintings in the Münter-Kandinsky Foundation in Munich, and four in the Paris collection; he painted seventeen in Moscow during the war. The total probably comes to around forty-five.

Until 1912 horses and riders occur in almost all groups of Kandinsky's works. But in some they are the central theme, which is treated in an increasingly abstract manner. A glass painting of 1908 (CC 660) with a lady in an old-fashioned German costume standing in front of the Frauenkirche in Munich continues the style of the early woodcuts; similarly, *Klänge* contains woodcuts executed before the book was written, which belong to his earlier works (*Horse and Rider Scene*, p. 39). The remaining glass paintings with horses and riders (*Cavalier*, 1912), and a few woodcuts in *Klänge* including the vignette on the last page (1912, p. 87) belong to the series of non-objective works.

Improvisation 3, with horse and rider (1909, CC 24) follows directly the *Funeral March*, and exists in two versions. The first is sketched with vehement brush strokes, and the rearing greenish horse in front of the egg-yellow house and the red sky supply the basic tone of the painting. The 1910 version (CC 619) is more rigid and calmer. Like *Funeral March* it represents a legendary exploit, although a much more dramatic one. Legendary also is *Pastoral* (color plate, p. 127) dating from the spring of 1911, when Kandinsky executed a few other quickly painted and successful works (*Nude*, CC 61; *Sunday*, CC 62; *Improvisation 19*, CC 57). But none of these has the captivating verve of this *fête champêtre* with four oversized Biedermeier figures in white, filling the entire right side of the painting, and the spring landscape at the left with horses being

Improvisation 10. ▶
1910, 101

watered and the shepherdess blowing her red pipe. A Paradise-like air pervades this bit of nature with its blue-green trees, violet-pink and yellow hills, and the white foal at the deep blue water. Yellow, red, blue are the main colors, but what abundance of intermediary tones, what gradations of white! It is a harmonious work, its centers of gravity and rhythms are distributed in such a way that its effect would be perfect even without any suggestion of objects.

Between *Improvisation 3* and *Pastoral* there are three loosely and heavily painted pictures representing horses and riders, which are naturalistic in appearance yet difficult to decipher. *Improvisation 4* (1911, CC 28), formerly in the museum of Nizhni Novgorod, becomes more understandable when compared with the woodcut in *Klänge*. Then we recognize a shying horse to the right of the slanting tree, and in the foreground three female figures involved in some indefinable action. In *Presto* (1910, CC 32), two riders gallop across an animated landscape, painted in the style of the Murnau gardens. *Improvisation 12, Riders* (1910, CC 43) which Kandinsky gave Franz Marc in exchange

Drawing for Composition III. 1910, 2

for one of the latter's paintings, might be a tribute to his friend: the type of the horse, and the rhythmic structure of the painting—a spherical triangle and a domed horizon— are in the style of Marc.

Lyrical, showing a race horse with a jockey, and reproduced as a color woodcut in *Klänge* (1911, CC 51) marks a high point. It has the conciseness of East Asian master-pieces, without a superfluous line or tone. The fairly large painting could almost have been executed in India ink. The lines delineating the horse can be counted, and yet it is more real than Degas' horses. The trees are as schematic as written characters; the landscape consists of a few colored spots—violet, blue, green. The woodcut is even more airy, the horse's neck is more slender, its mane indicated with a few strokes—it is a hieroglyphic of the transient, as are the watercolor and the woodcut *With Three Riders,* in which only the lines of movement remain (CC 687). A week earlier Kandinsky had painted *Romantic Landscape* (CC 48) showing three blue-green riders on horseback sweeping down a slope, a white landscape with a red sun, and a black fir tree in the foreground. The whole is both real and unreal, the red spot of the sun is placed in front of the hill instead of over it, the white suggests winter, and the green at the upper right summer, and yet everything is true if it is seen with the "inner eye."

Dating from about the same time as these two paintings is *Arab II* (CC 54), a fantasy of Arab riders, with Arab women and a child in front of a gate at the right (the painting is subtitled *With the Gate*); at the center there are free forms tending in different directions, straight lines (spears) and bent lines (shadows). A third painting of 1911, titled *Arabs* (CC 60), shows a contest of horsemen. It is based on formal analogies; only the objects in the foreground are recognizable (a harem woman with a pitcher), static elements which contrast with the dynamic ones.

Improvisation 16 and *Improvisation 18,* with their crystalline natural forms belong together. *Improvisation 18* (1911, CC 56) is subtitled *With Tombstone:* the gray prisms are a graveyard, the tree is a weeping willow, the half circle a dome, the rider perhaps a saint. In *Improvisation 16* (1910, CC 46) the horse has become Pegasus, the two arcs on the sides are mountains, as on the cover design of the Blaue Reiter catalogue of 1911. A composition not listed in KK shows horsemen galloping uphill; the empty center is framed in thick lines, the lower ones suggesting a horse's back; at the upper left there is a village with domed churches, and below a landscape with a horse (1911, CC 625). This composition is on the whole identical with *Improvisation 20* (1911, CC 65), a painting subtitled *Horses,* which Kandinsky left in Russia; these horses can barely be discerned as such. The form of a frame in the center is the same as that in the composition, but the horses galloping above it have disappeared, while the horses in the lower half of the painting have become recognizable. The last canvas with a leaping horse and rider is *Sketch* of 1912 (p. 275) painted in bright, luminous colors; the rider is recognizable (upper right), while the other forms suggest landscape and animal elements—hills, trees, houses, birds, fishes. It may represent a kind of paradise, like the last painting Kandinsky executed in 1909 (CC 31), showing Murnau mountains in the most varied blues with pink clouds, and nonnaturalistic figures in the foreground.

It was almost taken for granted that the cover of the Blaue Reiter catalogue and the binding of the Blaue Reiter almanac would be decorated with designs showing horses and riders. The catalogue cover of 1911 (p. 67) shows a rider taking a hurdle, reduced to a few lines as in *Lyrical.* The external form serves as frame; the inner form, approximating a triangle, is a mountain, as in *Improvisation 16.* For the Almanac Kandinsky made as many as ten preliminary sketches (CC 672-681); he chose the tenth, but omitted the word "Almanac" on the binding. Most of the watercolor sketches are done in the style of the Murnau paintings on glass. Once again we have the exact triangle, the mountain, the wavy lines indicating the ground with accompanying hatchings, the clouds and stars, and the peacock. A great deal is also taken over from the All Saints and Resurrection pictures, but brought into a more decorative arrangement suitable for the present purpose. Kandinsky uses sinuous arabesques inside which he places the pictorial action, half circles, and diagonal divisions. The next to the last version comes very close to the definitive one, but he doubtless thought it was too like the catalogue cover; the final one is more powerful and more pictorial, and does not have the character of a cover design. It shows a saint on horseback, St. Martin with a beggar at his feet. The colors—blue, orange, black—express excitement.

The landscapes Kandinsky called "Improvisations" occupy a special place in his works of the transitional period 1910–1912. They come closest to the ideas he developed in *On the Spiritual in Art*. The strict canon of the human figure is less amenable to new conceptions than the landscape, which can be treated with greater freedom.
The Waterfall (not listed in KK, CC 606) is an intricate complex of curved forms (trees, hills, rocks), although it was executed as early as 1909. *Improvisation on Mahogany* (1910, color plate, p. 71) seems at first glance quite nonobjective, yet gradually two figures emerge from the tapestry-like pattern at the right, and, at the left, churches with domes. They are attuned to the adjacent forms and the various reds and blues, merely echoing them, and do not disturb the warm, festive mood of this southern, almost oriental "landscape."
Improvisation 7 (1910, CC 34 and 620) exists in three versions—one in Russia, one at Yale University, and one (more sketchy) in Paris. We sense the presence of mountains, houses, and a few figures; but these are no more than sensed. The clearest version is the Russian one, the most balanced the one at Yale. All the forms are of equal value and interrrelated, without regard for meaning. The so-called *Etude* (1910, not in KK, CC 621) can be interpreted with the help of the *Klänge* woodcut (p. 97): the four parallels near the half circle indicate the branches of a weeping willow, and below it are four figures. *Improvisation 10* (1910, color plate, p. 113) has a complicated rhythm and is richer than *Etude:* three verticals intersect circular arcs which may indicate rocks and sky; at the right there are black and green bent lines arranged concentrically (branches), and above them red domes on a whitish rectangle (rock); a curve running downward from left to right, indicating the ground, finds its counterpart in the carmine red zigzag shape rising at the right, and its structural and chromatic termination in the egg yellow cone rising at the left. The graphic and flat elements are exactly balanced, as well as the colors: the yellow between the red and the blue has the effect of a flourish of trumpets, but the secondary colors dampen the brightness of this cheerful painting. Its harmony is the more euphonious because instrumentation and syntax meet half way.
Improvisation 14 (1910, CC 45) differs greatly both from the expressive *Interior (With G. Münter and M. v. Werefkin,* CC 42), which precedes it, and from *Composition III,* which follows it. Such sudden changes in style are characteristic of Kandinsky's evolution in this period. Around a large sky-blue area at the center (a lake) we see various forms

Autumn I. ▶
1911, 123

—landscape and figure elements in tender green and red—moving toward it; the austere form of a tree appears at the left. Its luminous green in conjunction with the dominant light blue achieves a maximum of brilliance of the kind sometimes to be observed on the shores of mountain lakes.

In *Impression 1*, dating from the beginning of 1911 (CC 50) and subtitled *Fountain*, only the fountain is treated realistically; the free elements are arranged along a diagonal line traversing the painting. *Improvisation 25* (1912, CC 72) is a "Garden of Love." A large watercolor study for the painting that was left in Russia supplies a key to the landscape type of composition. At the right we see a garden with couples under the trees; at the left, water with a rowboat reduced to a few formal indications. Essential is the division of the picture plane into two zones which relate to two different zones of experience: the circular, brightly toned forms at the right express the world of feeling; the angular forms at the left belong to the outside world. The latter are more rigid in the oil painting than in the watercolor. A second "Garden of Love" is *Improvisation 27* (CC 74), which the photographer Alfred Stieglitz bought at the Armory Show (New York, 1913). This was one of the first works—along with those acquired by Arthur Jerome Eddy of Chicago—to go to America. Stieglitz had a tiny gallery at 291 Fifth Avenue, through which he had been acquainting the United States with modern art since 1910. The starlike red spot in the watercolor study for *Improvisation 25* has become a yellow sun in *Improvisation 27* and has moved to the center; the water at the bottom and the reclining couples have been moved to the periphery.

The forms in *Improvisation 26, Oars* (1912, CC 73) are extremely free. In the preliminary watercolor study (p. 40) three men in a rowboat, a fir tree, and a spherical tree at the top are fairly recognizable. In the painting, the oars have been reduced to slightly diverging diagonals, and the boat to a semi-circle. Everything else has been reduced to graphic elements, and can be variously interpreted. The color areas do not keep inside the linear boundaries, but lie underneath, so that two planes are produced, one tangible and graphic, the other imaginary and colored. The same theme is very freely treated in a woodcut for *Klänge:* the pairs of oars have become three forceful downward strokes, the boat is a three-quarter circle, the water a wavy line. The process of emancipation from the object and its translation into a language of free forms is particularly obvious here; without tracing back the forms it would be difficult to relate them to the things originally intended. Does Kandinsky still intend them at all? It seems that by this time he recognized only the phenomena of the mind as real; though not yet entirely eliminated, external reality survives as no more than a residue, and pure essences are on the way to taking its place. Here as elsewhere Kandinsky displays extreme caution in moving toward abstraction: he was still conscious of the dangers of sheer ornamentalism. Only very gradually does his sensibility steer him toward what Husserl (writing about the same time) called "the awareness of something." This gives the paintings of 1912 a quality of utmost honesty.

The first three Compositions were executed in 1910, *Composition I* being the first painting executed that year (p. 265). *Composition II* had been begun late in 1909, but was not completed until the spring of 1910 (CC 35), and *Composition III* was finished on November 15 (p. 268). *Composition I* was destroyed during the war, and we possess no color reproduction of it; *Composition II and III* were in the collection of Baron von Gamp. A large study for *Composition II* is in the Solomon R. Guggenheim Museum, New York (color plate, p. 109). In February 1911, Kandinsky painted *Composition IV* (color plate, p. 123), in the Nina Kandinsky collection. That fall he began *Composition V* (CC 89, p. 270), and finished it on November 17. *Composition VI* was painted in the spring of 1913 (completed on March 3), and *Composition VII* (p. 276) was painted between October 25 and 28, after many preliminary studies. Kandinsky describes it as the most important work of this pre-war period. The two last-named Compositions are

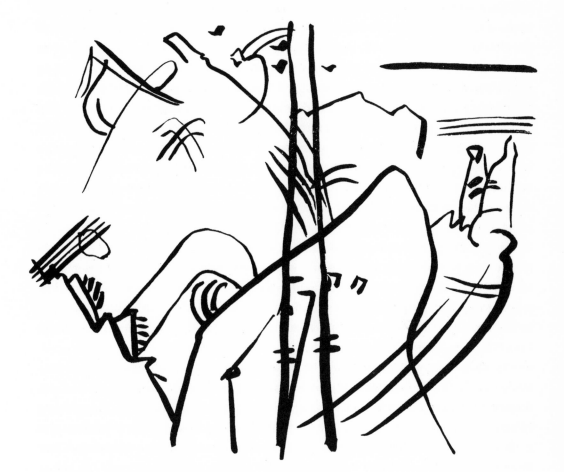

Second drawing for Composition IV. 1911

in Russia, and no color reproductions of them are available. The fact that his seventh Composition, over which he labored longer than on any other painting, should have remained in Russia distressed him a great deal. After these works falls an interval of ten years: not until 1923, at the Bauhaus, did he paint *Composition VIII*. The ninth dates from 1936, and the tenth and last dates from 1939.

Kandinsky looked upon the Compositions as his major works, his symphonies, which he prepared with the greatest care, both spiritually and technically. In some cases he made partial or complete preliminary drawings, watercolors, and oil studies. According to Thomas von Hartmann, Kandinsky noted his first ideas for the Compositions on

119

small notebook pages, but no such drawings seem to have been preserved. How sparing he was with the title "Composition," can be seen from the fact that several works which he had planned to call "Compositions" were not given that name, because they failed to come up to his standards, because they were not rich and balanced enough either in relation to individual forms or the totality of the relationships expressed. The "sacred shudder," which he mentions in *Backward Glances* epitomizes Kandinsky's acute sense of artistic responsibility.

Composition I is of modest dimensions, yet crowded with action and violent in expression; as a result it is somewhat overburdened. It has often been observed that the beginner's enthusiasm (and Kandinsky only began to be Kandinsky in 1908) leads to excess: he wants to do too many things at once. We must also keep in mind that *Composition I* chronologically comes between *Group in Crinolines* and *Presto*. In its over-all effect it reminds us of *Improvisation 9,* with the giant: it shows two overlapping rocky, terraced mountains; at the top are domed churches and houses, and at mid-height there are trees, as well as roads running in a direction opposite to the rightward movement of the mountain (intersecting diagonals). In the foreground are meadows, stones, bridges, various figures. In the middle distance three horses and riders partly conceal the mountains behind; the leaping horse and rider at the top appears here probably for the first time in this schematic form, while the one below and to the left is almost the same as the horse and rider in *Blue Mountain,* and the horse to the right is the same as the horse in *Funeral March*. The arabesque-like lines of the mountains, roads, and trees envelop the scene of horses and riders as much as the robe of the Madonna with the Mantle envelops the worshipers. The outer edges of the picture remain fairly empty; Kandinsky has built from outside in and from the top down. The *Composition* seems suspended, and produces an effect of hovering, of lightness. The colors are somewhat loose and expressive, particularly in the landscape elements; at the center they are quieter, neutralized.

Composition II shows a festive scene, a hilly wooded landscape with two leaping horses and riders facing each other at the center, a group of children playing and a couple reclining at the right, white rocks and standing figures at the left, a reclining figure below, and at the top a hill with domed churches, a mountain peak with trees, and bizarre clouds. The differences between the study and the painting are extensive. The study was done late in 1909; the painting, begun in 1909, was completed in the spring of 1910. Contrary to Kandinsky's usual habit, the study is the less naturalistic and more daring, but the painting has been more thoroughly worked out, and is more self-contained and harmonious. In 1930 when *Cahiers d'Art* prepared a monograph on Kandinsky, the artist sent a photograph of the study to serve as illustration for *Composition II*. Did he do this because he thought the study was more significant, more in line with his subsequent intentions? Elsewhere, too, photographs of the study have been reproduced as *Composition II,* both in Kandinsky's lifetime and since his death.

In the more naturalistic, later version the tree trunk at the center is a real tree trunk, extending to the upper edge of the picture, while in the study it resembles a leaning tower, some distance from the upper edge. This is also the case in a preliminary drawing in India ink, which indicates the essential lines of force (p. 107). In the painting, the ground line is clearly indicated above the horse and rider on the left, but the study shows at that place a curious figuration, a sort of ghost horse and rider, which overlap with the architecturally treated white trees. The children, the adults, and the reclining couple are all more angular in form, more simplified, and more closely attuned to each other in respect both to line and plane in study; the group of four figures at the left is shaped like a series of identical cylinders, and only the sleeping woman in the foreground has more body and is more tangible than in the painting. With regard to color, the study is more lively and richer in contrasts than the painting. The color harmonics are based on white, vermilion, red, and sky blue, secondary colors being emerald-green, green, violet, and egg yellow, with a bit of black. The bright harmonies make a festive music, suggestive of a summer morning, a symphony of cheerful, dew-drenched nature. The main theme in white (horseman and tower) echoes the white of the weeping willow and of the figures at the right; the colorful scherzo of the playing children is a phrase in itself; the adagio of the reclining figure in front is a third phrase; the jagged lines of the clouds drape the scenery as with a curtain. The simultaneity of the events depicted brings into focus the transitions from white to red and blue, from the verticals and diagonals to the intersecting half-circles of the horses and the arcs of the children.

There is a partial study (not in KK, CC 622), which probably was done at the same time as the study of 1909. It resembles the latter in individual forms; the reclining couple is flatter than in the painting, where the woman looks like one of Henry Moore's reclining figures. The woodcut in *Klänge* (p. 99) translates the whole composition into graphic terms, taking the last version as a model.

Composition III looks like a single gigantic rock articulated into small blocks; the middle one is blue. Bright "rocky forms" at the bottom grow upward like figures, there is a white horse at the left. At the center, between taut forms reminiscent of trees, are human figures and heads of horses. A drawing (p. 114) confirms the hypothesis of two figures at the bottom and indicates more clearly the horse at the left, and contains further clues that the painting does not supply. It is a composition which confirms Kandinsky's observation about the tragic element in his art; we are also reminded of Franz Marc's *Animal Destinies* of 1913: a tremor runs through the work, suggestive of a mood of catastrophe.

Composition IV was the most successful of the series, the reproduction of a watercolor study for it in the Blaue Reiter Almanac possibly helping its appreciation. Kandinsky made several preparatory studies for this painting, including two drawings, two watercolors, and an oil study (Tate Gallery, London) treating the left half of the finished painting. Increasingly the artist made more and more such studies for his compositions, trying out his conceptions both of the individual forms and of the over-all design. The definitive painting shows a mountain landscape. At the center is a blue mountain with a castle; at the left, an escarpment, and between them a rainbow; above the rainbow we see a combat between mounted horsemen, at the right a reclining couple, and on the ridge of one hill two standing figures. The whole is cut by two tree trunks, which extend from the very top of the painting to the bottom edge.

The first preliminary drawing (p. 122) shows some of the main lines, and already has the same proportions as the painting; the second (p. 119) contains all the details. The first watercolor study must be the one with a network of lines drawn in view of possible enlargement; it resembles the final version even though some details are lacking. The second watercolor study (CC 683) is similar to the reproduction in the *Blaue Reiter Almanac* that was reworked for this purpose, and differs from the painting in many respects. The staccato-like escarpment is like the one in *Winter II;* the blue mountain with the red-roofed houses is like the one in the Murnau landscapes of 1911. The fragment at the Tate Gallery (CC 52) is more epic, being extended in width, with "windows" in the castle and ornamental flashes of lightning in the sky.

With respect to subject matter, several details become clearer when we learn that *Composition IV* was subtitled *Battle,* presumably because of the horsemen in combat at the upper left; these figures are represented only by an ideogram, a cluster of lines of great suggestive force, their original meaning barely recognizable. One might call them lines of conflict; they are intensified by straight lines, mounting like arrows or spears in the direction of the battle scene. The ideograms for the horsemen are almost colorless: this emphasizes their dynamism, all the more so because they are placed above a brilliant rainbow. At the center (blue mountain) there is repose; the two trees separate the battle scene from the peaceful one on the right, with the oversized reclining figure.

*First drawing for
Composition IV. 1911, 3*

We see once again how Kandinsky moved step by step in the direction of free forms; without the help of the landscape they would be impossible to identify. Kandinsky's forms will soon take on independent existence, without reference to natural models. The long 3-form of the reclining woman, the "spears," the curved line of the horse-whip (a recollection of childhood games), the arched lines of the arms, the semi-circle of the mounted man, the parallel half-circles of the rainbow, the divergent verticals of the trees, will recur throughout the series. This is also true of the colors—the earthy yellow, the fairytale blue of the mountain, the vermilion of the houses, and the abstract white that occurs whenever Kandinsky approaches the frontiers of the absolute. In later contexts these forms will have other meanings too, many of them tending progressively to assume the significance of ideal essences.

In *Backward Glances* Kandinsky gives what he calls a "subsequent definition" of *Composition IV*. His analysis is revealing. He first speaks of the masses: at the lower center blue, at the upper right blue, red, yellow; at the upper left the knotted black lines of the horses, and the long drawn-out lines at the lower right. Second, he refers to the contrasts: between masses and lines, between the precise and the blurred, between the knots of line and the knots of color. The principal contrast is that between sharp, pointed movement (battle) and bright cold-sweet colors. Third, he mentions how the color flows over the outlines, and finally he says that the composition has two centers—the knots of line and the sharp peak of blue. Kandinsky clearly avoids emotional or symbolic interpretation. The viewer, however, while aware of the directions he is given, will inevitably go beyond them. Man has an innate tendency to transcend immediate experience, particularly in the realm of art, and to relate it to a general system of aesthetics, philosophy, religion, or a personal view of life.

Composition IV. 1911, 12

The counterpart of *Composition IV* is *Composition V* (p. 270) dating from the end of 1911. Black and gray predominate in it, and there are few color accents. The dominant form is a dynamic black whip line, which stretches across the entire surface like a Chinese dragon, so that the suggestions of landscape, a mountain with Kremlin towers, seem almost accidental. Most of the forms have no relation to natural objects— conical shapes in the middle, zigzag lines, arches of a bridge, triangles (bottom center). By stretching our imagination, we may recognize the horn-like forms in the upper corners as trumpets of the Last Judgment, as they appear in the painting on glass titled *Resurrection* (1911, CC 666); also the geometric triangle is there. The extended form next to it bears a certain similarity to the saint holding his head in his hands. This painting was, in fact, repeatedly referred to as representing the Last Judgment, and there is much in it to justify this interpretation. A sketch for *Composition V*, which Kandinsky gave his friend Thomas von Hartmann, cannot be used for comparison because it has remained in Russia.

Improvisation 22 (CC 67) and *Improvisation 23*, Kandinsky's last painting of 1911, are much less "objective" than the Compositions. The former was hung at the first Blaue Reiter exhibition next to *Composition V*, and the latter at the Sturm exhibition in 1912 with the first three Compositions. Thus Kandinsky regarded these paintings as especially significant, both the one with the zigzag line intersecting the floating planes like a flash of lightning, and the one subtitled *Troika*, which is very similar in formal structure, but not amenable to associative interpretation. The three lines at the bottom could be a troika, the clusters of lines at the center are reminiscent of those in *Composition IV*, as also the semi-circles of the domes at the top. This is also true of the first painting of 1912, *Improvisation 24* (CC 71). During the weeks preceding and following Christmas, Kandinsky must have thought a great deal about Moscow, which he had so recently visited.

The watercolors and drawings of this period are more advanced than the paintings. Late in 1919 he painted his first abstract watercolor (color plate, p. 101); it is very different from the other works done about the same time. He must have found this watercolor exciting, for he signed it with his full name and dated it. It has no discernible affinity with his paintings, apart from the conical form at the center, which cuts through a circle and is repeated in *Study for Composition VII* (CC 94) three years later. Also the tangles of color somewhat remind us of the couples of lovers in *Improvisation 25* (Garden of Love), but they suggest no natural objects. On an ivorylike ground, red-blue forms are seen floating loosely, without overlapping, occasionally with graphic signs in the style of incisions. The arrangement is approximately circular, and an energetic, slightly bent tangent runs from the upper left to the lower right. The structure is still as undecided as the individual forms, but the study which expresses a playful delight in fabulation, has great charm.

The watercolor studies are remarkably imaginative. The watercolor illustrated on p. 74 contains echoes of *Composition IV* (reclining couple, clusters of lines, central verticals), but also of *Improvisation 26*, with the oars, the boat, and the wavy lines. The same may be said of the watercolor CC 682 (mountain, reclining couple, oars, and

Saint George ▶
1911, 128

boat). Those of the watercolors which are entirely independent of the paintings, are as daring as some of the India ink drawings of the same period (p. 149), which we would today call "*tachiste*." Often the watercolors are preliminary studies for Improvisations that were not executed, for instance, the one reproduced p. 76, in carmine pink and light blue, with the zigzag line in the middle. These studies are full-fledged paintings.

Kandinsky still had a long way to go before producing Compositions VI and VII. In the interval he executed at least a dozen works that are scarcely inferior to them. The year 1913 is even richer than 1912 during which he produced a number of important works, including *Black Spot* (CC 77), *With the Black Arch* (p.273), *Sketch* (CC 80), *Improvisation 29* (CC 81), and a painting which is known as *Improvisation 28* (color plate, p. 131); it is probably the last painting Kandinsky executed in 1912. It has no title in his private catalogue.

Black Spot remained behind in Russia after Kandinsky's departure. In it there are no references to natural objects, apart from the suggestion of two triangular mountains with domed churches. It is a powerful work that Kandinsky himself valued very highly. When we look at the three "continents" shown here, colliding with one another, with the vermilion-red star at the left, and the connecting black arcs, we cannot help recalling the passage from *On the Spiritual in Art* which describes the act of painting as a thunderous collision of worlds. Here the collision is very violent, because the forms are different at the points of contact, and their colors clash—steel blue against violent red and vermilion. The tension is not allayed by the black arc bent at its center of gravity; the arc does not span, it looks dangerous. The clusters of lines and the green spots of color, yellowed, remain attached to the "continents." There is nothing that links one to the other; the overlapping lines, too, soar by the giants. Some have interpreted this austere painting as an anticipation of the First World War, as a prophecy in the sense of Jung's theory of art (Debrunner).

In a sketch in the Dotremont collection (CC 80) the elements are still more unleashed and it is understandable that it should be subtitled *Deluge*. As in the more objective Krefeld *Deluge* (p. 274), we find suggestions of drowning people and animals, and a flash of lightning coming down diagonally from the upper right; the overlapping of the translucent planes must have been deliberate, as it produces an effect of movement. The lines are even more flowing and have a more loosening effect in the related watercolor (CC 686). The horseman with the trumpet in the Krefeld painting recalls the glass paintings of 1911, and it must have been executed before the sketch, though it bears a later number in the catalogue. *Improvisation 29* (CC 81) was executed between the two Deluges; it is subtitled *The Swan,* from the form resembling a swan's neck at the center, which we find also in a glass painting executed at about the same time.

The last painting of the year (untitled, color plate, p. 131) for which we have a fairly accurate sketch executed in watercolor technique (CC 690) is related to *Composition IV,* with its verticals, the conical mountain, the church at the right and the cluster of spearlike parallels, but it is more somber (a great deal of black, gray, and white, the other colors neutralized), and the forms are less recognizable. The diverging

Pastoral. 1911, 132

bars at the left are oars as in *Improvisation 26,* and the Baroque vortex under them stands for foam, but the dented wheel forms and the wavy lines at the upper right are mere signs of excitement, which Kandinsky would ascribe to inner necessity, to the expressive character of the work. The brilliant sketchiness of the painting, and the large amount of white used both as a ground and as a color leaves it open to many interpretations. Perhaps only its vehemence is unambiguous.

For Kandinsky, as for many another European painter, 1913 was the most fruitful of the prewar yars. He has now mastered the abstract style of expression, and is in possession of the full range of his pictorial means. When so-called "similarities" emerge, he does not entirely reject them, but minimizes them, as he did in a letter to Arthur Jerome Eddy, dealing with *Improvisation 30* (color plate, p. 133), his first painting of 1913. He says in it that the designation "Cannon" which he adopted for private use (the origin of all Kandinsky's subtitles) should not be interpreted as a description of the content of the painting. The content, he goes on to say, is that which the beholder experiences under the impact of the colors and forms. The center, somewhat below the middle, is formed by an irregular blue plane (the blue color) and counteracts the impression caused by the cannon. The gray spot below is the second center of almost equal importance. The four corners, terminal points of a cross, are heavier than the two centers, and differ from each other. This veils the construction. The allusions to natural objects are mere incidental echoes. The presence of forms resembling guns, which came into being unconsciously, may be accounted for by the fact that at the time the painting was executed there was much talk of war. Nevertheless, Kandinsky says, he did not intend a war picture, which would have required altogether different means. All this, Kandinsky adds, is an analysis of a work which he painted in a state of strong inner tension. Occasionally, he gave himself spoken orders, such as "the corners must be heavy." In such cases, one must ponder all the facts, for instance, the element of weight. Precisely where feeling can be sufficiently relied upon to paint a composition correctly, schematism and consciousness do no harm; on the contrary, Kandinsky concluded, they are very beneficial.

It is instructive to see what Kandinsky was aiming at, and the letter just summarized is the more valuable because it was not intended for publication but was addressed to an art lover, who, judging by his book (*Cubism and Post-Impressionism,* Chicago, 1914), experienced paintings as intensely as their creator. The letter also accounts for the subtitles—they were meant only for the artist's personal use, to avoid confusion. Kandinsky did not like to use them because they diverted the viewer's attention from the essential. If it is true that the forms of guns made their way into the painting because there was so much talk of war, we realize to what extent "reality" penetrates even abstract works. This reality is unquestionably a psychic one, though inspired by facts. The abstract forms are only the external covers of inner intentions, but to the artist who is always primarily interested in form they become the most important thing. The letter makes no mention of the steep mountains with the domed churches, nor of the intersecting clusters of lines in the lower left with the "heads," or of the balustrade curves with accompanying cross hatching at the right; the emphasis is placed on the

Study for Landscape ▶
with Two Poplars.
1911

128

cross, the corners, the blue main center, the light blue of the middle. No mention is made of the other colors, though they help to determine the blue—the red of the house, the red-brown running knots, the graduated whites, the black. No doubt Kandinsky felt that a more exact analysis would shatter the painting's wholeness and falsify its meaning. Of course, such an observation does not apply only to Kandinsky's works. In analyzing an El Greco, also, we must confine ourselves to those formal and expressive features that veil and disclose the content.

A counterpart to *Improvisation 30* is *Improvisation 31* (CC 83) subtitled *Sea Battle*. Its effect is essentially cheerful, not at all threatening, with luminous orange, pink, and various blues. If you like, you may recognize a heaving sea, masts, and sails; in other words, reminiscences are present, but they do not determine the structure, which is notably loose. Compositionally, like the related watercolor (CC 694), the painting resembles a luminous cone broadening at the base. Possibly this work too refers to a personal experience, the battle of Tsushima; Kandinsky's beloved stepbrother died in the Russo-Japanese war of 1905.

Kandinsky was fond of another painting of 1913, *Small Pleasures* (color plate, p. 137), and in 1924 he returned to the subject, in a work which he called *Backward Glance,* in memory of 1913. *Small Pleasures* was painted at Murnau in the summer. At first, it brings to mind the All Saints pictures: it shows a mountain with domed churches, above it another mountain with two jumping horses and riders, figures in the clouds, and at the right a raging sea with a boat and three bars indicating oars. This is not, however, an "objective" painting, even though all these references are implied in the forms. The watercolor *Small Pleasures* (p. 94) is somewhat wider, and as a whole, brighter, freer, more sketchy: even the mountain, the domes, and the boat are only suggested, and two arched lines are boldly traced across the center. The painting is more detailed and throughly worked out. The black cloud shifts the center of gravity upward, the right side of the painting is somewhat ponderous, the left side with its brightly colored zoomorphic forms is playful. At the upper left there is a pink sun, the lightest point of the whole. The shifting of weight is in line with Kandinsky's theory, and is achieved in terms of color, the distribution of contrasts being particularly well calculated.

There is a baffling preliminary drawing for this painting (p. 130), which is completely abstract and geometric, showing an isosceles triangle, a circle, straight and broken lines, and perfect curves. It could be easily taken as a preliminary drawing for *Backward Glance* of 1924, but the drawing is dated 1913. Was this a slip on Kandinsky's part? I share Lindsay's opinion (*The Art Bulletin,* 1953) that the drawing actually dates from 1913, and that Kandinsky here had a presentment of things to come in his own development. We find exact triangles and circles as early as 1911, but no work that is completely geometric. A comparison with *Backward Glance* shows surprisingly identical details: Kandinsky must have had a mental picture of the work eleven years before he executed it. In 1924 he enriched the sketch with a few retrospective additions, absent in the drawing—geometric domed churches, and the line of the horse's back. It is a curious case of prophetic vision. The painting and the drawing were executed before his departure for Russia, so that influence by Russian painters is out of the question.

Drawing for Small Pleasures.

Improvisatio
1912, 160

It is not clear why Kandinsky called *Improvisation 33* (CC 87) *Orient,* and repeated it (*Improvisation 34,* CC 93). Possibly he was induced to do so by the arabesque-like lines in the foreground, "the reclining couple," and the "oriental" color scheme. He must have regarded this "couple" as his main theme, for he returned to it in *Improvisation 34.* Should the flowing lines to the right be interpreted as hanging gardens? *Painting with Green Center* (CC 92) has the same flowing forms, but there is a perfect polygon at the center, and to the right of it a dividing line that cuts the picture in two, but in a manner different from the dividing line in *Composition IV.* The frequently reproduced *Dreamy Improvisation* (CC 99), on the other hand, derives compositionally from the circle, as does the watercolor *In the Circle* of 1911 and the watercolor *Red-Blue* of 1913. The colorful forms revolve and change as in a kaleidoscope, their centrifugal forces being stronger than the encircling curves. The graphic element consists of wittily scattered *aperçus;* the vitality of the work springs from the revolving play of colors.

Kandinsky has given us his own detailed comments on *Painting with White Border* (CC 90) in his book *Backward Glances.* The two oil sketches (p. 276 and CC 82) are separated from the definitive version by five months, during which Kandinsky pondered the problems. He says that he hit on the solution when he thought of the white border that extends from mid-point at the bottom to the upper right, and emerges for the last time in the left corner, in the form of white zigzags. In the first oil study the upper left corner is filled up with the three lines of the troika; the study must have been conceived in Moscow in December 1912, and recorded in Munich, in January 1913, on a vertical canvas. Roughly speaking it corresponds to the left half of the final version, but is more graphic and spontaneous, a little like the related watercolor. But the second version, done on a horizontal canvas, discloses some uncertainty and emptiness in the right third of the painting; it is actually a preliminary sketch.

Painting with White Border ($55^1/_8 \times 78^3/_4$") is a triumphant work, a kind of apotheosis of Moscow; there are no architectural elements, but the troika has become a dynamic symbol. There are two centers—the blue-red at the left, and an articulated black curve with a white edge at the right, imbedded in blue: an independent realm, which "grows like a flower" in the painting. At the lower left there is a combat in black and white, suggesting an "inner seething in unclear form." The border is described by Kandinsky: "at the lower left an abyss, a white wave rising from it, which falls suddenly, and then encloses the right side of the painting in a lazily winding form, traces a lake at the upper right, and disappears at the upper left corner in order to emerge one last time and definitively as a white zigzag. Since this white border was the solution of the problem, I named the whole painting after it." It is thus that Kandinsky always looked at his own works, not "romantically," as they are so often interpreted. He omits a great deal, the white bar between the two centers, for instance, and the yellow brown desert extending over the right side as far as the white border. At the very beginning of his description he warns against too much explanation: "described in that way, these assembled forms acquire a wooden expression that fills me with disgust." He relies on the effect of the forms and colors. The viewer will note restlessness in the painting rather than repose, the staccato of the jagged lines, the whiplash force of the

Improvisation 30. ▶
1913, 161

flowing lines, opposition between the smooth and the rough surfaces, as well as the overflowing of the white border beyond the edge of the picture. As in the case of music, the artist's directions determine our sensations only up to a certain point.

Kandinsky made one sketch (CC 84) and a watercolor (p. 94) preliminary to the *Painting with White Forms* (color plate, p. 135). The sketch corresponds to the left side of the painting, while the watercolor includes the full composition. The sketch contains echoes of domed churches; the watercolor, of Murnau landscapes; the final version has none of them. The main form at the left, which gives this painting its name, looks almost like a tombstone, and the curved lines might be ground lines. The soaring round forms which are jagged on one side make their first appearance here, and remind us of amoebas. Graphic elements predominate in the right half, colors in the left. Ultramarine, next to white, is the dominant color; red appears only once but in strong contrast. The weight is shifted to the single white form, which emerges from its heavy ultramarine surroundings as the spatially foremost spot of the picture plane.

Compositions VI and VII are the chief works of 1913 (CC 89 and p. 279). There are more than two dozen preliminary studies for *Composition VII*, and as for *Composition VI*, Kandinsky tells us in one of his three analyses of paintings contained in *Backward Glances*, he pondered it for a year and a half before he ventured to paint it.

The starting point of *Composition VI* was the image of the deluge, he says, hence the subtitle. The first version was a painting on glass (unknown), which must have been fairly "objective," since Kandinsky speaks of nudes, animals, palms, flashes of lightning, and rain. The glass painting was followed by several sketches, probably destroyed, abstract and objective. None satisfied him; the expressive element stood in the way, he found "the inner sound" only when he had "paid heed to the expressive force of the word 'deluge'." But at the end of his analysis Kandinsky says that the painting must not be interpreted as the representation of an event. What, then, can be the meaning of the "expressive force of the word 'deluge'?" We are reminded of the Biblical "In the beginning was the word;" i. e., Kandinsky's conception of the deluge is not based on the image or idea of it, but on the evocative connotations of the word, which for him contains virtually all the possibilities of Becoming, or, as Franz Marc would have said, "re-emergence at another place."

Only a few of the preliminary studies have been preserved. We have two drawings (p. 94 and CC 753); one shows the four basic directions of the composition; the other, the network at the bottom left. One oil study, which was in the B. Köhler collection, was destroyed toward the end of the Second World War; there is another in the Münter-Kandinsky Foundation in Munich (CC 626). To same extent it serves to replace the painting, which has remained in Russia, although there are great differences between the two. The painting in Munich is a color study of overflowing power, almost without graphics elements. The colored forms glow against the dark ground like tropical vegetation, and at the bottom dissolve into a kind of surf. The study lacks the third center, which is the most important, according to Kandinsky.

The main center of the picture, to the left of the middle, is a surface foaming with pinks and whites, which is situated neither on the ground plane nor on an ideal plane,

Painting with White ▶
Forms. 1913, 166

but "somewhere else" (Kandinsky). This "somewhere else" determines the inner tone of the whole. At the left is the second center (pink), while at the right, a little higher, is a third (red-blue, strong, angry lines). The other forms are small, simple, done in festive strokes. The dramatic lines are tempered by a fugue of pink spots, counterpointed by blue spots with a warm effect. The color has been laid on in varying thicknesses. But the final effect is one of balance. The whole is not a tragedy; a great decline, says Kandinsky, is also a song of praise, "a hymn to the new birth that follows decline." Vantongerloo, in his *L'art et son avenir* (1924) reproduces *Composition VI* next to Bruegel's *Fall of the Angels* in the Brussels Museum, and it is amazing to see how similar the flat and pointed forms of the two paintings are when we disregard Bruegel's naturalism, and how closely related their structures and rhythms are. In Bruegel too there is a decline and a hymn. True art meets across the centuries, as Kandinsky says in *On the Spiritual in Art*.

Kandinsky's own catalogue lists four oil studies and two fragments as preliminary to *Composition VII: Sketch 1* (color plate, p. 139), the most important and most complete, he gave to Paul Klee in exchange for one of the latter's paintings; *Fragment 1* (p. 278) is in the Museum of Modern Art, New York; *Fragment 2* (CC 94) is in the Albright Art Gallery, Buffalo; *Sketch 2* (CC 95), *Study* (CC 96), and *Sketch 3* (CC 98) are in the Münter-Kandinsky Foundation, Munich, which also has four watercolors (p. 96 and p. 153), and three drawings (p. 96 and p. 153); two other drawings are in Paris. Incidentally the *Study*, which in the Foundation is referred to as a sketch for *Composition VII*, seems to me to belong to the group of the *All Saints* or *Resurrection* pictures, and to date from 1911. The preliminary studies are very different, and it is not always easy to relate them to the final version, so that possibly still other drawings or paintings belong with *Composition VII*. Kandinsky tried all possibilities in order to carry out his intentions without omissions. According to Münter-Eichner he painted the final version during November 25 to 28.

Sketch 1 shows the whole design (somewhat abridged at the right) in rough outline, but there are also some divergent individual forms. With its burning red and brown colors, and its nervous forms, the painting suggests a play of dark powers. Explosive forces are released in the middle, and move from the lower left to the upper right over-running the many smaller centers of energy. *Fragment 1* contains the center, and at the left the triangular swinging form, which is placed at mid-height to the right in *Sketch 1*. *Fragment 2* is a variant of the central part of *Sketch 1*, painted loosely and fuzzily, and effervescent in expression. *Sketch 2* and *Sketch 3* contain the entire stock of formal ideas that Kandinsky used in *Composition VII*, but arranged differently and in louder colors. In both sketches the center is situated higher than in the painting, the individual forms are less precise, the lower parts more misty, and in general the sketches are less inhibited, more airy. The watercolors differ from the final version almost more than the oil studies, and they are as interesting in themselves as the preliminary studies. The one shown on p. 96 (27) is nearly identical with *Fragment 1*. The one illustrated on p. 96 (25) belongs with *Sketch 2*, and the one shown on p. 153 is a fragment. As for the drawings, the complete sketch (p. 96 [27]; after Eichner) with the indications of color given in Russian, definitely belongs to the final version. It shows the design: a long

Small Pleasures. ▶
1913, 174

oval, rising from left to right, and curves surrounding the oval like orbits of satellites. The two other drawings are free studies of details. How long Kandinsky worked on the painting can be seen from a watercolor (CC 684) which he himself dated 1911, and which already shows the central forms as well as some secondary forms of *Composition VII.*

The main center of the painting is situated at the left below the middle point. It is a form approximating the oval, cut by a wedge and two arrows. One might think of an egg, of a development "*ab ovo,*" as Klee titled an abstract work of his in 1917. This form lies within an area bounded by lines and extends to a second center at the left with a triangular form which frequently recurs in the painting. This second center reaches out to the lower left corner with the "oars." All the weight is situated in the lower left quarter of the composition. The lower right is similar to *Painting with the White Border:* it includes sailing forms, and other forms below them. The diagonal running from the lower left to the upper right divides the whole into a nervous upper half and a calmer lower one. All the smaller forms—circles, wedges, triangles, bars, and arabesques are on the left side. Associations lead to no more tangible interpretation than a feeling of dramatic action, with energies and tensions as protagonists. What we have here is one of many possible worlds; it is the artist who introduces fate into the painting, and who uses the various formal elements and connections in order to state how he experiences the world.

The colors come closest to giving us information about the "content." The fiery quality of *Sketch 1* has been preserved in *Composition VII,* whose over-all character suggests a blazing fire, an approaching disaster, an exaggerated tempo. The red above the diagonal, the blue under it, the yellow, all are disquieting and threatening; the black opens up like a dangerous precipice, and there is no reassuring green. If Kandinsky had previously had war on his mind, this painting may well be a foreboding of its outbreak a year later. Once we engage in such speculations, further associations become possible, not with objects and memories, but with contrasting ideas, such as those of alarm and peace, flight and immobility, sharpness and bluntness. Even then the interpretation of the painting cannot be more definite than that of a symphony, the *Eroica,* for example.

Late in 1913 Kandinsky painted another two light, cheerful works—*Bright Picture* (CC 100) and *Black Lines* (color plate, p. 141). For the first of these he made a wash drawing (p. 93, 20), which corresponds to the painting. Small sheaves of lines which look like stars—carmine-red, green, and blue—are distributed on the yellow ground; diagonals, most of them running from the lower left to the upper right, show similar sheaf-like hatchings. One thinks of a celestial landscape, every form is so light and so starry. *Black Lines* has linear effects, similar to those Klee employed very often in the 1920s. They are placed on irregularly round spots of color, as though with India ink, and these red, blue, yellow, green, and white spots float on the white-yellow ground, like exotic flowers on the surface of the water. A jagged line introduces a staccato movement in the "pattern of strewn flowers," a suggestion of Chinese pointed mountains. A comparison to oriental paintings done in India ink with brush would not be too far-fetched.

138

Sketch 1 for ▶
Composition VII.
1913, 179

In 1914 Kandinsky's work was interrupted by the war. KK lists only eight paintings and four panels for an American collector. In 1915 he did not paint at all, and he did not resume work until 1916.

Some of the paintings are directly related to *Painting with White Border. Small Painting with Yellow* (CC 101), acquired by J. Arthur Jerome Eddy in Chicago, *Improvisation with Cold Forms* (CC 102) left behind in Russia, *Painting with Three Spots* (CC 105), and *Painting with Blue Border* (CC 104) are, structurally, as though carried by a wave, which pushes the dynamism in a definite direction, and provides a zone of emptiness and repose contrasting with the dramatic zone.

Painting with Red Spot (color plate, p. 143) and *Improvisation 35* (p. 282), purchased by Arp, are remotely reminiscent, with their arching bridges, of the much austerer work, *With the Black Arch,* of 1912; they are in somewhat the same relation to it as a cheerful capriccio is to the titanic finale of a symphony. In *Painting with Red Spot,* which has a yellow ground, the bridge connects the red area at the left with the bouquet of colorful, gay, small forms imbedded in black. Underneath, near the center, there is a line, with a purple-red border, of mountains with two peaks; but this line is pure form, it is not meant to suggest mountains. We must "take a shape only as a shape", what interests us being not its derivation, but its function in the painting—and here this function is structural. The symmetry has been deliberately complicated by a broken white band which runs toward the lower left, separating the left zone with the big red spot within a cloudy blue from the more earthly and eventful goings-on at the right. The left side acquires a quality of remoteness from the earth, the right is in mood reminiscent of the All Saints pictures. It would not be surprising if in the upper right corner there appeared the form of an angel's trumpet. *Improvisation 35* resembles *Painting with Red Spot* not only in the arching bridge, but also in its balance between large and small figures, although the whole has been transposed from red into green: it is spring rather than summer. The forms sprout, the lines quiver. Instead of the supporting scaffolding, there are intersecting diagonals.

Even more than in these two works the tendency to soar and fly is apparent in *Fugue* (color plate, p. 147), which Kandinsky called "a controlled Improvisation." It would no doubt be useless to look for three voices: the title refers less to polyphony than to a strict interlocking of themes. For instance, the way in which the round forms are echoed by the pointed forms beyond the wavy line, is something like the way in which the musical theme is answered by its counter-theme. Even in a strictly contrapuntal statement, Kandinsky was primarily guided by his feelings. The title occurred to him only later, when he ascertained that the order was polyphonic. Once again, there is relative repose in the lower half, and excitement above the black waves; the network of intersecting white lines suggests a collision of antagonistic forces.

It is hard to assign a place to the highly spontaneous *Improvisation* (not in KK, CC 627; formerly in the F. Müller gallery). The border relates it to other paintings with borders; some details also occur in *Painting with Round Forms* of 1914 (CC 103), and it may date from that year. The Münter-Kandinsky Foundation has three more unnamed Improvisations (CC 628, 631) not listed in KK; their titles are uncertain. One of them, called *Ravine,* may actually have been given that name, for we have a pencil study for it in a

Black Lines. ▶
1913, 189

sketchbook of 1914, which was called *Weir* (dated June 22, 1914). It was painted after Kandinsky went to see the canyon of Höllental, and it did not come off too well. The free forms are mixed with naturalistic ones—a waterfall, a landing pier, and a couple in Bavarian costume. Was the painting conceived in the spirit of a recollection?

Kandinsky's last work in Munich before he left Germany was the four panels he painted for Mr. Edwin Campbell of New York. Two of these are in the Museum of Modern Art in New York, and the two others, under different titles, in the Solomon R. Guggenheim Museum. Lindsay identified them from their dimensions and told his story of the work in *Art News* (1955). The panels were hung in the entrance to Campbell's apartment at 635 Park Avenue, in 1916; because of the war they had to be shipped via Sweden. The price Kandinsky noted in his catalogue was 500 Marks per panel.

All the panels are of the same height, but vary in width with the walls of the room in which they were hung. The two narrower ones bear the numbers 3 and 4 on the frames, the two others are unnumbered. Preliminary studies for this work include a watercolor for the narrowest panel, No. 4 (p. 153, 30); a drawing, a watercolor (p. 153, 31), and two oil studies for No. 3 (CC 632, 633), and one oil study for each of the two remaining panels (CC 634, 635). Also the painting in the Solomon R. Guggenheim Museum known as *Composition 1914* (not in KK, CC 630) seems to be a study for No. 3; at all events, the principal form in it is the same.

The four panels are untitled in KK. Lindsay proposes that we should call them after their dominant colors *Spring* (4), *Summer* (3), *Fall* (1), and *Winter* (2); and these titles would not be incompatible with the colors and forms. Titles such as *Fall* and *Winter* occur in 1912, and as early as 1913 Kandinsky called one of his paintings *Landscape with Rain*. Kandinsky himself would probably have called the panels "Improvisations." The narrower two have the radiant quality of a morning in the mountains. No. 4 is the most cheerful of the four, the tones of carmine and yellow, vermilion and green being wholly in a major key; the color forms are loose, and surrounded by linear play like vocal ornamentations for a soprano. In the watercolor sketch the lower blue violet form is reminiscent of the reclining couple in *Composition II*, but on the panel all resemblance has been eliminated. No. 3 is firmer, and if it denotes summer, it also denotes midday. It shows a rock and trees as in the large study for *Composition II*, with clouds and the familiar parallel lines of rain. Green, blue, and white predominate over red, and the white has a warm effect; black accents rather oppose the light upward movement. The triangle is like a roof, the mottled spots of color next to it are like a bed of flowers. No associations would be possible without the cloud. The drawing for this panel is presumably the preliminary sketch, and it comes closer to the watercolor than to the painting. The watercolor is somewhat more naturalistic than the panel: the black form under the rain could be a cloud, the bristly form at the upper right looks like a sea horse, and the parallel curves at the right suggest a rainbow. In the first oil study, which is rich in contrasts, the horizontal forms at the center are absent. The second oil study did not have the desired width and probably for that reason was not used. It is somewhat empty and less precise than the other preliminary works.

In the oil study for Panel 1 the dimensions and outlines of the finished work are indicated fairly accurately, while the oil study for Panel 2 develops a few important

Painting with Red Spot. ▶
1914, 192

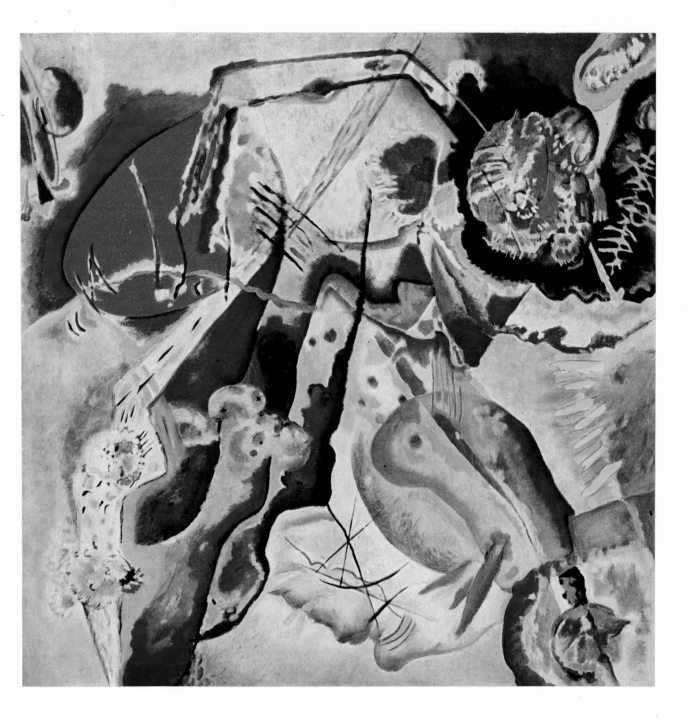

forms that occur in the final version, for instance, the ragged form at the center, which also occurs in *Composition 1914*. The crucial colors in Panel 1 are yellow, orange, ocher, brown red, brown black, and cold blue; the broad forms at the top could be mountains, whose crest line has been transformed into contours with intersecting short lines, reminiscent of stitching or fences. We are similarly tempted to recognize lines of mountains, trees, rain, or a waterfall in *Composition 1914,* but the ragged form at the center (whitish, within a blue-black semi-circle) precludes associations even more completely than it does in Panel 1.

Panel 2 is a chaotic furioso with many blue tones, setting carmine against emerald green; as a matter of fact there is nothing very wintry about this work. At the top, rays are emanating as from a star; at the bottom, lines eddy around the main form. The expression is strong but the meaning unclear. In Panels 1 and 2 the forms are arranged around a center, in 3 and 4 the arrangement is vertical; although 3 and 4 are rhythmically attuned to each other, 1 and 2 are not. Hung in pairs in the entrance hall of an apartment, the lighter narrow panels and the heavier broad panels must have made a striking contrast, which had doubtless been intended.

Between 1912 and 1914, in addition to his paintings, Kandinsky executed drawings and watercolors which are even more daring than the paintings of those years. "*Tachiste*" drawings like the one of 1911 mentioned above occur in 1912 and 1913 (p. 149), but there are also drawings which are composed with carefully placed but loosely drawn lines (line accompaniments and line intersections, p. 90). One drawing of 1912 (No. 1) is a preliminary study for the cover of *Backward Glances*. A few other drawings were made in preparation for the woodcuts of *Klänge*. "A line can say everything," Kandinsky wrote in a sketchbook of 1914. "Drawing, which, strictly speaking, is nothing but line, can express everything." The abstract drawings in this sketchbook prove this. It is difficult to assign precise dates to certain undated watercolors. The one in the Germanic Museum at Nuremberg (CC 691) is certainly of 1913; the spider web at the upper left is a development of the lefthand tower and the domed shape in *Improvisation 30*. The rest looks like a flower opening, not unlike the form in a watercolor, in the Solomon R. Guggenheim museum, and we may infer that it also dates from 1913.

As for the woodcuts in black-and-white and in color, Kandinsky went back to the medium and made a series of ten one-color woodcuts for *On the Spiritual in Art,* apparently all of them in 1911, and a large number, forty-three black-and-white and twelve color woodcuts for *Klänge*. While those for *On the Spiritual in Art* are homogeneous in style, and, except for the title page woodcut, almost abstract, those for *Klänge* were done in different years in different styles. Among the latter are some illustrative ones that recall the Biedermeier woodcuts of 1903, such as the *Fountain,* or the Russian ones of 1906 and 1907 (the first woodcut in the book with the purple-red ground and the two medieval horses and riders, p. 39,9). Kandinsky wrote in the publisher's prospectus: "The woodcuts go back to 1907. The period adapted the form to the 'content,' which became increasingly refined." Almost all of Kandinsky's periods are represented. *Inprovisation VI* (1909), *Etude* (1910), *Composition II* (1910), *Last Judgment* (1911), *Lyrical* (1911), *Red Spot* (1912), the watercolor *With Three Horses* (1912), and several other works appear as woodcuts. In such cases the painting must have served

144

Drawing. 1912, 4

as a model or starting point; other woodcuts in *Klänge* are independent of the paintings or refer to them only indirectly. The most impressive are the abstract ones, which resemble the Improvisations. The treatment in the black-and-whites is uncommonly skillful. Kandinsky bubbles over with ideas, as though he had only been waiting for an opportunity to return to graphic work, and the printing of his poems gave him that opportunity. The woodcuts are scarcely related to the poems; the poems are one thing, the woodcuts another. *Klänge* was successful: the book was reviewed favorably in *Graphische Künste* (Vienna, 1914), though only the woodcuts were praised.

Now that we have surveyed the paintings of Kandinsky's most fruitful period, both individually and in relation to the types they represent, we may in conclusion add a few remarks on the artistic problems and achievements of this period. How did Kandinsky come upon the new pictorial form, and what is its significance? What were his expressive means, and how shall we characterize his technical exploitation of color, line, surface, space? What kind of world had he in mind—a space-time, a universal, a romantic-intuitive world? What was the relation between the conscious and unconscious elements? How are these works related to music and poetry? Is Kandinsky's art European or is it a synthesis between the East and the West? Was "the great abstraction" that Kandinsky discovered in those years valid only for him, or has it become the turning point of a new era?

It is only with the greatest caution that Kandinsky made the transition to abstract forms. Had he been guided by theory alone, he could easily, after he wrote *On the Spiritual in Art* (i.e., from 1910 onward), have completely eliminated naturalistic elements from his painting. In actual fact it took him four years to reach that point, and he was still painting landscapes as late as 1913. Kandinsky did not want to paint decorative works, states of mind, or music. He consciously aimed at the pictorial, and for this reason he had to try to retain the forms he had intuitively discovered, but at the same time he filled them with the content of his lived experience. This was confirmed from outside, by friends like Marc, as well as by developments that took place in other intellectual spheres (the splitting of the atom, theosophy, Schönberg's music, Maeterlinck's poetry, Worringer's philosophy of art).

Since Kandinsky was a visual type, extremely sensitive to optical impressions, and endowed with total recall, he was compelled to express himself in sensory images, and at the same time to liberate color and line from their earlier embodiments. He had to reconcile the irreconcilable, and he did this, first, by reducing the object to its essential elements, and then by gradually shifting to forms derived from this reduction. Of the troika, all that remains is three arched lines, which, in the context of the other formal elements still denote the troika, although these will eventually become three lines only, which, in harmony or in contrast with other forms, stretched, bent, or involuted, will acquire new meanings, signifying now movement or hindered movement, stages in the process of breaking away or collision, and now a self-evident lightness, a surmounting of gravitation. The horse and rider theme was at first reduced to a flat spatial schema; then this became a linear schema—semi-circle and two broken curves like forearms (in *Composition IV*, for example)—and finally, a hieroglyph subordinated to the whole formal pattern as a word or a letter is subordinated to its surrounding text. The reclining couple of *Composition II* becomes an arabesque which is, as regards form and position, a distant echo of the original figures, but in the end it loses the character of abstraction from something else. Often it is only because Kandinsky made abbreviated sketches for certain paintings—for instance, for the painting *Nude* (1911) he drew (in KK) a diagram of the nude, a curve in four parts—that we recognize any provenance whatever for the actual elements of design in the finished works.

His elimination of the object was thus not a consequence of theoretical considerations, but the result of a development that began with Monet, was continued by the Neo- and Post-Impressionists, and had for the time being ended with the Fauves. At the moment when Matisse took a step backward, the Russian ventured a leap into the unknown, relying on the unlimited potentialities of his pictorial means of expression. This was the same moment when the Cubists, at their most "hermetic," were also clinging to the object, although no more obviously than Kandinsky in *Composition III* (1911). On the one hand, we note an objective analysis of space and time, on the other, an intuitive self-absorption in the eternal essence of the object, in the recording of the immediate experience.

As a result, matter became a kind of mind to Kandinsky. But the mind, too, simplifies, if only by the use of words; the things themselves have an even more secret life, hence art must be "the expression of mystery in terms of mystery." Kandinsky was one of those naïve souls who are able to see, hear, and think in a manner, as it were, virginal. According to Bergson (*Le Rire,* 1900), were the naïveté, the emancipation from habit, complete; were the soul no longer connected with active life through any of its perceptions, we would have an artist such as the world has never yet seen. Such an artist would perceive all things in their pristine purity: the forms, colors, and sounds of the physical world no less than the subtlest movements of the inner life. And Bergson goes on to say:

"Hence, originally, the diversity of arts ... This one applies himself to colors and forms, and since he loves color for color and form for form, since he perceives them for their sake and not for his own, it is the inner life of things that he sees appearing through their forms and colors. Little by little he insinuates it into his own perception, baffled though we may be at the outset. For a few moments at least, he diverts us from the prejudices of form and color that come between ourselves and reality. And thus he realizes the loftiest ambition of art, which here consists in revealing to us nature." (in *Comedy*, ed. Wylie Sypher, Doubleday & Co., New York, 1956, p. 161)

If the term "nature" is here taken in the sense of "universe," this passage applies to Kandinsky better than to any other artist. It shows that Kandinsky was not concerned with art for art's sake, but with the world in a deeper sense. According to Bergson, the painter, unlike the poet, seeks to grasp psychic states in their original purity, and to show us some of his insights in order to stimulate us to do the same work; just as the musician compels us to notice certain rhythms of life and breathing, which are hidden in man more deeply than his innermost feelings. Art aims at showing us the very face of reality. This insight, too, brings us close to Kandinsky, though the latter would not

146

Fugue. 1914, 193 ▶

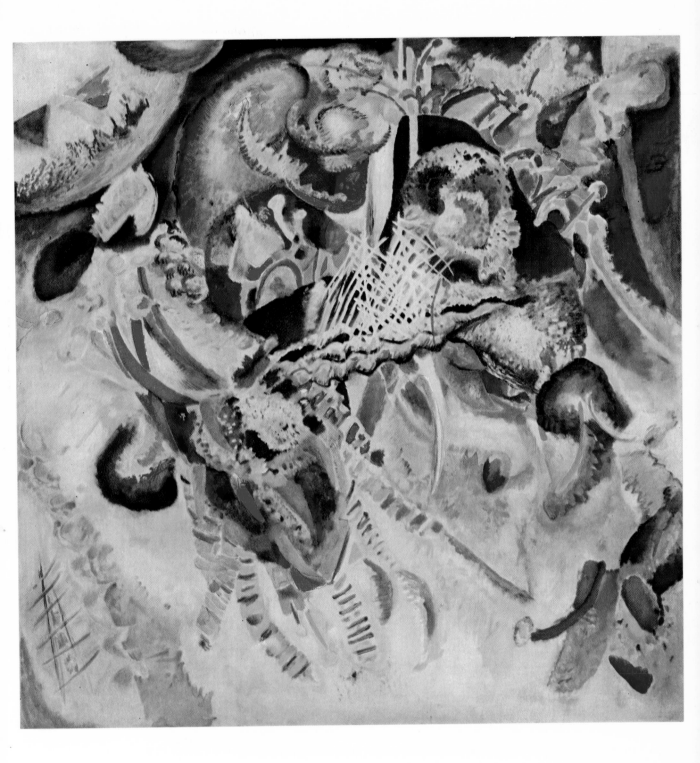

have accepted this classification of the arts, and would have applied Bergson's remarks on poetry and music to his own art.

Thus the question of the object could not, for Kandinsky, be a "matter of principle," nor could abstraction be nonsensory, even when the painting as a whole became "unreal." But it could be regarded as "unreal" only by the standards of the world of objects. His world is created by his creative imagination, or, as Rimbaud says, by the creative impulse. We infer existence from pictorial elements, not the other way round; like Apollinaire's *mots évocateurs*, they are charged with tension and create contents. If colors and forms were like sounds, i.e., if they could be expressed in terms of numbers, and at the same time in terms of values, if they could be defined both physically and psychologically, it would be easier for the beholder to make sure that the painting "makes sense." Hans Kayser, who asserts the existence of harmonic relations between sounds and colors, but rejects further inferences, describes in *Klang der Welt* (1937) a "harmonic" painting as follows: different points of view, different perspectives, autonomy of the painterly and draftsmanly elements, a dialectical exchange between nature and spirit. Like Kandinsky, he does not absolutely exclude the object, and, again like Kandinsky, he aims at "a boundless reality."

In the Murnau paintings the colors are predominantly expressive, not unlike the colors of other Expressionist works of the period. Kandinsky did not use local colors, although modeling and shading play a very subordinate role. As used in individual forms, the colors suggest analogies to objects; as used in the work as a whole, they produce harmonies that may suggest, for example, a Bavarian village with church, or a street in the light of an autumn noon. Color, without being descriptive, helps to show the most intensive aspect of the object. As abstraction progresses, color becomes absolutized, and its specific character asserts itself; to the extent that while there are still echoes of objects, they have become raw material, and are now subordinate to the total effect intended. Since color can be effective only if it is present in sufficient quantities, Kandinsky now works with large colored surfaces, giving preference to the complementaries, either in their pure or approximate tones *(Improvisation 6)*. In 1910 he discovered white as the color of eloquent silence, of the transcendent *(Composition II)*. In many of his works it has all the "sonority" of a golden ground in Byzantine painting, not only giving rhythm to the composition, but separating and bridging, functioning as a break and a transition.

As Kandinsky's intention "to touch the beholder's soul," to communicate his own "psychic vibration" becomes clearer, his color becomes more transparent. Whereas in the Murnau landscapes it could still be seen as surface, now that the object has been eliminated, it can be seen *through;* it leads an ethereal life of its own. Kandinsky works exclusively with its inherent qualities, light and dark, cold and warmth, seriousness and cheerfulness, smoothness and roughness, softness and hardness, eccentricity and concentricity, aggressiveness and restraint, and so forth *(Improvisation 13, 1910)*. Since language is poorer than music in designating possible vibrations, Kandinsky occasionally resorts to musical metaphors. He speaks of paintings as being "in a dark minor key" *(Composition II),* or in the key of C major *(Improvisation 10),* of paintings with "the sonority of the organ," and again of "violins." The paintings dating from 1911 on evoke a color space of a kind that had never existed before; it is a space that cannot be measured, but that can be experienced, for example, in *Deluge* or *Small Pleasures*. Space has become a psychic phenomenon. Occasionally such paintings may evoke a tower or some other figure (*Improvisation 1912*, color plate, p. 131), but in the sense that memory is one of the dimensions of psychic space.

Free colors and forms can be combined in countless ways to energize the composition. In many paintings they attain the level of universality: they express coming-into-being and passing away, love and hate, lyrical and dramatic events. Many subtitles can be accounted for only by the unintended symbolism of various colors and forms, for no object in these works justifies appellations such as *Orient, Garden of Love, War,* etc. For instance, blue has always a tendency to suggest depth, and in Kandinsky's paintings it is actually the color of the sky, as we might imagine it on hearing the word "sky." It is significant that Kandinsky correlates the color blue with the form of the firmament. Such a correlation is by no means arbitrary, nor is Kandinsky unique in this. An objective, universal element is present in his artistic personality: Kandinsky is also a medium.

Drawing. 1911, 3

In the paintings of the Munich years space and time undergo the same changes as color and form. Kandinsky speaks of a material surface, the picture surface, and ideal surface, which can be created and "used as three-dimensional space." He identifies the left side of the painting with "what is distant," the right with what is close, and in

On the Spiritual in Art he says that the artist who confines himself to the actual surface of the canvas restricts his possibilities.

The Murnau landscapes unquestionably contain suggestions of depth, but *Improvisation on Mahogany* is uniformly flat; in *Composition II* the meaning of space changes. The painting moves upward; although objects are still present, it almost completely avoids effects of distance or depth. Yet the carmine red lies on a different plane than the white, and the blue on a different one than the green. Looking at the paintings of 1913, it would occur to no one to speak of distance or depth, yet space is there.

Paradoxically the picture surface has become imaginary, and the constellation of colors and lines has resulted in "a finite, but unlimited" space, in which everything is in motion, and there are no fixed points. The colors are meaningful in themselves and in relation to the other colors; the lines are signs that create an order and give directions, both individually and in chorus with other linear elements; their distribution on the surface denotes weight, not location. But it is the imponderable, nonmeasurable quality of these elements and their combinations, that accounts for the characteristic mysteriousness of these paintings. We are not in a position to say (though we sometimes do so describe paintings, for the sake of vividness) that such or such things are moving or standing still, that one thing is in the foreground and another in the background, that one is opaque and another is not: everything seems transparent. The old standards no longer apply, for the painting has acquired a life of its own.

Today it is a commonplace to refer to the disappearance of perspective in art after 1900, and the introduction of the dimension of time in painting. J. Gebser, in his *Ursprung und Gegenwart* (Stuttgart, 1949 and 1953) proposes a new view of the world, which has surprising scientific and artistic implications. The nonrational concept of time, which he calls *"Zeitfreiheit"* or "time-freedom" is treated as a prelude to the emergence into consciousness of a world without perspective, characterized by totality and integration. Clock time and three-dimensional perspective would have no place in it, being replaced by "time-freedom" which involves rather such notions as those of biological duration, rhythm, relativity, and psychological energy. This time-freedom manifests itself as the unity of past, present and future, but also as creativity, and (in physics) as the fourth dimension. A mutation of the mind is supposed to have taken place, "a sudden actualization of latent potentialities that have always existed," which would not exclude, but would integrate, the old potentialities.

Gebser argues that the nonperspective world is already manifest in certain disciplines and arts. "Music creates a common order between man and time"—this statement by Stravinsky is to be understood as pointing to the surmounting of old forms of time. Schönberg in 1911 moved toward complete freedom with respect to harmony, melody, rhythm, and form; in his twelve-tone scale, music became spherical and four-dimensional; in the younger composers (according to Krenek) it has become parabolic, without beginning or end. In poetry the same change in the structure of consciousness may be noted: time as a literary theme, language as a primeval phenomenon, new syntax for creating the unity of this world and the beyond (Rilke); the integration of time with eternity in Gottfried Benn and T.S.Eliot ("things that will happen already happened"). And Gebser quotes Eddington to the effect that events do not happen, they are there, and we encounter them on our way. The observer merely comes across the events in question.

In modern painting, too, Gebser finds time an active presence, and dualism being transcended by nonperspective, nonrational elements. Already with Cézanne, pictorial space began to be spherical. The Cubists inaugurated the multiple view, and the simultaneity of two or more views implies abolition of the temporal sequence; the painting is made transparent by space-time structures. Without knowing anything about "space-time-freedom" Klee wrote: "What artist would not like to live where the central organ of all spatial and temporal movements—whether it be called the brain or the heart of creation—sets all functions going?"

Kandinsky certainly knew about these matters as little or as much as his friends, but new light is cast on many of his theoretical ideas: "inner necessity," for example, and his references to music as a phenomenon analogous to painting, his recourse to cosmic events in explaining creative activity, his emphasis on the relativity of forms and colors, and so on. His terminology is very free, he senses what is at stake, though he resorts to artistic paraphrases, to musical, psychological, physical, and often even theosophical concepts. How else could he express in writing "mystery in terms of mystery?"

He can do it in his paintings; the problem of space and time, which he barely mentions in his writings, is solved in the Blaue Reiter period in such a way that one feels the presence of time. In *Composition II* (1910) he is still undecided, in *Composition IV* (1911) the blue cone at the center is in the foreground, despite its color, while the reclining couple almost protrudes over it; the castle is transparent, letting the clouds appear behind it; the scene of horse and rider above the rainbow eludes the spatial definition of the spear-like lines, and bends to the left, curving the picture surface. Dating from the same period are quite differently structured paintings, such as *Saint George I* (1911). Here Kandinsky escapes the problem of space by use of a great amount of white, which is at once mystical and so transparent that it seems to be trying to let us glimpse the finiteness of unlimited space. In *Improvisation* of 1912 (color plate, p. 131) the relativity of the forms asserts itself: the rhythm is vehement, the harmony difficult to describe, and there is no frame of reference. As for *Painting with White Forms* (1913) and *Composition VII* (1913), it is hard to find where these pictures begin or end. They are excisions from the whole of the world, from the creative process which has no beginning or end; "events do not happen, they are there," and Kandinsky comes across them. The actual surface of the canvas bounded by the frame is the only static element bypassed by the events. What can be identified as space, and what as time, in *Black Lines* (1920)? We are reminded of what Krenek called the "parabolic" element in the new music: the painting has no beginning or end, no differentiation between space and time, "unless our mind moves along time" (Wells, quoted by Gebser). We are living in "the central organ of all spatial and temporal movements" of creation. *Fugue* (1914) is no longer outside the beholder; we move within the painting, just as Kandinsky had dreamed of making us do; we are surrounded by it, we are inside it.

As painter, Kandinsky was in advance of the theoretician, painting better than he knew. Only in his aforementioned lecture, shortly before the close of this stage in his development, did he indicate that he had become conscious of the great mutation in which he was taking part. After a few introductory sentences about his development, he observed that because colors are intrinsically of different weights, "the variety of the inner surfaces gave my paintings a depth which brilliantly replaced the former perspective depth [Klee's 'multidimensional simultaneity']. I distributed the masses in such a way that no architectural center was visible." In other words, spherical space, simultaneity, a constellation of points, replace the center. He goes on, speaking of individual color tones, that he cooled warmth or warmed coldness, and that a composition can thus be made of a single color. He speaks at greater length about his discovery of white in the sultry heat of the summer of 1911. Nature, he says, seemed white to him, and he showed and spread the white everywhere. He learned from this fundamental color how the inner character of each color can be "redefined" by varied application. The possibility of obtaining infinite series exclusively by the combinations of a single color value opened wide for him, he says, the gates of absolute art.

"Cosmic tragedy" and his shifting of the "center" to the sphere of the "divine" (Lecture) provide us with a clue. And we can read other things in On the Spiritual in Art, for instance, the sentence in the introduction: "An art that does not contain within itself the powers of the future . . . is a castrated art. It is short-lived." Thus the potentialities of the future are brought into the present.

Kandinsky's painting have a great deal in common with poetry and music. It would be quite possible to put them beside certain poems by Pound and certain compositions by Schönberg in such a way that the three art forms would elucidate one another, for instance, Pound's wordplay on the name "Itys" and Painting with White Forms, in which the round blue form with the zigzags has the same effect as the call "Itys" of the swallow in a few lines of verse. Schönberg wanted to express "a novel in a single gesture"; Kandinsky wrote, "My paintings become gradually more concise." The arts confirm one another, and Kandinsky casts light on Schönberg and Pound, as their works illuminate his.

The creative process, too, is everywhere the same. For instance, Stravinsky "discovers" the work "link by link, stitch by stitch." The chain of discoveries provides the continuing stimulation, and the latter spells out the steps of the creative process.

Kandinsky's propensity to clothe his thoughts in mysterious words occasionally produces a false picture of his mentality, and his references to "the unconscious" strengthen the impression that he was a shallow thinker. On the other hand, he was repeatedly criticized in his own lifetime for his "rationalism," even for his "intellectualism," the more so because his arguments are often pedantically thorough, and his technique of composition extremely exact.

Kandinsky was an artist. On the one hand, he always insisted that artistic entities which have not been produced spontaneously are worthless and of no use to him, while on the other hand, he repeatedly assured his pupils that thinking has never harmed an artist. In the course of a poll organized in the 1920s (P. Plaut, Psychologie der produktiven Persönlichkeit, 1929) he answered three questions: (1) How does the artist come to conceive? (2) What is the path leading from the idea to the completed work? and (3) Does conscious thought play a leading part in the process? At that time

28 *Watercolor for 'Composition VII', 1913*
   Aquarell zu ›Komposition VII‹
   Aquarelle pour «Composition VII»
   Acquerello per ‹Composizione VII›

29 *Pen drawing for 'Composition VII', 1913*
   Federzeichnung für ‹Komposition VII‹
   Dessin à la plume pour «Composition VII»
   Disegno a penna per ‹Composizione VII›

30 *Sketch for panel 'Spring', 1914*
   Entwurf zu Paneel ›Frühling‹
   Projet pour panneau «Printemps»
   Abbozzo per il pannello ‹Primavera›

31 *Sketch for panel 'Summer', 1914*
   Entwurf zu Paneel ›Sommer‹
   Projet pour panneau «Eté»
   Abbozzo per il pannello ‹Estate›

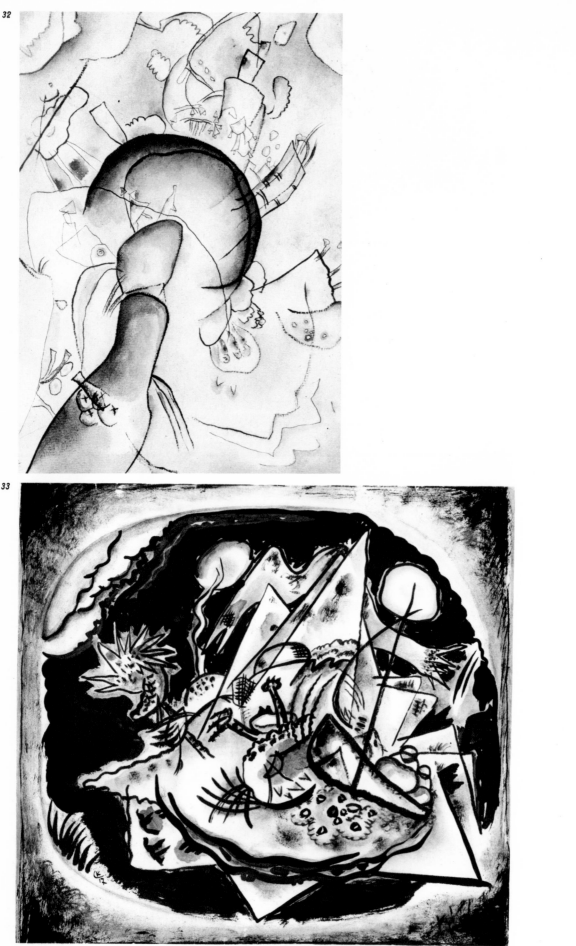

32 Watercolor, 1917
    Aquarell
    Aquarelle
    Acquerello

33 Watercolor, 1917
    Aquarell
    Aquarelle
    Acquerello

34 Lithograph, 1923
    Lithographie
    Lithographie
    Litografia

35 Calm Bend, 1924
    Ruhige Biegung
    Courbure calme
    Curva calma

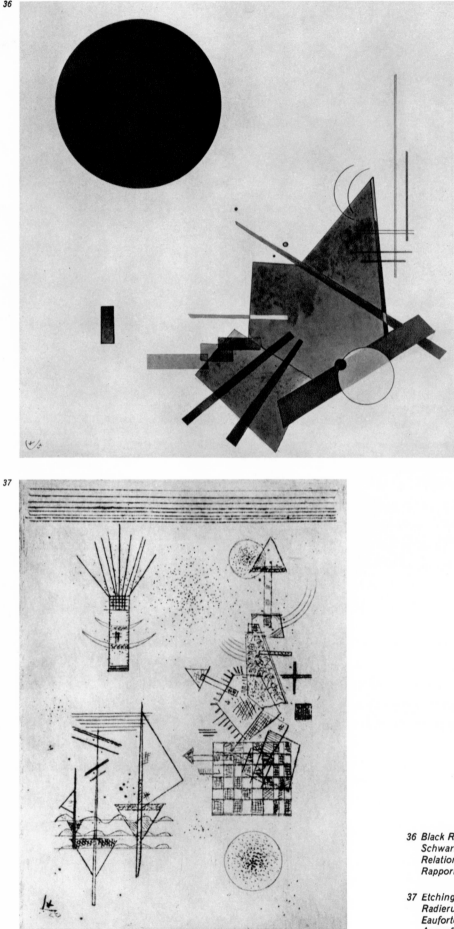

36 Black Relation, 1924
Schwarze Beziehung
Relation noire
Rapporto nero

37 Etching, 1926
Radierung
Eauforte
Acquaforte

Kandinsky was in a cold, constructive period, and his statements are doubly valid for the preceding years. His answers were: (1) The initial idea may have various origins; sometimes it is released by an external impression—a yellow mailbox, noises or musical sounds, the murmur of a stream, the sound of a harp, or Johann Sebastian Bach, a smell, a tactile sensation. Then there are inner stimuli, a good mood that is expressed in artistic ideas. These ideas are exclusively pictorial and cannot be described in words. The tensions between the elements, particularly the colors, are "inseparable" from the conception. (2) Sometimes one sees the painting as it will be when completed; sometimes one merely grasps what its fundamental character will be, and one is still wondering how to express the main idea (aggressive, hidden, for example). This is a mood that can be concentrated on one or several works. "Often one experiences that one is being dictated to during the work, and one must obey the dictation to the letter." The dictation may push one in a direction quite different from that originally intended, "and in such cases one must follow unreservedly." (3) Consciousness plays no part at all in the original conception. "During the actual labor my brain keeps still, but when I am not engaged in [actual] pictorial work I am extremely fond of theorizing." Much theory, he said, went into his work, and if he today is fond of circles, the reason for this is not in the geometric form, but in his past experience of the circle (as earlier, his experience of horses). But such circumstances do not influence him during the actual process of work: "I do not consciously choose the form, the form spontaneously chooses itself in me."

What artists say or write is not always or necessarily true of their works. From my own observations, I should judge that Kandinsky's answers correspond to the facts, but since they were meant for publication, they are less spontaneous than his statements in the undelivered 1914 lecture.

Kandinsky sometimes spoke of a work as yet unpainted as though it were completed. Occasionally, he spoke of a mere idea or a single new form, or a minor experience, as though it were a work. The degree of intensity of his experience may be discerned from the way he communicated it. The events he mentioned were often unimportant in themselves, such as his encounter with an accordion player, some disappointment, or some pleasure he looked forward to. The accordion might have had folklore associations for him, and the contraction and expansion of the instrument might have given rise to reflections on space. The pleasure looked forward to might be no more than the gift of a picture to a friend whom Kandinsky wanted to touch in a specific way. Plaut's inference from Kandinsky's answers to his questionnaire, that the emotional experience is a product of the act of creation, applies only to the actual labor, not to the stage of conception. Kandinsky was quite justified in claiming that "the form spontaneously chooses itself in me"—the form that he needed during the actual labor of painting, a manifestation of the unconscious, of the mood that set him to work in the first place.

Everyone knows about the Chinese artist who stepped into his own painting and vanished. It is striking that the Far East is better equipped to understand Kandinsky than we are. Far Eastern philosophy, particularly Zen, has many points of contact with Kandinsky. In the West intellectual forms predominate; in the Far East sensory intuitions. These are plentiful in Kandinsky, and his Eastern origin may explain them. Kandinsky sometimes strikes one as a wise and cultivated Asiatic, and occasionally he was himself aware of this. In the course of a difficult conversation he once said: "You are a European and you think logically. I do too, but I think in images as well."

A painting such as *Black Lines* looks Chinese, although it contains no direct references to Chinese painting, unless in the combination of color with the India ink brush (although here Kandinsky did not use India ink but oil). Many viewers see flowers in the cloudy patches of color, and this is understandable: the naïve viewer looks for associations and usually finds them where he looks for them. But it is quickly apparent that the flowers are of his own imagination, however insistent, for he relates everything to his own rational and three-dimensional world, not to the integral, transparent total world.

Kandinsky's affinities with Far Eastern art, which I pointed out in a volume published by *Cahiers d'Art* (1930) are still more marked in works of his Bauhaus period. What is pertinent here, is his affinity with the spirit of Far Eastern culture, its sense of man's identity with the universe, the "heaven within." "Until we study Zen, mountains are mountains, rivers rivers. When we gain insight into the truth of Zen, mountains are no longer mountains for us, and rivers are no longer rivers. But later, when we have really arrived at the peace of repose, mountains are once again mountains, and rivers rivers." (Suzuki, *Essays*, I)

Kandinsky's development in Russia and at the Bauhaus casts light on the preceding years. In the Blaue Reiter period Kandinsky was a European with some oriental features, primarily Russian, derived from Russian folklore, icons, music, and poetry. While he lived in Munich Kandinsky always kept one eye on developments in his native land. Moscow was his "tuning fork"; his family and friends remained there, and he visited them regularly. He also attached great importance to having his works exhibited in Russia and to his relations with the art dealer Izdebsky in Odessa. Possibly Kandinsky would have become a pro-Westerner in Moscow; in Munich he remained a Russian. He always kept something of the joyful Russian spirit, but also something of the universal breadth of the wider Eastern world. But his methodicalness, and his bent for theorizing, which occasionally went to the point of pedantry, are perhaps traceable to his German ancestors.

Kandinsky had much in common with Russian composers, his contemporaries, such as Scriabin and Stravinsky: both were interested in theosophy in their youth, and Scriabin's program music took some of its cues from the theories of Blavatsky. After *Rites of Spring* Stravinsky moved away from these influences (like Kandinsky); they shared an admiration for the Russian poet Konstantin Balmont. Stravinsky's cantata *Zvezdoliki* was composed to a text by Balmont. It is full of religious loftiness, the vision of an astral countenance, cosmic storms, ecstatic crowds, and is characterized by a dissonant chromatic style (H.H. Stuckenschmidt, *Frankfurter Allgemeine Zeitung*, No.137, 1957): this is the spirit of the All Saints and Resurrection pictures of 1911. Scriabin's efforts at synesthesia, among them the *Prometheus* symphony, which was conceived for expression simultaneously in sound and in color, as well as his striving for an intellectual synthesis, his mingling of exuberance with precision, coincide with Kandinsky's ideas for a total work of art, as envisaged in *Der gelbe Klang*.

Kandinsky was at the height of his creative activity, when the war interrupted his work, and doomed him to a long period of idleness. The interruption was a severe blow to him, for Kandinsky had been producing one work after another, almost in a trance. Not only German artists were hit hard by the war: the climate which had everywhere been favorable to art between 1910 and 1914 and had resulted in some very great achievements was shattered. Subsequently, it would be only in a few isolated places, such as the Bauhaus in Weimar and Dessau, that Kandinsky would find again an atmosphere as congenial as prewar Munich.

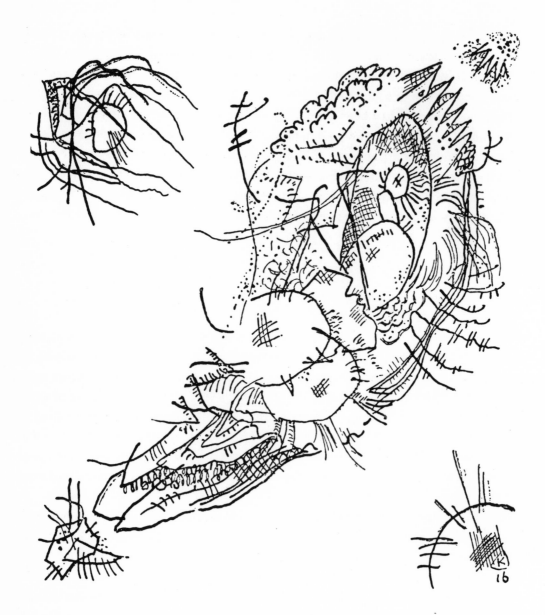

Preliminary drawing for an etching. 1916

IV Return to Russia

Art and Politics

1914-1921

It might at first appear that Kandinsky did not greatly suffer from the military and political events in Russia, but he was inhibited psychologically during those years by his separation from Gabriele Münter, and increasingly uncertain as to his position as an artist. In 1915 he did no work at all; in 1916 he executed eight paintings, five of which have remained in Russia; in 1917 nine, all of which he was obliged to leave behind; in 1918 six, in 1920 ten, and in 1921, the year he returned to Germany, eight. This is not an enormous output, even if we add a number of drawings, watercolors, and paintings on glass, a medium to which he resorted willingly because it became more and more difficult to get canvas and oil paints.

After the outbreak of the Revolution, his daily life was filled with time-consuming and troublesome occupations; all the most indispensable things were in short supply. Kandinsky later recounted that on one occasion it took him two weeks to obtain a document authorizing him to buy a pair of shoes, only to be told that there were no shoes. This despite the fact that from 1918 on he worked in various Soviet cultural agencies, and enjoyed a number of special privileges. Nor was he subjected to any political pressures prior to his departure toward the close of 1921; it was only in mid-1921 that the Communist government turned against modern painting. As it was, Kandinsky obtained permission for a three-month stay in Germany—in itself a great distinction, a reward for his close collaboration with the authorities in various cultural projects. When he failed to go back to Russia, he lost his citizenship, and for the next few years he was a stateless person.

According to the existing data, thanks in part to records kept by Gabriele Münter (Eichner), Kandinsky left Munich on August 3, 1914. He first went to Rorschach in Switzerland by way of Lindau, and then to Goldach on Lake Constance where his landlady in Munich owned a house. There he stayed for about three months; it was generally believed at the time that no modern war could possibly last longer than a few weeks. While at Goldach he made careful notes concerning formal problems, which he later used for *Point and Line to Surface*. On November 16 he went to Zurich, and from there across the Balkans to Odessa, where he arrived on December 12; on

December 22 he reached Moscow. Gabriele Münter, meanwhile, went back to Munich from Zurich. In the summer of 1915 she set out for Stockholm, where Kandinsky met her for Christmas. On February 1, 1916 Kandinsky, and on March 1 Gabriele Münter had exhibitions at Gummeson's. On March 15, 1916, Kandinsky was back in Moscow having traveled via Petrograd. This was the last time Kandinsky saw Gabriele Münter; presumably their meeting in Stockholm was facilitated by the plans for art exhibitions, and by personal invitations, which included one from Prince Eugene, the king of Sweden's brother and a painter of some note. Late in 1916, Kandinsky met the young daughter of a Russian general, Nina de Andreevsky whom he married February 11, 1917. The marriage was a happy one, and ended only with his death.

When life in Russia calmed down somewhat after the revolutionary events, and orderly work again became possible, the Commissariat for Public Instruction (Fine Arts Division) named Kandinsky member (July, 1918), and that fall appointed him Professor at the Art School (Government Art Workshops). In 1919, Kandinsky founded the Museum for Pictorial Culture; in 1920 he was appointed professor at the University of Moscow (but he never actually taught there), and in 1921 he founded the Academy of Aesthetics, becoming vice-president. Thus, from 1918 on he was busy with administrative matters and other organizational business, as well as lectures. His activities were by no means confined to Moscow, for as chief of the government purchasing commission for art, he had to supervise the provincial museums, of which he created twenty-two new ones between 1919 and 1921. This was a tremendous accomplishment, about which we learn, however, only from his own notes. To all appearances he devoted himself willingly to this work, for he was now in a position to carry out long-cherished ideas and to let others profit from his experiences.

As for his writings during this period, we have only the preface to the catalogue of the Münter exhibition in Stockholm, and the enlarged Russian version of *Backward Glances*, published in 1918 by the Commissariat for Public Education. In addition, there were his administrative projects for combining the functions of art teacher and cultural leader.

The reason Kandinsky painted nothing in 1915 may be that he needed some time to get his bearings in Russia. It has repeatedly been said that Kandinsky made his transition to his later, colder, style in Moscow, and that he did this under the influence of Constructivism, the movement associated with Vladimir Tatlin and his disciples, which had been gaining adherents since 1913. But, in the first place, there were strictly geometric elements in Kandinsky's art even in the Munich period (for instance, in the preliminary drawings for *Small Pleasures* of 1913, based on "pure" forms); and in the second place, the works of his Russian years down to 1921 reveal no Constructivist influence whatsoever. Subsequently, when he was at the Bauhaus, he often observed that Constructivism was alien to him. He was impelled to say this all the more firmly because Constructivist tendencies markedly asserted themselves at the Bauhaus from 1921 on.

Kandinsky had not, however, been wholly unfamiliar with what had been going on in Russia from 1910 on; when the Blaue Reiter was founded, he established contacts with Russian artists, and in the first exhibition of 1911 included a Cubist head by

V. Burliuk, and in the second exhibition the Cubist *Peasant Head* by Malevich. At the end of 1914, when Kandinsky arrived in Moscow, Russian Futurism and the Cubism of the Burliuk brothers were already a thing of the past; Marinetti had been received rather coldly on his second visit to Moscow, in 1913. Everybody was now talking about Malevich, who in 1913 had sent to an exhibition a single neatly drawn square, done in pencil. The term associated with his name was Suprematism (the supremacy of pure invention in art); there was also a great deal of talk about Vladimir Tatlin, who in 1913 had executed an abstract relief out of unusual materials, somewhat like Picasso's *Guitar,* composed about the same time. Naum Gabo and Antoine Pevsner joined Tatlin when they went back to Russia in 1917, but unlike the latter they remained interested in artistic problems only, not in political ones, and they left Russia for good at about the same time Kandinsky did.

Kandinsky, of course, met all these artists while he was in Russia, and, presumably, taught alongside them at the Art School for some time. However, he was not especially interested in their work. Kandinsky's paintings after 1922 are referred to as Constructivist only because of their austere structure and unmistakably geometric forms, not because of their aesthetic spirit. It is noteworthy that the Constructivists, in Russia down to 1921 and in Germany after 1921, had no close ties with Kandinsky, and tended to regard him as an opponent. He went his own way. He was very definitely attracted to Klee, just as Klee was to him, and though the differences between the two are very great, Kandinsky had much closer affinities with Klee than with the Constructivists, or than with the partisans of De Stijl, whose painting was similarly oriented. Fanina Halle reports (*Kunstblatt,* 1922) that for all his official activities Kandinsky remained fairly isolated as a painter while in Russia, and that during the years of the Revolution was much less prominent there than a number of successful Moscow painters.

This much is certain: the artistic atmosphere of Moscow no longer stimulated Kandinsky, whereas during his short stay in Stockholm he produces four paintings, half his entire output for 1916. These works do not differ essentially from his last paintings in Germany. We are already familiar with the centrifugal main form of *Painting with Two Red Spots* (CC 107); in *Painting on Light Ground* (CC 108) the border encloses the painting proper on all sides in such a way that the composition, unlike that of 1913, floats on the surface like an island with plastically articulated forms. *Painting with Orange Border* (CC 109) remains closer to the surface, the border extending over it and even pushing "the medallion" a little backward; only the center, where there is a play of pointed forms and curves, comes forward toward the viewer. It is a fluid balance. The border motif was often used again in 1917 and 1919, and tends increasingly to serve as a contrast. In *Gray Oval* (1917, CC 114) the dramatically animated landscape floats on a black ground, which lies considerably deeper than the gray surroundings. One may fancy one sees a boat over mountain peaks, on waves, or at least derivations of these; they are more recognizable in the painting that in the related watercolor (1917, CC 705). In *Red Border* (1919, CC 115) the border has the effect of a window through which we look out upon a stormy sea, with forms that can be traced as far back as 1911.

Reminiscences of this kind still occur. In *Blue Arch* (1917, CC 110) which is aptly subtitled *Ridge*, one recognizes, though vaguely, the steep cliff with domes, clouds, rain, pointed roofs, the boat with oars, and the hieroglyph of the rider. And in the water-color study dating from the same time (p. 154, 32) we even find figurative suggestions. Just as Kandinsky in Munich had liked to think of Moscow, so in Moscow he remembered Munich. The dramatic quality of the Blaue Reiter period has not yet disappeared. *Overcast* (p. 283) and *Entrance* (CC 111) have the effect of cosmic disasters; *Twilight* (CC 112) and *Clarity* (CC 113), on the other hand, have something exotic in their forms and expressions, something Chinese. Is it an attempt to dodge the pressure of events? These works were executed in September 1917, that is, when the Republic was proclaimed.

Between November 9, 1917, when the Bolsheviks seized power, and July 1919, for more than a year and a half, Kandinsky did not produce a single painting; but between 1915 and 1919 he did produce a number of drawings, watercolors, and paintings on glass many of which are related to his canvases *(Ridge* and *Gray Oval),* while others are independent works. The watercolors of 1915 are so varied that we have the feeling that Kandinsky must have been experimenting. Not all of them are dated or titled, and some may have been executed earlier or later. The drawing *Exotic Bird* (which was acquired by the Russian government) must have had another name; it is remotely related to the panels discussed in the last chapter. One watercolor of 1916 (CC 702) uses some forms from *Composition VII,* another (CC 703) comes toward the viewer and vibrates like a Calder mobile, every stroke, as through on springs, enlarging the pictorial space, on which spots of color (red, green, blue) appear as points in space. Most of the watercolors executed in this period date from 1918. These, too, have little in common with each other, unless it is a somewhat more marked cheerfulness and animation both of line and color. One watercolor (CC 706) is like a Chinese landscape; pictorial forms, whenever they have a basis in reality, lead to analogies with existing things, though these are often very remote.

In 1916, during his stay in Stockholm, Kandinsky painted a series of fourteen Biedermeier watercolors, "Trifles," which he entitled *Birds, Horsemen, Lady in Crinoline,* and which he sold to the art dealer Gummeson. They go back to the style of the early woodcuts, and are of a baffling naiveté. In the same style are the seventeen glass paintings that Kandinsky executed in Moscow in 1917, and most of which are still there. Even the titles remind us of the early woodcuts—*With a Golden Cloud, With a Green Lady, Amazons*—and just as he had done earlier he includes gold and silver among his colors, and introduces Neo-Classical temples and Russian churches as landscape elements (CC 671). To a series of abstract etchings (p. 160) which he had printed in Stockholm, he added, as the sixth in the series, *Young Woman* (p. 165), which is a mixture of Biedermeier and satire. Obviously Kandinsky executed these works to sell. He also sold all the paintings on glass: as he noted when he listed them, this was not a time when he could support himself by his paintings. In 1918 he produced one watercolor (Solomon R. Guggenheim Museum) and a drawing preliminary to it (p. 167), which playfully combine naturalistic and abstract forms, as he had done in 1914 and in his painting *Ravine.*

Young Woman. Etching. 1916

In the case of certain works, for instance, *St. George* (CC 636) and *Archers* (CC 637) which remained in Russia, it is difficult to decide whether they were executed in Munich or in Moscow; also, a painting titled *View of a Russian City* in the Gemeente-museum in The Hague is listed as dating from 1907. According to Nina Kandinsky, however, this picture represents the view from one window of the apartment she occupied in Moscow with her husband, and was painted in 1919. Another painting, now in Moscow (CC 638) shows the same view but without the Kremlin.

In Stockholm he had, very much against his usual habit, written a preface for the catalogue of the Gabriele Münter exhibition, but without any very extravagant flattery of the painter. Was it because he wanted to stress his differences from her? In any case, all that was printed was a discussion on the original artist and the virtuoso, a theme which he had already touched upon in *Backward Glances*. The virtuoso is the man who is acted upon by external stimuli, who "popularizes the dream of the original creator . . . On the other hand, the artist-creator comes into the world with his own soul's dream." The latter, Kandinsky said, is onesided, stubborn, uninfluenceable; the inner world and the artistic means are inseparable in him. The public, unfortunately, sees only the form, and turns it into a fashion. And probably out of consideration for Gabriele Münter, Kandinsky made a concession to objective painting at the end of the preface, comparing it rather boldly with vocal music, which, he says, although it no longer attracts the composer, retains "in its retrospective form, the capacity to arouse emotions." In the passages that were not printed, he referred to Gabriele Münter as a genuine artist, "attached to an innocent conception of the world and nature," one who always remained herself. He would have been embarrassed to recall a passage in *Backward Glances* where he said that the virtuoso is the artist who creates from nature, while the creator is the "compositional" artist, who like the composer produces objective works "arising out of themselves." In the preface, however, he said that the artist who transforms external nature into "his own inner nature" is also a creator. Was this the expression of a conviction (Degas, Monet, Renoir were still alive), or merely a compliment? At all events, Kandinsky deleted the passage in question.

In July 1919, Kandinsky resumed work, executing several watercolors and six paintings. We have already mentioned *Red Border* with its effect of depth; in it the border still plays a part. This compositional motive, which has now developed into a means of balancing the strict rectangular surface of the canvas with the pictorial construction, is also used in *White Oval* (CC 116), further in two watercolors (CC 707 and 708) and particularly the study for *Green Border* (1920, CC 123). After this, it disappears. The pictorial work is not always completely adjusted to the shape of the canvas; the linear scaffolding and the colors, the pictorial rhythms and accents are often set within boundaries that do not outwardly coincide with the frame. That is one of the reasons why Kandinsky from 1925 onward occasionally switched to oval canvases. In 1913 the border was part of the pictorial form, while later it served to bridge inner and outer limits. In *Green Border* and the watercolor study for it, the curved lines at the left are supported by the line of the frame, extending on to give the picture tension and elasticity. Some of the forms now become more geometric. *White Oval* (1919, CC 116) is built up, as so often happens in Kandinsky's works, diagonally from lower left to upper right in violent forms both pointed and blunted, which are crossed by a nervous black line. Here, too, Kandinsky takes the shape of the canvas into account when he pushes the border back a little at the upper right. *Two Ovals* (p. 284) is a very Russian, optimistic, almost exuberant work, which strikes one as a prelude to further exploits. *In Gray*, on the other hand, is very complicated and confusing in its richness, and was probably executed in an exploratory mood.

The chief painting of 1920 was *Pointed Hovering* which Kandinsky originally planned to call *Composition VIII*. It was bought by the Russian government, and in 1922 was loaned to the Van Diemen gallery for the Russian Art Exhibition in Berlin. It is a curiously ambiguous painting with deliberately contradictory forms. At the lower left there are hill-shaped arched lines with antenna-like scaffoldings; near the middle there is a rectangular body seen in perspective; at the left a complex hovering Baroque structure consisting of round and angular forms, and at the right a figuration partly covered by an exact basket weave oval in shape. It is spatially situated in the nearest plane, and behind it are many other planes. The soaring ornamental forms appear and disappear like orbiting meteors pointing to space sequences in which locations and directions are relative. If the title is intended as an aid, it suggests a case of borderline movement, for the pointed and the hovering forms are dissociated from each other.

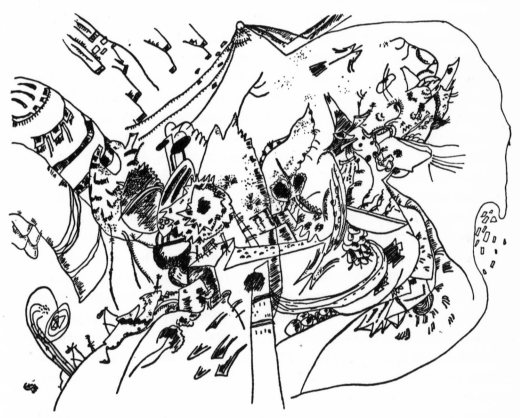

Drawing. 1918

It is as though Kandinsky were primarily concerned with the problem of space: his interest in the psychological elements of color, form, content, and expression is now less marked. By this time he was over fifty, and occupied a responsible post in a government that recognized only "objective" values. This is not to say that the government followed a specific policy in relation to modern art movements; that came later. But the very fact that the private collector had been eliminated along with, more generally, that portion of the population most receptive to art, may have brought new potentialities into Kandinsky's field of vision, quite apart from his personal development. Seen from Moscow, the Blaue Reiter must have looked like German Romanticism to him; a shift had occurred in ways of envisaging artistic problems. The task of bringing order out of chaos may now have appeared more urgent to him that the spiritualization of art with which he had been concerned for ten years. The next step would have to be the stabilization of the spiritual in its pictorial and compositional aspects, and the problems of space, color values, and form would have to be formulated anew. Kandinsky recalled his notes on this subject made at Goldach, which still had to be revised and completed. His professional work at the People's Commissariat must also have spurred him to cope with these problems. He had no sufficient leisure to write, and it was painting that for the time being offered the only chance to solve these problems.

White Background (1920, CC 118) is an austere work. Between fluttering bands we see symbols of order, a dictatorial black line, a checkerboard shaped like a trapeze, a tricolored band. These three formal elements are parallel to one another. The core of the painting, but not its center, is an irregular red oval with an inscribed star, its projections indicating the cardinal points. There are still free graphic elements, but there are also squares. The title leaves interpretation open, but unquestionably white here means extreme objectivity, the elimination of expressive elements. *Red Oval* (CC 120) is even more austere. The bright yellow quadrangle is placed in front of the cloudy blue green ground, setting it off, and carries the vermilion red oval, shifted a little from the center, which is counterpoised by the jagged form at the right. *White Line* (CC 125) is constructed differently: the main form bursts like a flash of lightning out of an immeasurable expanse furrowed by movements, standing still for a little space, and then at once going back into the spherical infinity, within which the firm straight lines serve as points of support and auxiliary structures.

The eight paintings of 1921 are all of the highest excellence. It is as though Kandinsky anticipated the end of his exile in his native land, now becoming foreign to him, and drew new strength from this hope. *Red Spot* (CC 127) is a sharply defined painting: the four corners cut the picture plane forming an irregular white octagon, which serves as stage for the pictorial event. Hooked and horn-shaped forms and a rounded red triangle are shown in restrained contact; and now for the first time circles appear, not accidentally, but as part of the design, strengthening the tension. At the upper left corner are dynamic white-on-black figures. The harmonies are rigid; the colors are atonal—the motives do not relate to a dominant tone. Still more rigid is *White Center* (CC 129), a complicated painting with a parabola, which runs rightward into the open, and a flash of lightning that runs toward the lower left corner, into a triangle made of parallel black stripes. Behind this scaffolding appears a view over a "mountain ridge" into space, emerging out of the center, but not directly—through a kind of pane of frosted glass we see pointed forms an incalculable distance away.

Blue Segment (CC 128) and *Black Spot* (CC 132) show the same mixture of free and exact forms, a whitish ground, which is, however, not identical with the picture surface but lies further back, and emphatic black accents: a cool climate. The middle form of *Blue Segment* is constructed like a steep mountain, with one segment of a circle crowning it, and with a large number of colorful triangles, quadrangles, and arcs at the edge, like some Surrealist architecture. The flying black forms in the nearest picture plane are not unlike snails. At the left there are troika lines, and at the right small colorful circles.

Variegated Circle (p. 285) is Kandinsky's first painting to use pure forms almost exclusively—the circle, the triangle, broad cross bars, smaller circles, semicircles and segments of circles; the freer curved ribbon alludes to no recognizable object. The colors are bright and cool; and the construction anticipates *Through-going Line* (1923). Despite the regularity of the parts, there is no resemblance to pictures of machines; the circle is neither a wheel nor a disk, and the change of color in the intersections of forms precludes mechanical associations. The whole is a dream of a world governed neither by mechanical nor psychological laws. It is a free and austere composition which is in accord with the experiences of the postwar years.

The last painting of the year was *Circles in Black* (p. 286). The term "circle" appears for the second time in a title. On the pink-white ground there is a black cone, with a rainbow (light blue, light green, yellow) enclosing it at its center. The two circles and the quarter-circle are white; the dented form, the intersecting horn-shaped forms, and the lines are also white; there are a very few carmine pink and blue accents. The painting has no beginning or end, yet it is entirely self-contained. The simplicity of the main forms, their vigorous dynamism, the reduction to black and white, all show that Kandinsky is on the road to a monumentalism, which Léger, too, was seeking in these same years, by different means.

Step by step, Kandinsky in Moscow was attaining a new pictorial form, harder and more objective, which was to surprise his old acquaintances when he showed it to them in Berlin. He aroused much the same reponse as Klee, whose friends were always suspecting that his latest development was an aberration.

What we know of Kandinsky's activities as an art teacher and administrator in Moscow does not amount to much. At the Commissariat for Public Instruction he was, according to his own statements, concerned with the reform of the art school; he was unable to prevent intensive mechanization and rigorous emphasis upon pragmatic goals. He was also concerned with the reform of art publishing and with the theater, but here he merely elaborated guiding principles that were worked out by the politicians. As teacher at the government art workshops, he had more to do with applied art than with art, and it is noteworthy that Kandinsky in 1919 sketched a dinner service for the government porcelain manufacture in Leningrad (p. 28). With respect to his museum work, he was interested both in purchases (which after 1918 were made solely by the government bureaus), and the new museums in cities such as Perm, Tobolsk, and Ekaterinburg. A large number of paintings by Kandinsky were at this time scattered all over Russia. At the Institute for Art Culture, which he founded in 1919, he worked with a number of artists and scholars on the elements of the various arts, their connections and affinities, and the possibilities of their synthesis, about which he had published several essays in Germany in the 1920s, and which he also discusses in *On the Spiritual in Art*. It is noteworthy that in his proposal to the Institute, he touched on poetry, music, drama, and ballet, and made suggestions for radical reform. With regard to poetry he referred to his *Gelbe Klang;* in music, to Scriabin and Schönberg. Science, too, was on his agenda: Kandinsky believed that science and art can help each other, although the artist must rely on his own experiences. In this connection he touched on Constructivism. The Constructivist, he says, can easily make the error of seeing mechanics as the answer to his question, and of identifying this solution with art (cf. *Wassily Kandinsky Memorial,* Guggenheim Foundation, 1945). Klee expressed similar ideas in conversations, and thought that Constructivism implied the danger of a new naturalism.

The program for the Russian Academy of Aesthetics, of which Kandinsky gave me a copy, deals mainly with problems he had dealt with in his projects for the Institute. New is the discussion of the reciprocal relation between art and society. Kandinsky himself was in charge of the "physico-psychological" division (basic elements, construction, composition). Most of all this remained on paper, for the government's attitude toward art changed, and the committees were disbanded. But in terms of Kandinsky's own development, the experience had not been in vain.

Drawing. 1923, 8

V The Bauhaus · Theory and Practice

A Weimar

1922-1925

At the end of December, 1921, Kandinsky and his wife arrived in Berlin with very little baggage, but with great hopes. He supposed that a new start in Germany would not be too difficult: had he not, in 1914, left about 150 of his works in Herwarth Walden's Sturm gallery, and the rest with Gabriele Münter in Murnau? This seemed to him an ample economic foundation for the future, but he was disappointed. Walden had sold nearly everything in the interval, but the German mark, under the pressure of the postwar inflation, had become almost valueless. What Kandinsky actually received was a negligible sum of money, and two canvases—*Painting with White Forms* (1913) and *Painting with Red Spot* (1914). As for the works stored in Munich and in Murnau, it was not until 1926 that Kandinsky was able, after long negotiations through intermediaries. to recover twenty-six crates of "prewar works, all of them in good condition" (letter to the author, July 4, 1927). Many paintings, studies, watercolors, drawings, and sketchbooks remained undelivered. His papers, including the manuscript of a lecture, did not come to light until February 1957, thanks to the Kandinsky-Münter Foundation and Eichner's book. Moreover, Kandinsky had been compelled to leave about fifty paintings behind in Russia—works bought by museums or entrusted to friends for storage. Kandinsky did not feel at home in Berlin, and the winter of 1921–1922 was particularly hard. The purchasing power of the mark had dropped to two pfennigs; the misery of the population was indescribable, the sanitary conditions were appalling. Kandinsky's friends were dead or widely scattered: Paul Klee and Lyonel Feininger were teaching in Weimar, Alexej von Jawlensky had recently moved to Wiesbaden, Marianne von Werefkin now lived at Ascona, and A. Sacharoff in Zurich. Kandinsky had no contact with the Brücke painters. Berlin was at this time as radical artistically and intellectually as politically, and in many respects the situation may have reminded him of Moscow. The questions that the Workers' Council for Art addressed to painters, sculptors, and architects in 1919—questions concerning art schools, exhibitions, and the artist's attitude toward society—had been answered by most of them in the spirit of socialism. The November Group (founded in November 1918) declared that it sided with the revolution, and that its motto was "Freedom, Equality, Brotherhood." Expressionism and its offshoots were dominant; there were few abstract painters or Constructivists, and almost all of them insignificant. The Dadaists (the Dada Almanac appeared in 1921) and the adherents of Neue Sachlichkeit were all the cry. None of this interested Kandinsky, and he wondered if the Bauhaus, where Klee was working, might offer some possibilities. His friends made efforts in his behalf, and the negotiations in Weimar were so successful that in June Kandinsky was able to move there and begin his activity as teacher. Before leaving Berlin he took part in the *Juryfreien* at the Glaspalast near the Lehrter Bahnhof, painting some large murals for it which kept him busy several weeks. In addition, he executed for the Propyläen Verlag, Berlin, a portfolio entitled *Small Worlds,* with four etchings, two color woodcuts, two black-and-white woodcuts, and four color lithographs; it was published the same year. In 1922 he completed six paintings and about twenty-five watercolors (Kandinsky began to keep a catalogue of his watercolors in 1922). Although he needed considerable time to adjust himself to his new circumstances, he accomplished a great deal. A sign that he had burned his bridges, and intended to stay in Germany forever, is the fact that early in 1922 he once again began to note the titles of his works in German (from No. 244 on in KK).

However, the year Kandinsky moved to Weimar was marked by an event that brought him into an emotional conflict, namely, the great Exhibition of Russian Art in the Van Diemen gallery (Unter den Linden), organized by the Russian Commissariat for Public Instruction and Art in conjunction with the Foreign Organization for Relief of Famine in Russia. In Sterenberg's preface (dated October) we read: "The works by the Leftist group illustrate the laboratory experiments that preceded the transformation of art." In other words, as early as 1922, "modern" art was being regarded as a thing of the past. Nevertheless, perhaps in order to maintain contact with the West, all the schools were exhibited, including the Traditionalists, the Impressionists, the painters of *Mir Iskustva,* the *Karobubs* with whom Kandinsky had repeatedly exhibited in Moscow, and the Union of Leftist Groups (Cubists, Suprematists, and Constructivists); in addition there were outsiders, belonging to no group. Edwin Redslob acting as *Reichkunstwart* welcomed the exhibition in the name of the German government, and mentioned the possibility of an exhibition of German art in Moscow.

The unsigned introduction by a Russian critic lists the artists from Right to Left, mentioning also Kandinsky, Chagall, Archipenko, Gabo, and Pevsner, i. e., artists who had left Russia, although it was not yet certain that they had left it for good. Realistic bourgeois paintings hung next to Malevich's famous *White on White,* Chagall's *Streetsweeper* next to Lisitsky's *Proun,* and Lentulov's *Cubist Women* next to Kandinsky's Compositions and watercolors from the Moscow period. The Leningrad porcelain industry was also represented.

The exhibition aroused much attention, though opinions differed. Some experts were enthusiastic about Kandinsky, Gabo, Malevich, and Tatlin, others about the painters of the new Social Realism (Pilonov). *Das Kunstblatt* (1922, pp. 493–498) says that the exhibition was a disappointment, and at the same time one of the most interesting artistic manifestations: there are no works of permanent value, the new ventures are merely radical, and the whole is an exhibition of artistic problems, not of works. The Russians, the article goes on to say, have reached the stage of fundamental grammatical concepts, but they have a long way to go before they achieve a language. In this company Kandinsky sticks out as a singular phenomenon, for he reflects neither the Russian convention nor Russian dialectics: his paintings are nonobjective, but contain a human component. His *Pointed Hovering* shows that it is the result of a long development, not a leap into the void. Kandinsky, forced to choose between his fellow countrymen and his former German friends, had obviously chosen the latter.

The idea of joining the Bauhaus seemed to appeal to him: he hoped to find a circle of colleagues of a high level, artistically and personally. He was not disappointed, and he remained faithful to his new friends until the last moment. As late as March 1933, shortly before leaving Germany, he planned to continue his teaching privately. Only in the summer of that year did he realize that he could not stay in Germany.

The Bauhaus came into being when Walter Gropius in 1919 combined the Weimar School of Creative Art with the School of Industrial Arts, and gave both schools a common curriculum. There was little money available and few teachers—the moment could scarcely have been more unfavorable—but enthusiasm was boundless. Gropius first invited Johannes Itten, Lyonel Feininger, and Gerhardt Marcks, then the architect Adolf Meyer (Gropius' collaborator), and Georg Muche. In 1920 he added Paul Klee and Oskar Schlemmer to the faculty, in 1922 Kandinsky, and in 1923 Moholy-Nagy. In April 1925, after the Bauhaus moved to Dessau, the faculty was augmented by the inclusion of several former students: Josef Albers, Herbert Bayer, Marcel Breuer, Hinnerk Scheper, Joost Schmidt and Gunta Stölzl. The new teachers supervised the preliminary courses, typography, the furniture workshop, wall painting, the plastic workshop, and the weaving shop. In 1928 Gropius withdrew from the direction of the Bauhaus to devote himself to his own work. Moholy-Nagy and Breuer left the school at the same time as Gropius. Schlemmer withdrew in 1929, and Klee in 1930, not because of disagreements, but because of other plans or appointments.

The Bauhaus was not an academy, but a school of creative art, and artists such as Kandinsky and Klee had no classes in painting in Weimar; only in Dessau were they permitted to teach painting. Their main activity consisted in imparting to beginning artists and designers a theory of form, which could serve as a kind of general canon or theory of "harmony-in-progress," similar to the one Arnold Schönberg had written for beginning composers. The principles and aims of the Bauhaus, which Gropius clearly expounded on several occasions, are well known, and the achievements of the school were so convincing that to this day both Germany and other countries continue to benefit from them. The catalogue of the Bauhaus exhibition held in the Museum of Modern Art in New York in 1938 gives us the best single insight into the diversity of these achievements and the spiritual foundations on which they rest.

It may be of some importance to note that the theory of form was not an isolated subject, but was taught in conjunction with crafts; every student had to follow courses by both a master craftsman and a master of form. Traditional teaching by masters as practised in the past was thus replaced in the Bauhaus by the simultaneous teaching of two disciplines whose unity had been lost in the century-long separation between workshop and studio. The ultimate goal was a synthesis of the two, of a sort Kandinsky had already sought in Munich, and later, again in Moscow. The word had a familiar sound to him, and he was ready to subscribe to the Institute's guiding principle: "The Bauhaus strives to gather all artistic creation into unity, to re-unite all artistic crafts into a new architecture as inseparable components of it. The ultimate, though distant goal of the Bauhaus is the unified work of art—the great style—in which there is no boundary line between monumental and decorative art . . . the gathering of the many arts into an indivisible whole, which is anchored in man himself, and which acquires meaning and importance only through living life."

The existing store of the elements of form and color and the laws governing them had still to be worked out, and it was fortunate that this task was assigned to two men as different as Kandinsky and Klee. They taught the grammar, so to speak, with the help of which everyone could give expression to his own ideas. Just as the musician or composer has at his disposal a "theory" with which he can work meaningfully whether he follows it closely, develops it, or deviates from it, so the painter and sculptor need a theory dealing with the laws of rhythm, proportion, measure, weight (light-dark), quality (color), space, and the like. Study from nature was not excluded; Kandinsky, for instance, would set up a still life composition and ask his students to work from it imitatively, analytically, or compositionally. As Klee also did, he once conducted the class working from the nude. But since the theory of form was closely connected with the crafts, Kandinsky also worked in the various workshops, for instance, in the class of wall painting, just as Klee worked in glass painting.

As for synthesis, he had been well prepared by the murals he did for the Juryfreie in 1922, and in the report on Bauhaus activities, *Staatliches Bauhaus Weimar* 1919–1923 (Bauhaus-Verlag, Weimar-Munich), he contributed an essay "On the Abstract Stage Synthesis," which harks back to the Blaue Reiter and *Der gelbe Klang*. He realized such a synthesis only once, at Dessau, in 1928, when he staged Mussorgsky's *Pictures at an Exhibition* for the local state theater. For the catalogue of the first international exhibition after the First World War (Düsseldorf, 1922) he wrote a preface beginning with the words: "We stand under the sign of synthesis . . . All roads which we have traveled separately until today have become one road, which we travel together, whether we like it or not." And in a letter from Weimar (to the author, October 5, 1924) he wrote: "To work in space, i.e., with architecture, is an old dream of mine (unfortunately the only larger attempt is my painting of the reception room of a museum of art, commissioned by the Juryfreie in 1922) which I hoped to realize when I went to the Bauhaus (but unfortunately have not as yet)." Significantly, Kandinsky goes on to say in his letter: "But in addition to synthetic collaboration, I expect from each art a further powerful, entirely new inner development, a deep penetration, liberated from all external purposes, into the human spirit, which only begins to touch the world spirit" —in other words, a painting fulfilled in all its aspects.

From the outset Kandinsky felt at ease in Weimar, for he was surrounded by men who understood him. His closest contacts were with Klee, who used the opportunity to experiment just as enthusiastically as Kandinsky, stimulated by intelligent experiments made in the preliminary course by Ittens, and later by Albers and Moholy-Nagy, who worked with the most varied materials and formal requirements. They were also

Drawing. 1922, 6

174

inspired by the works made by both teachers and students (masters and apprentices) in the various classes. They were interested in Hirschfeld-Mack's investigations of color and light, in the techniques of weaving, in Oskar Schlemmer's stage experiments and triadic ballet, and not least in the study of spatial problems by architects. Everybody learned from everybody else, the students from the teachers and vice versa, and Kandinsky felt as Klee did when he said that actually he should be paying tuition to his pupils. Albert Bloch, a member of the Blaue Reiter group, has written me from Lawrence, Kansas (January 29, 1957) that Kandinsky had confessed to him in one of his last letters from Neuilly (1935) that he owed a great deal to his pupils, adding: "a man who has not had such an experience is a bad teacher, and no artist at all."

It is not easy to ascertain in detail what stimulus influenced a given picture; it is clear, however, that Klee's *Fugue in Red* (1923) was influenced by Hirschfeld-Mack's explorations, and Kandinsky's transparent areas by his experiences with the techniques of painting on glass. It is impossible to enumerate influences due to the many painters, musicians, and scientists who came to visit the Bauhaus or to give lectures there, men such as Oud, Berlage, Adolf Busch, Igor Stravinsky, Bela Bartok, Wilhelm Ostwald, and Hans Driesch. The intellectual life of the community was so intense, so filled with inner and outer conflicts, that the objection that the Bauhaus simply wanted to create a new "style" completely misses the point. The Bauhaus was "an idea" (Mies van der Rohe), and was based on aspirations toward a new way of life.

This was the starting point for many attacks on the part of the petty bourgeois local population: since Goethe's death Weimar had become an increasingly provincial town. The new ideas were branded as "immoral" or as politically "radical," and the school —teachers and students alike—was attacked with increasing violence, until it was finally dissolved on December 26, 1924. Kandinsky, too, was attacked, all the more so because he was a Russian and a refugee from the Soviets. The People's Party in the Weimar government attacked him in the same language as later (in 1932) the National Socialists in Dessau.

In a letter (to the author, September 1, 1924) from Wennigstedt on the North Sea, where he had gone for his summer vacations, Kandinsky asks whether anything cannot be done about the shameless slanders printed in the *Braunschweigische Landeszeitung*, which referred to him and his wife as Communists and dangerous agitators. "I have never been active in politics," he wrote, "I never read newspapers . . . it's all lies . . . even in artistic politics I have never been partisan . . . this aspect of me should really be known." In other provincial towns, the situation was just as bad as in Weimar, and early in 1924 (letter to the author, May 23) Kandinsky considered leaving Weimar for a big city, and moving to Dresden, possibly as a teacher at the Academy. In Dresden, he wrote, he had friends and collectors, and even at the Academy there were signs of a renewal, and he would not be disinclined to teach "free art" and do a number of things that could not be done at the Bauhaus.

In Weimar Kandinsky and his wife lived in modest circumstances, first occupying a tiny apartment at No. 7 Cranachstrasse, then a larger one, at No. 3 Südstrasse. His salary was small, and until the end of 1923 the inflation raged on. When the Bauhaus exhibition of August 1923 opened, a million marks was worth only 1.47 gold marks; four

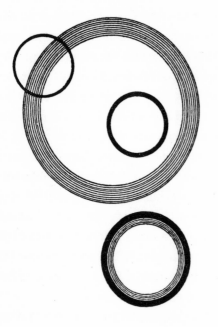
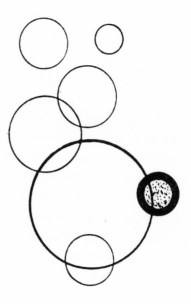

Drawing. 1923, I

months later one of the latter had to be counted in the billions. Even crates necessary to ship pictures to exhibitions present a problem to Kandinsky, for they were too expensive for him. He had a hard time, and when a collector (Otto Ralfs) had the idea of founding a group of subscribers, a kind of Kandinsky society, each of whose members was to receive a watercolor at the end of the year, Kandinsky agreed readily (as Klee had earlier to the formation of a Klee society). As he wrote in a letter (to the author, June 24, 1925), it always meant an additional few thousand marks a year.

He could no longer afford long trips, although to the end of his life he liked nothing better than to spend his vacations traveling. He twice visited the Timmendorf beach (on the Baltic); in 1924 he went to Wennigstedt (North Sea), and in 1925 to Binz auf Rügen. In 1924 he gave paid lectures in Vienna and in a few German cities (among them Wiesbaden, Braunschweig, Erfurt, Dresden, Leipzig). Trips abroad were too expensive, and besides, Kandinsky's passport was of little use. He did not become a German citizen until March 8, 1928. During his Weimar period he had exhibitions in New York, Hannover, Weimar, Dresden, and Wiesbaden. While he was at Weimar, too, the Blue Four group was organized at the suggestion of Galka Scheyer (who later settled in Los Angeles). The Blue Four, i.e., Kandinsky, Klee, Feininger, and Jawlensky exhibited together in the United States, and sold some paintings.

Like Klee, Kandinsky had to work hard on his courses, for there were no textbooks on which they could base themselves. Both prepared their lectures carefully, and published parts of them in the series of Bauhaus books which were printed by Müller and Langen in Munich. Kandinsky's *Point and Line to Plane* was published in 1925; Klee's *Pedagogic Sketchbook,* after the Bauhaus moved to Dessau. Kandinsky'y book is a short excerpt from a much longer course; it is doubtful whether it can be published in toto. For *Bauhaus-Buch* 1919–1923, Kandinsky wrote two short theoretical essays—"The Basic Elements of Form," and "Course in Color, and Seminar," and in addition, a paper "On the Abstract Stage Synthesis." In 1922, Kandinsky took part in a symposium, "A New Naturalism"; in 1923 he wrote "Yesterday, Today, Tomorrow" for Wertheim's *Künstlerbekenntnisse;* in 1925, "Abstract Art" for *Cicerone;* and in 1926 the essay "The Value of Theoretical Teaching in Painting" for the first issue of the Bauhaus magazine.

In these writings Kandinsky clarifies his earlier insights with a view to a formulating a general canon for artists and lovers of art. At the Bauhaus he primarily addressed his own students. He approaches the problem of abstract art from the most various points of view; for instance, in the symposium mentioned above, he is concerned with the effects of the postwar situation in Germany. The return to naturalism seems to him a symptom of weariness after a somewhat feverish epoch, and also of a desire for comfort. Kandinsky does not discuss the topic of the Neue Sachlichkeit, as might have been expected, but Realism which he had discussed earlier in the Blaue Reiter Almanac, and which, he thinks, will be of use to abstract art. The content, he says, must create the form, but since the general content of the period is still incapable of creating a general form, abstract art need not be recognized as the only art today. The two paths lead of themselves to one and the same goal. Kandinsky makes a similar point in his essay, "Yesterday, Today, Tomorrow." "Two movements running in opposite directions lead to one goal," he wrote: the analytic and the synthetic movement, the materialistic and the spiritual, the intuitive and the theoretical. In other words, we should not say "either-or" but "and" (cf. his paper "And" in the Dutch periodical *Internationale revue i 10,* 1929).

"Basic Elements of Form" is an excerpt from *Point and Line to Plane,* whereas "Course in Color, and Seminar" is a chapter from a planned sequel. The main ideas are familiar: color in isolation, purposeful combination of colors in the structure (construction), and the subordination of them to the artistic content of the work (composition); the combination of color and form; and, finally, the practical application of the results to the various Bauhaus problems.

In his paper "Value of Theoretical Teaching" Kandinsky, in line with the spirit of his courses, distinguishes between painting as an end in itself, and painting as a con-

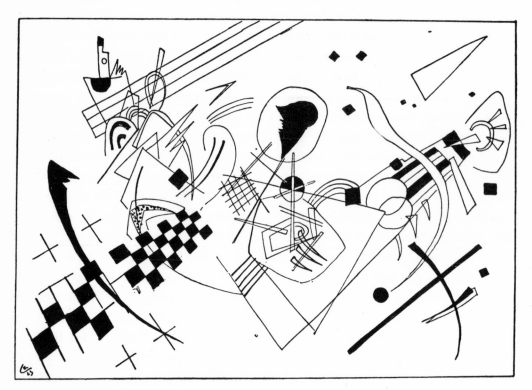

Drawing. 1923, 4

tributory organizing force. The latter, he says, is the basis of instruction in painting at the Bauhaus. Everywhere today the analytical approach is presupposed, the more strongly because overemphasis on intuition in the past has done a great deal of harm. To feel the affinity between the elements and the laws of nature is to gain insight into the elements and laws of the arts as well, and paves the way for a synthesis of all arts of the spirit, transcending specialization in the name of true "culture." An advanced school such as the Bauhaus has the duty to train the artist in such a way that he will be able to realize his "dream" with the highest degree of precision. At the Bauhaus, painting is the most suitable educator, for it has a place in all its workshops and it has been ahead of the other arts for decades and has enriched them.

In "Abstract Art" Kandinsky touches on the "transvaluation of values" hinted at in *On the Spiritual in Art,* now regarding it as possible that the center of the development will shift from the West to Russia, where "spiritual values" are predominant even in the realm of law. The French, he says, have analyzed the external matter of art (from Impressionism to Cubism), and now they will again recede into the background. Analysis of the pure means of expression in the various arts will lead to insight into their universal content, and to a synthesis that will clearly disclose "the purely artistic" in all fields. Referring to his program for the Russian Academy for the Study of Art, Kandinsky says that "minimal differences between the various kinds of art release maximal forces," and should reveal the differences among art, nature, and the world soul, despite their common roots. This clearly favors abstract art, synthesis, and the victory of "the spirit."

Point and Line to Plane, Kandinsky's major theoretical work of the Bauhaus period, makes emphatic use of the analytical method without losing sight of synthesis. The book deals with the elements of graphic art. It is a fragment, the sequel to it was planned but never written. Kandinsky, after having turned back again and again to the notes he made while at Goldach in 1914, wrote to the author, on July 16, 1925: "Here I, too, at least have a special room for my writing, and I have set to work on my book. The combination of theoretical speculation and practical work is often a necessity for me, but it is at the same time a great joy. I am also convinced that such a combination is the direct line to the future: we must keep them hitched together." And as though feeling guilty about theorizing when he might be painting—the following year he would be sixty—he returned to this question several times in his letters. On November 3, i.e., three months later, he wrote: "I have just finished the book, and I hope it will soon go to press. I'll be glad to get the manuscript out of the way, for otherwise I'll never stop revising it. For three months now I haven't painted as I should, and all sorts of ideas are begging to be expressed—if I may say so, I suffer from a kind of constipation, a spiritual kind." A few days later, Kandinsky wrote that people had been telling him more and more frequently lately that he was a theoretician: "As a matter of fact, I should like people to see what is *behind* my painting (for this is really the only thing I care about; the so-called question of form has always played a subordinate part with me, see the Bl. R.!!!) and not content themselves with saying that I use triangles or circles. I know that the future belongs to abstract art, and I am distressed when other abstract artists fail to go beyond questions of form ... By now, it should be clear that for me form is only a means to an end, and that I spend so much time on the theory of form because I want to capture the inner secrets of form." And he goes on to say: "Once you referred to 'Romanticism,' and I am glad you did. It is no part of my program to paint with tears or to make people cry, and I really don't care for sweets, but Romanticism goes far, far, very far beyond tears. Today there is Neue Sachlichkeit; why should there not be a (or the) New Romanticism? I once set out to write about it, intending to devote a chapter to it in the new edition of *On the Spiritual in Art.* But since then my plan for the book has changed. Instead, I want to produce a series of books—*Point and Line to Plane* is the beginning. But it may be a long time before I get to Romanticism. It is very interesting that Germans especially are afraid (AFRAID!) of this word. The

Russians are, too. On this point, at least, the somewhat hidden affinity between the two nations emerges. The meaning, the content of art is Romanticism, and it is our own fault if we mistake a temporal phenomenon for the whole notion. Please don't tell me that I give too broad a meaning to this term. Or don't you mean this? If you do, we understand one another perfectly. In 1910, if I am not mistaken. I painted a 'Romantic landscape' that had nothing in common with earlier Romanticism. I intend to use such a title again. Up until now I have been calling my things 'Lyrical Triangles' (for this I was exposed to incredible abuse in the press), 'Lyrical Structure,' etc. The old gulf between these two concepts no longer exists: where is the boundary line between Lyricism and Romanticism? The circle which I have been using so often of late is nothing if not Romantic. Actually, the coming Romanticism is profound, beautiful (the obsolete term 'beautiful' should be restored to usage), meaningful, joy-giving— it is a block of ice with a burning flame inside. If people perceive only the ice and not the flame, that is just too bad. But a few are beginning to grasp. Forgive my wretched style! There are so many things to tell you . . ." (To the author, November 21, 1925)

It is most instructive that Kandinsky spoke so frankly about the meaning and purpose of his art just at the moment he had sent off the manuscript of *Point and Line to Plane* to the publisher. True Russian that he was, he had gone rather far with his analytic and systematic exposition, and perhaps was too much influenced by his Bauhaus students, who were disposed to carry questions to the very frontiers of knowledge. He comforted himself with the idea that he would go on to write a sequel dealing with color, Romanticism, and abstraction. But the constant conflicts about art, both inside and outside the Bauhaus, and, eventually, political developments prevented him from carrying out these plans. Early in 1933, there were new worries to plague him—the move to Paris, and the awareness that he was approaching seventy and had no time to lose.

Kandinsky opens *Point and Line to Plane* with a defense of theory. Hostility toward it, he says, rests upon an underestimation of the elements and their forces. Music has long had a well-founded theory, and today painting is at last ready to concern itself with theoretical questions. Analysis can do no harm, although it must be granted that its application to works of the past presents great difficulties. Such investigations answer a deep human need, and in art they serve to elucidate the relations between intuition and calculation.

The theme of the book is stated in these terms: "Through pedantic investigation of each separate phenomenon—both in isolation and interaction with other phenomena— to draw comparisons and general conclusions." If Kandinsky's material is scarcely sufficient for arriving at general conclusions, he was able to make a very careful investigation of the basic "graphic" elements—point and line.

He begins with the point, "the zero point," which has various properties, for it brings together silence and discourse. Emancipated from its practical uses (in script), it becomes an independent entity (painting). The encounter between the instrument [brush or pen] and the picture surface is a productive interaction. Out of the relative magnitude and external form (relative boundary) of the point, life arises. This very

least of the formal elements achieves the most concise statement, setting up ten-

Drawing. 1924, 10

sion—and the work thrives on tensions. Theoretically speaking, a work could consist of a single point: the single point in the center of the picture surface is "the archetype of pictorial expression." By moving it around and repeating it, we progress to awareness of the chord where point and surface meet. This chord is also to be found in nature, in architecture, in sculpture, and in music. As Kandinsky is discussing the graphic elements, he does not confine his remarks to painting, but also investigates the character of the point in etching, in woodcuts, and in lithography, together with the various treatments by which "the sound" of this smallest element may be modified.

Whenever an outside force shifts the point on the surface in any direction, there arises a new entity with its own laws—the line. When a single force is applied, a straight line is produced; when two forces are applied simultaneously or successively, a zigzag line or a curve is produced.

The straight line has both tension and direction. As a horizontal it is cold and flat; as vertical it is warm; as diagonal it is lukewarm. Lines may occupy central or a-central positions. A-centrally positioned free (diagonal) straight lines are conducive to color and lie loosely on the picture surface, whereas horizontals and verticals are conducive to black and white, and are more firmly related to the picture surface.

The straight line is lyrical; whereas, wherever two forces operate, drama arises. When the forces work alternately, angular lines are produced (acute, obtuse, and right angles); when they work together, curved lines result. The right angle tends to red, the 60-degree angle to yellow, the obtuse to blue. The same may be said of the plane surface formed by these lines in combination—squares, triangles, circles. However, often the sum of the tones produces something different than might have been expected of the individual tones. This is a previously unknown law, and Kandinsky illustrates it with a reference to differing national and racial sensibilities, which, in the end, produce the same result.

While two forces acting in alternation produce zigzag lines, two simultaneous forces, of which one is stronger than the other, result in curves. Straight, zigzag, and curved lines are to each other as birth, youth, and maturity. Every curved line bears in it the germ of a surface. When the curve goes back to its starting point, we have a circle; when the force operating from the inside predominates, we have the spiral. The circle, as a surface, is "the opposite" of the triangle, and other such pairs of opposites are the straight line and the curve, the colors yellow and blue. Kandinsky looks forward to the formulation of a corresponding grammar for the other arts, and for art as a whole.

Drawing. 1925. From Point and Line to Plane (1926)

Kandinsky deals with curved lines in great detail. They may be geometrically wavy, freely wavy, or combinations of the two; also, they can be flat or ascending, emphasizing direction by swelling their degree of arc (bulges), and so forth. Bulging lines may also result in plane surfaces, but Kandinsky stresses that it is by carrying the elements to their limit that we obtain "a powerful means for compositional ends." The primal source of every line is the force behind it, the living element that engenders and determines tension.

Complexes of lines belong to the theory of composition, but Kandinsky ventures a few examples, so as to suggest the wealth of possibilities to be achieved through repetition, opposition, convergence, and divergence.

The line is not only an element in painting and the graphic arts, but also in music (notation), in poetry (meter), in technology (Eiffel tower), in nature (crystals, tissues, skeletons). Like Klee, Kandinsky points to analogies with and divergencies from the forms of nature. For instance, in painting, though not in nature, a line can run freely, "without being externally subordinated to the whole, without having an external relation to the center." In art, consequently, the subordination of line has the effect of being "natural."

In canvases bounded by two horizontals and two verticals, the predominance of height or width determines whether the predominant tone is cold or warm. The most objective form of the surface is the square. The artist must treat with great responsibility the divisions between upper and lower, and right and left. The top of the picture surface is where there is relaxation, lightness, freedom, where all inhibitions are reduced to a minimum. The bottom is the place of condensation, gravity, and dependence, but the artist can deviate from this law for the purpose of differentiating the organism. The right is to the left as the bottom to the top, as heaviness to lightness. The left side of the picture surface is movement away from; the right side, the place of movement homeward. The "square of tensions" is thus defined as Heaven, Earth, Home, Distance. Arrangement of the pictorial elements can emphasize the character of the picture surface or obliterate it—in the latter case, the elements "are suspended" in space. Spatially, the actual picture surface can be moved forward and backward like an accordion, chiefly by means of color.

And so Kandinsky goes on to divide and fill up the picture surface, obtaining lyrical and dramatic tensions, harmonious and unharmonious shapes. The concentric or the excentric may predominate, according to the character of a given artist and his epoch. Art may adjust itself to the epoch or transcend its boundaries, and anticipate the future, as abstract art is doing. However, there are also things that cannot be accounted for in such "positive" terms. There are also invisible and intangible factors about which it is impossible to speak.

Surfaces that are not rectangular are more complicated. The circular surface is at once the simplest of these and at the same time the most complicated. This is because, first, in it the pressure of the boundaries is everywhere equal, and, second, while the upper part flows leftward and rightward, the right and the left parts flow downward. Passing on to the oval, we finally reach free surfaces, which transcend the boundaries of geometric form as do angular forms.

The material surface may be of various textures—smooth, rough, grainy, shiny, dull, and these properties may strengthen the energy of the pictorial elements or be in contradiction with them. Likewise, the material forms may be of various textures and modify the relation to the surface, either lying solidly on it or floating as though in an indeterminate space. The viewer's collaboration is necessary to perceive this space, respectively, to keep it flat. Here, too, the purpose of theory is "to discover the living elements, to make their pulsations perceptible, and to ascertain the laws governing them." To draw consequences from these data is, according to Kandinsky, "the task of philosophy, and it is synthetic work in the highest sense. This work leads to spiritual revelations within the limits of a given epoch's capacities."

A small collection of reproductions at the end of the book facilitates understanding of the text and shows on the one hand how boundless are the possibilities of abstract art, and on the other, how much their effect depends on the activity of the viewer. A new world creates new organs, both in the artist and in the beholder, but since the artist leads the way, it may take a long time for him to be understood.

Kandinsky refers to his years in Weimar as pictorially cold and restrained, with reference to color. On January 31, 1924, he wrote to the author: "In 1921 my cool period began, from which I now often emerge." But the works of 1922 are scarcely cooler than those of 1921, and the term applies best to 1923, and to *Composition VIII. The Blue Circle* (CC 133) with its dramatic, slightly curved diagonal has a rigid center, but the light waves and ornamental forms at the lower right prevent it from properly asserting itself, and the sky-blue circle at the upper right is poised above the reinforced end of the diagonal. Even more animated is *Blue-Red* (CC 136) in which tension runs inversely, from the lower right to the upper left, and is held fast by two stripes on the two long sides, as though for the purpose of restraining the painter's enthusiasm. Kandinsky attached particular value to his *White Zigzags* (CC 135), the first painting he executed at Weimar, because it brought a large number of contrasts and contradictions into unity, the white staccato lines and the isolated steep pink curves, the smoothness of the geometric planes and the roughness of the free forms, the cool colors and the explosive character of the construction. In a letter to the author dated January 31, 1924, Kandinsky wrote: "When you go to Berlin, will you please look at my picture No. 244 *(White Zigzags)* at Nierendorf's (Graphisches Kabinett J. B. Neumann). They are going to photograph it . . . I wish you would mention this picture in your essay." Kandinsky had it reproduced several times. It is, incidentally, the first of his works bearing a German title.

As mentioned above, while Kandinsky was in Berlin, he painted murals for a reception hall (CC 641-645), which were exhibited at the Juryfreien in 1922. The hall had four walls, three of them with a single door each; narrow panels in the four corners broke up the wall surfaces. Kandinsky's mural for the wall facing the entrance was the most animated, the frothy forms reminding us of his Blaue Reiter period. The diagonals have the effect of a flourish of trumpets, the parallel waves that of galloping horsemen. It is the most passionate picture that Kandinsky painted during the postwar years, with luminous colors on a black background, Russian in character. The remaining three walls repeat the main formal motives: polygon, wavy lines, clusters, while enlarging the range of themes to include the checkerboard, the basketweave, the circle combined with an arrow, circles grouped around a steep scaffolding of lines, and the isolated curved line, which goes back to the reclining couple of *Composition IV*. The thematic material is used in accordance with musical ideas—repetition, inversion, variation, dynamic crescendos and diminuendos, alternating rhythms, coda. The effect of the whole is at once cheerful and solemn—an effect suitable for the purpose in hand, for the paintings were intended for the reception hall of a modern museum. Unfortunately the room Kandinsky decorated was not really suitable for displaying his functional intentions, and his aim of synthesizing architecture, painting and music was not fully realized.

Altogether fantastic are the twelve prints made for *Small Worlds* (CC 758), which Kandinsky set to work on as soon as he arrived in Weimar. As though he had been impatiently waiting for just such a commission, in a very few weeks he had made four color lithographs, four woodcuts (two of these in color), and four etchings on copper. In these he did not draw on the formal vocabulary of the paintings and watercolors executed in the same period, but for the most part anticipated boldly, drawing upon

Drawing for Intimate Communication. 1925. From Point and Line to Plane (1925)

the past only in a few instances, as in the sail forms of *Litho II,* and in print *No. VI* which is a variation of *Circles in Black* (1921). He wisely cut down the number of colors used to red, yellow, and blue, save for one use of the color harmony violet-ocher-green, a combination he would often employ again in works of the Paris period. Meshwork, checkerboard, and circle, conical forms and freely curving lines are the main elements, and their combinations are richly diversified. In the etchings he improvised in the manner of his drawings, experimenting with tonal values.

Like his early works, Kandinsky's paintings of 1923 and 1924 fall into a number of types: pictures constructed along diagonal lines, some of these freely curving; square pictures with "accented corners," pictures with some circles, and pictures with nothing but circles, among others. Each work is fundamentally unique, and it is only for survey purposes that we presume to group them at all.

Accented Corners (CC 138), the first work of 1923, belongs with On White (1923, p. 287) and Yellow Accompaniment (1924, CC 158). In each of these works the four corners are "accented," in the last-named painting by free spaces between the violet cross bars. The grounds are whitish or yellow, the graphic elements are black, the central forms brown. In Yellow Accompaniment, the central form is violet with a a vermilion-red rectangle in the middle. The color tones of this painting which has a yellow ground give a very un-European effect, Chinese rather than Russian, in deliberate contrast with the over-all design. This is true to a lesser degree of Accented Corners, while On White emphasizes the essential elements of the composition with the greatest precision, omitting all ornamental forms. There is a preliminary, not too literal, drawing for the black zigzag line, which in the painting serves as geometric counterpart to the free curve.

From 1923 on Kandinsky made more drawings than he had for several years: he listed fifteen for this year, eleven for 1924, and twenty-five for 1925. After this the number decreases again, and in 1930 rises to twenty-one, and in 1931 to forty-six. Some of these are schematic outlines for paintings, containing all essential components. The number of watercolors also increased. We have twenty-five dating from 1922, sixty-five for 1923, sixty-seven for 1924; in 1925 the number drops to twenty-two, in 1926, when Kandinsky moved to Dessau, to three; and beginning with 1927 the number rises rapidly, reaching ninety-one in 1928. Some of these watercolors also are studies for paintings, for instance, Accented Corners (1922, 32), Black Circle (1922, 38), On White (1922, 42), Circles within a Circle (1923, 52), Through-going Line (1923, 65), In a Black Square (1923, 84), Animated Repose (1923, 105), to mention only those done before the end of 1923. However, a majority of the watercolors, like most of the drawings, are free conceptions, independent of the artist's other works and equal to them in importance. Occasionally Kandinsky made preliminary studies for lithographs in watercolor; in 1923, for example, Nos. 60, 63, and 83 were obviously of this kind.

In 1923, closest in spirit to the square pictures with emphasized corners, are such constructions as Black and Violet (CC 145) with its excentric linear composition, Diagonal (CC 141) with its arrow-like points at the right, Without Support (CC 152), which is indeed a rather unstable construction, and Red Square (CC 151). A watercolor done during the same months, which Kandinsky entitled Lyrical, is almost mechanistic, yet for all its mathematical content somehow suggests a parade with flags by the sea.

The circle of some paintings is a contributory factor in the construction. In Black Form (CC 143), In the Black Square (CC 147), and Open Green (CC 150) circles and segments of circles give off greater intensity than the triangles, rectangles, and the other graphic elements, through they are transparent and restrained. The dynamism of the paintings is now occasionally enhanced by modifications of the picture surface: corners are cut off, another rectangle is inscribed within the frame, vigorous black-

and-white accents are employed, or there is an alternating use of smooth and rough (dotted) areas. The circle dominates *Arrow Form* (CC 146), a work Kandinsky reproduced in color in the *Bauhausbuch* 1919–1923. It shows a black sun bordered in red, with some white inside; and as though far off, another, yellow sun; behind it a red-tipped arrow, which passes behind another, smaller, black circle. The ground is pink; at the lower right, there is an almost playful figuration, resembling the inscription that is an integral part of many Chinese paintings.

Drawing for Lithograph. 1925, 22

Finally, the circle pictures themselves, *In the Black Circle* and *Circles within the Circle* (CC 148, 714), foreshadow the works of 1926, of which Kandinsky was especially proud. In a letter (to the author, October, 12, 1930) looking back on these years, he wrote: "You mention the circle, and I agree with your definition. It is a link with the cosmic. But I

187

use it above all formally. Have I sent you the few lines I wrote for you way back in April? I have just come upon them again.—Why does the circle fascinate me? It is

(1) the most modest form, but asserts itself unconditionally,

(2) a precise but inexhaustible variable,

(3) simultaneously stable and unstable,

(4) simultaneously loud and soft,

(5) a single tension that carries countless tensions within it. The circle is the synthesis of the greatest opositions. It combines the concentric and the excentric in a single form, and in balance. Of the three primary forms [triangle, square, circle], it points most clearly to the fourth dimension."

And in answer to a psychologist's poll of artists (Plaut, 1929), Kandinsky cast further light upon these remarks: "If I make such frequent, vehement use of the circle in recent years, the reason (or cause) for this is not the geometric form of the circle, or its geometric properties, but my strong feeling for the inner force of the circle and its countless variations; I love the circle today as I formerly loved the horse, for instance —perhaps even more, since I find more inner potentialities in the circle, which is why it has taken the horse's place... In my pictures, I have said a great many "new" things about the circle, but theoretically, although I have often tried, I cannot say very much."

In the Black Circle, which is a square canvas, has inscribed within it another, circular one, which is the painting proper. It rather evokes a landscape on some other planet. By contrast, *Circles within a Circle* consists formally and expressively only of circular forms on a square white picture surface, which is cut diagonally by two lines. The circles move like fixed stars against the firmament, shining through each other, over-lapping, or free and independent. A light scaffolding of intersecting diagonals is thrown over them like a net, forcing the movement inward. The same observations apply to the watercolor study.

Dating from 1923 also is a Composition almost two yards in length, titled *Composition VIII* (color plate, p. 189), which Kandinsky regarded as the high point of his postwar achievement. In this work geometry becomes number, but number transformed into magic, as Thomas Mann wrote in *Doctor Faustus*. The hero of this novel, Adrian Leverkühn, has a conversation with his friend Serenus Zeitblom, about creative free-dom, mentioning the problem of the artist who, despairing of the possibility of being creative out of himself, seeks shelter and security in "the objective." Freedom, says Leverkühn, "always inclines to dialectical reversals. She realizes herself very soon in constraint, fulfils herself in the subordination to law, rule, coercion, system—but to fulfil herself therein does not mean she therefore ceases to be freedom... Organiza-tion is everything. Without it there is nothing, least of all art." In "strict composition," Leverkühn goes on to say, "every note, without exception, has significance and function according to its place in the basic series or its derivatives. That would guar-antee what I call the indifference to harmony and melody." No element is a function of the others, as in Romanticism; all of them are to be developed separately from each other, and made to converge. Opposition between the polyphonic fugue style and the homophonic sonata form is thus eliminated; a basic motive chosen in advance deter-

Composition VIII. ▶
1923, 260

mines the development, and every element stands in strict relation to it. This results in cosmic order, law, and aesthetic gratification. Although the task of composition is subordinated to the nature of the material, harmony is not left to blind chance, but is determined by "the constellation" of the elements. But is not the rationalism of such a system incompatible with the concept of "the constellation"? "Reason and magic," says Leverkühn, "may meet and become one in that which one calls wisdom, initiation; in belief in the stars, in numbers . . ." [Thomas Mann, *Doctor Faustus*. Translated from the German by H. T. Lowe-Porter. Alfred A. Knopf, New York, 1948. pp. 190 ff.] *Composition VIII* is constructed in accordance with this strict compositional technique. The circles, triangles, and checkered figures, the linear elements—straight lines, angles, curves, semi-circles—stand side by side, occasionally overlapping, seemingly unconnected. Colors are reduced to a minimum; the ground of the upper right is whitish, that of the lower left light blue; the only exception to primary blues, reds, yellows is the violet inside the black circle at the upper left, which dominates the picture. The pink aura around the circle fixes its position in space. But does the black circle recede into or protrude from the picture plane? The vermilion red circle tangential to it makes it seem to protrude, while the violet circle at the center makes it recede. The pink aura contributes to the ambiguity. The rest of the composition is flat, and it is impossible to say whether the variously colored smaller circles create depth, or are merely points of rest in the staccato movement of the predominantly linear design. The color areas around the linear elements contribute to the airiness of the painting. In the checkered figures blacks and whites predominate counterpoising the small vermilion-colored circles and the light blue triangle. The resulting balance is nonetheless enigmatic, or perhaps we should say that the angle standing in the middle makes all the elements converge in harmony.

Through-going Line (CC 144), also monumental in size, reveals a purity of means which makes it look like a preliminary study for *Composition VIII*, although the individual forms, apart from the arched figure, are entirely different. Even the dominant black circle is of a different character. It seems hollow, more sphere than circle, with various inscribed details. Upon the brown trapezoid at the left lies a smaller white one, which is "a picture within a picture," as Kandinsky titled another work. The rigid diagonal which runs to the upper right, but which does not touch the edge the better to create tension, separates the more crowded right half, in which round forms predominate, from the left half in which rectilinear forms predominate. At the same time the diagonal serves as link between the two, thus reinforcing the function of the yellow triangle between the trapezoid and the sphere. What strikes the eye as a violet oval with dots of variegated color, nevertheless belongs.

Kandinsky remained fascinated with the circle throughout 1924 and 1925. Early in 1926, he painted the major work in this group, *Several Circles*. The most important works of 1924 are *Black Accompaniment* (color plate, p. 193) and *A Center* (p. 288), both vertical, and filled with dramatic tensions. The watercolor study for *Black Accompaniment*, though small, contains all the details of the large composition, including the colors; Kandinsky did not, however, merely make a mechanical enlargement. The white-bordered brown circle provides a warm center among predominantly cold colors: ultra-

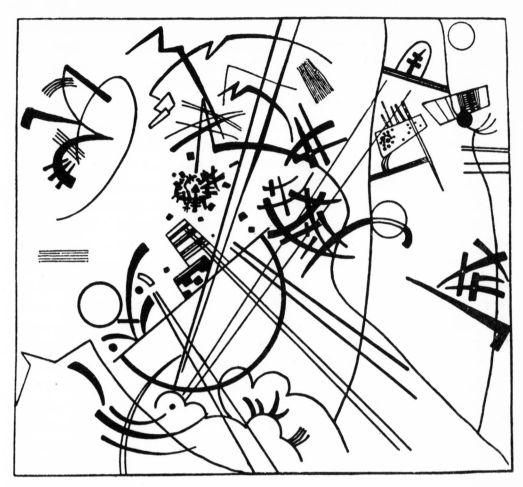

Drawing for Little Dream in Red. 1925. From Point and Line to Plane (1926)

marine blue, violet, and yellow; even the red is cold, as a result of mixtures and counter-tones. The pointed sticks, even the cursives, are cold. Animation derives not so much from the construction as from the passion and consistency of the treatment. The painting swirls with the most heterogeneous elements, and the forms near the edges appear to be flying outward. Only the little color chart at the lower right is still, a symbol of repose. There is a great deal of artistic understanding in Kandinsky's works of this period; they remind us of Balzac's saying, "The heart must lie in the region of the head." *A Center* is warmer in color, and the cursive forms swing outward from the black circle in the middle in an ever widening circle, whose transparency veils rather than discloses. Only the points in the upper left corner are aggressive, pushing threateningly toward the glass ball, but these points too are subdued by the flaky way in which the paint has been applied.

In certain paintings Kandinsky combines the circle with whiplash lines, either capricious (*Capricious Lines*, CC 167), or jagged like the letter Z (*Green Sound*, CC 168). Elsewhere the circles, lightest elements of the construction, contribute to the upward movement of the other forms (*Heavy Red*, CC 164). There are circles in almost every

191

painting, but their functions vary in importance, sometimes being reduced to mere accompaniment. In *Yellow Point* (CC 154) the circle mitigates the clash of the dominant triangles. In *Cheerful* (CC 153) it balances the repose at the right and the carnival-like variegation at the left. How carefully Kandinsky composed these works can be seen in *Blue Picture* (CC 155) in which the circle of the preliminary study (watercolor) was moved from the upper left to the lower right, giving more prominence to the diagonally ascending arrow. In *Contrasting Sounds* (CC 169) the blue circle at the top contrasts with the blue zigzag line at the bottom, as the standing triangle contrasts with the checkerboard. In *Calm Tension* (CC 174) the circle at the upper left balances the cluster of round forms below it. The contrast between forms is reduced to the simplest in *Contact* (CC 172), in which the standing narrow triangle cuts into a light circle at the top, and touches a dark circular segment at the bottom, as though to show how expressive basic forms can be in themselves, without the help of intermediate forms. Even in such compositions, the subsidiary motives, which are numerous, do not divert attention from the main theme, but merely vary it rhythmically or tonally. In this picture, this function is performed by the curve, the little bars, and the little inverted triangles at the bottom, all of which are ornaments rather than structural elements.

Texture once again enhances expression: Kandinsky sets flakily painted parts next to smooth ones, contours are both soft and hard, the circles and triangles have both broad and narrow colored borders, or no borders at all. The circles often suggest planets or stars, and the flat areas set in relief the other elements. Purely painterly elements intensify the design. The mathematically varied *White Pentagon* (CC 173) is chilly against a cloudy ground, while the thickly painted pentagon in *Quiet Harmony* (CC 162) has a soft, vegetable character in juxtaposition with the smoother, partly transparent circles and triangles. The more "Constructivist" the picture, the greater the effort to differentiate the treatment. *In Red* (CC 156) has a flaky texture throughout, and even the geometric elements become flexible in consequence. The texture of *Horn Form* (CC 163) is almost grainy, underlining the nocturnal effect of phantasmagoria. The painting *Silent* (CC 166) has similar effects: a tidily constructed scaffolding appears against a cloudy ground which is enclosed between brown areas painted just as cloudily. Some acrobatic stunt is evoked; actually there is a figure in the scaffolding which suggests a tight-rope walker.

Kandinsky himself was opposed to such associations. Doubtless he feared that the public would be only too ready to pervert abstract painting into its opposite, and invent an all-too facile symbolism of the forms, for the time was not yet ripe for understanding his work in terms of abstract art. Nevertheless, it may be assumed that the "spontaneously arising" forms originated in an unconscious, in which image and idea were linked. A circle is a circle first, but by Kandinsky's own definition it is at the same time more than a circle. One of his ink drawings of 1923, for instance, incorporating a number of pure circles (p. 176), suggests a planetary phenomenon far more stimulating to the imagination than anything in geometry. A drawing showing a circle and a ruler (1925, p. 187) implies a structure similar to that of Klee's *Steerable Grandfather* (1930); possibly Klee in this and similar cases was inspired by Kandinsky—we know that the two artists, for all their differences, freely shared their experiences. Most

Black Accompaniment. ▶
1924, 270

people will interpret a watercolor such as *Tender Yellow* (1927) as a city in Tunisia, and the circle at the top as the moon, although Kandinsky did not definitely intend anything of the kind.

Another instructive work dating from 1924 is *Backward Glance* (CC 157), which Kandinsky so named because it was built up like *Small Pleasures* (1913) and like the abstract drawing that served as preliminary study for the latter, and that is so different from other works of that period. At all events, the drawing is less closely related to *Small Pleasures* than to *Backward Glance*. In the painting of 1924, we recognize outlines of steep mountains, on the lower slopes of these the Kremlin with its domes (now circles), and towers; the triangle, in a sense, summarizes the idea of roofs. At the right of the slope, where formerly were a boat with oars and breaking waves, there is a form suggesting a sailboat and wavy lines, and where there had formerly been horses and riders, we now have a wavy line. Not that it is meant to suggest horses and riders, but the painter must have regarded the movement as related. At the lower left, *Backward Glance* shows an oval with the three oars of the boat, which are to be found in *Small Pleasures* (it appeared for the first time in 1912), and there are more of such parallels. Differences are greatest in respect to the colors—the painting of 1924 has a white ground with light, almost unbroken colors, while the 1913 one still reflects an expressive and varied color treatment. However closely Kandinsky kept to the geometric drawing of 1913, in his painting of 1924, he had *Small Pleasures* present in his mind and heart, and was recasting a bit of his past in the mold of new ideas. And the relation between form and motive proves that although the forms remain forms, they are linked to the ideas of things by an umbilical cord.

Not uninteresting in this context is one print by Kandinsky in a portfolio that members of the Bauhaus faculty presented to Walter Gropius in 1924 on the occasion of his fortieth birthday. Each of the artists was to execute one variation on a photograph in an illustrated newspaper showing a loudspeaker (a funnel) with a crowd of listeners behind it. Klee painted a funnel, an arrow emerging from it, and an ear above it. Kandinsky painted a triangle (funnel) directed at the "crowd," a curve accented at the bottom, and at the upper left a concentric circle surrounded by a number of smaller circles. The individual forms have no relation to the "motives," yet the results seem nevertheless to be as well in accord with the task as his colleagues' solutions.

It would be erroneous to generalize, to attempt to discover objective origins of the forms in each instance; *Backward Glance,* like *Small Dream in Red* (1925), is an exception. In such cases, as well as in the case of Z-shaped curve, the forms continue for a long time to be related to the reclining couple in *Composition II,* but for the most part the forms are emancipated more and more from the motives, and enter into new combinations, so that as early as the 1920s they can be traced back only to general feelings, such as Kandinsky expressed when he described the circle. The romantic spirit Kandinsky referred to in his letter of November 21, 1925 is still alive, however: "The circle . . . is nothing if not romantic . . . the coming Romanticism . . . is a block of ice with a burning flame inside."

In June 1925, when Kandinsky moved to Dessau, his work was interrupted, and he did not

settle down to it again until January. During the first six months of 1925, he executed thirty-four paintings. Some of them, of oval shape and in oval frames of the type used for family portraits, suggest a degree of personal communication: *Intimate Communication, Oval, Whispered, For Nina* (CC 196, 197, 199, p. 292). They were painted on special occasions for his wife, and must have had a private sense, as suggested by the gold brown ground, the Andreas Cross, the soft plaited curves, the Russian colors and the general mood of the pictures. *Small Dream in Red* (p. 290), too, is an "intimate" painting, evoking an earlier romanticism in the conical mountain form at the right, the zigzag lines and the curves, the horseshoe arc, the structures on the slanting half-circle, and the border of half-circles. This work is the only one reproduced in color in *Point and Line to Plane:* we may infer that Kandinsky particularly liked it on account of the memories it evoked. The diversity of design is rather notable in 1925. First, circles reappear. *Blue Circle* (CC 176) has an atmospheric effect, the firmly outlined circle standing within a concentrically arranged mist, but the black bar underneath points to pure invention, just as the calligraphic ship form in *One Spot* (CC 201) eliminates any idea of a mist around the moon. In other paintings a pointed wedge cuts deep into the circular form, or else the basic conception is enlarged by ornamental forms, nets, tablets. Often the circle is pushed to the background and reduced to an accompaniment. In *Steady Green* (CC 190) the cross dominates the moon and the half-moons, and in *Brown Silence* (CC 203) the dominant color nullifies the effect of the circle. In *Double Ascension* (p. 289) the parallel arrangement of the two scaffoldings results in something like an acrobatic feat: the expressive energy of the forms, despite the negation of visual appearance, implies a reality appealing to the totality of our experiences. Just as in music, formal analysis incorporates experience, both objective and subjective. At this time Kandinsky was preoccupied with the triangle in combination with the circle and half-circle (*Abstract Interpretation*, CC 183, and *Bright Unity*, CC 194); and in such works we may often feel that we have to do with unconscious expression of the complex of the masculine-feminine. The tangle of pointed wedges in the flakily painted *In the Bright Oval* (CC 198) also points in this direction.

Next to these we have more "Constructivist" paintings like *Black Triangle* (CC 204), a structure of stilts with an irregular rectangle and a slicing diagonal that looks like a balancing rod. The artist's and the viewer's ideas may easily not agree about these works. *Shaking* (CC 178) is for us far less balanced than *Black Triangle;* in *White Point* (CC 187) the point does not seem to us sufficiently emphatic to give the name to the painting: we are more affected by the transparent triangle and Z-form at the right; and we experience *Red Depth* (CC 200) as a passionate and dangerous play of heterogeneous forms. The titles are often mere identification marks. *Above and Left* (CC 181) and *Pointed and Round* (CC 180) are titles that scarcely characterize the paintings: the former suggests ascent and flight, tension between the rising red disk and the yellow arrow pointing downward, and between the cold rectangle and the broken curve above it. Kandinsky was often asked by collectors and dealers to change his titles, but he always refused to do so. "My titles are supposed to make my paintings uninteresting, boring. But I have an aversion for pompous titles. No title is anything but an unavoidable evil, for it always has a limiting rather than a broadening effect—just like 'the object'." (Letter to author, November 1928).

The two most important paintings of 1925 are surely *In Blue* (CC 175), the first work of that year, and *Yellow-Red-Blue* (color plate, p. 197) which approaches the great Compositions in size and significance. The preliminary sketch, a carefully executed watercolor, contains the design in somewhat simplified form, while the corresponding drawing (1925, 11, p. 198) is strongly divergent. The left side of the painting is brightly lit, graphic, and rectilinear; the right side is dramatic and heavy, with a large dark blue circle and a curve opening to the left. The two centers of the painting are linked by their frank contrast—it is an 'Either-Or' that becomes an "And." This was a problem with which Kandinsky was greatly concerned at this time—the synthesis of apparent contradictions into integral plenitude. The earthy yellow signifies firmness; violet and blue convey movement, which this time, violating the basic rules, emancipates itself in the direction of the upper right. It is noteworthy that the left side is framed in cloudy blue, the animated part at the right is superposed on yellow, while the central axis is gray. But the viewer does not calculate all this—rather he "enters into the picture," as Kandinsky phrased it in *Backward Glances,* and experiences the order of the whole with its contrasts and congruences. In doing this he is now on the picture surface, now in the upper air, now in the space that is bounded by the blue circle and the forms connected with it, a space that, as Kandinsky would say, is "indefinable."

The drawings and watercolors Kandinsky made between 1922 and 1925, while always in harmony with the paintings, are nevertheless more than mere supplements to them. Among the drawings are impromptu ones that display the same spontaneity and sureness of touch that characterized Kandinsky during the eventful period of 1913. Those done with brush and India ink especially are of an admirable vehemence and even colorfulness (1928, 8 and 15; 1925, 9). Next to these we have very precise drawings for "pictures" which were never painted, mostly done with the pen, and so fully realized that they could have served as blueprints. When they were not so used, it was simply because Kandinsky never got around to them again (1923, 4; 1924, 4; 1925, 19). The watercolors, apart from the preliminary studies for paintings, are independent works, and many collectors value them as highly as the paintings. From the Weimar period on, they have been eagerly collected, and today they are scattered all over the world. Kandinsky often tried out new ideas in the watercolor medium, as they occurred to him, and did not always use them later. For instance, *The Two* (1924, 179) is a conception that is quite unique within his entire work. What the viewer sees, is apparently the plan of a city with main thoroughfares and side streets, the various quarters and parks, and a neighboring town at the right; this was almost certainly not what the artist had in mind, but the watercolor can be read that way provided the association respects the construction, which is independent of any objective interpretation. On the whole, Kandinsky's watercolors and tempera paintings in their transparency meet the artist's imagination more than half way: they give him the opportunity to realize "the indefinable space" as if it were definable. This transparency provides a glimpse into the "limited infinite," as if it might one day become visible and measurable.

Drawing for Yellow–Red–Blue. 1925, 11

B Dessau

1925-1932

The move to Dessau brought many changes in Kandinsky's outward circumstances, but not in his art: he continued to work and teach. Some of his former students came along from Weimar; the faculty, too, was partly the same as before, and the fact that it included former students made it all the more homogeneous.

Dessau, which since 1341 had been the residence of the princes of Anhalt, was not without culture. It had a state theater, a small art gallery, a castle with wings that had been added by Frederic's architect G. W. von Knobelsdorff, and a late Gothic church with paintings by Lucas Cranach the Younger. The Oranienbaum castle is near-by, as well as the Wörlitz castle, built by F. W. von Erdmannsdorff in the Neo-Classical style.

In 1925 Dessau was a modern industrial city. The Junkers airplane factory was created there. Around 1900 Messel had built a palace there, which was used for cultural purposes in the 1920s. In April 1925, when Fritz Hesse, Mayor of Dessau, proposed to Walter Gropius favorable conditions for his school, Gropius accepted. He did this all the more willingly because the regional and municipal authorities undertook to erect a new building with workshops and dwelling units (designed by Gropius) for the faculty on the outskirts of the city in the Burgkühnauer Allee. From 1926 on, Kandinsky and Klee occupied the double house at Nos. 6 and 7, living wall to wall, and delighted to have large, well-lighted studios and comfortable apartments with view of the park. The artists often took walks in the valley of the Elbe, and on one occasion Kandinsky wrote enthusiastically about an incredibly beautiful mist-enveloped landscape, "Whistler could not paint this, nor could Monet" (to the author, November 22, 1925). Financially, too, teachers and pupils were better off in Dessau: the Institute disposed of larger funds than in Weimar, and the income derived from original models developed at the Institute, both for large industry and for the crafts, was not inconsiderable. The newly founded Bauhaus Inc. handled such commercial enterprises as a furniture factory (Marcel Breuer), a manufacture of lighting fixtures (Marianne Brandt), a printing plant (Herbert Bayer); the Bauhaus wallpapers had an unexpected success. A Bauhaus periodical was launched, which reported on studies, laboratory research, and new designs, as well as on world events connected with Bauhaus activities. The

199

first issue was published on the occasion of the Bauhaus' official inauguration, December 4, 1926, and was dedicated to Kandinsky on his sixtieth birthday. In the meantime *Point and Line to Surface* had been printed. A Society of Friends of the Bauhaus was formed to support Bauhaus production and aid its members; the board included prominent personalities from the various professions, such as H.P.Berlage, Albert Einstein, Arnold Schönberg, Gerhart Hauptmann, Adolf Busch. In the first issue of the periodical Gropius gave a chronological account of the development of the Bauhaus: the preliminary work had begun in September 1925, the masonry was completed in March 1926—including the school building with offices, workshops (with glass walls), studios with dwellings for students and common rooms, the auditorium, the dining room, and the stage for Schlemmer's theatrical experiments. All furnishings were produced by the Bauhaus workshops. The houses for the teachers were ready and occupied by July 1926; until then the teachers had apartments in the city. Kandinsky lived at No. 7, Moltkestrasse, and Klee shared the premises.

Besides teaching, Kandinsky had other duties as one of the executive directors of the Institute. In a letter from Paris much later he said that while at Dessau he never had more than three days a week for his own work, and that now he enjoyed at last being able to paint undisturbedly. Paul Klee, also, made something of the same complaint when he left the Bauhaus. Nevertheless, the two artists never regretted having sacrificed their time to a community that produced so much fruitful work and offered so much stimulation. Kandinsky felt at home in Dessau, having quite adjusted to it in two weeks. "Man is the most unfaithful animal," he wrote to the author on July 16, 1925. After occupying his own house, on July 4, 1926, he wrote: "We live as if we were in the country, not in the city: we can hear chickens, birds, dogs; we smell hay, linden blossoms, the woods. In a few short days we have become different people. Even the movies don't attract us [Kandinsky was an enthusiastic movie-goer, his favorite being Buster Keaton], and this is saying a great deal."

In these months he was involved in correspondence relative to various exhibitions in honor of his sixtieth birthday. He was thus reminded of his age, but not upset by it. On November 21, 1925, he wrote to the author: "In a Russian novel there is this sentence: 'The hair is dumb: ignorant of the youth of the heart, it turns white.' So far as I am concerned I neither respect nor fear white hair . . . I'd like to live, say, another fifty years to be able to penetrate art ever more deeply. We are really forced to stop much, much too early, at the very moment when we have begun to understand something. But perhaps we can continue in the other world." Klee declared himself ready to draw up a catalogue for the birthday exhibition. In his preface, he writes:

"He developed in advance of me. I could have been his pupil and was, in a sense, because more than one of his remarks managed to illuminate my quest beneficently and confirmingly. Needless to say, his words did not lack the resonance of deed (Kandinsky's early compositions) . . . Emotional connections remained, it is true, uninterrupted, but also unverifiable, until Weimar realized my hope for a fresh encounter, which was further enriched by common educational activity, and which is now to be continued in Dessau. In the meanwhile, an occasion for celebration draws near: his sixtieth anniversary. But this has nothing oppressive about it for anyone able to follow his development, and who in addition sees him daily. Many artists complete their work speedily (Franz Marc), others are able even in their fifties to take bold strides into unexplored territory and richly to develop the results they have achieved. This is not sunset, it is simply action ... which by the richness of its achievement transcends not only the life span of artistic experience but also the epoch. What could be done successfully yesterday, can also be done tomorrow, even after sixty—the achievement of a work that concentrates all tensions within it."

Kandinsky's life in Dessau was not too eventful externally. Old and new friends came to see him; the conductor Leopold Stokowski paid him a visit and bought some paintings; also Solomon R. Guggenheim, the American collector. There were visits by German and foreign artists: Marcel Duchamp, Amédée Ozenfant, Albert Gleizes, and there were lectures by scientists such as Wilhelm Ostwald, Hans Prinzhorn, Hans Driesch. Kandinsky experienced many such stimulations and profited from them, while his visitors studied the development of his work and that of the Bauhaus. Further contacts with the outside world came through exhibitions, the one-man exhibitions which gave him pleasure, and the exhibitions in which he was represented by only a few paintings, and which he cared less for, feeling that they often gave a completely false idea of his work (cf. List of Exhibitions, P. 424). All over Germany there were artistic societies and independent groups that sought the participation of prominent artists in their enterprises. Since Kandinsky was not yet properly appreciated abroad, he particularly welcomed invitations from foreign galleries. In 1926, anniversary exhibitions of his works were held in Dresden, Berlin, and Dessau; in 1927, in Mannheim, Munich, Amsterdam, and Zurich; and in 1928, in Francfort, Brussels, and Krefeld. In 1929 he finally had an exhibition in Paris (Zack gallery), and in 1930 another at the Galerie de France. In 1929, more interest began to be shown in Kandinsky outside Germany; in that year he had exhibitions in Paris, The Hague, Brussels, Antwerp, Basel, and Oakland, California, as well as as in other American cities with the other members of the Blue Four. Sales of his paintings reached figures that were not equaled later when he had moved to Paris, owing to the world economic crisis. His works were now also being bought by museums: among others, the Dresden gallery, the National Gallery in Berlin, and the Kunsthalle in Hamburg. The dealers, however, still hesitated, continuing to favor the Brücke, Kokoschka, and Beckmann, although public opinion and the Museumverein exerted a favorable influence on his sales. There were still occasional attacks, but they were insignificant and failed of effect. Not until the summer of 1932 did all this change.

Drawing. 1929, 10

Kandinsky could now travel again, and he spent his summer vacations wherever he liked. On March 8, 1928, he and his wife became German citizens (letter to the author, March 11, 1928), and he was able to travel abroad on a regular passport. In 1925 and 1926 he could only afford modest holidays on the Baltic Sea (Binz and Müritz); in 1927 he went to the Wörther See in Carinthia (where he met Arnold Schönberg) and to Guéthary near Biarritz (Klee was spending his vacations in near-by Bidart); in 1928 he went to the French Riviera, in 1929 to Belgium where he paid a visit to James Ensor at Ostend. In 1930 he spent a few days in Paris and went on to Cattolica on the Adriatic, also visiting Verona, Bologna, Urbino, Ravenna, and Venice: "I have finally

201

seen Ravenna, and what I saw was beyond all my expectations. They are the best, the most powerful mosaics I have ever seen—not only as mosaics but as works of art" (to the author, September 16, 1930). In 1931, Kandinsky took a cruise through the Near East (Klee had been in Egypt in 1928), visiting cities in Egypt, Syria, Turkey, and Greece; in 1932 he spent his vacation at Dubrovnik (Yugoslavia).

Then disaster struck the Bauhaus. Early in September 1932 the Anhalt government, in which the Nazis had gained a majority, closed the Bauhaus. Appropriations for it had been cut earlier, in 1931. On December 10, Kandinsky moved to Berlin (staying at No. 19 Bahnstrasse, Südende); not until the following summer did he make up his mind to leave Germany in view of the political developments. A last attempt to keep the Bauhaus going had failed, for the Nazi government had stepped in here too. On Christmas 1933, he was in Paris, having made a preliminary trip in October, to determine whether he would be able to live and work there.

During his years at Dessau, Kandinsky accomplished an enormous amount of work; down to 1930 the number of his paintings and watercolors grew steadily, although his teaching and administrative duties made great demands on his time and energies. He wrote a number of articles for newspapers; in 1928, he staged Mussorgsky's *Pictures at an Exhibition* for the Dessau theater, and in 1931 prepared a wall design in ceramics for the Architectural Show in Berlin. The latter two works are an organic part of his painted *oeuvre,* and contributions to that "synthesis of the art" with which Kandinsky was intensively concerned during these years.

In "And, Some Observations on Synthetic Art," printed in the first issue of the Dutch periodical *i 10* (1926), he expressed his despair at the slowness of the human spirit, which, he says, judges everything new by the specialist standards of the nineteenth century. There are few signs clearly pointing to the emergence of a new order: for instance, painting has made a good beginning with the principle of inner necessity, with the recognition that form is a bridge to inwardness. The church, the theater, and architecture retain remnants of an ancient spirit of synthesis, but they are of little value, for each epoch must find its own forms. Painting, Kandinsky went on to say, has aroused interest in the basic elements of all art, thus creating the foundations for an organic union of two arts, such as Scriabin anticipated in his *Prometheus.* Kandinsky himself took a step toward synthesis in *Der gelbe Klang,* while others also made attempts in the theater. What is still lacking, completely lacking, is the insight that science and technology both can co-operate with art; this is done only at the Bauhaus, to the extent that there art, technology, and science are the cornerstones of the curriculum, and that the universal man is the educational ideal. In the near future, Kandinsky predicts, the roots of the various disciplines will be reduced to a common root, and this will facilitate the achievement of synthesis.

An example of synthesis in the theater was given by Kandinsky in Dessau when he staged Mussorgsky's *Pictures at an Exhibition,* performed on April 4. He reports on this in *Kunstblatt* (1930). The composition was based on sixteen pictures, probably realistic watercolors, which Mussorgsky translated, however, not into program but pure music. Kandinsky, created stage designs (p. 28, fig. 31-33) stemming from the same root, namely, pictorial counterparts to the music, by following the movement of the musical phrases with colorful forms and animated plays of light. Dancers appear in only two scenes. In Scene 4, for instance *(The Old Castle),* the stage is open and dark. "At the first *espressivo* only three long vertical strips appear in the background. They vanish. At the next *espressivo* the great red perspective is introduced from the right (double color). Then, from the left, the green perspective. The middle figure emerges from the trap door. It is illumined with an intense colored light . . ." In other words, music and pictures intensify and clarify each other, forming a harmonious whole. Georg Hartmann, the director of the theater, saw in Kandinsky's work, not entirely without justification, a development of Tairov's ideas; he could also have pointed to the fact in the late 1920s there were stage designs of a high level in Germany as well as in Russia, and that painters such as Kokoschka, Schlemmer, and Baumeister were striving for a new style, particularly in the opera. Thus Kandinsky's stage synthesis belongs to a period which was most receptive to such experiments.

In his theoretical articles of the Dessau period, Kandinsky returns repeatedly to the problem of synthesis. His "Analysis of the Primary Elements of Painting" (*Cahiers de Belgique,* 1928) is a chapter from *Point and Line to Surface,* with special reference to the connection between reflection nad intuition, and the identity of structural laws in nature and art. In "Teaching of Art" (Bauhaus magazine, 1928) he discusses the need to develop the whole man, criticizes specialization, particularly in art schools, and demands a curriculum based on philosophical ideas. The process of creative work, he says, is the same in art, science, and technology. While creative art cannot be taught, and the teacher cannot impart the intuition required for creation, teaching is needed notwithstanding, for the mastery of compositional technique is wholly barren without intuition.

"The Bare Wall" (*Kunstnarr,* 1929) deals ironically with the so-called "painters' disease" at the Bauhaus, namely, the passion of all students, including the architects, for painting secretly, although this was in principle discouraged. For the Bauhaus was proud of not being an "art school"; the wall without pictures was almost a moral principle (consequence of functionalism in architecture). But Kandinsky sees in this reaction against purism an affirmation of the human need for art.

"The Blaue Reiter (Retrospective)" (*Das Kunstblatt,* 1930) and "Farewell to Paul Klee" (Bauhaus magazine, 1931) are more personal in character. The two essays, like the one on Franz Marc in 1936, are devoted to reminiscences, and their content, as regards the Munich period, is already familiar to the reader. "Farewell to Paul Klee" is a human document. Kandinsky's friend was about to join the State Academy at Düsseldorf, leaving the faculty at Dessau and his friends of the Burgkühnauer Allee—a painful separation after so many experiences shared in common. Fortunately for both, it was not as bad as had been feared. Klee was unable to find a suitable apartment in Düsseldorf, and did not move until the spring of 1933, when everything had come to an end at Dessau, and Kandinsky, too, was preparing to leave.

The last essay Kandinsky wrote in Dessau is entitled "Reflections on Abstract Art," and was published in *Cahiers d'art* in 1931. In 1929 and 1930 Kandinsky had had exhibitions in Paris, and no doubt had seen for himself to what extent abstract art was alien to the French, although Mondrian, Kupka, Vantongerloo, and Doesburg were living and working in Paris. Christian Zervos, the publisher of *Cahiers d'art,* had asked him to write on this subject, and Kandinsky welcomed the opportunity. He said that he has been put in the position of a criminal defending himself before the court, for he is supposed to prove that "nonobjective painting is really painting and that its existence is as justified as any other kind of painting." It would be more proper, he says, to ask the objective painters to prove that their painting is the only true one. Is the object really more important to them than color and form? History proves the opposite, and the charge of intellectualism applies only to untalented abstract painters. Needless to say, reason alone is not sufficient, as the source of all art is intuition, and reason is secondary. Even the Constructivists, when they are true artists, cannot dispense with intuition. The use of geometric forms no more leads necessarily to a geometric art than still life compositions with flowers lead to a botanical art. The circle is a pictorial means as legitimate as Adam's finger in Michelangelo's fresco, and abstract painting provides us with the opportunity "to hear a sound in the stillness." It does not preclude all connection with nature, but one must learn to see the content behind the unaccustomed form, just as we must look beneath nature's surface to grasp her essence.

Kandinsky was now over sixty, and his style more aphoristic than before. Often he merely suggests his ideas without developing them, seeming to feel that the reader can think for himself. Nor does he shy away from occasional witticisms, intimating that he is weary of speaking always in dead earnestness. After all, he implies, people should look at the pictures, expose themselves to the impact of the works, be interested in the effects and not the causes.

As regards his paintings, Kandinsky began the year 1926 with *Sketch* and the canvas *Several Circles,* once the proud possession of the Dresden National Gallery. This was a productive year, with forty-eight paintings, though few watercolors, which he once more produced in quantity only after 1927. Altogether, during his stay in Dessau he produced 251 paintings and 289 watercolors. We arrange them chronologically merely to introduce some order in this wealth of material. The development of the themes is not strictly chronological. Paintings based primarily on the circle are found as early as 1927 (*Heavy Circles,* CC 262), 1928 (*Deepened Impulse,* CC 284), and 1929 (*Circle with Brown,* CC 304). The circle continued to play a significant role even in Paris, but the circle paintings of between 1926 and 1929 constitute a separate group.

Most viewers will interpret them as cosmic metaphors; and while Kandinsky wanted his circles to be regarded primarily as circles with all the potentialities inherent in this form—the "countless tensions," "the synthesis of the great contrasts" (soft-loud, stable-unstable, concentric-excentric)—he acknowledged the reference to a cosmic symbolism in the letter to the author (1930) quoted above. This is also true of his "relation to the fourth dimension" which, according to Paul Valéry, is for the artist "the sum of all possibilities," and for Kandinsky the transcendent. He could scarcely have meant anything less when, in his letter of 1925 he referred to the circle as "Romantic"

Several Circles. ▶
1926, 323

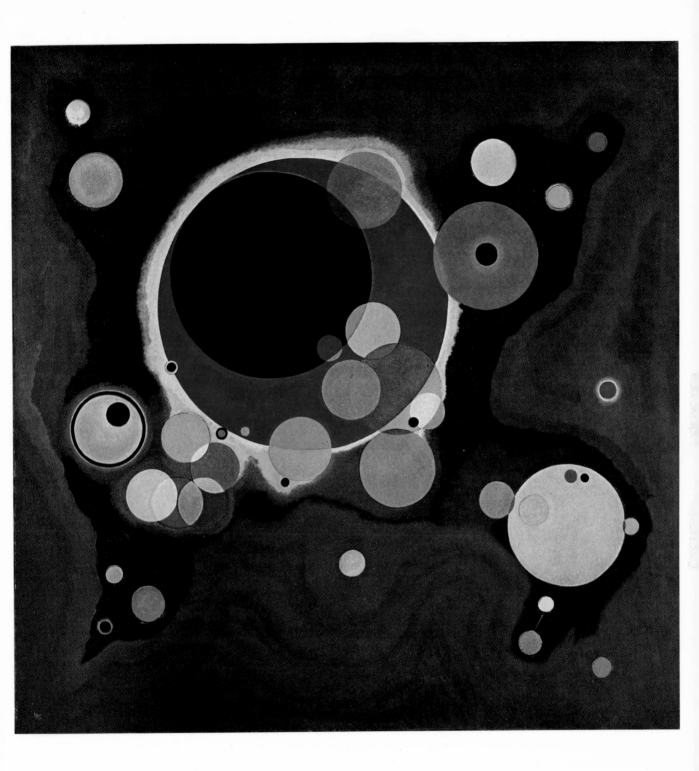

and spoke of a future "Romanticism." Publicly he was reluctant to encourage such interpretations, but in private he was a little more willing.

In *Several Circles,* the ground is black, not blue as it appears in most reproductions; the aura around the great sky-blue circle is almost white; the dark circle inscribed into it is deep black—a noteworthy austerity, not only with respect to color. The scale of the dimensional relations and the changes of color suggest a starry sky, all the more because it is cloudy. The white protuberance of the main circle has an atmospheric effect, and the transparent intersections of the circular forms lead the eye into the distance. The surface is elastic, the movement of the circle varying in size and color takes place in three dimensions, but the whole has the effect of a "limited infinite," as we have encountered it before, of something imaginary. The ambivalence of the circle extends to the entire composition; it is hard to say which circles are closer and which are more removed from us, for the constellation continually changes according to whether the eye focuses on one or another part. For instance, the milky blue is no more distant than the violet, and not all the red points are on the same plane.

Most closely related to this painting are *In Itself* (1926, CC 210), *Black Increasing* (1927, color plate, p. 213), and *Deepened Impulse* (1928, CC 284). In these works Kandinsky imbeds all or some of the circles in a color zone of the same or a different color, so that, according to the color tones and their contraries and the manner in which these zones are placed on the ground, he produces a cosmic-romantic impression, or, as in *Black Increasing,* a floral impression, a kind of still life, which is not too far removed from Odilon Redon's "spectral" floral poems. The two vase forms at the bottom, and the combination of light violet, green, and light blue enhance the suggestiveness. All magic is *Blue* (1927, CC 258), in which the circle becomes a constellation emerging from the mist of color and then receding back into it when looked at for a longer time. Its position can be indicated only "approximately," the bright point at the lower right being the only fixed position to which the indefinable space can be attached. Magic is also involved in *Heavy Circles* (1927, CC 262). The competition of the two large circles, the sudden overlappings, the contrast between rough and smooth, even the dotted surfaces, and the light emanating from the circles and spheres, along with the impulse starting from the lower left, all combine to produce some heroic cosmic process which it is impossible to look at unmoved.

Occasionally Kandinsky fixes the location of the circle by means of small forms. These are sometimes placed in the front plane like a signature (*Closely Surrounded,* 1926, CC 240); sometimes they have the effect of toy buildings (*Simple,* 1927, CC 242; *A Circle A,* 1928, CC 281). On one occasion he contrasts hard and soft (*A Circle B,* 1928, CC 291); on another, he neutralizes the circle with a number of forms placed within it, which are reminiscent of a page in an illustrated book, and locates it with the aid of tangent rectangles. By this means its movement is arrested.

Does *Accent in Pink* (1926, CC 207) with the many circles on the rectangle inscribed in the surface belong to this group? The painting has always attracted much attention at exhibitions, and been interpreted in many ways, some of which were recorded by Debrunner: a world of worlds with cosmic bodies approaching and moving away again, and an accumulation of elements at the center, possibly a reminiscence of

Kandinsky's visits to the peasant houses in the Vologda government: the small red lamp that hangs before the images of saints, for example. Others have interpreted it as a meditation, which requires an inner emptiness in the beholder, who can only thus receive its radiance. Formally, we are aware of circles dominating the precarious balance between the irregular fair-sided figure and the restful square inside it as movement dominates rest and life death, less summarily than words can say, with a great richness of nuance in the colors, the dimensions of the circles, and their positions in relation to one another. The pink of the largest circles has something comforting and reassuring among so many obscurities, an almost religious quality as compared with the earthy brown of the square, the shrill white at the center, and the emerald green of the dots unassertive against it. The painting contains both mathematics and mysticism, but the oppositions are bridged by their common root, by a kind of meditation that is to be found in the religious exercises of the Far East. It is hard to say whether there is a connection with the mandala, but the possibility of a psychological archaism cannot be entirely ruled out, and seems more likely than a connection with Russian icons.

It is not impossible that *Accent in Pink* and the circle paintings refer to Indian and Eastern Asiatic archetypes of concentric forms, the mandala, in which the transcendent manifests itself in the phenomenal world. In such archetypal paintings, not only circles but also quadrilateral figures, as in *Accent in Pink,* serve to embody cosmic and religious relationships: they are representations of the whole of the universe, of the One, from which realities emanate; conversely, the mandala circle, arising from meditations, can lead to the contemplative knowledge of the One. In other words, the purpose is to unite the opposites in symbolical form, to achieve Kandinsky's "And" instead of the "Either—Or," the unity of consciousness and life, a kind of Tao. After all, the mandala is not alien to Western culture, being found in medieval representations of Christ and the four Evangelists, and also in the writings of Jakob Boehme. Jung called our attention to such connections between the East and the West in his preface to *The Secret of the Golden Blossom* (1939).

In works where the circle is not the only dominant form, its confrontation with the triangle is noteworthy (*Conclusion,* 1926, CC 235). Kandinsky himself pointed out the fruitfulness of this contrast and probably here, too, had the higher unity in mind. *Hovering* and *Variegated in the Triangle* (1927, CC 259 and 273) are clear proofs of this assertion, and the netlike interlocking of the corner circles with the smaller inner circles and the acute angles diclose both sensitivity and understanding of art. On the other hand, *On Points* (p. 297) is so designed that the triangles become rockets sending the circles into cosmic space, while the sparingly distributed red and violet spots on the opalescent blue of the ground assume a threatening character (watercolor, 1928, 263, is a preliminary study for this painting).

Quiet (1926, color plate, p. 209) is the most "romantic" work of the group. The loosely contoured pink circle and the branching wavy line with the pointed oval appendages have the effect of a plant. The blue circle with the red point at the center and the dark blue circle at the lower right are very precisely drawn, but their geometrical effect is nullified by the open design in the gray-green ground; also the green-black triangle

207

is without harshness. The impression of vegetation is all the more emphatic because the forms shown at the left are to those shown at the right as passing-away is to coming-to-be. The white figuration on the ocher-colored spot suggests decay, the grained pointed ovals are like earth, and visitors to the Erfurt museum, which acquired the painting soon after it was executed, saw plants and nature in it. Kandinsky, of course, would have pointed out the values immanent in the colors and forms, and would have warned against far-fetched associations; on the other hand, he never forbade his viewers to extend the relevance of universal ideas to the more restricted area of personal experience.

As austere as *Quiet* are *Rift* (1926, CC 237) and *Loose-Fast* (1926, CC 239), which date from about the same time. The circle, the crescent, free curves, the triangle, the rectangle, and the pentagon are loosely constructed, the "rift" between the two sides of the painting is almost painfully felt, for the world at the right is light and airy, that at the left heavy and architectonic. Kandinsky was fond of confrontations of this kind at this time; in *Cool* (1926, CC 225) and *Variegated Accompaniment* (1928, CC 288) he plainly set circle against triangle, and on another occasion checkered squares against circle (*Counterweights,* 1926, CC 214). He was very fond of the checkered forms, which in India signify cosmographic elements. Sometimes they are small rectangles reminding us of Mondrian's compositions, while in other works they remind us of Klee's "magic squares." In other paintings, the checkered areas have the function of a tuning fork or color chart, stating the key values of the work, as in *Asserting* (1926, CC 231), a broad six-sided figure with three inscribed transparent squares. It looks like the entrance to a temple hewn out of sheer rock; the circle at the upper right has the force of a religious symbol.

Also dating from 1926 are a few "intimate" paintings—*For Nina* (p. 292), *Easter Egg* (CC 322), *Discreet* (CC 218); *Dark Impulse* (CC 224)—which Kandinsky obviously painted for his wife to commemorate experiences they had shared. Forms and colors are emphatically Russian. In *For Nina* there is a Russian cross, the lower part of which becomes a triangle; at the left, we see moons and halfmoons, in enamellike colors on black related to Russian folk art. Kandinsky still makes his pictorial means convey quite personal messages; it might be more accurate to say that specific colors and forms result from specific psychic dispositions.

The numerous paintings produced between 1926 and 1928 may be conveniently classified in groups according to certain characteristics. There are pictures in which arrow forms dominate (No. 350, 1926, p. 291; *Arrows,* 1927, CC 254), others in which crosses dominate (*Red Cross,* 1927, CC 247), some in which pointed conical forms are the most striking elements (*Theme Point,* and *Pointed Structure,* 1927, CC 249 and 263), others in which trellises figure (*Trellis Form,* 1927, CC 261), some with bars (*Mottled Bars,* 1928, CC 292, and *Veiled Glow,* 1928, CC 282), some with various square structures such as Josef Albers used in his Bauhaus work (*Square,* 1927, CC 246), and finally some with thorny forms (*Thorny,* 1926, CC 232). Few, if any, of these repeat themselves, for at the very least the expression changes. If *Pointed Structure* suggests an engineer's blueprint, *Points in Arc* (1927, p. 295) suggests at once a musical fugue and a Chinese village. There is no connection between these two impressions,

208

Quiet. 1926, 357 ▶

yet both are possible according to whether the viewer focuses on the formal development or the expression. In certain works of these years, we find jagged streaks of lightning, menacing in effect (*Angular*, 1927, CC 252) and in others freely curving lines such as in *Red Bar* (1927, CC 265), in which Kandinsky used the curve much as he prescribed in *Point and Line to Plane,* in conjunction with half-circles, bars, and arrows. In some paintings the constructive elements are exaggerated (*Small Yellow*, 1926, CC 206) as if the artist had occasionally to come back to the formal values stripped of all else. In others the constructive elements suggest architecture: a city with many-storied houses (*Repose*, 1928, CC 278), a festively illumined Ferris wheel (*Dark Coolness*, 1927, CC 248), a window for the staircase of some scientific institute (*Tension in Red*, 1926, CC 208).

Pointed Accents (1926, CC 222) and *Rose in Gray* (1926, CC 229) are especially complicated: in these paintings, as in his Compositions, Kandinsky has subordinated several centers or points of gravity to the total conception, and the pictorial ideas in them are only loosely connected. These works, even more than the others, must be seen in color to be understood; for instance *Two Sides Red* (1928, CC 294) will appear a cold canvas to anyone unaware that the whole work is painted in red and dark brown tones of violet. Far from being crystalline, this painting is inherently dynamic, yet without the red even the division at the center must seem expressionless.

In a few of these works, Kandinsky has stressed fluidity rather than rigidity, e. g., in *Shifted* (1926, CC 238) and *Disturbance* (1927, CC 245). The titles are of little help here. This is not always the case. There are a few works in which a new reality is born of the configuration: a kind of Viking ship in *Woven* (1927, CC 255), an excavation site in *Three Places* (1928, CC 286). No archaeological associations are directly suggested, as in Klee—there are only triangles, circles, and rectangles—and yet this work with its three centers of gravity somehow evokes a prehistoric site.

During the last years in Dessau, from 1929 to 1932, Kandinsky constantly gained in assurance and lightness of touch. A joy of living is perceptibly felt in his work. In certain paintings there is even a kind of philosophical humor. It is not that he works less strenuously, but now he has mastered his craft so completely that he can paint at any time of day, he can break off work and resume it at the next occasion. He does not have to change into working clothes in order to work, but is able to paint anywhere at any time, without waiting for outside stimulation.

To what extent did Kandinsky enlarge his expressive means and develop new conceptions during the Bauhaus years? Not only are his means very flexible, he transforms them endlessly. This is also true of his use of color in ever more unexpected and unfamiliar combinations. He sometimes uses black and white alone, and also simplifies the forms. The numerous studies, drawings, and watercolors are invariably exact, and in structure and expression equivalent to the paintings, although not everything in the former proves usable in the latter. The splatter technique, for example, which from 1927 on often turns up in Kandinsky as in Klee, is not adapted to oils.

What distinguishes the paintings prior to 1933, is first of all the spirituality with which the mathematical and "Constructivist" elements are treated, the unprecedented empathic response to forms derived from mathematical physics, and their adaptation to the realm of pictorial invention. In 1929, most notably, he produces a large number of phantasmagorias with circles, which go beyond his own earlier "cosmic" circle paintings. Today they make us think of such later developments as artificial satellites and the exploration of outer space. *Hovering above Firm* (1929, CC 300) suggests an artificial planet; *Taciturn* and *Pink Sweet* (1929, CC 311 and 333) arouse not merely general feelings, but scientific ideas. *Circle and Spot* (1929, CC 298) juxtaposes the exact geometric circle with the loosely drawn one, as we have seen before, but the crystalline forms at the bottom, the scaffolding at the left and the parachute at the right point in the direction of super-technology. *Disintegrated Tension* of 1930 (CC 356) might be an electronic brain, although Kandinsky had never heard of one. And there are a few other works of this type dating from these years.

For Kandinsky art was always invention, never reproduction, and these pictures can best be interpreted as prophetic symbols. It would not be surprising if Kandinsky had had a glimpse of the future in the late 1920s, as he had had prior to World War I. The anticipatory reality of these works is enigmatic and imaginative, and we might remember that even the scientist cannot construct models of it, but merely record it in mathematical formulas. In both cases we are dealing with symbols. Regarding this content, upon which Kandinsky always placed such emphasis, the least we can say is that it is not exhausted in general feelings, nor even in highly differentiated feelings. We must conclude that these works contain new facts and new truths expressed in the language of painting.

Anyone is free to experience these works purely in in terms of form and color, concentrating upon the qualities and tensions inherent in the connections between these two elements. These qualities and tensions are infinite in number. It is the sum total of the various relationships among line, plane, rhythm, melody, both at the formal and the spiritual or psychological level. More and more the paintings become phenomena that elude simple analysis: words cannot do justice to the multidimensional character of so free a conception.

Except for *Circles in Brown* (1929, CC 329), the paintings in which the circle predominates are differently expressive than those of 1926. They have a kind of "electronic" romanticism: *Gentle Stress* (1931, CC 393), for example, suggests a system of mental wiring, a switchboard for thinking in entirely new categories. Of course, painting as yet possessed no means analogous to those of a latter-day "electronic music," and Kandinsky found the vocabulary he invented sufficient for his symbolism. However, he carried his vocabulary to the extreme limits of the communicable, and sometimes employed his circles and triangles in ready-made configurations—of the type employed today by composers of *musique concrète*.

The variations on circles, such as *Upward* (1929, CC 323), *Unsteady Balance* (1930, CC 348), and *Gray Mood* (1933, CC 426) also contain allusions to cosmic ideas. The disks with their divisions and the inscribed points or lines, resemble the equations of astrophysics, rather than stars, seeming to emanate from cosmic speculations rather than from empirical findings. Theirs is a symbolic truth, no less than the medieval mandala of the four Evangelists. Meditations, speculations lead to such manifestations of the absolute, they result less in communications than in insights, glimpses into spatio-temporal being that at the same time are emanations of inward being.

For Kandinsky, ideas about the universe were always linked with ideas about human existence and fate, as in Asian thought. He stands between East and West: familiar both with the scientific and philosophical ideas of Europe, and with the cosmogonies and myths of the Far East. This is why the viewer is often tempted to see affinities between the mathematical relations in Kandinsky's paintings and oriental symbolic figures. It is unlikely that when Kandinsky painted *Unsteady Balance* he had in mind what the title suggests, but rather a geometry of concentric circles and interpenetrating triangles like the one to be found in the Tantras; but in Kandinsky (as in Klee) the symbolic elements are more subjective. Wherever stars appear, they are not to be taken in a Biblical or Copernican sense, but in that of present existence and immediate psychological effect. The artistic results become more and more complex and poly-valent, so that it is possible for some to interpret Kandinsky's paintings on the basis of their formal structure, and for others as the myth of our era—if such an expression may be used for the explorations and the fictions of physicists, chemists, and biologists. The drawings in today's scientific journals, like earlier scientific drawings of microscopic worlds resemble nothing so much as Kandinsky's pictures.

Another group of paintings of these years brings to mind technological inventions, the blueprints of engineers and architects. *Diagonal* (1930, CC 360) is a subtle diagonal cross with indications as to how it might be set in motion. *Within Three Points* (1930, CC 352), a network of complicated tensions, is not unlike a flying machine. *Up from the Half Circle* (1931, CC 409) contradicts the laws of balance, and yet it is per-fectly plausible—this is also true of the vertical figures in the designs for rooms at the Architectural Exhibition of Berlin 1931. *All the More* (1933, CC 421; preliminary study in watercolor, 1932, 497) suggests a scaffolding; and a painting with ladder forms, *Upward Through Blue* (1930, CC 344) looks like a high scaffolding in process of being erected. Graphic elements predominate, the colors are confined to the surface design, and form an imaginary space whose effect is psychological: its extension is indefinable, and hard linear facts contrast with the vivid spontaneity of the intense purplish reds and purplish greens. In *One-Two* (1929, CC 320) the colors are toned down to pink with contrasting light blue and lemon yellow planes.

In 1929 and 1930 zigzag lines and angular constructions appear repeatedly in drawings, watercolors, and paintings; in 1932, they appear in an etching for the Society of Friends of the Bauhaus. Kandinsky used them in the most varied ways, as in a geo-metric version of the Chinese dragon (watercolor, 1929, 355), as a broken rhythmic series (*Angular Swing*, 1929, CC 326), as masterful gestures (*From-To*, 1930, CC 358), as a blueprint design against a light blue ground, with a topographic plan of colorful quadrilateral planes (*Angular Structure*, 1930, CC 370).

Based on plane structures are *Slowly out* (1931, CC 407), *Rightward-Leftward* (1932, CC 414), and *Development in Brown* (1933, p. 301; watercolor sketch, 1933). Unlike the previous paintings, these are restrained, taciturn, melancholy in color as well as in the careful overlapping of the planes. In *Slowly out* the variously nuanced blue-green planes lie on a green-brown ground; the small amount of violet-red seems merely

212

juxtaposed rather than complementary, while the pointed triangles have nothing aggressive about them, rather serving to articulate the elegiac mood. "Abstract art as the expression of stillness," as Kandinsky said. Somewhat more dynamic is the structure of planes in *Rightward-Leftward;* the ornamental form at the left is reminiscent of a figure on stage—an echo of Kandinsky's staging of Mussorgsky. *Development in Brown* is the most contemplative, the luminous center with the variegated triangles and half moons is somehow like a backward glance at happy youth, but the crucial elements are the overlapping planes in solemn brown tones, in an arrangement suggesting the rhythm of a funeral march.

The paintings organized in bands, of 1930 and 1931, also come forward from the flat surface. They bring to mind the structure of Kandinsky's stage designs, and occasionally contain ornamental forms echoing his figures for Mussorgsky. *Green-Empty* (1930, CC 357) is expectant; at the upper left there is the staccato of the cloud bands— or should we say pizzicato? At the lower right is a closed door. *Cool Stripes* (1930, CC 374) has an opening in front similar to the one in *Rightward-Leftward;* it is superimposed on the four fairly empty planes of the picture surface; the circle, however, and particularly the mandala above it, point to magic. This mandala form occupies the dominant central place in *Erect* (1930, CC 362), and it has a still more mysterious aura. It is not out of the question that a painting such as *Balance-Pink* (1933, CC 422) with its maze of spatial interlockings, reminiscent of rock tombs, may have been inspired by Mozart's *Magic Flute*. Kandinsky's trip to Egypt may also have some bearing.

In all these cases, we are not dealing with associations of the Klee type. Rather, Kandinsky's form-creating power leads to entities of a higher order, inherently related to formal rather than naturalistic preoccupations. The clock cannot be turned back in art any more than in science; after Kandinsky had come to understand and express reality in a form such as the circle, and in a color such as blue, a new and truer reality arose from this form and this color. It may occasionally resemble the reality familiar to us, but it is never the same. It is a creation in its own right, with a significance different from that of familiar reality. It may occasionally evoke a stage design with figures or a backdrop, just as it may suggest a cosmic fantasy, but the pictorial achievement is always a higher order of symbolism. The stage designs are not stage designs, the figures are not figures, the satellites are not satellites, but all of these in combination convey a vision of the world, employing pictorial signs occasionally analogous in this way. Kandinsky refused to entitle one of his stage designs "The Magic Flute," on the ground that even though the allusion would have been appropriate, it would denote only a part of the intended whole. He would much more willingly have given that title to a painting completely unrelated to Mozart's opera, but which would have expressed the meaning of those words in its own terms.

It is noteworthy, however, that even before the Paris days a pictorially objective reality penetrates the paintings, which might be called "concrete." *Bridge* (1931, CC 390; watercolor sketch, 1930) is a construction based on two vertical forms connected by an arch. In earlier works, arches of this type often signified rainbows, just as rectangles signified towers, or triangles mountains. The meanings never completely "covered" the pictorial content, and now they "cover" the content even less completely. "Bridge" is just not enough, although Kandinsky gives this name to this painting. The title is meant to convey also the notions of bridging, reconciliation, the union of opposites. In this case, the arch transforms the construction into an imaginary form, which gratifies the human need to participate in the transcendent. The flags and pennants in *Dense* (1929, CC 310) and *Fluttering* (1930, CC 345) are flags and pennants, not because they are simply "there" as such, empirically, but because Kandinsky's art is permeated by a form-creating energy that arrives at such empirical facts by following its own

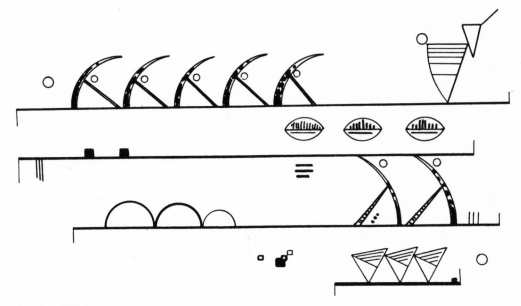

Drawing. 1931, 6

bent. Perhaps a certain cheerfulness or festive spirit predominated when Kandinsky created these paintings, just as fear may have been dominant when he painted the hallucinatory *Pointed Black* (1931, CC 389).

Dating from the same time are a number of paintings which almost inevitably suggest some sort of mechanical ballet, although the figurations are completely nonnaturalistic. Nevertheless, the mechanism of the dance is unmistakable, and occasionally takes on a grotesque quality. In *Two Black Stripes* (1930, CC 385), in *Moody* (1930, CC 383), and in many watercolors of 1930 and 1931, the dancing or the acrobatics is more striking than the setting in which they occur, i. e., than the sum of the other pictorial elements. The drawing No. 14 of 1932 can scarcely be understood otherwise than as a piece of clowning.

The titles of the paintings sometimes give a clue to the humorous element—this is the case with *Moody*. A number of paintings dating from 1929 to 1932 are obviously cheerful, humorous, or witty: *Jocular Sounds* (1929, CC 336), *Eight Times* (1929, CC 340), *Serious-Joke* (1930, CC 363), *Jolly* (1930, CC 392), *Both Striped* (1932, CC 416). Kandinsky was happy and successful at this epoch, sharing in his students' activities and amusements, and fond of motion pictures (Buster Keaton especially). The eight large rhomboid figures in *Eight Times,* which are aligned along a horizontal (string), like a family of eight, are droll; *Both Striped,* two ovals tapering upward, the smaller one yellow and red, the larger blue and green, suggest Pat and Patachon, without being anything but geometric forms. In *Jocular Sounds,* however, and in *Serious-Joke,* the humor lies in the arrangement as a whole, in the play of forms, the lightness of the structure, the rhythm, and the colors. In *Cold* (1929, CC 318), there is an amusing effect in the opposition between the two irritating main forms, and in the relation between the outline and the form inside. Kandinsky, as anyone who knew him can vouch, had a rich sense of humor and loved both to tell and to be told funny stories, so we should not be surprised to find humor in his art.

Humor has been defined as a metaphysical attitude toward the rational and the irrational, a definition that applies to Kandinsky. He does not rob the serious of its seriousness, and while he occasionally celebrates the accidental or "unnecessary," he does not abolish "inner necessity." Since the work process consists in the invention of forms, the psychic tensions that constitute humor result from discrepancies between expectation and actual event. In *Green Empty* the discrepancy is between the setting and anticipation of the scene and its nonoccurrence; in *Eight Times,* between the elaborate arrangement of eight figures and the fact that they are not really used. In another instance, humor derives from the sketching in, say of a Falstaff figure, and its sudden breaking off, its failure to be completed. It is as though the artist were saying: Look, I am sticking to my method even if you believe that I am telling you a story in twelve chapters—in *Levels* (1929, CC 307), for instance; but you can't read my hieroglyphics that way—they are pictorial signs, not words. Why didn't you look more carefully at the various reds on the bottle green ground? It may remind you of birds in an aviary, but it would be more natural to hear their voices raised in song.

A contrast to such works is provided by the black-and-white paintings produced between 1930 and 1932, to which Kandinsky attached particular importance. As early as the Blaue Reiter period he called attention to black and white as colors, and, encouraged by the success of an exhibition of black-and-white works arranged by Ferdinand Möller (Berlin, 1931), he wrote about their intense color values in a preface to a catalogue (Saarbrücken, 1931). He knew a dozen blacks and about as many whites, and many who looked at these pictures failed to notice the fact that they were "not in color." How carefully he worked at them can be seen from a drawing for *White on Black* (1930, CC 378; drawing No. 21, 1930, p. 217), a preliminary sketch that can be scarcely understood without further explanation. It contains the internal "magnetic fields" of the picture and looks like a kind of equation. When we see it in the finished painting, the graded juxtaposition of white squares, both large and small, suddenly makes sense as design. The conscientiously balanced weights result in a fugue-like structure whose main theme is defined by the four great squares. The black of the ground lies behind the picture plane, the white in front of it, but the sizes and positions of the squares imply movement from left to right and from front to back, giving the illusion of a fourth dimension. *Black-White* (1931, CC 404) meets the movement in space halfway, by means of its circle segments, and *White-Soft and Hard* (1932, CC 415; watercolor sketch, 1932, 8) by means of the flying forms at the right. *Lightly Touched* (1931, CC 405;

Drawing. 1932, 14

216

drawing No. 17, 1931), and two works extremely sparing in color, *Heavy and Light* (1930, CC 376) and *White* (1930, CC 361) are painted according to the same principle.

In addition, there are dozens of paintings of these years that cannot be grouped, because each expresses a distinct conception. Kandinsky was extremely fertile, exploring in every direction. Sometimes it was discontinuity that interested him, and he scattered his inventions without any apparent interrelation over the surface (*Isolated*, 1930, CC 382). At other times he was concerned with the problem of achieving stability through the inhibition of movement (*Stable*, 1931, CC 388; *Secure Position*, 1932, CC 412). At still other times, he was trying to conceive movement as movement (*Fixed Flight*, 1932, CC 411). He painted pictures in which a single color determines the character of the work (*Decisive Pink* 1932, CC 413), and nebulous pictures in which we look in vain for a dominant color (*Surfaces and Lines*, 1930, CC 369). The works of the Dessau years are characterized by incomparable richness, for all that they also have greater unity than the works of the Blaue Reiter period or those of the last years in Paris.

Drawing for White on Black.
1930, 21

If the Blaue Reiter period was romantic, the Bauhaus period was classical. Kandinsky himself described his Weimar works as "cool." The climate grows warmer in the Dessau pictures, and there is no sharp break between them and the first Paris pictures, for which they are a preparation.

The works executed between 1922 and 1933 are unequivocally severe and lucid, determined by number and measure, more graphic than pictorial, even disclosing a certain naturalism, a naturalism of mathematical forms. The revolution after the First World War had a cooling effect; romanticism was succeeded by its opposite, and by Surrealism, which is a kind of romanticism in reverse. Kandinsky could have salvaged his rich Munich experiences and incorporated them within his newer conceptions, despite a more self-conscious compositional technique; if he did this only very partially, it was because he knew that he had accomplished the tasks he set himself before, and that new tasks now faced him.

Intense creative periods cannot last long, and Kandinsky almost abruptly launched on a new path, on the basis of additional insights. Life is transformation of forms, but it is also permanence in change. Kandinsky for all his new insights and achievements remained Kandinsky; neither his intuition nor his inspiration deserted him. What happened was that the subjective element merged into the universal, and the result was a development toward objectivity. This does not transform art into science, as Flaubert had prophesied, nor does it quite confirm the words of Edgar Degas, who described painting as the result of "computing operations," calculations subtle and hard to formulate but nevertheless calculations. Kandinsky might have agreed with Degas, but he would have insisted on alloting a minimum five per cent to the role of intuition.

Although the term he used is "forms," he might more aptly have used that of "organisms," which, as in nature, develop according to structural laws from "inner necessity." And in both cases the lower forms are integrated into the higher ones. Perhaps this approach will make it easier for the viewer, faced with Kandinsky's almost unsurveyable richness of individual forms, to reduce them to a common denominator and to order them, i. e., to replace a vocabulary with a basic plan. Although there are primary forms out of which the higher develop, "the great difference nevertheless discloses the common striving," "their original identity." This process does not preclude "a guiding hand," i. e. rational work: bringing the parts together to form a whole, organizing the elements in co-operation with the artistic understanding. Kandinsky, it is true, felt that he must not hinder the free growth of details, but also that he must be concerned with the organization of the whole. Only in this way, he believed, do objective works arise, beings as independent as the works of nature. "Art, another nature, just as mysterious, but more understandable, for it springs from the understanding," Goethe said. The laws of art and nature, Kandinsky infers, will ultimately lead to understanding the laws of the world's composition. That is how he justified his point of departure, his belief that artistic creation is like the creation of the world.

It would be a hopeless undertaking to attempt a systematic ordering of the elements out of which Kandinsky formed the great organism of his art. We would soon be at a point beyond description. Only this much is evident, that he obtained his greatest tensions from opposing the geometric elements to the free, and, so to speak, living elements, and by this means arrived at more comprehensive higher forms. Even these are not his ultimate goal, however, for here color both of itself and in co-existence is also present. Other essential tensions were obtained by Kandinsky from opposing exact forms both flat and linear to deliberately inexact ones, complete forms to fragmentary forms, main forms to merely ornamental ones, organic amoeba-like elements to elements suggesting technology (serrated forms), static elements to dynamic, symbolic forms (cross) to everyday forms (ladder), and so on. In addition there are other contrasts, such as those between smooth and rough, transparent and opaque, full and empty, the one and the many (the number of centers), harmonious arrangements and unharmonious ones.

Color plays an essential part throughout. Kandinsky's sense of color aims at variety and nuance in the works of the Bauhaus period, and achieves a range of tones and harmonies which we cannot even begin to describe for lack of terms.

In contrast to earlier periods, the emotional and expressive character of color takes a subordinate place in these works, color no longer representing a psychic element, but becoming more than ever a thing, a quality in its own right. This is characteristic of the paintings of 1920s. However, as early as 1912 Kandinsky Saw that this independence of color, as well as the oppositions and contradictions created by combinations of color, were adequate for his purpose, This conviction grew stronger in the course of the years, and he was less and less preoccupied with color harmony, being in this regard as in others faithful to necessity. This necessity is expressed differently in each picture, and does not repeat itself; but there remain favorite "sounds," such as carmine pink and blue green, light sky blue, and egg yellow, whereas formerly the combination of steel-blue with gray and of vermilion red with lemon-yellow had been favored. Including intermediate tones and values, occasionally more than one hundred combinations are found in a painting. Each single tone, by its reciprocal relationships with the other tones, becomes a chord, giving rise to an endless variety.

"Constructivist" paintings like those of the Bauhaus period might be expected to follow a certain norm in the choice of colors and combinations of color. This expectation is only partially fulfilled. In *Composition VIII*, for instance, no single color could conceivably be replaced by another, yet it would be impossible to show why each circle has a different circle, or why the linear elements are in different blacks. Nevertheless a representative exhibition of the works of these years, such as was held at the Maeght gallery in Paris in 1953, does not produce an effect of heterogeneity; this would tend to show that the color chords used within a given period are interrelated. A room displaying paintings from the period 1911–1914 similarly strikes us as a self-contained whole with respect to color. However, "inner necessity" can no more be computed than genius; and Klee's definition of genius as "a flaw in the system" may also be applied to Kandinsky's "inner necessity," which is a mystery that is only to a slight degree accessible to logic.

It might be supposed that the spatial relationships in the works of 1920s can be reduced to system, in view of the precision that characterized them. But here, too, it is hard to arrive at demonstrable results. As early as 1912 Kandinsky spoke of both picture surface and ideal plane in terms of swelling and tapering lines, overlappings, and the projection and interpolation of colors as a means of representing space. In *Point and Line to Plane* he discusses a new feeling of space, which requires the viewer "to become active and to experience the pulsation of the painting with all his senses." Until 1914 the abstract works had contained general elements that enabled the viewer to associate freely, to evoke psychological and poetic ideas. In the works of the Bauhaus period the viewer is guided more strictly, obliged to keep to the technical compositional indications if he would avoid arbitrary interpretation. The picture space is filled with elements in tension that seem always to have existed, and that we, the viewers, are merely running across for the first time. This picture space surrounds us on all sides, for it seems to have no center. It is scarcely possible to distinguish between the spatial and the temporal, for everything is movement and in movement toward movement. We are "in the central organ of all spatial-temporal movement, which governs all functions" (Klee). Kandinsky is as sensitive to space as he is to forms and colors, and it is only the concept of inner necessity that saves us from the embarrassment of charting the spatio-temporal scheme.

Drawing. 1932, 12

These works have been called "architectural"; but are they really? In his 1914 lecture, Kandinsky said: "I scattered the weights in such a manner that no architectonic center was visible." But Kandinsky was still talking about "the centers" of his paintings much later, and centers are certainly there; but does this suffice to make the paintings "architectural"? They are certainly tectonic, though there are exceptions. *Composition VIII* has three centers of gravity; of these the black circle is only relatively tectonic; the blue angle at the left and the checkered angle at the upper right might be so in relation to the many triangles, circles, and half circles. However, it is easier to find one's way in *Composition VIII* than in *Yellow-Red-Blue*, where the left side with its angular geometric forms is firmly anchored, while the right side with the transparent free forms and the blue circle is not. The contrast produces a fluctuating balance, which is however steadied by the cloudy bluish tone at the lower left edge. No matter

21

how closely we follow the artist, and experience the picture's rhythms with every sense alert, we nevertheless feel ourselves on firmer ground in the left half than in the intensely dynamic zone at the right. However, this feeling relates to only one component of the painting, namely, to structure. There are other components to be considered, the color relations, the forms, the accents (staccato at the left, legato at the right), the "melodies" (the black curve leading to the arc and the circles). Multidimensional simultaneity cannot be formulated in words, unless the total phenomenon Kandinsky were to be analyzed from a single painting. Even then many questions would be left unanswered, with Kandinsky's full agreement, for he never prescribed the details of the viewer's experience. We can now understand his aversion for "poetic" titles and his predilection for bare characterizations. *Yellow-Red-Black* can be interpreted in various ways: we can focus on the experience of space, or on the over-all harmony of the colors, or, under ideal circumstances, on the multidimensionality of the full conception. It is not impossible that we should find discontinuity persisting among the ultimate formal problems. If so, time would be transformed "from an extended measurable dimension into an element of intensity with effects that cannot be determined in advance" (Gebser). This definition seems to apply to the works of the Bauhaus period.

Occasionally a kind of veil lies over these paintings, through which we now glimpse and now lose sight of their wealth of levels and hidden depths, their interlocking, inexplicable qualities. To the extent that the unintelligible element cannot be explained, that this element is not the painting itself, the latter approaches the status of symbol. Kandinsky's subsequent development in Paris will follow this direction.

VI The Paris Years

A Writings and Travels

1933-1944

Kandinsky's first impression of Paris was that of a city to work in. All his other problems—finding a place to live and work, earning a living, making new friends—paled before this certitude. Klee was now in Bern, Feininger in Berlin, Jawlensky in Wiesbaden. Nearly all Kandinsky's friends and collectors were still in Germany, although a few of the most influential and helpful were in Switzerland and in America. He now depended on America, for the French scarcely knew or understood him. The only one who helped was Christian Zervos, publisher of the *Cahiers d'art,* at No. 14 Rue du Dragon. In October 1933, Kandinsky moved into a hotel in the Rue des Saints-Pères, near by, and began to look for an apartment. He found a suitable one with three rooms in Neuilly, at No. 135 Boulevard de la Seine, on the sixth floor, with a view on Mont Valérien, only a few steps from the Bois de Boulogne. The Bois would remind him of his country surroundings in Weimar and Dessau, and it was there he always took his walks. The largest room of the apartment became his studio; as there was not much space, he had also to store his works and install his desk there. He leased the place for one year only, because he was unsure of political developments in Germany. "We are not leaving Germany for good—I couldn't do that; my roots are too deep in German soil" (to the author, December 4, 1933). Nevertheless, he furnished his apartment with great care, making the tiny dining room look exactly like the one in Dessau, and whatever old furniture and mementos he had been able to keep he installed in the small drawing room.

Kandinsky had to economize; although he had reduced his prices, he sold few paintings. In his letters at this time, he never failed to mention his success at exhibitions or with sales. In most cases, he had only "moral successes"—"the only kind of morality to be found in the world today" (letter to the author). He comforted himself with the reflection that art was in an economic slump everywhere in the world.

The French painters were having a better time of it, however. Most of them had permanent contracts and collectors who kept on buying, while the Germans, intimidated by Nazi policies with regard to art, had stopped collecting. Kandinsky tried to make contacts with Paris artists, but they kept aloof from the foreigner. His art seemed to them very Russian and problematic. Significantly, it was with foreigners that he most easily became acquainted, with Miró, Mondrian, Chagall, Magnelli, Max Ernst, Brancusi, and Pevsner. Among the French, he found the most candid artists to be Léger, Arp, and Delaunay. They didn't "strike poses." "It was very pleasant at Léger's yesterday, and I was very much impressed by him—he is definitely a man with sound roots, from which his art, original and vigorous, grows organically." He saw a good deal of Arp and Sophie Täuber-Arp, as well as Magnelli. Among "the younger artists," he was most impressed by Miró. "This little man who always paints large canvases is a real little volcano, constantly erupting paintings. Fabulous strength and energy" (letter to the author, December 2, 1935). He of course met many other painters at openings, but few such meetings led to closer acquaintance; after all he was nearly seventy, and in old age, as he wrote more than once, old friendships matter more than new ones. He was more impressed by exhibitions of earlier art down to Cézanne than by those of modern painters; at the same time he felt the lack of young talents to carry on his own ideas. This was to come about only after his death. When the Second World War broke out, and the Germans had invaded France, many of his colleagues left Europe. Léger, Chagall, and Mondrian went to America, Arp to Switzerland. Kandinsky, however, stayed in France; in 1941, he refused to leave his new home to which he had become attached. He did get away from Paris for two months shortly after the entry of the Germans, staying at Cauterets (Hautes Pyrénées). After that trip he traveled no more, the French capital compensating for all his privations, including the fact that he could not go to concerts or to the theater; he gave up all social life.

Prior to 1939, he took several summer holidays with his wife, and traveled to attend his own exhibitions. In 1933 he went to Les Sablettes (Var), in 1934 to Normandy (Le Home, Calvados), in 1935 to Napoule near Cannes, in 1936 to Forte dei Marmi (Pisa and Florence), in 1937 he went to an exhibition in Bern, where he also visited the sick Klee, and in the summer of that year to Brittany (Carnac Plage). In 1938 he stayed near Aix-les-Bains and spent that summer in St. Jean-Cap Ferrat (Alpes Maritimes), and in 1939 went to La Croix (Var). Everywhere he enjoyed with youthful enthusiasm the beauty of the landscape and the sea, the light and the colors. He rested on his holidays, working hard right up to the day of departure and resuming work the moment he was back in Paris.

He was gratified to exhibit, of course, but every such occasion meant hard work, for he had no dealer to take care of the practical details for him. He had many invitations from Stockholm, Milan, London, and New York (see Bibliography). Unfortunately, the political situation prevented him from taking advantage of this increasingly worldwide recognition. With the outbreak of war, the art world came to a standstill. Kandinsky worked in complete seclusion in Neuilly, hoping that he might live to see the end of the catastrophe and a better future.

During his Paris years, Kandinsky wrote more than a dozen articles of varying length for periodicals, and prefaces to catalogues, portfolios, and so on (cf. Bibliography). Again and again, he returned to the problem of abstract art and its cultural justification. He was well aware of the resistance it still encountered: skepticism about the absence of the object, about standards of appreciation. He was tireless in his efforts

Relations. 1934, 604 ▶

to prove what cannot, after all, be proved, what can only be experienced. He repeated himself in his arguments, examples, and quotations at this time, but—particularly in answers to direct questions—he often expressed himself more clearly and persuasively than before: as when, referring to the *douanier* Rousseau (who had more than once said that "the voice of his dead wife" was the guiding thread of his artistic activities) he reformulated "inner necessity" as "inner dictation." For the artistic "crisis" he chiefly blames the viewer's inability to grasp nature and the world as a whole, his tendency to fasten on pictorial details, his unwillingness to see with the eyes of his own epoch, instead of with those of the past, his imprisonment in "matter" and his inability to see the "unreal," which is "true reality."

Certain passages are well worth quoting. "Man cannot renounce his milieu, but he can emancipate himself from the object." Just as the musician can compose a sunrise without using the sound of the crowing cock, so the painter can paint a morning with purely pictorial means. "This morning—rather, the whole of nature, life, the whole world surrounding the artist, as well as the life of his soul—is the only source of his art." Reality and dream create the work. The purpose remains unconscious, in order that the painter's interest can be turned to form ("Today's art is more alive than ever," 1935). Elsewhere Kandinsky speaks of the inward view and of perceiving the interrelationships between great and small. A work's structure is not dictated by fragments of nature, but "by the totality of natural laws governing the cosmos." ("Two Currents," 1935.) The world as a whole is the content of abstract art, which Kandinsky would prefer to call "real" art, for it creates a real world. The future belongs to this "real" art, for it is the only "current" that has remained contemporary ("Abstract Painting," 1935). It alone has "the ability and energy to say what life necessarily passes over in silence." His painting, he says, is not a special language. He has merely freed painting from irrelevant "noises." Once the true form has been brought out, it takes care of the content, for in the last analysis the content of painting is painting. He is not dismayed when a natural form slips in, for "Who can tell, perhaps our [abstract] forms are natural forms, though they are never objects of daily use." ("Approach to Art," 1937.) His aim is not to create "fantastic objects," but to create "the pure pictorial fairytale" out of "the material reality of the pictorial means." And he refers to these in almost poetic terms: "A black circle—a distant thunder, a self-contained world seemingly unconcerned for all else, a withdrawal inward, an on-the-spot conclusion, a slowly and coolly uttered, 'I am here'." And all these voices together compose a great polyphony. ("Empty Canvas," 1935.) Time and again he emphasized the synthesis of head and heart, the importance of intuition, inner dictation. We may be reminded of Brückner's statement that the adagio of one of his symphonies was suggested to him by God in a dream.

Two essays of 1938 discuss the expression "concrete art," which Theo van Doesburg had launched in 1930, and which was taken up later by Arp and Max Bill. Every new work expresses a new world, adding an artistic world to the natural world, a world just as real, just as concrete. "I prefer the term, 'concrete art' to that of 'abstract art'." ("Abstract or Concrete," 1938.) Kandinsky had long regarded the term "abstract" as being too negative, and his painting at this time is "concrete" rather than "abstract."

Two Green Points. ▶
1935, 616

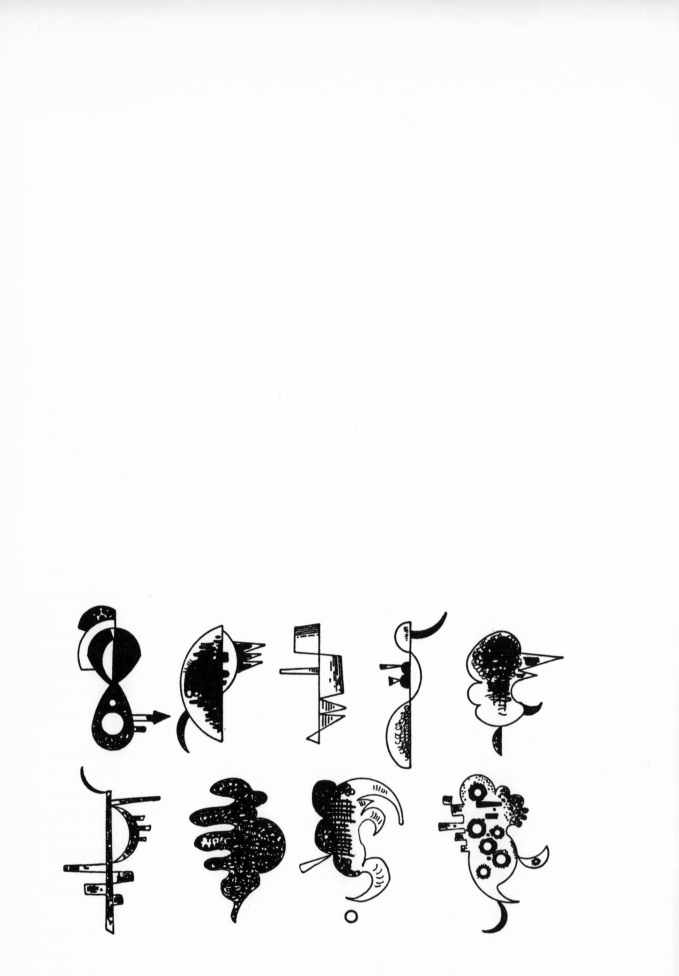

Drawing for Each for Itself. 1934

B The New Conception

Kandinsky had painted his last work in Germany—*Development in Brown*—in August 1933. He resumed work in Paris in February 1934. He was to enjoy eleven more years, and during them, he produced 144 paintings. Between 1934 and 1941 he painted 208 watercolors and gouaches; he produced one more in 1944. From 1940 on, the watercolors have no titles. They are scarcely less intense than the paintings, but they scarcely represent a major change in Kandinsky's art. Many were sold because they were less expensive than the paintings, a consideration of some importance during these troubled years. A large number of them are fairly accurate preliminary studies for paintings. Kandinsky produced drawings until 1944, but fewer than in Dessau: two only in 1935, twenty-seven in 1939, and seven in 1944, the year of his death. Many of these are sketches for paintings or watercolors.

The first Paris painting, interestingly enough, is called *Start*. After some months of not working, Kandinsky felt rested, and was full of youthful optimism, for all his sixty-seven years. We feel the zest of the Paris climate, as well as the passion with which he made a fresh start. The calm solemnity of which he writes in his essay "Empty Canvas" is not yet perceptible. This and the other canvases painted in Paris are works of old age, but more in the sense of a last maturity than of a last effort.

The works of the Paris years have been described as expressing a superior synthesis; in Kandinsky's language, this would mean that they reflect a union of head and heart, of compositional technique and intuition, but also a branching out toward other sensory experiences, particularly toward music, and even a symbiotic relationship with scientific thinking—the latter, after all, also originates in "the central organ of all spatio-temporal movement." It is even more difficult to group the works of the last years than those of the preceding ones, and if we introduce a break in 1940, it is more for convenience than for any other reason. Thus we will treat the works of the war years separately from those of 1934–1940, as a "last period."

The non-European, Russian or Asiatic splendor of the colors in the Paris paintings is the most striking thing about them. In any Kandinsky exhibition showing works from different periods, this is what everyone notices. It is not the individual color, but their total effect that conveys something of the spirit of Moscow as Kandinsky described it, something of the spirit of the East. In design, these works have subtle relationships to icons; the divisions of the paintings are related to the contrast between the large and the small forms. The epic breadth of the horizontal canvases is reminiscent of the Chinese paintings on rolls, and the passionate curves of the surging waves in Chinese or Japanese pictures. And in both cases we are tempted to look for deeper meanings. The spirit of cheerful mastery breathes in the Paris paintings, bringing to mind Goethe's *West-östlicher Divan*. Even the last ones contain no trace of melancholy. Unlike Klee, Kandinsky had no premonition of his end.

The year 1934 produced works in which we perceive echoes of old themes alongside new ones. There are no more emphatically "Constructivist" paintings. *Graceful Ascent* (March 1934, CC 433) is severe in structure, but the delicacy of the lines and the enamel colors (pink, light green, light brown) bring to mind jester's bells or spring in Paris. The same contrast between severity of structure and delicacy of color characterizes *Blue World* (1934, CC 437), on a Mignonette green ground with fluttering forms. For the first time, Kandinsky has added fine sand to his oil paint, a procedure he will employ more and more often to differentiate between color planes and individual forms. The paintings thereby acquire both materiality and something of the quality of Chinese embroidery on silk. Seven of the fifteen paintings of 1934 use this technique, including *Dominant Violet,* first in the series of works featuring flying forms and swinging curves. The three principal pictures in this group are *Balancing Act* (1935, p. 306), *Rigid and Bent* (1935, CC 451), and *Dominant Curve* (1936, color plate p. 231), all of them in the Solomon R. Guggenheim Museum. The two Arp-like forms in *Balancing Act* will occur quite frequently in later works. In many of these contexts they suggest Matisse's leaf forms; they are developments of Kandinsky's amoeba forms of 1913. The whiplash line on the light blue ground is familiar to us from earlier paintings and drawings, having appeared for the first time in *Composition D* of 1913, but it was never before this used with such magistral cheerfulness. In *Rigid and Bent* the form is doubled and has become two figures winding around each other; in *Dominant Curve,* the largest and richest of these works, the broadly designed curve dominates its surroundings like some exotic creature its native forests or temple stairs. The small hieroglyphic forms are like inscriptions on the larger figures. There is a tablet with signs at the upper left, and three black circles at the upper right, which serve as a poetic and technological accent, conveying an impression of Baroque strangeness. After the romantic chords of the Blaue Reiter period and the classical ones of the Bauhaus period, we now encounter these chords of Baroque richness. *Center with Accompaniment* (1937, color plate, p. 239) has tiny forms which swarm like living creatures over the rectangles and the bright ground, in the most varied color tones, held together by the grandiosely curved main form. Another rich painting is *Composition IX* (1936, color plate, p. 229). In it, the dominant curve shrinks, so to speak, to a heart-shaped form toward which the fluttering smaller ones are attracted. The four diagonal stripes are blue, red, and yellow, their countless gradations in tone creating unusual, constantly mounting tensions. The pink on the light green at the right strikes a different chord than the

Composition IX. ▶
1936, 626

same pink on the egg-yellow at the left. The rhythm of the linear elements is free and infinitely varied.

The bipartite division is a frequent compositional device in the works of these years, the division being nearly always into equal parts, for instance in *Triangles* (1936, CC 457). The two halves, however, have a completely different scheme of composition and color. In *Two* the heraldic objectivity of the two Asiatic "flags," light blue on black, and black on white, respectively, is relieved only by the two simple bent lines, opposed to each other, which reach over the line of separation like samurai swords. *Penetrating Green* (1938, CC 470) on cloudy violet of varying intensities brings together the two diverging mollusc-like creatures by means of a fine network of lines and repetition of the forms. *In Between* (1934, p. 303), however, shows the central twin forms set one against the other. The result is almost always concord, and the painting *Unanimity* (1939, CC 481) is divided in a particularly obvious way. Two times two does not invariably come to four in art, as Kandinsky once observed, and in the last analysis *Two Surroundings* (1934, p. 304) and *Red Knot* (1936, CC 456) are also divided into halves, held in balance by means of color values and mediating linear elements. A small emerald-green form can very well balance the carmine-rose form three times its size thanks to the arrangement of the various other forms. Kandinsky added the word "ambiguity" in parenthesis to the title of *Complex-Simple* (1939, CC 477), thus underlining his awareness of the ambivalence of the figures, outwardly so different, but inwardly so closely related.

It is not easy to decide whether *Composition X* (1939, color plate, p. 241), a painting nearly two yards in width, belongs with this group. Certainly the two main forms are related to each other in the contradictory relation of loose to firm, or of warm to cold; at the left the inner forms are pictorial signs, and at the right they are ribbons or bands. The dark violet ground encompasses the figures, none of which touches the edge. This is now the case with nearly all the paintings: the pictorial elements are allowed to float freely in every direction and on the colored ground. They are spatially localizable only in so far as depth is occasionally indicated by overlapping and transparency.

Several large works of these years are scarcely inferior in intensity or in compositional technique to *Composition X. Clear Tensions* (May 1937, CC 462) is a delicate painting consisting of transparent trellis forms in light green with one red accent; *Multiple Forms* (1936, CC 453) is just as loose and as full of verve, but made more mysterious by the presence of a dark ground. *The Good Contact* (1938, CC 468) with its odd wheel form, which we will encounter again in *Band with Rectangles* (1944), and with its checkered area and the fluttering "flag," its snail form and the bent line suggesting an animal, is a kind of ballad celebrating the adventures of weird "thing-like" creatures.

Black Points (1937, p. 310), like *Red Circle* (1939, p. 313), is a painting apart. It looks quite Chinese with its rocklike points and figures. The mottled dots and the parallel bent lines at the lower right are possibly a last reminiscence of the reclining couple.

Few pictures of this period are tectonic. *Two Green Points* (1935, color plate, p. 225; watercolor study 1934, 535), a large horizontal canvas with a light ground, displays figurations inscribed in rectangles which overlap transparently at the left. But this structure of suspended planes cannot be called severe, for the two green dots (for which Kan-

Dominant Curve ▶
1936, 631

dinsky named the painting) inject ambiguity into the composition, areas of which have been made grainy by the addition of sand. Quite different in effect is *Fragile Fixed* (1934, CC 439), in which the familiar leaf forms are used like figures in some temple frieze or like oval masks decorating a proscenium. The whole looks like a design for an early Greek temple, although no detail in itself suggests such an interpretation. But such associations will now become more frequent. *Animated Stability* (1937, p. 312) with its rectangles clearly suggests a mechanical structure, anchored in the violet circle at the right.

Movement (1935, p. 308) is generally interpreted as representing stars and banks of clouds, and the scattered dots on the green ground and on the cloudlike red, violet, and gray green patches, do encourage such an association. But there are also other forms—circles, squares, and polygons—that look like astronomical figures, and all the formal elements are directed upward. Also open on all sides is *Relations* (1934, color plate, p. 223), although this composition on a white pink ground is filled with metamorphic forms, with geometric, arabesque-like, and zoomorphic structures that might be living creatures in some imaginary world. One is reminded of birds' heads and swimming creatures, of the bird-fish motive of Amerasian art, and of the Siberian animal style (with which Kandinsky must have been familiar). The use of sand, the sharp setting off of the intensely colored elements against the ground, the use of enamel-like colors—all this evokes the nomadic style, which began in the Altai region in the first millennium B.C.

In *Variegated Black* (1935, CC 447), a great many figurations arranged like constellations are set off against an irregularly dark ground, like islands on the surrounding sea. Similarly, *Many-colored Ensemble* (1938, CC 469) and *Environment* (1936, color plate, p. 233) are islands in the oceans of imaginary worlds, the first thickly strewn with colorful pearls and archaic forms of life, the second filled loosely with stony structures.

The search for variety of forms and at the same time for a firm unifying order leads Kandinsky to create paintings divided into horizontal or vertical strips, or into nine, twelve, fifteen, or thirty quadrilateral fields. This gives rise to charming and lovely compositions. *Striped* (1934, p. 305) and *Succession* (1935, p. 307) tell stories in rich arabesque forms, the first in vertical, the second in horizontal arrangement. *Striped* might well have been painted after a stay at the seaside, for it has star fish, sea horses, snails, creeping plants, and the colors which have been mixed with sand run from ocher tones, through red brown and orange to dull blue and blue-green. *Succession* develops its forms out of the arabesque and the jagged leaf, which, here as elsewhere, approach human and animal forms. The divisions of *Division Unity* (1934, CC 440) are arranged diagonally. The picture might be a recollection of the painted ceiling in the Omayyad palace at Quseir Amra. *Thirty* (1939, CC 460) is filled with purely geometric forms, *Sweet Trifles* (1937, p. 235) shows zoomorphic and abstract forms. *Fifteen*, a gouache of a kind frequently painted from 1938 on, was used by the Gobelins factory at Aubusson as a model for a rug (as were three other gouaches—1923, 69; 1939, 633, and 1940, 642). These are modern designs which, in abstract and metamorphic language, give the illusion of a world as open as that of music. The illusion is most

Environment. ▶
1936, 633

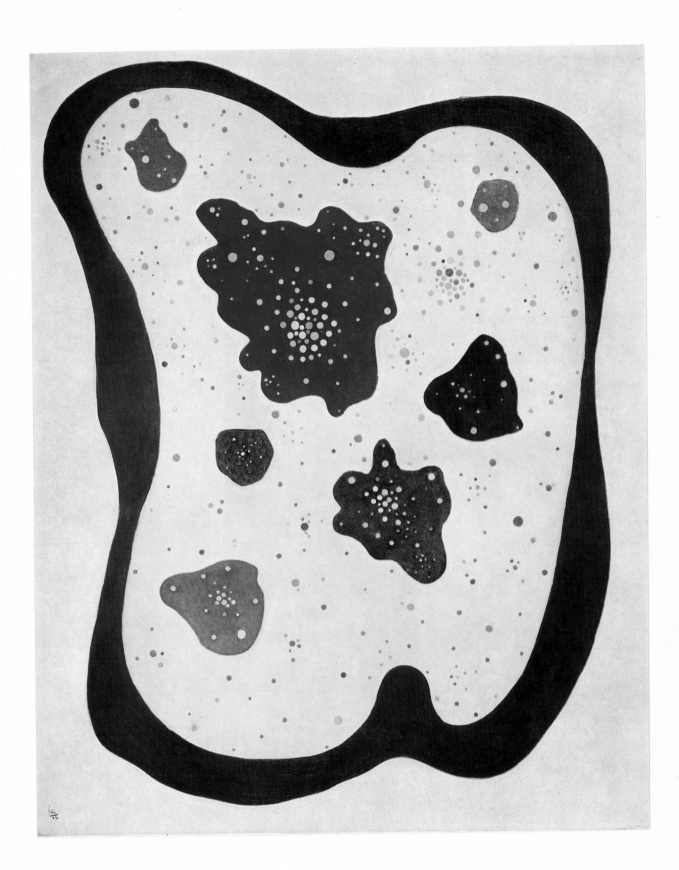

plausible in the relevant drawings, such as 1939, 7 and 1939, 16, the latter a preliminary sketch for *Sky Blue* (p. 236).

It was in the conviction that he was creating a "concrete art," opposing a purer reality to the given reality, that Kandinsky painted such works as *Green Figure* (1936, CC 454) and *One Figure Among Others* (1939, p. 314). The latter is a kind of dance scene with a tall "figure" in the blue green area at the left and with large and small signs, which might have been taken from a puppet show. A notable gaiety animates the dancing, a gaiety of gestures, such as also characterizes the circus-like picture that Kandinsky titled *Serenity* (1938, CC 473). It is hard to explain how such associations arise, or why *Capricious Forms* (1937, CC 463) suggests dragon heads and snake-like creatures, or why *Elan* (1939, CC 478) and *Cheerfulness* (1939, CC 483) suggest, respectively, a stage scene with a man-bird, and a vista glimpsed through a gateway. The individual forms are pure inventions, and yet the whole does constitute a reality; this reality has nothing in common with our habitual experience and yet it does have the effect of carrying it on at another level. This starry sky is not the starry sky, these animals are not real animals, this theater is not a real theater, and so on. There is no relation to the completed forms of nature, but there are definite analogies to their laws of growth and organization.

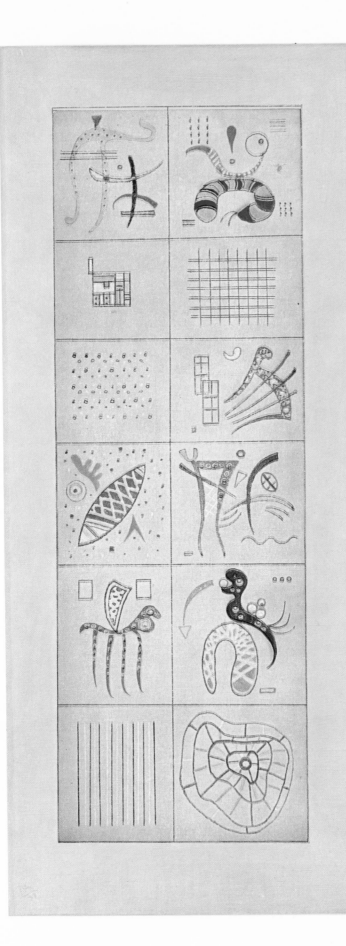

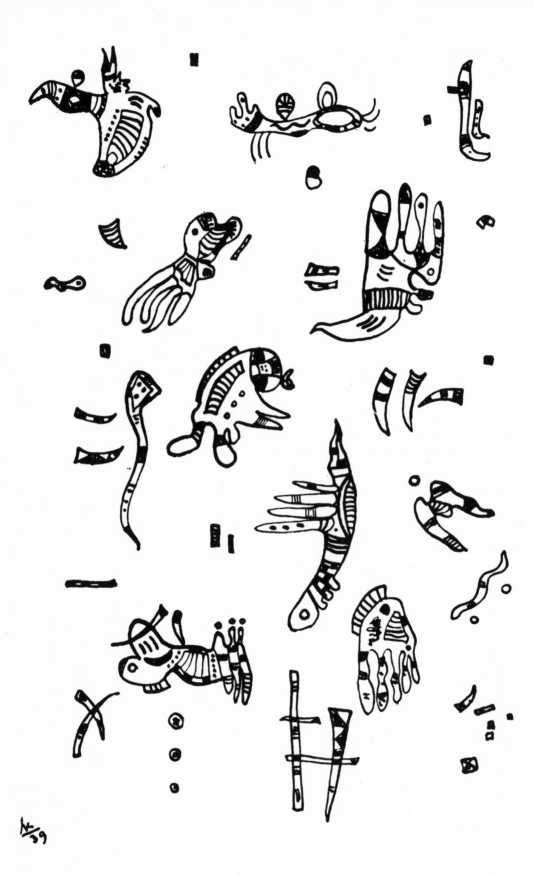

Drawing for Sky Blue. 1939, 16

C The Last Years

The last five years, from 1940 to December 1944 were nothing if not difficult ones, but the restlessness and tragedy of the period are not manifest in the paintings of these years. Similarly, during the First World War and during the Russian revolution, Kandinsky's works did not reflect what was going on outside the studio. Kandinsky lived in a different world, as he always had, keeping himself informed about all that was happening, but taking from the outside world only what he needed and reshaping it in his art.

Down to the middle of 1942 Kandinsky continued to paint quite large canvases, but after that produced only small works on wood or cardboard, the most frequent dimensions being 22¾ × 16½". His supplies were dwindling, and it became impossible to obtain large canvases. He prepared his own paints. With these last works he did not create fundamentally new conceptions, but he went to the limits of communicability within the existing ones, exploring ever more exhaustively the sphere of the symbolic. For many of these works he made preliminary drawings or watercolors, most of the latter in 1942, but he painted others without preliminary studies.

Drawing. 1939, 3

Paintings that are still tectonic, like *Light Construction* (1940, CC 488) suggest musical instruments rather than machines; the later *Netting* (1942, CC 510) and *Thin Threads* (1943, CC 524) are looms of the imagination drawn on air. The fanlike compositions of 1943, *Fanlike* (CC 513) and *Two Rays* (CC 522)—a continuation of *Light Tension* of 1935 (CC 445)—are delightful Chinoiseries, a sort of playing at cards; *Darkness* (p. 326) translates flatness into roundness, and the result is a festival of lanterns.

The great compositions executed between 1940 and 1942—*Ensemble* (1940, p. 315), *Various Parts* (1940, p. 316), *Around the Circle* (two versions, 1940, p. 317 and CC 489), *Various Actions* (1941, p. 319), *Round Accent* (1942, CC 497), *Reciprocal Accord* (1942, color plate p. 243), and *Delicate Tensions,* the last large canvas (1942, CC 499)—are of the greatest vigor. Every one deserves the title "Composition" which Kandinsky used so sparingly. *Ensemble* (preliminary drawing 1940, 12, and gouache 1940, 534) is, like *Various Parts,* composed of rectangular fields of unequal size, within which Kandinsky records the pictorial action. The central field of *Ensemble* is like the structure for a high-wire trapeze act, and arrows point out the direction the acrobats are to take. *Various Parts* is more capricious, suggesting a country fair in the style of the early Stravinsky. The colors are Russian; in the central field they are raspberry pink on pale Mignonette green, dark green, and a bit of violet accented with vermilion; the field below is of the palest violet, while to the left is a dull light brown and to the right a bright purple. This particular color harmony had never before appeared in Western art. The forms suggest inflated flying animals and tiny figures, with more abstract elements in the brown field. *Around the Circle* (the two version differ very little) throws together burlesque forms in a kaleidoscopic jumble on a black and green ground, with only a red circle for point of support. *Various Actions* with its blue-green ground and carmine red accents is the most Russian of all these paintings. The jagged hanging leaf-forms produce a falling rhythm, while the graphic elements between the flat forms produce a rising one. It happens to have been painted in September, and it does have the quality of a sunny autumn morning, recalling Kandinsky's earliest landscapes in the Akhtyrka Park just outside Moscow. That recollections of the past should emerge in the seventy-five-

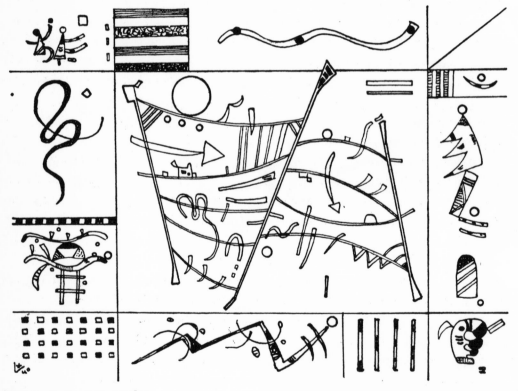

Drawing for Ensemble. 1940, 12

year-old artist is only normal, but we may note that the memory is far more intense and Slavic than the reality was. We may recall the Firebird and the native folklore, but this extraordinary mastery of composition is the result of decades in Europe. In *Reciprocal Accord* (1942, color plate, p. 243) and *Round Accent* (1942, CC 497; drawing 1942, 8) Kandinsky still pursues his explorations, but now they are more secure and more sensitive; in both, black is set against the most delicate greens, pinks, and light blues.

Center with ▶
Accompaniment.
1937, 641

There are also more fan paintings and paintings divided into rectilinear fields, although the fields now vary in size and accents, and are filled with zoomorphic creatures—exotic birds or fishes. They might represent primal stages of growth, from which almost anything could develop (*Division-Unity*, 1943, color plate, p. 245; *Seven*, 1943, p. 324, drawing 1943, 1; *Five Parts*, 1944, CC 527). *A Conglomerate* (1943, p. 327) shows the fields in a golden yellow table, a kind of easel, which is in turn set off against a freely contoured blue area. The fields present a great variety of scenes, including a large hand, a puppet, and two seated figures.

Figurations that involve a concrete idea are now frequent in the paintings as well as in the drawings and watercolors. Where the latter have not been given titles by the artist (from 1940 on) we often find that their owners have given them names such as *Little Boats* or *Paper Dragon*. Kandinsky was more reserved on this score, but he called one such painting *Fluttering Figure* (1942, CC 500; drawing 1942, 12), and the impression it makes does justify the title. Elsewhere he prefers to call a Ferris wheel with puppet-like figures, *Junctions* (1942, CC 508), and a penguin-like figure with a tight rope act *Balancing* (1942, CC 496), and loosely stretched wires with small forms on them, *Little Accents* (1940, CC 486). *Sky Blue* (1940, CC 487; drawing 1939, 16) is a captivating painting on a blue ground with figurations that might be called "Scenes of Childhood"; *Reduced Contrasts* (1941, p. 318; watercolor 1941, 721) is a ballet scene consisting of three large and two small figures, and a chimaera-like creature at the left under the gray-green moon; *Circle and Square* (1943, color plate, p. 247) shows five actors performing in an exotic theater constructed, like the dancing figures in *Reduced Contrasts,* of free forms and triangles. *Three Variegated Figures* (1942, p. 320; drawing 1942, 11) shows three differently characterized figures; the oval of the central head is beflagged, some sort of parade is going on. Once again, the pictorial elements in these works do not in the slightest resemble previously known forms, but they are so constructed as inevitably to suggest these associations. In *Accord* (1943, p. 323) we imagine we are looking at the heads of mammoths, although the two jagged main forms derive from the jagged leaf. In *Fragments* (1943, p. 325) a very similar form lies on a blue-black ground as in a grave, around which is set a mosaic of brightly colored stones. This mosaic has three small hollows in it with hieroglyphlike offerings to the dead, and the whole is surrounded by a violent brown border. Forebodings?

A number of Kandinsky's last works treat the subject of flying or climbing. In *Dusk* (1943, CC 520) the seed forms rising toward the upper right detach themselves effortlessly from their confinement. *White Figure* (1943, p. 321) has the effect of a nightmare, the bright flying figure in *Arrow* (1943, p. 322) that of a solemn promise. *White Balancing Act* (1944, CC 530) was interpreted as a "die and be reborn," the longish creatures being contrasted with the dark round ones and unlike them, victorious over gravitation. *Band with Squares* (1944, p. 328) is very mysterious with its black ground, the fiery red wheel at the top, the blue exclamation mark, and the iridescent head of a bird at the upper left; it is pictorial writing of a mystical character, for there exist no objects corresponding to them. The ladder, too, is no ladder, but rather a religious idea, pointing to something sacred. The figure in *Brown Impetus* (1943, CC 517) is a spiritual bird, a

Composition X. ▶
1939, 655

symbol of the Holy Ghost, in Christian terms; and Kandinsky's last painting, *Tempered Elan* (1944, color plate, p. 249) shows a flying figure, not unlike an angel, at the upper left, over the large border that separates the upper region with its starlike squares from the lower one with the zoomorphic forms. This figure occupies the same place as the angel in Rembrandt's *Sacrifice of Manoah*, which was Kandinsky's first and most overwhelming experience of art. The dull violet of the picture surface suggests gentle grief, and the muffled browns and blues of the other forms do not work against the violet.

In a tribute to Kandinsky written on the occasion of an exhibition in San Francisco (1931), the painter Diego Rivera observed that Kandinsky's art is not a reflection of life, but life itself; that he is the most realistic of painters because his works contain everything that exists plus his own discoveries, and that they foreshadow the advent of a new universal order. With these words an artist whose work is very different from Kandinsky's expressed a great truth. To be sure, Kandinsky repeatedly pointed out that abstract art can express more than nonabstract art, and that the future belongs to it, but what he called "abstract" does not denote the life of the forms, but life—and not life here and now, but a new order in the universe, a new reality.

In a letter to the author Kandinsky used the term "pure realism" in speaking of abstract painting. He said of it that it leaves the conventional realism of objective painting far behind. And this art, he went on to say, is situated "outside space and time" (April 3, 1933). The reader will recall his earlier references to a "nonperspective" world and a new kind of time, in which past, present, and future dissolve into the transparency of the ages. Every comparison with the accidental stages of being is to be eliminated, and we are led on to total visions. Kandinsky might have used here the term "synthesis."

The whole man radiates in the works of his last years. Kandinsky speaks out of the innermost depths of consciousness, and creates analogies to the world as a whole in the language which he invented and developed, a language which renounces ties with the visible, but not with limitless reality. The late paintings are echoes of a transparent and transitory world, which we may think we recognize, but which eludes us when we try to grasp it. The painter's work has become a kind of participation in the universal process. The pictorial elements keep the initiative, and when analogies arise—we have very frequently noted them—they always point to a higher world. What we are confronted with is not dragons or people, but potential figurations, whose form, rhythm, and color polyphonically produce a highly plausible original myth. So long as we remain aware of the distance between the two worlds, we may relate this myth to our own memories and ideas. *Russian Country Fair* pointed the direction in which the "other" was to be sought, for the painter's world, too, contained both familiar, human things, and things infinitely remote.

Space and time are incorporated in this myth and cannot be separated from "the objects." The spatio-temporal relationships are dominated by simultaneity and multi-dimensionality. Everything is present at once. We must imagine a continuum, within which events cannot be localized in time or in space, or an inner cosmic space within

Reciprocal Accord. ▶
1942, 687

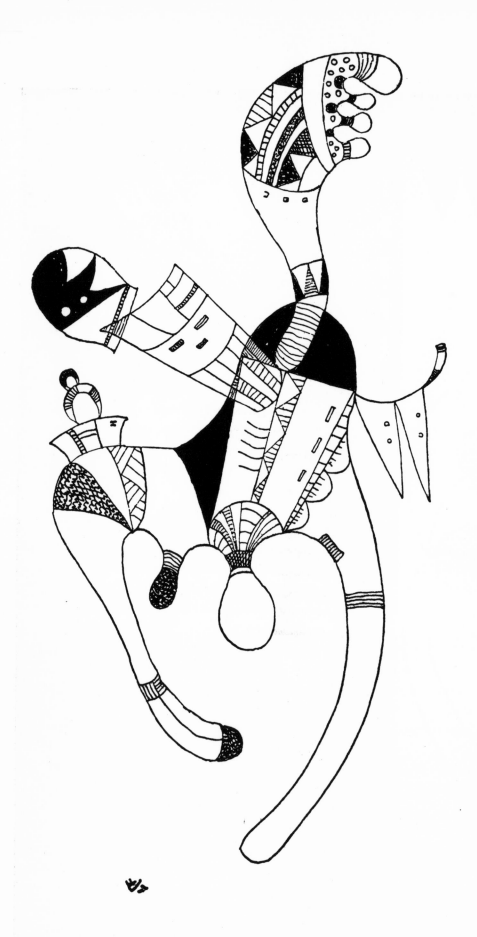

which everything is open to everything else. However that may be, in the Paris paintings the colorful figurations are to space and time what the positive is to the negative; we might say that the two factors condition each other. This is the source of that notable repose which Kandinsky himself felt to be characteristic of his late works.

It may be assumed that his mental and racial kinship to Asia contributed to the character of Kandinsky's forms and composition, and probably also to his symbolism. The writer stressed this point in the Kandinsky issue of *Cahiers d'art* (1930), Possibly the relationships are less direct than I supposed at the time (circle, trellis, fan forms, etc.) and more Amerasian than Asian. The affinity is both spiritual and emotional. Like Kandinsky, the Chinese painters never speak of "things," but of their living spirit and rhythm. They paint what they feel, admire precision, relate every detail to the whole, and their art is symbolic. "The spiritual in art" is taken for granted by the Chinese, as is the dependence of the elements upon each other and upon the whole, and their relevance to the over-all meaning.

The meaning behind Kandinsky's forms comes from unfathomable depths, but Moscow and Asia are more distinctly perceptible than Western Europe, even in the works of the Bauhaus period. This meaning is not dragged in from outside, but, as in the *Book of Changes* (I Ching), serves as a force through which the artist's work becomes significant. "Feeling is identical with force, force is identical with spirit, the spirit is identical with the beyond." It is less the details that point to Asia in Kandinsky's paintings, than the works as a whole, their formal rhythms, their color chords, their sensual irreality, their purity and unconditionality of expression, the wisdom with which Kandinsky, within the limits of painting, makes us sense the eternal.

Kandinsky's late works have points of resemblance to Mexican and Peruvian art, but more often they evoke the art of the Altai region, especially the abstract branch of that art, which gave rise to the arabesque; the formalized animal of the Scythians, the bird-fish motive, the landscape forms of the silk weavers of Noin Ula all are repeatedly echoed in Kandinsky, through scarcely with the same significance. At all events, future studies will have to concern themselves with this relationship, and with the Chinese affinities as well. In the Smithsonian Institute in Washington there is an example of the calligraphy of Ch'en Haoien Chan (fifteenth century) that is strikingly similar to Kandinsky's sign language.

Symbols remain symbols only so long as they are pregnant with meaning and yet irreducible. Kandinsky's symbolism is very much alive, still far from being a thing of the past, and the viewer must resign himself to the fact that he still cannot look "behind the phenomena." Kandinsky's art proclaims a truth that can be expressed only in this and no other way. But by retracing his artistic processes back to their origins, we should be able to come closer to the truth, to the conjuring up of the absolute.

Kandinsky continued working until March 1944, when he fell ill. Nine months later, at 8 P.M. on December 13, he died. The cause of death was a sclerosis in the cerebellum. He did not suspect that his condition was serious, and right up to the end kept on making plans. Among other projects he conceived a ballet for which his friend Thomas von Hartmann was to write the score, and he also planned a film comedy. On his last

Circle and Square.
1943, 716

birthday he was still fully conscious, and sang Russian songs with his wife Nina, confident that he would recover by Christmas time.

He was buried in the Neuilly cemetery, only a few persons being present at the funeral. On the large stone slab that covers his grave appear these words only: Wassily Kandinsky, 1866–1944. Had he any belief in afterlife, it must have appeared to him as it did to Novalis, as life enhanced by absolute mystery. The artist who throughout his life had tried to express mystery in terms of mystery had now entered the ultimate realm of the mysterious.

Memorial exhibitions were held as early as 1945. On March 15, the Guggenheim Foundation in New York opened a Memorial Exhibition with 227 works, which later went on tour to Chicago and Pittsburgh. Basel, Zurich, Paris, and Amsterdam followed. In the fall of 1949 an exhibition of the Blaue Reiter group was organized in Munich (cf. Bibliography). The artist's widow, Nina Kandinsky, took care of the artistic and literary works he left, and in 1946 established an annual Kandinsky Prize for promising young painters.

Kandinsky's fame is still growing, and to the young painters of all nations he may be coming to mean more than other twentieth-century masters. Translations of his books have multiplied, and the number of books and articles about him increases every year. We are coming to a more just appreciation of his heroic life and of his work, the uniqueness and greatness of which were grasped by very few during his lifetime.

Tempered Elan. ▶
1944, 738

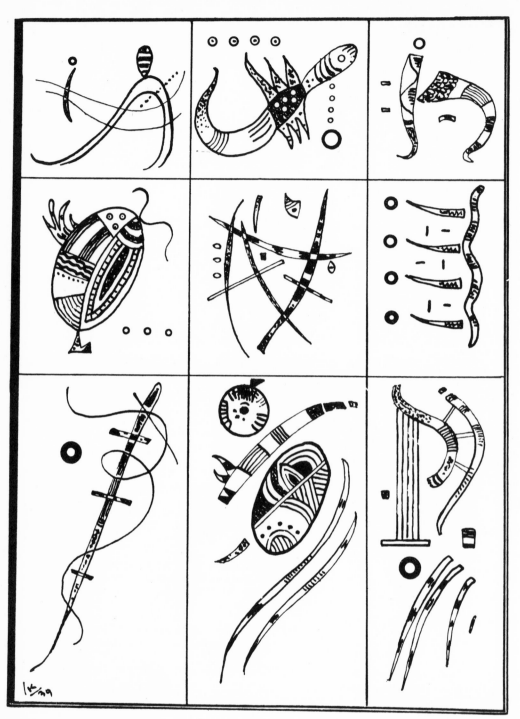

Drawing 1939. 7

Biographical Summary

1866 December 4: Kandinsky born in Moscow.

1869 Goes to Italy with parents.

1871 Family moves to Odessa.

1886 Begins law studies in Moscow.

1889 Ethnographic expedition to Vologda province. Visit to Hermitage in Petersburg where he is impressed by Rembrandt. Trip to Paris.

1892 End of university studies. Second trip to Paris.

1893 Appointed lecturer.

1895 Visits exhibition of French Impressionists in Moscow.

1896 Declines appointment as professor at University of Dorpat. Moves to Munich, begins to study painting.

1897–1899 Azbé School, Munich.

1900 Studies under Stuck at Munich Academy.

1901 Founds Phalanx group.

1902 Elected president of Phalanx. Teaches at Phalanx school, meets Gabriele Münter. Several oil studies and tempera paintings. Earliest woodcuts.

1903 Phalanx school closed. Visits Venice, Odessa, Moscow.

1904 Phalanx group dissolved. Trips to Holland and Odessa. From December 1904 to April 1905 stays in Tunisia. Several tempera paintings. *Poems without Words* (woodcuts).

1905 Trip to Odessa. Exhibits at the Salon d'Automne and the Indépendants in Paris. From December 1905 to April 1906 stays at Rapallo.

1906 *Xylographies* (woodcuts). From June 1906 to June 1, 1907: Sèvres near Paris.

1907 Trip to Switzerland. From September 1907 to April 1908: Berlin.

1908 Return to Munich. Apartment in the Ainmillerstrasse No.36. Meets Jawlensky and Maria v. Werefkin. First Murnau sketches.

1909 Acquires house at Murnau. Murnau landscapes. Foundation of Neue Künstlervereinigung, president Kandinsky. First *Improvisations*.

1910 First *Compositions*. Meets Marc. Writes *On the Spiritual in Art*. Visits Moscow, Petersburg, Odessa.

1911 Meets Klee, Arp, Macke. Founds Blaue Reiter with Marc. First Blaue Reiter show (Munich, December 15–January 1, 1912).

1912 Publication of *On the Spiritual in Art*. Second Blaue Reiter exhibition in Munich. Blaue Reiter show at the Sturm, Berlin. Exhibits at Moderner Bund show, Zurich. Trips to Odessa and Moscow.

1913 *Klänge. Blaue Reiter Almanac. Gelber Klang.* Exhibits at First German Salon d'Automne, Sturm gallery, Berlin.

1914 Goes to Meran with his mother. After outbreak of war goes to Rorschach. Stays three months at Goldach on Lake Constance, then proceeds to Odessa and Moscow.

1915 December 1915 to March 1916: Stockholm.

1916 Separates from Gabriele Münter.

1917 February 11: marries Nina Andreevskaya.

1918 Post with Department of Fine Arts, Commissariat of Public Education. Teacher at government art workshops.

1919 Founds Museum for Pictorial Culture. Organizes twenty-two provincial museums.

1920 Appointed professor, University of Moscow.

Drawing. 1942, 702

Maria Krushchov · Maria Krustschoff · Maria Kroustchoff · Maria Krushov, 1900

264   *Arabs I (Arab Cemetery)* · *Araber I (Arabischer Friedhof)* · *Arabes I (Cimetière arabe)* · *Arabi I (Cimitero arabo), 1909, 85*

Improvisation *Composition I* · *Komposition I* · *Composition I* · *Composizione I, 1910, 92*

Im 274 *Deluge I · Sintflut I · Déluge I · Diluvio Universale I, 1912, 159a*

Sketch · Skizze · Esquisse · Schizzo, 1912, 160a

Sketch for 'Painting with White Border' · *Skizze zu ›Bild mit weißem Rand‹, 1913, 162*
Esquisse pour «Tableau à bordure blanche» · *Schizzo per ‹Quadro con bordo bianco›*

Landscape with Church I · Landschaft mit der Kirche I · Paysage avec église I · Paesaggio con chiesa I, 1913, 168   277

Fragment I (Composition VII) · Fragment I zu ›Komposition VII‹, 1913, 180

278 *Fragment I pour «Composition VII» · Frammento I per ‹Composizione VII›*

Composition VII · Komposition VII · Composition VII · Composizione VII, 1913, 186

a Panel (Spring) · Paneel (Frühling) · Panneau (Printemps) · Pannello (Primavera), 1914, 201
b Panel (Summer) · Paneel (Sommer) · Panneau (Eté) · Pannello (Estate), 1914, 200

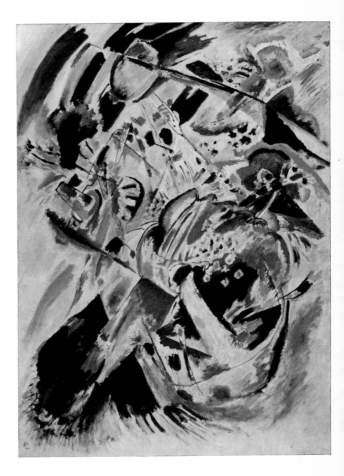

a Panel (Autumn) · Paneel (Herbst) · Panneau (Automne) · Pannello (Autunno), 1914, 198

b Panel (Winter) · Paneel (Winter) · Panneau (Hiver) · Pannello (Inverno), 1914, 199

Improvisation 35 · Improvvisazione 35, 1914, 197

Murky · Trübe · Sombre · Tetro, 1917, 211

284   *Two Ovals · Zwei Ovale · Deux ovales · Due ovali, 1919, 218*

Variegated Circle · Bunter Kreis · Cercle multicolore · Cerchio multicolore, 1921, 238

286   *Circles in the Black · Kreise im Schwarz · Cercles sur noir · Cerchi in nero, 1921, 241*

On White · Auf Weiß · Sur blanc · Su bianco, 1923, 253

288   *A Center · Ein Zentrum · Un centre · Un centro, 1924, 285*

Double Ascension · Doppelter Aufstieg · Ascension double · Doppia ascesa, 1925, 301

289

290   *Small Dream* in Red · *Kleiner Traum in Rot* · *Petit rêve en rouge* · *Piccolo sogno in rosso, 1925, 311*

Hommage à Grohmann · Omaggio a Grohmann, 1926, 350

292   *For Nina · Für Nina · Pour Nina · Per Nina, 1926, 364*

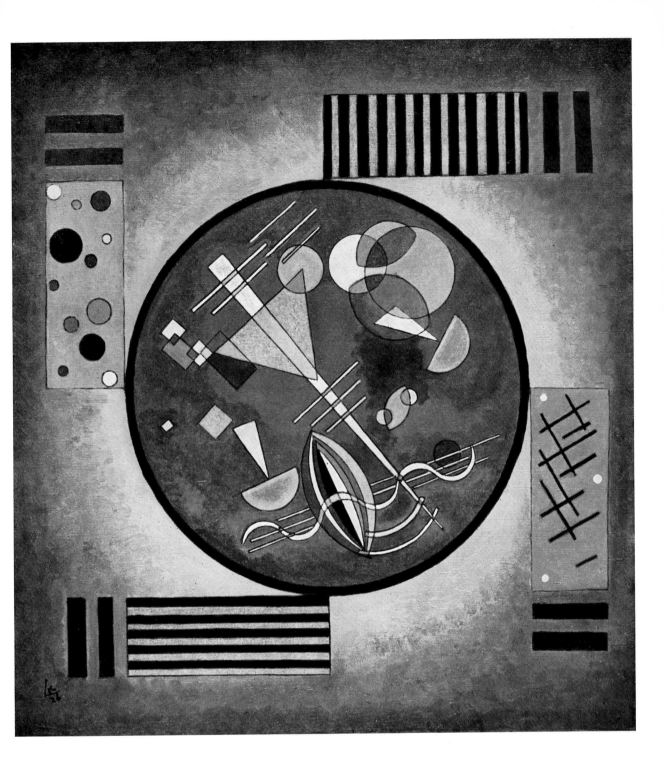

Chat · Plauderei · Causerie · Conversazione, 1926, 368

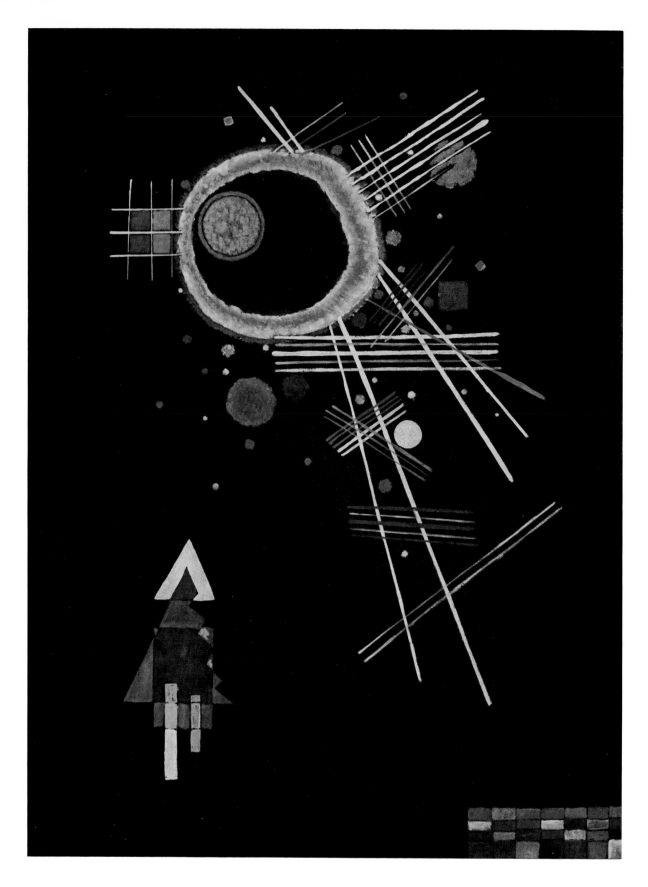

294   *Radiating · Strahlenlinien · Lignes de rayons · Linee a raggi, 1927, 401*

Points in the Arc · Spitzen im Bogen · Pointes en arc · Punte nell'arco, 1927, 407

296   *Lyrical Oval · Lyrisches Oval · Ovale lyrique · Ovale lirico, 1928, 421*

On Points · *Auf Spitzen* · *Sur pointes* · *Sulle punte, 1928, 433*

298 *Picture within Picture · Bild im Bilde · Tableau dans le tableau · Quadro nel quadro, 1929, 467*

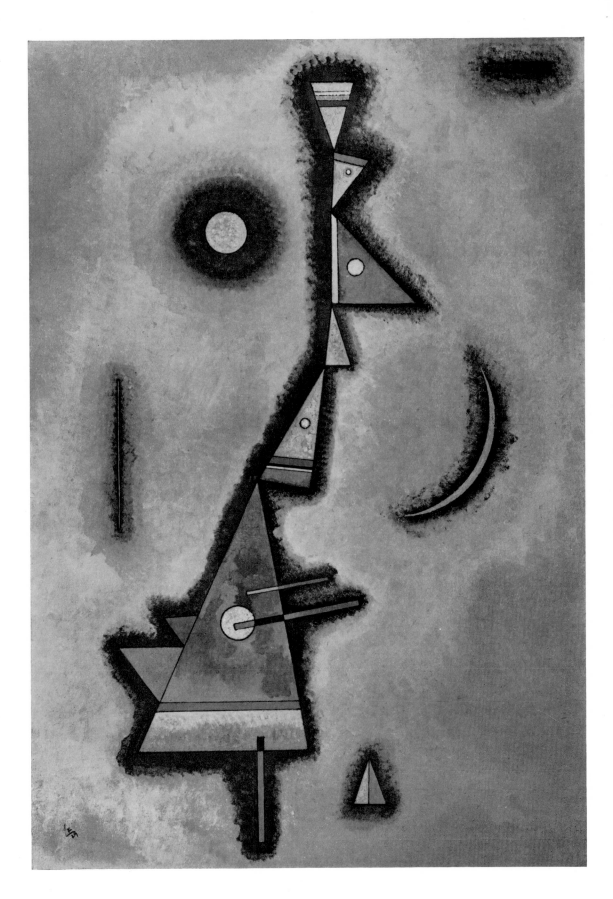

Stubborn · Hartnäckig · Obstiné · Ostinato, 1929, 474

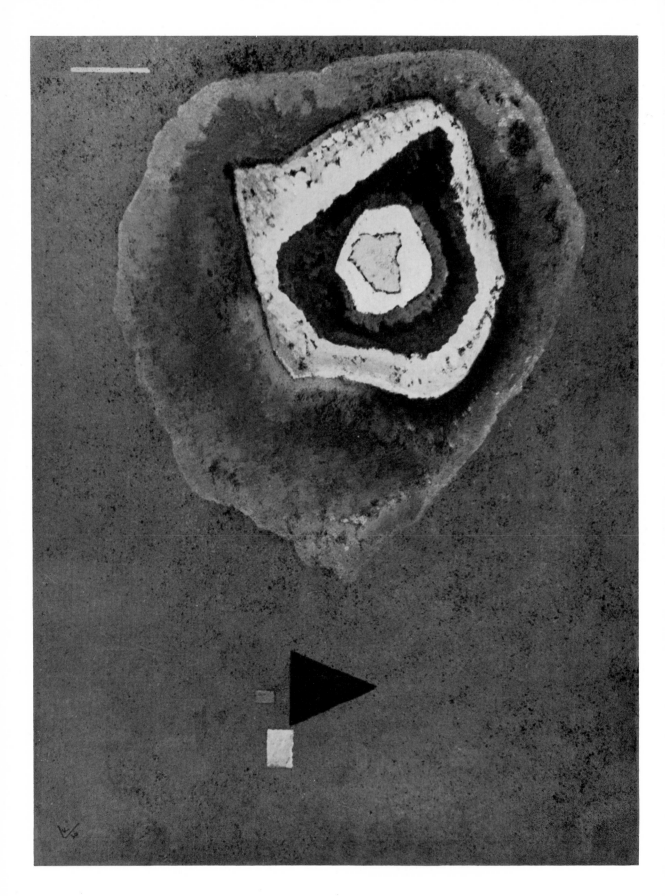

300   *Cool Condensation · Kühle Verdichtung · Condensation froide · Condensamento freddo, 1930, 518*

Development in Brown · Entwicklung in Braun · Développement en brun · Sviluppo in bruno, 1933, 594

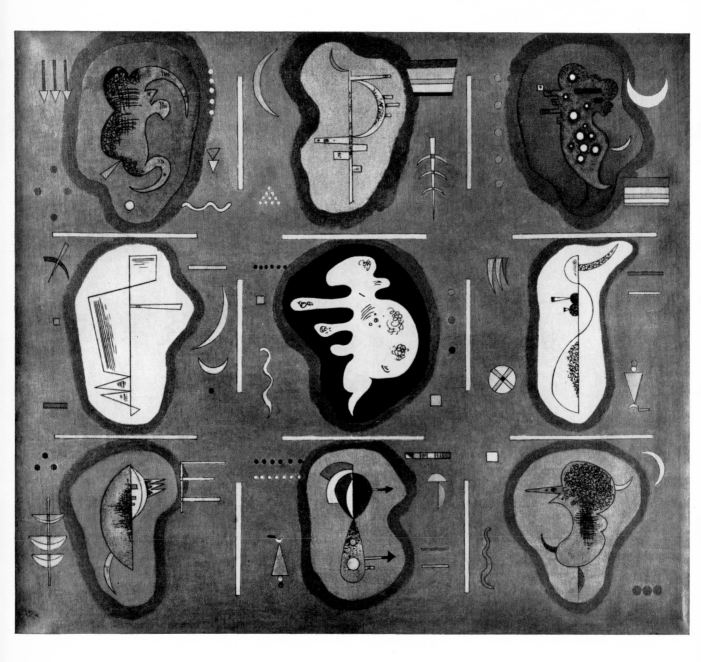

302   *Each for Itself · Jedes für sich · Chacun pour soi · Ognuno per sè, 1934, 598*

In Between · Zwischen Zweien · Entre-deux · Fra due, 1934, 601

304 *Two Surroundings · Zwei Einfassungen · Deux entourages · Due ambienti, 1934, 608*

Striped · Gestreift · Rayé · Rigato, 1934, 609

306   *Balancing Act · Schwung · Voltige · Volteggio, 1935, 612*

Succession · Aufeinanderfolge · Succession · Successione, 1935, 617

308   *Movement I · Bewegung I · Mouvement I · Movimento I, 1935, 618*

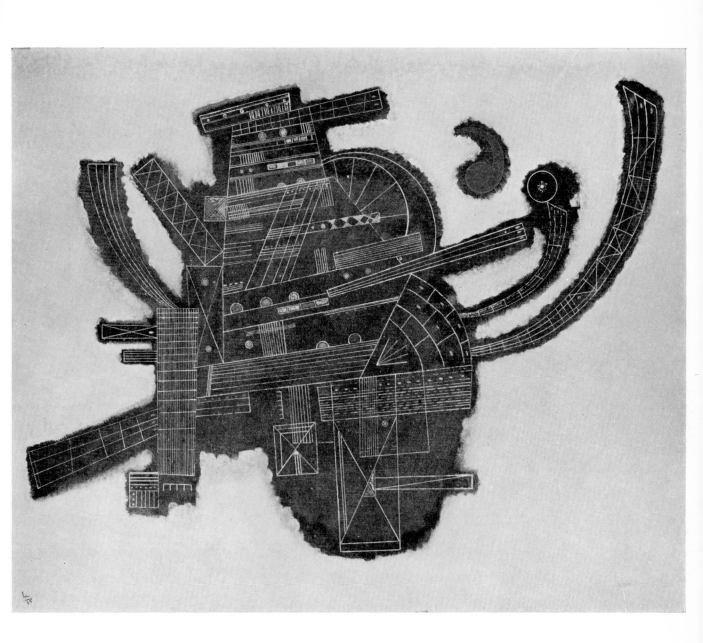

Green Accent · Grüner Akzent · Accent vert · Accento verde, 1935, 623

309

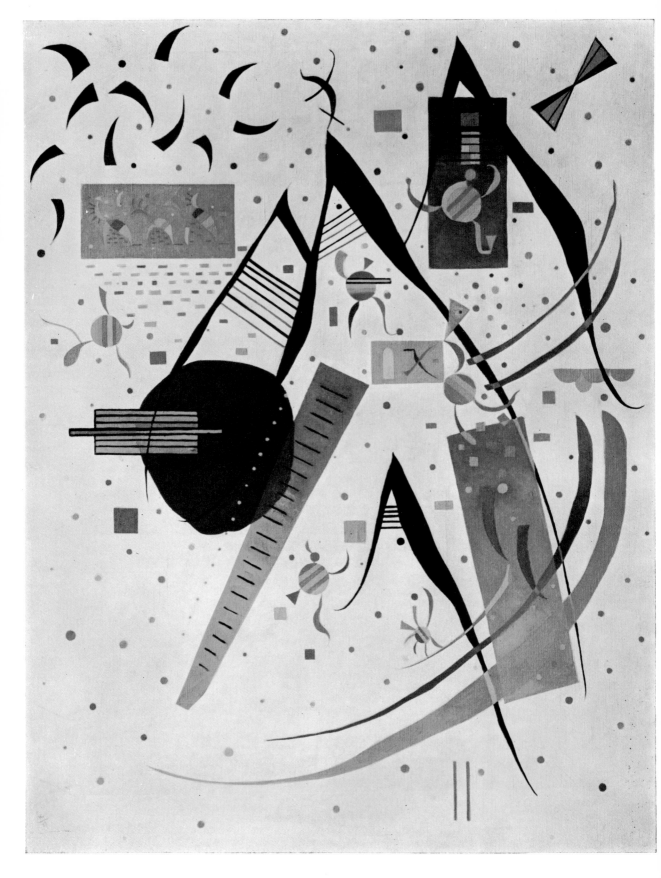

310   *Black Points · Schwarze Spitzen · Pointes noires · Punte nere, 1937, 637*

Two, Etc. · Zwei usw. · Deux etc. · Due ecc., 1937, 642

311

312　*Animated Stability · Belebte Stabilität · Stabilité animée · Stabilità animata, 1937, 646*

Red Circle · Der rote Kreis · Le rond rouge · Il cerchio rosso, 1939, 661

314   *One Figure among others · Eine Figur unter anderen · Une figure entre autres · Una figura fra altre, 1939, 665*

L'Ensemble · L'insieme, 1940, 671

316   *Various Parts · Verschiedene Teile · Parties diverses · Parti diverse, 1940, 672*

Around the Circle · Um den Kreis · Autour du cercle · Intorno al cerchio, 1940, 677   317

318   *Reduced Contrasts · Reduzierte Kontraste · Contrastes réduits · Contrasti ridotti, 1941, 681*

Various Actions · *Bunte Aktionen* · *Actions variées* · *Azioni varie, 1941, 683*

320 *Three Variegated Figures* · *Drei bunte Figuren* · *Trois figures bigarrées* · *Tre figure multicolori, 1942, 702*

White Figure · Weiße Figur · La Figure blanche · Figura bianca, 1943, 705

322   *The Arrow · Der Pfeil · La flèche · La freccia, 1943, 711*

Accord · Accordo, 1943, 713

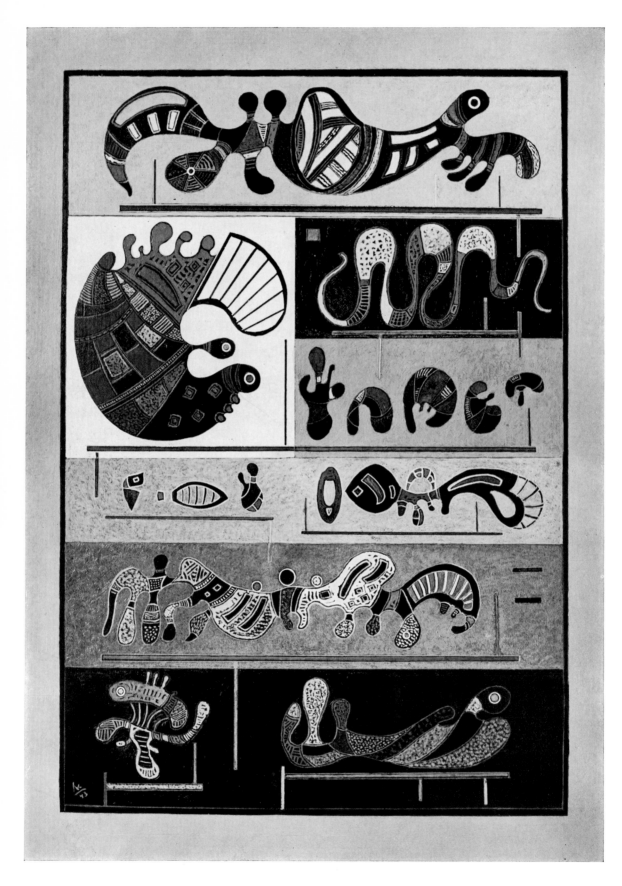

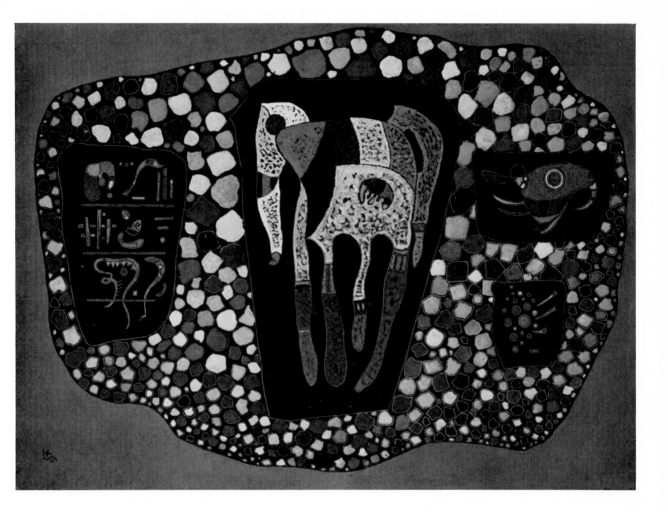

Fragments · Fragmente · Fragments · Frammenti, 1943, 718

Darkness · Finsternis · Ténèbres · Tenebre, 1943, 721

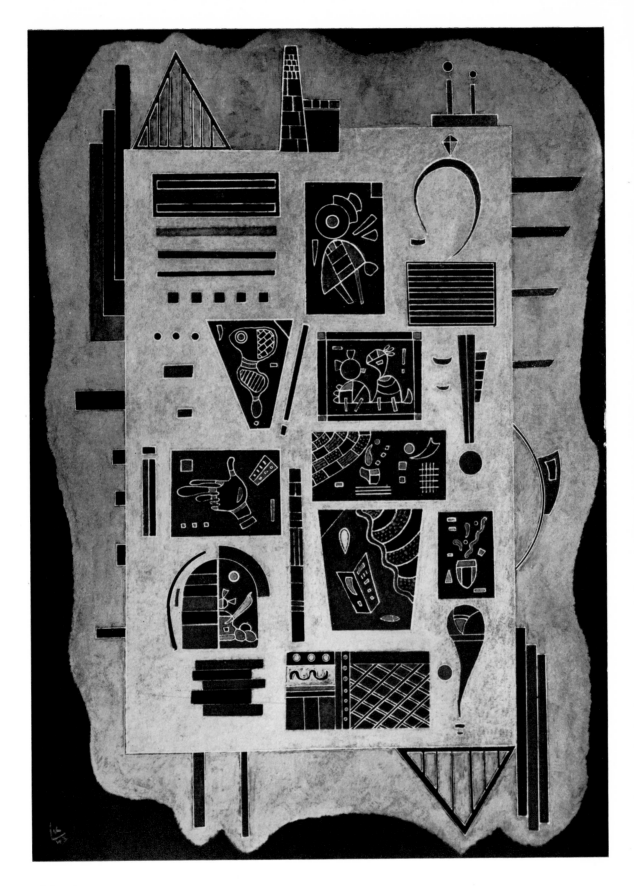

A Conglomerate · Ein Konglomerat · Un conglomérat · Un conglomerato, 1943, 728

328   *Ribbon with Squares · Band mit Vierecken · Ruban aux carrés · Nastro quadrettato, 1944, 731*

Catalogue of Works

(Based on Kandinsky's handwritten catalogue)

The data, whenever available, are given in the following order:

1. Number in Kandinsky's private catalogue (= KK).

2. Title.

3. Medium.

4. Dimensions (when preceded by letter "F", with frames).

5. Signature: "Kandinsky", "∠K", or "⚠" (cf. note on Signatures). Abbreviations: l. l. = lower left; l. r. = lower right; c. b. = center bottom, etc.

6. Owner. In some cases replaced with Kandinsky's own notation. Abbreviations: NK = Collection Nina Kandinsky, Paris; GMF = Gabriele Münter Foundation, Städtische Galerie, Munich; SRG = Solomon R. Guggenheim Museum, New York; MMA = Museum of Modern Art, New York.

7. Where exhibited (in parenthesis). Only the most important exhibitions are listed.

8. Reference to reproduction (page number) or Classified Catalogue (CC-number).
Works not listed in KK and discovered after the artist's death are given separately in the Supplement (p. 343).

The contents of the original manuscript are as follows:

Notebook 1:

List of paintings numbered 1 to 73 (1900–1909), in German.

List of prints numbered 1 to 39 (1902–1907), partly in French.

List of oil studies numbered 1 to 108 (1900–1908). The entries are in German, undated, and for the most part without accompanying sketches.

List of "Color drawings", i. e., tempera paintings, numbered 1 to 132 (1901–1907), undated.

Notebook 2:

List of paintings numbered 62 to 370 (1909–1926). Titles 62–243 are in Russian, the rest in German, Additional pages contain a list of the *Trifles* (1915 and 1916) numbered 1 to 18, and a list of paintings on glass (1918) numbered 1 to 17.

Notebook 3:

German version of nos. 62–204 with explanatory subtitles added; nos. 62–186, 202, and 203 were copied by Gabriele Münter.

Notebook 4:

List of paintings numbered 371 to 738 (1927–1944). The titles up to no. 594 are in German, from no. 595 on in French.

Notebook 5:

List of watercolors numbered 1 to 647 (1910–1944). Untitled from no. 635 on.

Notebook 6:

List of watercolors numbered 648 to 730 (1940–1944).

Paintings

1900

1a *Port of Odessa*. Tempera.
1b *After the Rain*. Tempera. Formerly collection Mrs. Abrikosov, Moscow.
1c *Fountain (Switzerland)*. Tempera. Formerly collection Mrs. Abrikosov, Moscow.

1901

1 *Trysting Place No. 1*. Tempera. (Phalanx 1901).
2 *Farewell*. Tempera. (Phalanx 1901, Odessa 1902, Moscow 1903).
3 *Promenade*. Tempera. 17^{15}/$_{16}$ × 27^1/$_8$". "Kandinsky" l. r. Collection Dr. Z. Goldberg, Zurich. (Phalanx 1901, Warsaw 1904). CC 1.
4 *Winter*. Tempera. Given away. (Phalanx 1901).
5 *Sunset*. Tempera. Given away. (Phalanx 1901).

1902

6 *Autumn Days No. 1*. Oil. (Phalanx 1902, Dresden 1905).
7 *Winter in Schwabing*. Tempera. Gift to his brother. (Phalanx 1902, Odessa, Petersburg, Moscow 1903). Cf. Supplement.
8 *Evening*. Tempera. Sold at Stettin. (Phalanx 1902).
9 *Sun Spot*. Oil. Sold in Russia. (Phalanx 1902).
10 *Pond in the Woods*. Lacquer. Destroyed. (Moscow 1902). Replaced with: Pond in the Woods. Oil on canvas. 13^1/$_4$ × 21". "Kandinsky" l. r. Private collection, Paris. CC 2.
11 *Girl on River Bank*. Oil. 32^{11}/$_{16}$ × 45^1/$_4$". (Berlin Sezession 1903).
12 *Old City (Rothenburg)*. Oil on canvas. 20^1/$_2$ × 30^7/$_8$". "Kandinsky" l. r. NK. (Phalanx 1902, Sal. d'aut. Paris 1906). CC 3.
13 *Bright Air*. Oil tempera on canvas. 13^3/$_8$ × 20^1/$_2$". "Kandinsky" l. r. NK. (Berlin Sezession 1902; Sal. d'aut. Paris 1906). CC 4.
14 *Autumn Sun*. Tempera. Given away. (Phalanx 1902).
15 *Autumn Days No. 2*. Oil. Sold in Moscow. (Phalanx 1902).
15a *The Sluice*. Oil on canvas. 31^1/$_4$ × 22". "Kandinsky" l. r. Collection R. Lee Feigen, Los Angeles. (Phalanx 1902). Cf. Supplement. CC 5.
16 *Before the Storm*. Lacquer. Destroyed. (Phalanx 1902).

1903

17 *Trysting Place No. 2*. Tempera on canvas. 35^1/$_2$ × 27^1/$_8$". Formerly collection A. J. Eddy, Chicago. (Phalanx 1903). CC 6.
18 *The Blue Rider*. Oil on canvas. 20^1/$_2$ × 21^7/$_{16}$". "Kandinsky" l. r. Collection Ernst Bührle, Zurich, formerly collection B. G. Citroën, Amsterdam. (Prague 1903, Paris 1904). p. 258.
19 *The First Poet*. Tempera. 18^1/$_8$ × 20^1/$_2$". (Wiesbaden 1903).
20 *Riding Couple*. Tempera on canvas. 29^1/$_2$ × 39". Destroyed. (Dresden 1905, Paris 1907).
21 *Dark Evening*. Tempera on canvas. F 60^3/$_8$ × 42^1/$_2$". (Cracow 1904).
22 *Summer Landscape*. Oil. (Paris 1904).

1904

23 *Spring.* Lacquer. (Cassirer, Berlin 1905).

24 *Promenade Party.* Tempera and lacquer. $23^5/_8 \times 35^7/_{16}''$. "Kandinsky" l. r. Collection Paul Citroën, Wasenaar (Holland). (Berlin Sezession 1904, Paris 1906). CC 7.

25 *Stormy Weather (Kallmünz).* Oil $29^{15}/_{16} \times 39^3/_8''$. Sold in Dresden.

26 *Child and Dog.* Oil. $29^{15}/_{16} \times 39^3/_8''$.

27 *Sunday (Old Russia).* Oil on canvas. $17^3/_4 \times 37^3/_8''$. Mus. Boymans, Rotterdam. (Munich 1904, Paris 1906). CC 8.

28 *The Last Rays.* Oil. $17^3/_4 \times 37^3/_8''$.

29 *Sunny Day (Kallmünz).* Oil study from nature. $19^{11}/_{16} \times 27^1/_2''$.

30 *Countryside.* Oil. $29^1/_2 \times 68^7/_8''$.

31 *Mountain Landscape (Upper Palatinate).* Oil. $33^7/_8 \times 45^1/_4''$. (Dresden 1905).

32 *Winter Twilight (Starnberg).* Oil. $17^3/_4 \times 22^1/_{16}''$. "Kandinsky" l. r. Collection Tage Bertelsta, Sdr. Aby, Denmark. CC 9.

33 *Kallmünz.* Oil on cardboard. $19^{11}/_{16} \times 27^9/_{16}''$.

34 *In the Woods.* Tempera. $8 \times 10^1/_4''$.

35 *Sunflowers.* Oil. $24^{13}/_{16} \times 39^3/_8''$.

36 *Sunflowers.* Oil. $23^1/_4 \times 23^5/_8''$.

37 *A Summer Day (The Yellow Lady).* Tempera. $18^7/_8 \times 20^1/_2''$.

38 *Cloudy Day.* Oil. $19^{11}/_{16} \times 27^9/_{16}''$.

1905

39 *Cheerful Visit.* Tempera. $39^3/_8 \times 59^1/_{16}''$. Destroyed.

40 *Arrival of the Merchants.* Tempera. $36^7/_{16} \times 53^3/_{16}''$. Sold in Berlin. (Paris 1905). CC 10.

41 *Quiet Water (The Blue Gentleman and the White Lady).* $26^3/_8 \times 38^5/_8''$. Sold in Odessa.

42 *The Rivals.* Tempera.

43 *Rapallo.* Oil on canvas. $9^7/_{16} \times 13''$. "Kandinsky 1905" on the back. Collection Verner Nielsen, Copenhagen. (Copenhagen 1914). CC 11.

1906

44 *Event.* Tempera. F. $46^1/_{16} \times 61^{13}/_{16}''$. (Paris 1906).

45 *Troika.* Oil on canvas. F $38^3/_{16} \times 49^3/_{16}''$. Private collection USA. CC 12.

1907

46 *Motley Life.* Tempera on canvas. $57^1/_{16} \times 63''$. "Kandinsky" l. r. Collection S. Slijper, Blaricum, Holland. (Paris 1907). p. 261.

47 *Sketch.* Oil. $21^5/_8 \times 23^5/_8''$.

48 *Morning.* Tempera on canvas. F. $48^{13}/_{16} \times 62^3/_{16}''$. Sold in Paris. (Paris 1907). Reproduced in *Backward Glances.*

49 *Panic.* Tempera on canvas. $38^3/_{16} \times 55^1/_8''$. (Odessa 1907). CC 13.

50 *Storm Bell.* Tempera on canvas. $35^7/_{16} \times 42^1/_2''$. CC 14.

51 *C. (Canvas?) with Nun.* Oil on canvas. $31^1/_8 \times 48^7/_{16}''$.

52 *C. with Blue Cloud.* Oil on canvas. $20^1/_2 \times 28^3/_8''$. (Paris 1909).

53 *C. with Yellow Cloud (Nuage montant).* Oil on canvas. $13^3/_8 \times 20^1/_2''$. (Paris 1908).

54 *C. with Green and Blue Cloud.* Oil on canvas. $19^{11}/_{16} \times 25^8/_{16}''$.

55 *C. with Red Clouds.* Oil on canvas. $43^1/_4 \times 43^1/_4''$. (Paris 1909).

56 *C. with Green Women.* Oil on canvas. $35^7/_{16} \times 71^5/_8''$.

57 *Autumn.* Oil on canvas. $37^3/_8 \times 50^3/_4''$.

58 *C. with Red Rider.* Oil on canvas. $31^1/_8 \times 48^3/_8''$.

1908

59 *White Sound.* Oil on cardboard. $28^1/_4 \times 28^1/_4''$. "Kandinsky" l. r. Collection Mr. and Mrs. Charles R. Lachman, New York, formerly collection Fernand Graindorge, Liège. (Berlin Sezession 1909). CC 15.

60 *Summer Landscape.* Oil on canvas. $28^1/_4 \times 38^3/_8''$. (Paris 1909).

61 *Autumn Landscape with Road.* Oil on canvas. $28^1/_4 \times 38^3/_8$. "Kandinsky" l. l. Private collection, New York. (Salon d'Automne, Paris 1909). CC 16.

1909

62 *Winter I.* Oil on canvas. $28^1/_4 \times 38^3/_8''$. – USSR. (Berlin Sezession 1909, London 1909). CC 17.

63 *Autumn Landscape with Boats.* Oil on canvas. $30^1/_8 \times 38^3/_8''$.

64 *The Crinolines.* Oil on canvas. $37^3/_8 \times 50^3/_4''$. "Kandinsky" l. l. USSR. Formerly Tretiakov Gallery, Moscow. (Odessa, Izdebsky 1910, Moscow 1920. CC 18.

65 *Hill with Pink.* Oil on cardboard. $27^1/_{16} \times 27^1/_{16}''$. (Odessa, Izdebsky 1909)

66 *Domes (Red Wall).* Oil on canvas. $33^1/_2 \times 45^5/_8''$. USSR, formerly Museum of Astrakhan. CC 19.

67 *Landscape with Tree.* Oil on canvas. $28^1/_4 \times 38^3/_8''$. "Kandinsky 1909" l. l. Museum of Düsseldorf. CC 20.

68 *Interior.* Oil on cardboard. $19^{11}/_{16} \times 25^8/_{16}''$. "Kandinsky" l. r. GMF Munich.

69 *Blue Rider.*

70 *Yellow Cliff.* Oil on canvas. $51^1/_8 \times 47^3/_{16}''$. Lost while being shipped. (Stockholm 1910)

71 *Painting with Boat.* Oil on cardboard. $31^1/_8 \times 48^3/_8''$. "Kandinsky 1909" l. l. Collection Tage Bertelsta, Sdr. Aby, Denmark, formerly collection Dr. Christensen, Stockholm. (Neue Künstlervereinigung Munich 1909). CC 21.

72 *Landscape with Tower.* Oil on cardboard. $29^3/_4 \times 39^3/_{16}''$. "Kandinsky 1908" (sic.) l. l. NK, Paris. (Neue Künstlervereinigung Munich 1909). p. 59.

73 *Painting with Houses.* Oil on canvas. $38^3/_{16} \times 51^1/_2''$. "Kandinsky 1909" l. r. Stedelijk Museum Amsterdam, formerly collection Marie de Vanstiden. CC 22.

74 *Painting with Archer (Study for 75).* Oil on canvas. $41^3/_4 \times 38^3/_{16}''$. Gift to D. Burliuk.

75 *Picture with an Archer.* Oil on canvas. $69^{11}/_{16} \times 57^7/_8''$. "Kandinsky" l. r. MMA, New York, Gift of Mrs. Louise Smith, formerly collection Tetzen Lund, Copenhagen. p. 262.

76 *Improvisation 1.* Oil on canvas. $31^{11}/_{16} \times 28^5/_{16}''$. Private collection, U. S. Cf. woodcut in *Klänge.*

77 *Improvisation 2 (Funeral March).* Oil on canvas. $37 \times 51^7/_8''$. "Kandinsky" l. l. National Museum, Stockholm, formerly collection Stenhammar, Stockholm. (Stockholm 1916). CC 23.

78 *Improvisation 3.* Oil on canvas. $37 \times 51^1/_8''$. "Kandinsky 1909" l. r. NK Paris, formerly collection Ibach, Ruhmeshalle Barmen. Cf. copy in Supplement. CC 24.

79 *Landscape with Green House.* Oil on canvas. $26^3/_4 \times 37^3/_8''$. "Kandinsky 1909" l. r. Leo Hofmann, Zurich. (Bern 1955). CC 25.

80 *Landscape with Church.* Oil on canvas. $26^3/_4 \times 37^{13}/_{16}''$. "Kandinsky 1909" l. l. Collection Mrs. James Eppenstein, Chicago. CC 26.

81 *Hills.* Oil on canvas. Formerly collection Karl Münter, Bonn. (Neue Künstlervereinigung Munich 1909).

82 *Sketch (Rider).* Oil on canvas. $26^3/_8 \times 39^3/_8''$. "Kandinsky 1909" l. l. Collection Frau Helene Lange, Krefeld. (Neue Künstlervereinigung Munich 1909). CC 27.

83 *Improvisation 4*. Oil on canvas. 42¹/₈×62⁵/₈″. "Kandinsky 1909" I. r. USSR, formerly Museum of Nizhni Novgorod. (Odessa, Izdebsky 1911; Stockholm 1916). CC 28.

84 *Blue Mountain*. Oil on canvas. 41³/₈×37¹³/₁₆″. "Kandinsky" I. I. SRG New York, formerly Staatl. Gemäldegalerie Dresden. p. 263.

85 *Arabs I (Arab Cemetery)*. Oil on canvas. 28¹/₈×38⁵/₈″. "Kandinsky 1909" I. r. Kunsthalle Hamburg. (Neue Künstlervereinigung Munich 1910). p. 264.

86 *Landscape, Murnau* (large study).

87 *Landscape (Church in Murnau*, large study*)*. Oil on canvas. 27⁹/₁₆×19¹¹/₁₆″.– Lost, replaced with small preliminary study. Oil on canvas. 17³/₄×13³/₄″. "Kandinsky" I. r. Collection Klaus Brommer, Stuttgart (destroyed). CC 29.

88 *Improvisation*.

89 *Group in Crinolines*. Oil on canvas. 37¹/₂×59¹/₄″. "Kandinsky 1909" I. I. SRG, New York, formerly collection Beffie, Amsterdam. CC 30.

89a *Sketch for Composition II*. Oil on canvas. 57⁷/₈×38³/₁₆″. "Kandinsky 1910" I. r. (in KK 1909). SRG, New York. Color plate, p. 109.

90 *Old Germany*. Oil on cardboard.

91 *Paradise*. Oil on cardboard. 27⁹/₁₆×38³/₁₆″. "Kandinsky 1909" I. I. Collection H. S. Stadler, Newcastle – on – Tyne, England. CC 31.

1910

92 *Composition I*. Oil on canvas. 47³/₁₆×55¹/₈″. "Kandinsky 1910" I. r. Collection Otto Ralfs, Braunschweig. Destroyed. (London 1910). p. 265.

93 *Improvisation 4a*. Oil on mahogany. 32¹¹/₁₆×45¹/₄″.

93a *Improvisation*. Oil on mahogany. 25×39″. NK, Paris. Color plate. p. 71.

94 *Improvisation 5 (Presto)*. Oil on canvas. 42¹/₈×37³/₈″. USSR, formerly Museum of Smolensk. (Sonderbund Düsseldorf 1910). Cf. Supplement. CC 32.

95 *Mountains (not recognizable)*. On back: *Study for Improvisation 8*. Oil on canvas. 37¹³/₁₆×27³/₈″. Collection Aimé Maeght, Paris. (Neue Künstlervereinigung Munich 1911). CC 33.

96 *Improvisation 6*. Oil on canvas. 42⁵/₁₆×37⁵/₈″. "Kandinsky" I. I. GMF, Munich. Color plate. p. 79.

97 *Improvisation 7*. Oil on canvas. 51⁹/₁₆×38³/₁₆″. "Kandinsky 1910" I. r. USSR, formerly Tretiakov Gallery, Moscow. (Stockholm 1916). CC 34.

98 *Composition II*. Oil on canvas. 78³/₄×108¹/₄″. "Kandinsky 1910" I. r. Formerly collection Baron von Gamp, Berlin. (Neue Künstlervereinigung Munich 1910/11). CC 35.

99 *Improvisation 8*. Oil on canvas. 49³/₁₆×28³/₄″. "Kandinsky 1909" (sic) c. b. Collection Herbert M. Rothschild, New York, formerly collection K. Munakata, Tokyo. (Moscow 1911). p. 266.

100 *Improvisation 9*. Oil on canvas. 43¹/₄×43¹/₄″. "Kandinsky 1910" I. r. Collection Franz Stadler, Zurich. (Neue Künstlervereinigung Munich 1910/11). p. 267.

101 *Improvisation 10*. Oil on canvas. 47³/₁₆×55¹/₈″. "Kandinsky 1910" I. r. Galerie E. Beyeler, Basel, formerly Prov. Mus. Hannover. (Moscow 1910). Color plate, p. 113.

102 *Improvisation 11*. Oil on canvas. 38³/₈×41¹⁵/₁₆″. "Kandinsky 1910" I. r. USSR. (Moscow 1920). CC 36.

103 *Garden*. Oil on cardboard. 26³/₈×20¹/₁₆″. – Collection Walter v. Scheven, Krefeld. CC 37.

104 *Landscape with Rain*. Oil on cardboard. 13×17¹⁵/₁₆″. "Kandinsky 1910" I. r. Private collection, Paris. CC 38.

104a *Landscape with Mountains*. Oil on cardboard. 12¹/₈×17¹/₂″. "Kandinsky" I. I. SRG, New York. (Neue Künstlervereinigung, Munich 1910/11). CC 39.

105 *Landscape with Factory Chimney*. Oil on canvas. 26×31¹/₂″. "Kandinsky 1910" I. r. SRG, New York. (Neue Künstlervereinigung, Munich 1910/11). CC 40.

106 *Lake (Boat Ride)*. Oil on canvas. 38⁵/₈×41³/₈″. "Kandinsky 1910" I. I. USSR, formerly Tretiakov Gallery, Moscow. (Sonderbund, Cologne 1912; Moscow 1920). CC 41.

107 *Interior (with G. Münter and M. v. Werefkin)*. Oil on cardboard. 19¹/₈×25⁹/₁₆″. – Collection Felix Klee, Bern. CC 42.

108 *Improvisation 12 (Riders)*. Oil on canvas. 38³/₁₆×41¹⁵/₁₆″. "Kandinsky 1910" I. I. Bayr. Staatsgemäldesammlung, Munich. CC 43.

109 *Improvisation 13*. Oil on canvas. 47³/₁₆×55¹/₈″. "Kandinsky" I. r. Collection Frau Mildred Crous, Krefeld, formerly collection H. Lange, Krefeld. (Blaue Reiter, Munich 1949). CC 44.

110 *Improvisation 14*. Oil on canvas. 28³/₄×49³/₁₆″. "Kandinsky 1910" I. I. NK, Paris. CC 45.

111 *Improvisation 15*. Destroyed.

112 *Composition III*. Oil on canvas. 74¹³/₁₆×98¹/₂″. "Kandinsky 1910" I. I. Formerly collection Baron v. Gamp, Berlin. p. 268.

113 *Improvisation 16*. Oil on canvas. 43¹/₄×43¹/₄″. "Kandinsky 1910" I. I. – (Karo Bube, Moscow 1912). CC 46.

113a *Last Judgment*. Oil on canvas. 49¹/₄×28³/₄″. "Kandinsky 1910" I. I. Galerie Maeght, Paris. (Blaue Reiter, Munich 1949). CC 47.

1911

114 *Impression II (Moscow)* (dated 1.1.1911 in KK). Oil on canvas. 47¹/₄×55¹/₈″. Collection Bernhard Köhler, Berlin. Destroyed. (Blaue Reiter, Munich 1911). p. 269.

115 *Romantic Landscape*. Oil on canvas. 37×51¹/₈″. "Kandinsky 1911" I. r. GMF, Munich. CC 48.

116 *Impression III (Concert)*. Oil on canvas. 37³/₄×41³/₈″. "Kandinsky 1911" I. r. GMF, Munich. CC 49.

117 *Impression I (Fountain)*. Oil on canvas. 37³/₈×53¹/₈″. "Kandinsky 1911" I. r. Collection Walter v. Scheven, Krefeld. Destroyed. CC 50.

118 *Lyrical*. Oil on canvas. 37×51¹/₈″. "Kandinsky" I. r. Boymans Museum, Rotterdam, formerly collection Tak van Poortvliet, The Hague. (Paris 1911). CC 51.

119 *Fragment for Composition IV*. Oil on canvas. 37×51¹/₈″. "Kandinsky 1910" I. r. (in KK listed under 1911). Tate Gall., London. CC 52.

120 *Painting with Troika*. Oil on cardboard. 27³/₈×38⁵/₁₆″. "Kandinsky" I. I. The Art Institute of Chicago, A. J. Eddy Memorial Coll. (Neuer Bund, Zurich 1912). CC 53.

121 *Arabs II*. Oil on canvas. 27⁵/₈×36³/₈″. "Kandinsky" I. r. Galerie Grosshennig, formerly collection Frau Gottschalk, Düsseldorf. CC 54.

122 *Winter II*. Oil on canvas. 26¹/₂×35³/₈″. "Kandinsky 1911" I. I. Collection Mr. and Mrs. Stanley Rogers Resor, New Canaan Conn., formerly collection Mies v. d. Rohe, Chicago. CC 55.

123 *Autumn I*. Oil on canvas. 28×39″. "Kandinsky" I. I. Collection Mrs. Lora F. Marx, Chicago. (Neuer Bund, Zurich 1912). Color plate, p. 117.

124 *St. George II*. Oil on canvas. 42¹/₈×37³/₈″. USSR, formerly Museum for Pictorial Culture, Moscow. (Paris 1911).

125 *Composition IV*. Oil on canvas. 63×78³/₄″. "Kandinsky 1911" I. I. NK, Paris. (Neue Sezession, Berlin 1911). Color plate, p. 123.

126 *Improvisation 18 (with Tombstone)*. Oil on canvas. 55¹/₂×47¹/₄″. "Kandinsky 1911" I. I. GMF, Munich. CC 56.

127 *Improvisation 19*. Oil on canvas. 38¹/₈×41³/₄″.– GMF, Munich. CC 57.

128 *St. George I*. Oil on canvas. 37³/₄×41³/₈″. "Kandinsky 1911" I. r. Collection Prof. W. Löffler, Zurich. Color plate. p. 125.

128a *Improvisation 19a*. Oil on canvas. 38¹/₈ × 41³/₄″. "Kandinsky 1911" l. r. GMF, Munich. CC 58.

129 *Portrait*.

130 *Landscape with Cemetery*.

131 *The Cow*. Oil on canvas. 37¹/₂ × 41³/₈″. "Kandinsky" l. r. GMF, Munich. CC 59.

132 *Pastoral*. Oil on canvas. 41 × 60⁵/₈″. "Kandinsky 1911" l. r. SRG, New York. Color plate, p. 127.

133 *Arabs III (with Pitcher)*. Oil on canvas. 41³/₄ × 62¹/₄″. "Kandinsky" l. l. USSR. (Moscow 1920). CC 60.

134 *Nude*. Oil on canvas. 59 × 37³/₄″. "Kandinsky 1911" l. r. J. K. Thannhauser Gallery, New York, formerly collection Morton D. May, St. Louis, Miss., formerly collection K. Munakata, Tokyo. CC 61.

135 *Sunday (Impression VI)*. Oil on canvas. 37³/₈ × 42¹/₄″. GMF, Munich. CC 62.

136 *St. George III*. Oil on canvas. 38¹/₄ × 42¹/₄″. "Kandinsky 1911" l. l. GMF, Munich. CC 63.

137 *Impression IV (Policeman)*. Oil on canvas. 37³/₈ × 42¹/₂″. GMF, Munich. CC 64.

138 *Improvisation 20*. Oil on canvas. 39³/₈ × 47¹/₄″. "Kandinsky 1911" l. r. USSR. CC 65.

139 *Improvisation 21 (with Yellow Horse)*. Oil on canvas. 39³/₈ × 43¹/₄″. "Kandinsky 1911" l. r. Private collection, Krefeld. (Sonderbund, Cologne 1912). CC 66.

140 *Improvisation 22*. Oil on canvas. 47¹/₄ × 55¹/₈″. "Kandinsky 1911" l. r. Formerly collection Otto Ralfs, Braunschweig. (Blaue Reiter, Munich 1911). CC 67.

141 *Impression V (Park)*. Oil on canvas. 41³/₈ × 61³/₄″. "Kandinski 1911" l. r. NK, Paris. (Paris 1911). CC 68.

142 *Sketch for Composition V*. Gift to Thomas v. Hartmann. Lost.

143 *Improvisation 21a*. Oil on canvas. 33¹/₄ × 41³/₈″. "Kandinsky 1911" l. l. GMF, Munich. Cf. 1913, 174. (Sonderbund, Cologne 1912). CC 69.

144 *Composition V*. Oil on canvas. 74³/₄ × 108¹/₄″. "Kandinsky 1911" l. l. Collection Dübi Müller, Solothurn. (Blaue Reiter, Munich 1911). p. 270.

144a *Murnau Winter Landscape with Locomotive*. Oil on canvas. 36¹/₄ × 41″. "Kandinsky 1911" l. r. Collection Morton D. May, St. Louis, Miss. Loan to Museum of St. Louis. Color plate. p. 271.

145 *Improvisation 23*. Oil on canvas. 43¹/₄ × 43¹/₄″. "Kandinsky 1911" l. l. Munson-Williams Proctor Institute of Utica, New York, formerly collection H. v. Garvens-Garvensberg, Hannover. CC 70.

1912

146 *Improvisation 24 (Troika Nr. 2)*. (Lost, replaced with study for Improvisation 24). Oil on cardboard. 18³/₄ × 26¹/₂″. "Kandinsky 1912" l. l. Formerly Reiff Mus., Aix-en-Chapelle. CC 71.

147 *Improvisation 25 (Garden of Love)*. Oil on canvas. 18³/₄ × 26¹/₂″. "Kandinsky 1912" l. l. USSR, formerly Museum of Smolensk. (Paris 1912). CC 72.

148 *Improvisation 26 (Oars)*. Oil on canvas. 38⁵/₈ × 42¹/₄″. "Kandinsky 1912" l. r. GMF, Munich. CC 73.

149 *Improvisation 27 (Garden of Love)*. Oil on canvas. 47¹/₄ × 55¹/₈″. "Kandinsky 1912" l. l. Formerly collection Alfred Stieglitz, New York. (Sturm Berlin 1912). CC 74.

150 *Improvisation 28 (War)*. Oil on canvas.

151 *Sketch for a Composition*.

151a *Sketch for Deluge*. Oil on cardboard. 13⁷/₈ × 20¹/₂″. "Kandinsky 1912" l. l. Galerie Bing, Paris. CC 75.

152 *Moscow Lady*. Oil on canvas. 42⁷/₈ × 42⁷/₈″. GMF, Munich. CC 76.

153 *Black Spot I*. Oil on canvas. 39³/₈ × 51¹/₈″. "Kandinsky 1912" l. l. Formerly Museum of Pictorial Culture, Moscow. (Stockholm 1916). CC 77.

154 *With the Black Arch*. Oil on canvas. 74 × 77¹/₁₆″. "Kandinsky 1912" l. l. NK, Paris. (Paris 1937). p. 273.

155 *Landscape with two Poplars*. Oil on canvas. 30⁷/₈ × 39¹/₂″. "Kandinsky 1911" l. r. (in KK, 1912). The Art Institute of Chicago. CC 78.

156 *Autumn II*. Oil on canvas. 23⁵/₈ × 32⁵/₈″. "Kandinsky" l. r. The Phillips Gallery, Washington. CC 79.

157 *Winter Landscape*.

158 *Blue Hill*.

159 *Sketch*. Oil on canvas. 37³/₈ × 42¹/₄″. "Kandinsky 1912" l. l. Collection Philippe Dotremont, Brussels. CC 80.

159a *Deluge I*. Oil on canvas. 39³/₈ × 41³/₈″. "Kandinsky 1912" l. l. Kaiser-Wilhelm-Museum, Krefeld. p. 274.

160 *Improvisation 29 (Swan)*. Oil on canvas. 37³/₈ × 42¹/₂″. "Kandinsky 1912" l. l. Philadelphia Museum of Art, Arensberg Collection. CC 81.

160a *Sketch*. Oil on canvas. 37³/₄ × 42¹/₈″. "Kandinsky 1912" l. l. Collection Mrs. Louise Smith, New York, New York. p. 275.

160b *Untitled (Improvisation)*. Oil on canvas. 44¹/₂ × 62¹/₂″. "Kandinsky 1912" l. l. SRG, New York. Color plate. p. 131.

1913

161 *Improvisation 30 (Cannon)*. Oil on canvas. 43¹/₄ × 43¹/₄″. "Kandinsky 1913" l. l. The Art Institute of Chicago, A. J. Eddy Memorial Collection. Color plate, p. 133.

162 *Sketch for Painting with White Border*. Oil on canvas. 39⁵/₈ × 30³/₄″. "Kandinsky" l. r. The Phillips Gallery, Washington, formerly collection Miss Katherine S. Dreier. p. 276.

163 *Second Sketch for Painting with White Border*. Oil on canvas. 27⁵/₈ × 41″. "Kandinsky" l. l. USSR, formerly Museum for Pictorial Culture, Moscow. (Herbstsalon Berlin 1913). CC 82.

164 *Improvisation 31 (Sea Battle)*. Oil on canvas. 55¹/₈ × 47¹/₄″. Collection Dübi-Müller, Solothurn. (Herbstsalon 1913). CC 83.

165 *Sketch for Painting with White Forms*. Oil on canvas. 39⁵/₈ × 34⁵/₈″. "Kandinsky 1913" l. l. Collection Frau Ferdinand Möller, Cologne. CC 84.

166 *Painting with White Forms*. Oil on canvas. 47 × 54³/₈″. "Kandinsky 1913" l. l. SRG, New York. (Deutscher Herbstsalon Berlin 1913). Color plate, p. 135.

167 *Landscape with Rain*. Oil on canvas. 28 × 31¹/₈″. "Kandinsky" l. l. SRG, New York. CC 85.

168 *Landscape with Church I*. Oil on canvas. 30³/₄ × 39³/₈″. "Kandinsky 1913" l. r. Mr. and Mrs. Charles Zadok, New York. (Blaue Reiter, Basel 1950). p. 277.

169 *Landscape with Church II (with Red Spot)*. Oil on canvas. 44⁷/₈ × 53¹/₈″. "Kandinsky 1913" l. r. Collection Mrs. Peggy Guggenheim, Venice. (Deutscher Herbstsalon 1913). CC 86.

170 *Improvisation 33 (Sketch for Orient)*. Oil on canvas. 34⁵/₈ × 39³/₈″. "Kandinsky 1913" l. r. Stedelijk Museum, Amsterdam, formerly collection van Assendelft, Holland. CC 87.

171 *Red Spot*. Oil on canvas. 39³/₈ × 34⁵/₈″. GMF, Munich. CC 88.

172 *Composition VI*. Oil on canvas. 76³/₄ × 118¹/₈″. "Kandinsky 1913" l. r. USSR. (Deutscher Herbstsalon Berlin 1913). CC 89.

173 *Painting with White Border*. Oil on canvas. 55³/₄ × 79″. "Kandinsky 1913" l. l. SRG, New York. (Deutscher Herbstsalon Berlin 1913). CC 90.

174 *Small Pleasures*. Oil on canvas. 43¹/₄ × 47¹/₄″. "Kandinsky 1913" l. l. SRG. New York, formerly collection Beffie, Amsterdam. Watercolor study, NK, Paris. Color plate, p.137.

175 *Landscape (Dünaberg in Murnau)*. Oil on canvas. 34⁵/₈ × 39³/₈″. "Kandinsky 1913" l. l. USSR. CC 91.

176 *Painting with Green Center*. Oil on canvas. 43¹/₄ × 47″. "Kandinsky 1913" l. r. The Art Institute of Chicago, A. J. Eddy Memorial Collection. CC 92.

177 *Improvisation 34 (Motive from KK 170).* Oil on canvas. 47^1/$_4$ × 55^1/$_8$''. "Kandinsky 1913" l. r. USSR, formerly Museum of Kazan. CC 93.

178 *Painting with White Lines.* Oil on canvas. 55^1/$_8$ × 43^1/$_4$''. – USSR, formerly Museum of Penza.

179 *Sketch for Composition VII.* Oil on canvas. 30^3/$_4$ × 39^3/$_8$''. "Kandinsky" l. l. Collection Felix Klee, Bern. Color plate. p. 139.

180 *Fragment 1 for Composition VII (Center).* Oil on canvas. 34^5/$_8$ × 38^5/$_8$''. Collection Mr. and Mrs. Harry L. Bradley, Milwaukee, Wisconsin. p. 278.

181 *Fragment 2 for Composition VII (Center and Corners).* Oil on canvas. 34^5/$_8$ × 39^3/$_8$''. "Kandinsky 1913" l. l. Albright Art Gallery, Buffalo NY. CC 94.

182 *Sketch 2 for Composition VII.* Oil on canvas. 39^3/$_8$ × 55^1/$_8$''. GMF, Munich. CC 95.

183 *Study for Composition VII* (probably a representation of the Last Judgment). Oil on canvas. 30^3/$_4$ × 39^3/$_8$''. GMF, Munich. CC 96.

184 *Improvisation with Red and Blue Ring.* Oil on canvas. 47^1/$_4$ × 43^1/$_4$''. "Kandinsky" l. r. CC 97.

185 *Sketch 3 for Composition VII.* Oil on canvas. 35^3/$_8$ × 49^1/$_4$''. GMF, Munich. CC 98.

186 *Composition VII.* Oil on canvas. 78^3/$_4$ × 118^1/$_8$''. "Kandinsky" l. l. USSR. (Moscow 1920). p. 279.

187 *Dreamy Improvisation.* Oil on canvas. 51^1/$_8$ × 51^1/$_8$''. "Kandinsky 1913" l. l. Collection Frau Ida Bienert, Munich. CC 99.

188 *Bright Picture.* Oil on canvas. 30^5/$_8$ × 39^3/$_8$''. "Kandinsky 1913" l. l. SRG, New York. (Gal. Thannhauser, Munich 1914). CC 100.

189 *Black Lines.* Oil on canvas. 50^3/$_8$ × 50^3/$_8$''. "Kandinsky 1913" l. l. SRG, New York. (Gal. Thannhauser, Munich 1914). Color plate, p. 141.

1914

190 *Little Painting with Yellow.* Oil on canvas. 30^3/$_4$ × 39^1/$_2$''. "Kandinsky 1914" l. r. Philadelphia Museum of Art, Arensberg Collection. CC 101.

191 *Improvisation with Cold Forms.* Oil on canvas. 47^1/$_4$ × 55^1/$_8$''. "Kandinsky 1914" l. r. USSR, formerly Museum for Pictorial Culture, Moscow. CC 102.

192 *Painting with Red Spot.* Oil on canvas. 51^1/$_8$ × 51^1/$_8$''. "Kandinsky 1914" l. r. NK, Paris. (Internat. Kunstausst. Dresden 1926). Color plate, p. 143.

193 *Fugue.* Oil on canvas. 51^1/$_8$ × 51^1/$_8$''. "Kandinsky 1914" l. l. SRG, New York. Color plate, p. 147.

194 *Painting with Round Forms.* Oil on canvas. 47^1/$_4$ × 43^1/$_4$''. "Kandinsky 1914" l. l. Formerly collection Walden. CC 103.

195 *Painting with Blue Border.* Oil on canvas. 63 × 78^3/$_4$''. "K 14" l. l. Collection Joseph R. Shapiro, Oak Park Illinois. CC 104.

196 *Painting with Three Spots.* Oil on canvas. 46^1/$_2$ × 42^1/$_2$''. "Kandinsky 1914" l. l. SRG, New York. CC 105.

197 *Improvisation 35.* Oil on canvas. 43^1/$_4$ × 47^1/$_4$''. "∠K 1914" l. l. Collection Hans Arp, Loan to Kunstmuseum Basel. Color plate, p. 282.

198–201 *Four Panels for Edwin R. Campbell, New York.* Oil on canvas. "K 1914" l. l. 1 & 2. Autumn and Winter, 63 × 47^5/$_8$'' each. SRG, New York. 3. Summer, 63 × 35^5/$_8$'', 4. Spring, 63 × 31^1/$_2$''. MMA, New York, formerly collection Edwin R. Campbell, New York. pp. 281, 282.

1916

202 *Painting with Two Red Spots.* Oil on canvas. 30^3/$_4$ × 39^3/$_8$''. "∠K" l. l. Formerly National-Gal. Berlin. CC 107.

203 *Painting on Light Ground.* Oil on canvas. 39^3/$_8$ × 30^3/$_4$''. "∠K 16" l. l. NK, Paris. (Kestner-Gesellschaft, Hannover 1923). CC 108.

204 *Painting with Orange Border.* Oil on canvas. 34 × 39^3/$_8$''. "∠K 16" l. l. Collection Otto Ralfs, Braunschweig. Destroyed. CC 109.

205 *Naive.* Oil on canvas. 20^1/$_4$ × 26^3/$_8$''. USSR, formerly Museum of Perm.

206 *Untitled.* Oil on canvas. 26^3/$_8$ × 23^5/$_8$''. USSR, formerly Museum of Voronezh.

207 *Untitled.* Oil on canvas. 26^3/$_8$ × 23^5/$_8$''. USSR, formerly Museum of Tobolsk.

208 *Ladies.* Oil on canvas. 26 × 30^3/$_4$''. USSR.

208a *Untitled.* Oil on canvas. USSR.

1917

209 *Untitled.* Oil on canvas. 26^3/$_4$ × 24^3/$_4$''. Sold to private collector in Russia.

210 *Blue Arch (Ridge).* Oil on canvas. 52^3/$_8$ × 41''. "∠K 17" l. l. USSR, formerly Museum of Leningrad. CC 110.

211 *Overcast.* Oil on canvas. 41^3/$_8$ × 52^3/$_4$''. "∠K 17" l. l. USSR, formerly Tretiakov Gallery, Moscow. p. 283.

212 *Entrance.* Oil on canvas. 35 × 41^3/$_4$''. "∠K 17" l. l. USSR, formerly Museum of Vitebsk. CC 111.

213 *Twilight.* Oil on canvas. 36^5/$_8$ × 28''. "∠K 17" l. l. USSR, formerly Museum of Leningrad. CC 112.

214 *Southern (Indian).* Oil on canvas. 28^3/$_4$ × 40^1/$_4$''. USSR.

215 *Clarity.* Oil on canvas. 39^3/$_4$ × 31^1/$_8$''. "∠K 17" l. l. USSR. CC 113.

216 *Horn.* Oil on canvas. 39 × 23''. USSR.

217 *Gray Oval (Gray Border).* Oil on canvas. 38^5/$_8$ × 52^3/$_8$''. "∠K 17" USSR, formerly Museum of Ekaterinburg. CC 114.

1919

218 *Two Ovals.* Oil on canvas. 42^1/$_8$ × 35^1/$_8$''. "∠K 19" l. l. USSR, formerly Museum of Leningrad. p. 284.

219 *Red Border.* Oil on canvas. 36^5/$_8$ × 28''. "∠K 19" l. l. USSR, formerly Museum of Vitebsk. CC 115.

220 *White Oval (Black Border).* Oil on canvas. 31^1/$_2$ × 36^5/$_8$''. "∠K 19" l. l. USSR, formerly Tretiakov Gallery, Moscow. CC 116.

221 *Violet Wedge.* Oil on canvas. 23^5/$_8$ × 26^3/$_8$''. USSR, formerly Tretiakov Gallery, Moscow.

222 *In Gray.* Oil on canvas. 50^3/$_4$ × 69^1/$_2$''. "∠K 19" l. l. NK, Paris. CC 117.

223 *Painting with Points.* Oil on canvas. 49^1/$_4$ × 37^3/$_8$''. USSR, formerly Museum of Leningrad.

1920

224 *White Background.* Oil on canvas. 37^3/$_8$ × 54^3/$_8$''. "∠K 20" l. l. USSR, formerly Museum of Leningrad. CC 118.

225 *Easter.* Oil on canvas. 35 × 23^1/$_4$''. USSR.

226 *Black Lines.* Oil on canvas. 22^1/$_2$ × 28''. "∠K 20" l. l. USSR. CC 119.

227 *Red Oval.* Oil on canvas. 28 × 28''. "∠K 20" l. l. SRG, New York. (Wallerstein, Berlin 1929; Thannhauser, Munich 1922; Stockholm 1922). CC 120.

228 *Pointed Hovering*. Oil on canvas. 53^1/$_2$×70^1/$_2$″. "∠K 20" I. I. USSR. (First Russian Exhibition, Gal. van Diemen, Berlin 1922). CC 121.

229 *Sketch (Red with Black)*. Oil on canvas. 38^1/$_8$×42^1/$_2$″. "∠K 20" I. I. USSR, formerly Museum of Tashkent. CC 122.

230 *The Green Border*. Oil on canvas. 47^1/$_4$×55^1/$_8$″. "∠K 20" I. I. USSR. (First Russian Exhibition, Gal. van Diemen, Berlin 1922). CC 123.

231 *Points*. Oil on canvas. 43^1/$_4$×36^5/$_8$″. "∠K 20" I. I. Collection S. Nakada, Tokyo. CC 124.

232 *White Line*. Oil on canvas. 38^5/$_8$×31^1/$_2$″. "∠K 20" I. I. NK. Paris. CC 125.

233 *On Yellow*. Oil on canvas. 34^3/$_4$×34^3/$_4$″. "∠K 20" I. I. USSR, formerly Museum of Turkestan. CC 126.

1921

234 *Red Spot II*. Oil on canvas. 51^5/$_8$×71^1/$_4$″. "∠K 21" I. I. NK, Paris. Loan to Kunstmuseum Basel. (Gal. Cahiers d'art, Paris 1934). CC 127.

235 *Blue Segment*. Oil on canvas. 47^1/$_4$×55^1/$_8$″. "∠K 21" I. I. SRG, New York. (Jeu de Paume, Paris 1937). CC 128.

236 *White Center*. Oil on canvas. 46^7/$_8$×53^7/$_8$″. "∠K 21" I. I. Collection Mrs. Hilla Rebay, Greens Farms, Conn. CC 129.

237 *Chessboard*. Oil on canvas. 65^3/$_8$×52^3/$_4$″. "∠K 21" I. I. SRG, New York. (Gummesons Konsthandel, Stockholm 1922). CC 130.

238 *Variegated Circle*. Oil on canvas. 54^1/$_2$×70^7/$_8$″. "∠K 21" I. I. Yale University Art Gallery, Coll. Société Anonyme, formerly collection Miss K. S. Dreier. (New York 1923). p. 285.

239 *White Oval*. Oil on canvas. 41^1/$_2$×39^5/$_8$″. "∠K 21" I. I. SRG, New York. CC 131.

240 *Black Spot*. Oil on canvas. 53^7/$_8$×47^1/$_4$″. "K 21" I.I. Kunsthaus Zurich. CC 132.

241 *Circles within Black*. Oil on canvas. 53^1/$_8$×47^1/$_4$″. "∠K" I. I. SRG, New York, formerly collection Miss K. S. Dreier. p.286.

1922

242 *Blue Circle*. Oil on canvas. 43×39″. "∠K 22" I. I. SRG, New York, formerly collection Miss K. S. Dreier. CC 133.

243 *White Cross*. Oil on canvas. 39^3/$_8$×43^1/$_4$″. "∠K 22" I. I. Collection Peggy Guggenheim, Venice. CC 134.

244 *White Zigzags*. Oil on canvas. 37^3/$_8$×49^1/$_4$″. "∠K 22" I.I. Gall. Internazionale d'arte moderna della città Venezia. (Fides, Dresden 1924). CC 135.

245 *Blue-Red*. Oil on canvas. 47^1/$_8$×43^1/$_4$″. "∠K 22" I. I. Private collection, Krefeld. CC 136.

246 *Black Grid*. Oil on canvas. 37^3/$_4$×41^3/$_4$″. "∠K 22" I. I. NK, Paris. (Bauhaus, Weimar 1923). CC 137.

1923

247 *Accented Corners*. Oil on canvas. 51^1/$_8$×51^1/$_8$″. "∠K 23" I. I. SRG, New York. CC 138.

248 *Untitled*. Oil on canvas. 36×29″. "∠K 23" I. I. SRG, New York. CC 139.

249 *In the Black Circle*. Oil on canvas. 51^1/$_8$×51^1/$_8$″. "∠K 23" I. I. Galerie Aimé Maeght, Paris. (Los Angeles, 1926). CC 140.

250 *Diagonal*. Oil on canvas. 27^5/$_8$×^{7}/$_8$″. "∠K 23" I. I. Collection Dr. Hermann Bode, Steinhude am Meer. (Loan to Landesmuseum, Hannover). CC 141.

251 *Black Form*. Oil on canvas. 43^1/$_4$×38^1/$_8$″. "∠K 23" I. I. Collection Hjalmar Gabrielson, Göteborg. CC 142.

252 *On Gray*. Oil on canvas. 47^1/$_4$×55^1/$_8$″. "∠K 23" I. I. SRG, New York. CC 143.

253 *On White*. Oil on canvas. 41^3/$_8$×38^5/$_8$″. "∠K 23" I. I. NK, Paris. (Jeu de Paume, Paris 1937). p. 287.

254 *Red Square*. Oil on canvas. 28^3/$_8$×21^5/$_8$″. "∠K 23" I. I. Collection Otto Ralfs, Braunschweig (presumably destroyed). (Fides, Dresden 1924).

255 *Through-going Line*. Oil on canvas. 45^1/$_8$×78^3/$_4$″. "∠K 23" I. I. NK, Paris, on loan to Kunstmuseum Basel. CC 144.

256 *White Picture*. Oil on canvas. 37^3/$_4$×41^3/$_4$″. "∠K 23" I. I.

257 *Black and Violet*. Oil on canvas. 30^3/$_4$×39^3/$_8$″. "∠K 23" I. I. Collection Hans and Walter Bechtler, Zurich, formerly collection James Wood, London. (Bauhaus, Weimar 1923). CC 145.

258 *The Arrow Form*. Oil on canvas. 55^1/$_8$×47^1/$_4$″. "∠K 23" I. I. SRG, New York. CC 146.

259 *In the Black Square*. Oil on canvas. 38^3/$_8$×36^3/$_4$″. "∠K 23" I. I. SRG, New York. CC 147.

260 *Composition VIII*. Oil on canvas. 55^1/$_8$×78^3/$_4$″. "K 23" I. I. SRG, New York. (Bauhaus, Weimar 1923). Color plate, p.189.

261 *Circles Within the Circle*. Oil on canvas. 38^1/$_8$×37^3/$_4$″. "∠K 23" I. I. Philadelphia Museum of Art, Arensberg Collection. (Bauhaus, Weimar 1923). CC 148.

262 *Animated Repose*. Oil on canvas. 23×29^5/$_8$″. "∠K 23" I. I. Louis Clayeux, Paris. CC 149.

263 *Open Green*. Oil on canvas. 38^1/$_4$×38^1/$_4$″. "∠K 23" I. I. SRG, New York. (Galerie Arnold, Dresden 1926). CC 150.

264 *Pink Oblong*. Oil on canvas. 41×37^3/$_4$″. "∠K 23" I. I. SRG, New York. CC 151.

264a *Without Support*. Oil on canvas. 37^3/$_4$×36^1/$_4$″. I. I. SRG, New York. CC 152.

1924

265 *Cheerful*. Oil on canvas. 25^3/$_4$×28^1/$_2$″. "∠K 24" I. I. SRG, New York. CC 153.

266 *Yellow Point*. Oil on canvas. 18^1/$_2$×25^3/$_4$″. "∠K 24" I. I. Collection Dr. Othmar Huber, Glarus. CC 154.

267 *Blue Picture*. Oil on canvas. 19^1/$_2$×20". "∠K 24" I. I. Collection Mr. Henry Cohen, New York. (Oakland 1926). CC 155.

268 *In Red*. Oil on canvas. 16×14″. "∠K 24" I. I. Collection Mrs. Hilla Rebay, Greens Farms, Conn. CC 156.

268a *Backward Glance*. Oil on canvas. 38^5/$_8$×33^1/$_2$″. "∠K 24" I. I. NK, Paris. (Cf. *Small Pleasures*, KK 1913, 174). CC 157.

269 *Yellow Accompaniment*. Oil on canvas. 32^3/$_4$×38^1/$_2$″. "∠K24" I. I. SRG, New York. (Braunschweig 1926). CC 158.

270 *Black Accompaniment*. Oil on canvas. 65^3/$_8$×53^1/$_8$″. "∠K 24" I. I. Galerie Maeght, Paris. Color plate, p. 193.

271 *Deep Brown*. Oil on canvas. 32^1/$_4$×28^3/$_4$″. "∠K 24" I. I. SRG, New York. CC 159.

272 *Self-Illuminating*. Oil on canvas. 27^5/$_8$×19^3/$_4$″. "∠K 24" I. I. SRG, New York. CC 160.

273 *Sharp-Calm Pink*. Oil on cardboard. 25^1/$_4$×19″. "∠K 24" I. r. Wallraf Richartz Museum, Collection Haubrich, Cologne. CC 161.

274 *Quiet Harmony*. Oil on cardboard. 34^1/$_2$×20^1/$_8$″. "∠K 24" I. I. Kunstmuseum Düsseldorf, Auction Ketterer 11.30.1955. CC 162.

275 *Horn Form*. Oil on cardboard. 23×19^1/$_4$″. "∠K 24" I. I. Galerie des 20. Jahrhunderts Berlin. (Esquisse, Paris 1944). CC 163.

276 *Heavy Red*. Oil on cardboard. 23^3/$_8$×19″. "∠K 24" I. I. Collection Richard Doetsch-Benziger, Basel. CC 164.

277 *Pink and Gray*. Oil on cardboard. 23^3/$_8$×19″. "∠K 24" I. I. Collection Mrs. Thomas von Hartmann, New York. CC 165.

278 *Silent*. Oil on cardboard. 27^1/$_8$×19^1/$_2$″. "∠K 24" I. I. SRG, New York. CC 166.

279 *Capricious Line*. Oil on cardboard. 27⁵/₈ × 19³/₈″. "∠K 24" l. l. Collection Diego Rivera, Mexico City. CC 167.

280 *Green Sound*. Oil on cardboard. 28 × 20.″ "∠K 24" l. l. SRG, New York. CC 168.

281 *Contrasting Sounds*. Oil on cardboard. 27⁵/₈ × 19³/₈″. "∠K24" l. l. NK, Paris. CC 169.

282 *Red*. Oil on canvas. 28³/₄ × 16¹/₂″. "∠K 24" l. l. Collection Frau Maja Sacher, Pratteln near Basel. CC 170.

283 *Quiet*. Oil on canvas. 31¹/₈ × 21⁵/₈″. "∠K 24" l. l. Galerie Maeght, Paris. CC 171.

284 *Contact*. Oil on cardboard. 31¹/₈ × 21¹/₄″. "∠K 24" l. l. NK, Paris. CC 172.

285 *One Center*. Oil on canvas. 55¹/₈ × 39″. "∠K 24" l. l. SRG, New York, formerly collection Kirchhoff, Wiesbaden. (Wiesbaden 1925). p. 288.

286 *White Pentagon*. Oil on cardboard. 30⁷/₈ × 21³/₈″. "∠K 24" l. l. Collection Leo Glass, New York. CC 173.

287 *Calm Tension*. Oil on canvas. 30¹/₈ × 21³/₈″. "∠K 24" l. l. NK, Paris. CC 174.

1925

288 *In Blue*. Oil on cardboard. 31¹/₂ × 43¹/₄″. "∠K 25" l. l. Collection J. B. Urvater, Brussels. (Internat. Kunstausstellung, Dresden 1926). CC 175.

289 *Blue Circle Nr. 2*. Oil on cardboard. 24 × 16¹/₄″. "∠K 25" l. l. Collection P. Brugniere, Paris. CC 176.

290 *Sign*. Oil on cardboard. 27¹/₈ × 19⁵/₈″. "∠K 25" l. l. NK, Paris. (Internat. Kunstausstellung, Zurich 1925). CC 177.

291 *Shaking*. Oil on cardboard. 27⁵/₈ × 19⁵/₈″. "∠K 25" l. l. Collection Mr. and Mrs. Victor Kiam, New York. CC 178.

292 *Several Points*. Oil on cardboard. 27⁵/₈ × 19⁵/₈″. "∠K 25" l. l. Galerie Maeght, Paris. CC 179.

293 *Pointed and Round*. Oil on cardboard. 27⁵/₈ × 19³/₄″. "∠K 25" l. l. SRG, New York. CC 180.

294 *Above and Left*. Oil on cardboard. 27⁵/₈ × 19⁵/₈″. "∠K 25" l. l. SRG, New York, formerly collection Ferdinand Möller, Cologne. (Internat. Kunstausstellung, Dresden 1926). CC 181.

295 *Three Elements*. Oil on cardboard. 27³/₈ × 19³/₈″. "∠K 25" l. l. Collection Alexandre Kojève, Paris. CC 182.

296 *Abstract Interpretation*. Oil on cardboard. 19¹/₈ × 13¹/₈″. "∠K 25" l. l. Yale University Art Gallery, Collection Société Anonyme. CC 183.

297 *Green and Red*. Oil on cardboard. 27³/₈ × 19³/₈″. "∠K 25" l. l. NK, Paris. CC 184.

298 *Loosely in Red*. Oil on cardboard. 27¹/₈ × 19³/₄″. "∠K 25" l. l. Private collection, Paris. CC 185.

299 *Red in Black*. Oil on canvas. 27¹/₈ × 19³/₈″. "∠K 25" l. l. Collection Frau Ida Bienert, Munich. CC 186.

300 *White Point*. Oil on canvas. 29¹/₂ × 27⁵/₈″. "∠K 25" l. l. Museum of Düren, formerly collection H. Berggruen, Paris. (Deutscher Künstlerbund Hannover 1928). CC 187.

301 *Double Ascension*. Oil on cardboard. 27³/₈ × 19³/₈″. "∠K 25" l. l. Collection Richard Doetsch-Benziger, Basel. (Internat. Kunstausstellung, Zurich 1925). p. 289.

302 *Green Wedge*. Oil on canvas. 27³/₈ × 19³/₈″. "∠K 25" l. l. SRG, New York. CC 188.

303 *Small Signs*. Oil on canvas. 27¹/₈ × 19³/₈″. l. l. Private collection, Paris. CC 189.

304 *Steady Green*. Oil on wood. 27³/₈ × 19³/₈″. "∠K 25" l. l. Collection Curt Burgauer, Zurich. CC 190.

305 *Balanced*. Oil on cardboard. 19³/₈ × 13¹/₂″. "∠K 25" l. l. Collection R. de M., Paris. CC 191.

306 *Blue over Motley*. Oil on cardboard. 27³/₈ × 19³/₈″. "∠K 25" l. l. NK, Paris. CC 192.

307 *Tempered*. Oil on cardboard. 27¹/₈ × 19¹/₄″. "∠K 25" l. l. Collection Louis Clayeux, Paris. CC 193.

308 *Bright Unity*. Oil on cardboard. 27¹/₂ × 19⁵/₈″. "∠K 25" l. l. SRG, New York. CC 194.

309 *Wavering*. Oil on cardboard. 19³/₈ × 13¹/₂″. "∠K 25" l. l. Private collection, Paris. CC 195.

310 *Intimate Communication*. Oil on canvas. 14⁵/₈ × 12⁵/₈″. "∠K 25" c. b. NK, Paris. CC 196.

311 *Small Dream in Red*. Oil on canvas. 13³/₄ × 16¹/₈″. "∠K 25" l. l. NK, Paris. p. 290.

312 *Untitled (Oval No. 2)*. Oil on cardboard. 13³/₈ × 11³/₈″. "∠K 25" c. b. NK, Paris. CC 197.

313 *In the Bright Oval*. Oil on cardboard. 28¹/₂ × 23″. "∠K 25" l. l. Alexandre Rabow Gallery, San Francisco, formerly collection Mrs. Ch. Mack, San Francisco. CC 198.

314 *Yellow-Red-Blue*. Oil on canvas. 50 × 78³/₄″. "∠K 25" l. l. NK, Paris. (Internat. Kunstausstellung, Zurich 1925). Color plate, p. 197.

315 *Whispered*. Oil on cardboard. 9⁷/₈ × 7⁷/₈″. "∠K 25" c. b. NK, Paris. CC 199.

316 *Red Depth*. Oil on canvas. 39³/₈ × 31¹/₂″. "∠K 25" l. l. Destroyed. CC 200.

317 *One Spot (Red on Brown)*. Oil on cardboard. 29¹/₂ × 21⁵/₈″. "∠K 25" l. l. Collection M. Beglarian, Paris. CC 201.

318 *Becoming*. Oil on cardboard. 29¹/₂ × 21⁵/₈″. "∠K 25" l. l. Galerie Maeght, Paris. CC 202.

319 *Brown Silence*. Oil on cardboard. 30¹/₄ × 25″. "∠K 25" l. l. Private collection, Paris. CC 203.

320 *Black Triangle*. Oil on canvas. 30⁷/₈ × 21¹/₄″. "∠K 25" l. l. SRG, New York. CC 204.

321 *Pointed-Round*. Oil on canvas. 28¹/₂ × 12⁵/₈″. "∠K 25" l. l. Collection Richard Mortensen, Copenhagen and Paris. CC 205.

1926

322 *Sketch for Several Circles*. Oil on canvas. 27⁵/₈ × 27⁵/₈″. "∠K" l. l. Collection Mme Anne Lewenstein, Paris.

323 *Several Circles*. Oil on canvas. 55¹/₈ × 55¹/₈″. "∠K 26" l. l. SRG, New York, formerly Staatl. Gemälde-Gal. Dresden. (Internat. Kunstausstellung, Dresden 1926). Color plate, p. 205.

324 *Small Yellow*. Oil on canvas. 16¹/₈ × 12⁵/₈″. "∠K 26" l. l. Yale University Art Gallery, Collection Société Anonyme. CC 206.

325 *Accent in Pink*. Oil on canvas. 39³/₈ × 31¹/₂″. "∠K 26" l. l. NK, Paris. CC 207.

326 *Tension in Red*. Oil on cardboard. 26 × 21¹/₄″. "∠K 26" l. l. SRG, New York. (Internat. Kunstausstellung, Dresden 1926). CC 208.

327 *Easter Egg*. Oil on cardboard. 10¹/₄ × 8⁵/₈″. "∠K 26" c. b. NK, Paris. CC 322.

328 *Fissure*. Oil on cardboard. 19⁵/₈ × 14⁵/₈″. "∠K 26" l. l. Formerly collection L. W. Gutbier, Dresden.

329 *Violet-Green*. Oil on canvas. 26 × 21¹/₄″. "∠K 26" l. l. Gift to Committee for Relief of Russian Prisoners of War, 1945, Paris. CC 209.

330 *In Itself*. Oil on cardboard. 19³/₈ × 13¹/₂″. "∠K 26" l. l. Private collection, Paris. CC 210.

331 *Cool Energy*. Oil on canvas. 28³/₄ × 23⁵/₈″. "∠K 26" l. l. CC 211.

332 *Connecting Green*. Oil on canvas. 33¹/₈ × 22⁵/₈″. "∠K 26" l. l. SRG, New York. CC 212.

333 *Extended*. Oil on wood. 37³/₈ × 17³/₈″. "K 26" l. l. SRG, New York, formerly collection Kirchhoff, Wiesbaden. (Kestner-Gesellschaft, Hannover 1927). CC 213.

334 *Counterweights*. Oil on cardboard. 19³/₈ × 19³/₈″. "∠K 26" l. l. Collection Gilda Fardel, Paris. CC 214.

335

335 *Yellow Circle*. Oil on cardboard. 27⁵/₈×19⁵/₈″. "∠K 26" l. l. SRG, New York. CC 215.

336 *Small Values*. Oil on cardboard. 17³/₄×13″. "∠K 26" l. l. NK, Paris. CC 216.

337 *Blue Cross*. Oil on cardboard. 16¹/₈×13″. "∠K 26" l. l. Collection M. Bruguière, Paris. CC 217.

338 *Discreet*. Oil on cardboard. 17³/₄×13″. "∠K 26" l. l. Collection Max Bill, Zurich. CC 218.

339 *Crescent*. Oil on cardboard. 16¹/₈×13″. "∠K 26" l. l. Collection Wilhelm Hack, Cologne. (Lucerne 1935). CC 219.

340 *Wedge on Circle*. Oil on cardboard. 16¹/₈×13″. "∠K 26" l. l. Private collection, Paris. CC 220.

341 *Sharp Hardness*. Oil on cardboard. 24×13³/₄″. "∠K 26" l. l. Collection Wilhelm Hack, Cologne. CC 221.

342 *Pointed Accents*. Oil on canvas. 31×49¹/₄″. "∠K 26" l. l. SRG, New York. CC 222.

343 *Three Sounds*. Oil on canvas. 23⁵/₈×23³/₈″. "∠K 26" l. l. SRG, New York, formerly Museum of Dessau. CC 223.

344 *Horizontal*. Oil on cardboard. 13×16¹/₈″. "∠K 26" l. l. Formerly Galerie Arnold (Gutbier), Dresden.

345 *Dark Impulse*. Oil on cardboard. 16¹/₈×13″. "K 26" l. l. CC 224.

346 *Little Whim*. Oil on cardboard. 16¹/₈×13″. "∠K 26" l. l. Formerly Collection Frau U. Voigt, Dresden.

347 *Cool*. Oil on canvas. 16⁷/₈×12⁵/₈″. "∠K 26" l. l. CC 225.

348 *Toward Pink*. Oil on cardboard. 27⁵/₈×10⁵/₈″. "∠K 26" l. l. CC 226.

349 *Discreet Blue*. Oil on canvas. 23⁵/₈×13³/₄″. "∠K 26" l. l. Private collection, Berlin. CC 227.

350 *Untitled (Hommage à Grohmann)*. Oil on canvas. 13³/₄×9⁷/₈″. "∠K 26" l. l. Collection Will Grohmann, Berlin. p. 291.

351 *Pressure*. Oil on canvas. 9⁷/₈×13³/₄″. "∠K 26" l. l. NK, Paris. CC 228.

352 *Rose in Gray*. Oil on canvas. 16¹/₈×20¹/₂″. "∠K 26" l. l. NK, Paris. CC 229.

353 *Cross Form*. Oil on canvas. 20¹/₂×17³/₄″. "∠K 26" l. l. Collection Frau Bally, Montreux, Switzerland, formerly Ruhmeshalle Barmen. CC 230.

354 *Above-Below*. Oil on canvas. 23⁵/₈×19⁵/₈″. "∠K 26" l. l. Private collection, New York.

355 *Asserting*. Oil on canvas. 17⁷/₈×21″. "∠K 26" l. l. SRG, New York. CC 231.

356 *Thorny*. Oil on canvas. 19¹/₄×24″. "∠K 26" l. l. CC 232.

357 *Quiet*. Oil on canvas. 19⁵/₈×18¹/₂″. "∠K 26" l. l. SRG, New York, formerly Museum of Erfurt. Color plate. p. 209.

358 *Beginning*. Oil on cardboard. 12¹/₄×15³/₄″. "∠K 25" l. l. (sic). NK, Paris. CC 233.

359 *Development*. Oil on cardboard. 12⁵/₈×15³/₄″. "∠K 26" l. l. Private collection, Paris. CC 234.

360 *Conclusion*. Oil on cardboard. 31¹/₂×15″. "∠K 26" l. l. Private collection, Paris. CC 235.

361 *Yellow Center*. Oil on cardboard. 17³/₄×14⁵/₈″. "∠K 26" l. l. SRG, New York. CC 236.

362 *Rift*. Oil on canvas. 39³/₄×32″. "∠K 26" l. l. SRG, New York. CC 237.

363 *Secure Square*. Oil on cardboard. 23¹/₄×22⁷/₈″. "∠K 26" l. l. Destroyed.

364 *For Nina*. Oil on canvas. 13×17⁵/₄″. "∠K 26" l. l. NK, Paris. p. 292.

365 *Thorn*. Oil on cardboard. 13×15³/₄″. "∠K 26" l. l. Lost.

366 *In Repose*. Oil on cardboard.

367 *Shifted*. Oil on canvas. 22⁷/₈×22⁷/₈″. "∠K 26" l. l. Collection Louis Clayeux, Paris. CC 238.

368 *Chat*. Oil on canvas. 22⁷/₈×22⁷/₈″. "∠K 26" l. l. SRG, New York. p. 293.

369 *Loose-Fast*. Oil on canvas. 43⁷/₈×39⁵/₈″. "K 26" l. l. SRG, New York. CC 239.

370 *Closely Surrounded*. Oil on canvas. 39³/₈×25¹/₄″. "∠K 26" l. l. private collection, Paris. CC 240.

1927

371 *Free*. Oil on cardboard. 19⁵/₈×14⁵/₈″. "∠K 27" l. l. Joan Miró, Mallorca. CC 241.

372 *Simple*. Oil on cardboard. 19⁵/₈×14⁵/₈″. "∠K 27" l. l. Collection Frau A. Müller-Widmann, Basel. CC 242.

373 *Black Increasing*. Oil on canvas. 23⁵/₈×19⁵/₈″. "∠K 27" l. l. Collection G. David Thompson, Pittsburgh. Color plate, p. 213.

374 *Leftward*. Oil on cardboard. 16¹/₈×13″. "∠K 27" l. l. CC 243.

375 *Supported*. Oil on canvas. 31¹/₈×20¹/₂″. "∠K 27" l. l. Collection Dr. and Mrs. Israel Rosen, Baltimore, USA. CC 244.

376 *Disturbance*. Oil on canvas. 19⁵/₈×16⁷/₈″. "∠K 27" l. l. NK, Paris. CC 245.

377 *Square*. Oil on canvas. 28³/₄×23⁵/₈″. "∠K 27" l. l. Galerie Aimé Maeght, Paris. CC 246.

378 *Red Cross*. Oil on cardboard. 20¹/₈×18¹/₈″. "∠K 27" l. l. Collection Clayeux, Paris. CC 247.

379 *Motley Figure*. Oil on cardboard. 23³/₈×9⁷/₈″. "∠K 27" l. l. Formerly collection Fernand Graindorge, Liège.

380 *Dark Coolness*. Oil on wood. 10¹/₄×7⁷/₈″. "∠K 27" l. l. NK, Paris. CC 248.

381 *Theme Point*. Oil on canvas. 31¹/₂×22¹/₂″. "∠K 27" l. l. CC 249.

382 *Sign with Accompaniment*. Oil on canvas. 30³/₄×20¹/₂″. "∠K 27" l. l. SRG, New York. CC 250.

383 *Arched*. Oil on cardboard. 16¹/₂×11³/₄″. "∠K 27" l. l. Formerly Gallery Castelli, New York.

384 *Sharp-Quiet*. Oil on cardboard. 16⁵/₈×22¹/₂″. "∠K 27" l. l. Galerie Aimé Maeght, Paris. CC 251.

385 *Cloudy Circle*. Oil on canvas. 35³/₈×27⁵/₈″. "∠K 27" l. l. Formerly Gallery K. Nierendorf, New York.

386 *Angular*. Oil on canvas. 22¹/₂×20¹/₂″. "∠K 27" l. l. NK, Paris. CC 252.

387 *Upper Blue*. Oil on canvas. 23⁵/₈×9⁷/₈″. "∠K 27" l. l. Destroyed by Kandinsky.

388 *Glow*. Oil on canvas. 20¹/₂×13¹/₂″. "∠K 27" l. l. Collection Mr. and Mrs. Harry L. Winston, Birmingham, Mich., formerly collection Rose, Hannover. CC 253.

389 *Arrows*. Oil on canvas. 34⁵/₈×30³/₄″. "K 27" l. l. Collection M. Beglarian, Paris. CC 254.

390 *Woven*. Oil on canvas. 19⁵/₈×27⁵/₈″. "∠K 27" l. l. NK, Paris. CC 255.

391 *Several Sounds*. Oil on cardboard. 13×16¹/₈″. "∠K 27" l. l. Private collection, Paris. CC 256.

392 *Hard in Soft*. Oil on canvas. 39¹/₄×19⁵/₈″. "∠K 27" l. l. SRG, New York. CC 257.

393 *Blue*. Oil on cardboard. 19¹/₂×14¹/₂″. "∠K 27" l. l. MMA, New York, Katherine S. Dreier Request. CC 258.

394 *Delicate White Lines*. Oil on cardboard. 22¹/₂×20¹/₂″. "∠K 27" l. l. Destroyed.

395 *Hovering*. Oil on cardboard. 18×21¹/₄″. "∠K 27" l. l. SRG, New York. CC 259.

396 *Black Strip*. Oil on cardboard. 21¹/₄×26″. "∠K27" l. l. Formerly Staatl. Schule für Textilindustrie Plauen. CC 260.

397 *Netting*. Oil on canvas. 27⁵/₈×23⁵/₈″. "∠K 27" l. l. Louis Clayeux, Paris. CC 261.

398 *Heavy Circles*. Oil on canvas. 22¹/₂×20¹/₂″. "∠K 27" l. l. The Pasadena Art. Museum, Calif., formerly collection Mrs. Galka Scheyer. CC 262.

399 *Pointed Structure*. Oil on canvas. 20¹/₂×28³/₈″. "∠K 27" l. l. Formerly collection Mrs. Galka Scheyer. CC 263.

400 *Dull Red*. Oil on canvas. 26×30″. "∠K 27" l. l. CC 264.

401 *Radiating Lines*. Oil on canvas. 39¹/₈×29¹/₈″. "∠K 27" l. l. SRG, New York, formerly collection R. Drouin, Paris. (Esquisse, Paris 1944). p. 294.

402 *Red Bar*. Oil on canvas. 36³/₈×20³/₈″. "∠K 27" l. l. SRG, New York. CC 265.

403 *Red in the Net*. Oil on cardboard. 24³/₈ × 19¹/₄″. "∠K 27" l. l. Formerly Galerie Percier, Paris. CC 266.

404 *Mild Hardness*. Oil on cardboard. 19⁷/₈ × 14⁷/₈″. "∠K 27" l. l. SRG, New York. CC 267.

405 *Black-Red*. Oil on canvas. 17³/₄ × 26″. "∠K 27" l. l. NK, Paris. CC 268.

406 *Warm-Cool*. Oil on canvas. 15 × 19⁵/₈″. "∠K 27" l. l. Galerie Maeght, Paris. CC 269.

407 *Points in Arc*. Oil on canvas. 26 × 19¹/₄″. "∠K 27" l. l. Collection Frau Ida Bienert, Munich. p. 295.

408 *Sharp Heat*. Oil on cardboard. 13³/₈ × 16¹/₈″. "∠K 27" l. l. Mus. Wuppertal-Elberfeld. CC 270.

409 *Line-Spot*. Oil on canvas. 14³/₄ × 10¹/₄″. "∠K 27" l. l. Santa Barbara Museum of Art, Calif., Gift of Mr. and Mrs. Ira Gershwin. CC 271.

410 *Soft Hard*. Oil on canvas. 13 × 16¹/₂″. "∠K 27" l. l. NK, Paris. CC 272.

411 *Variegation in the Triangle*. Oil on cardboard. 19⁵/₈ × 14⁵/₈″. "∠K 27" l. l. Collection Bernard Maeght, Paris. CC 273.

412 *Several Cool*. Oil on canvas. 11 × 12⁵/₈″. "∠K 27" l. l. CC 274.

413 *Red Circle*. Oil on canvas. 13 × 16¹/₈″. "∠K 27" l. l. Formerly collection Bucher, Paris.

1928

414 *Bipartite*. Oil on cardboard. 13³/₄ × 16¹/₈″. "∠K 28" l. l. NK, Paris. CC 275.

415 *Little Black Bars*. Oil on wood. 10¹/₄ × 7⁷/₈″. "∠K 28" l. l. Private collection, Cologne. CC 276.

416 *Square Lyrical*. Oil on cardboard. 13 × 9″. "∠K 28" l. l. Formerly collection Mrs. Galka Scheyer, Los Angeles. CC 277.

417 *Repose*. Oil on canvas. 20¹/₂ × 31¹/₈″. "∠K 28" l. l. SRG, New York, formerly National-Gal. Berlin. CC 278.

418 *Red-Cornered*. Oil on canvas. 18¹/₄ × 14³/₄″. "∠K 28" l. l. Collection Mme Dina Vierney, Paris. CC 279.

419 *Mild Happening*. Oil on canvas. 15³/₈ × 26³/₄″. "∠K 28" l. l. NK, Paris. CC 280.

420 *A Circle A*. Oil on canvas. 13³/₈ × 9⁷/₈″. "∠K 28" l. l. NK, Paris. CC 281.

421 *Lyrical Oval*. Oil on canvas. 13³/₈ × 11³/₈″. "∠K 28" l. l. Private collection, Paris. p. 296.

422 *Veiled Glow*. Oil on cardboard. 30¹/₄ × 24³/₈″. "∠K 28" l. l. Collection Mr. and Mrs. Victor Kiam, New York. CC 282.

423 *Variegated Signs*. Oil on canvas. 9⁷/₈ × 17³/₄″. "∠K 28" l. l. Collection Louis Clayeux, Paris. CC 283.

424 *Deepened Impulse*. Oil on canvas. 39³/₈ × 29⁷/₈″. "∠K 28" l. l. Private collection, Mexico City, formerly collection Otto Ralfs, Braunschweig. CC 284.

425 *Dull-Clear*. Oil on canvas. 25 × 7⁷/₈″. "∠K 28" l. l. Collection Orjan Lüning, Stockholm. CC 285.

426 *Three Places*. Oil on cardboard. 17³/₄ × 24³/₄″. "∠K 28" l. l. Private collection, Paris. CC 286.

427 *To and Fro*. Oil on canvas. 13³/₈ × 20¹/₂″. "∠K 28" l. l. Private collection, Paris. CC 287.

428 *Variegated Accompaniment*. Oil on canvas. 11³/₄ × 7⁷/₈″. "∠K 28" l. l. Private collection, Paris. CC 288.

429 *Determining*. Oil on cardboard. 13³/₄ × 7⁷/₈″. "∠K 28" l. l. Collection Miss Evelyn Mayer, San Francisco.

430 *Red Figure*. Oil on cardboard. 19⁵/₈ × 14³/₄″. "∠K 28" l. l. CC 289.

431 *Powerful Red*. Oil on cardboard. 15³/₈ × 12⁵/₈″. "∠K 28" l. l. CC 290.

432 *A Circle B*. Oil on canvas. 13³/₄ × 9⁷/₈″. "∠K 28" l. l. CC 291.

433 *On Points*. Oil on canvas. 55¹/₈ × 55¹/₈″. "∠K 28" l. l. NK, Paris. (Hamburger Kunstverein 1928). p. 297.

434 *Mottled Bars*. Oil on cardboard. 22¹/₂ × 16¹/₂″. "∠K 28" l. l. SRG, New York. CC 292.

435 *Red Repose*. Oil on cardboard. 16¹/₈ × 13″. "∠K 28" l. l. Collection M. de Montbrison, Paris. CC 293.

436 *White Grids*. Oil on cardboard. 16¹/₂ × 12⁵/₈″. "∠K 28" l. l. Formerly collection M. Panier, Paris.

437 *Two Sides Red*. Oil on canvas. 22³/₄ × 17¹/₈″. "∠K 28" l. l. SRG, New York. CC 294.

1929

438 *Rigid*. Oil on woods. 24³/₈ × 13³/₄″. "∠K 29" l. l. Collection Mrs. Hilla Rebay, Greens Farms, Conn. CC 295.

439 *Thin*. Oil on cardboard. 14¹/₈ × 10⁵/₈″. "∠K 29" l. l. Formerly collection Mrs. Galka Scheyer, Los Angeles.

440 *Loose Connection*. Oil on cardboard. 17³/₈ × 13″. "∠K 28" l. l. Collection Alberto Magnelli, Paris. CC 296.

441 *A Bit of Red*. Oil on cardboard. 15³/₈ × 12″. "∠K 29" l. l. SRG, New York, formerly collection Otto Baier, Cologne. CC 297.

442 *Circle and Spot*. Oil on canvas. 29⁷/₈ × 26″. "∠K 29" l. l. NK, Paris. CC 298.

443 *Light Blue*. Oil on canvas. 21 × 26³/₈″. "∠K 29" l. l. SRG, New York, formerly collection Ferdinand Möller, Cologne. CC 299.

444 *Hovering above Firm*. Oil on cardboard. 16¹/₂ × 22¹/₂″. "∠K 29" l. l. Collection Helmut Beck, Stuttgart. CC 300.

445 *Whitish*. Oil on canvas. 20¹/₂ × 28³/₈″. "∠K 29" l. l. Stolen from exhibition in Los Angeles. CC 301.

446 *Round Accent*. Oil on cardboard. 17³/₄ × 13¹/₈″. "∠K 29" l. l. Private collection, USA. CC 302.

447 *Inner Bond*. Oil on cardboard. 26 × 29⁷/₈″. "∠K 29" l. l. Collection Robert Brest, Buenos Aires. CC 303.

448 *Circle with Brown*. Oil on cardboard. 19⁵/₈ × 14⁵/₈″. "∠K 29" l. l. – CC 304.

449 *Ladder Form*. Oil on canvas. 19⁵/₈ × 19⁵/₈″. "∠K 29" l. l. Collection Dr. E. Friedrich, Zurich. CC 305.

450 *Cheerful Yellow*. Oil on canvas. 13³/₄ × 9⁷/₈″. "∠K 29" l. l. CC 306.

451 *Whitebound*. Oil on canvas. 14¹/₈ × 18⁷/₈″. "∠K 29" l. l. Collection Mme Marcella Ascarelli-Ziffer, Rome. CC 446.

452 *Levels*. Oil on canvas. 22 × 16¹/₈″. "∠K 29" l. l. SRG, New York. CC 307.

453 *Condensation*. Oil on canvas. 39³/₈ × 31¹/₂″. "∠K 29" l. l. Private collection, USA. CC 308.

454 *In the Clear Blue*. Oil on canvas. 39³/₈ × 24³/₈″. "∠K 29" l. l. Gift by Nina Kandinsky to the House of Youth, Copenhagen. (Documenta, Kassel 1955). CC 309.

455 *Dense*. Oil on cardboard. 12⁵/₈ × 16¹/₈″. "∠K 29" l. l. CC 310.

456 *Taciturn*. Oil on cardboard. 13¹/₂ × 9¹/₂″. "∠K 29" l. l. SRG, New York. CC 311.

457 *Light in Heavy*. Oil on canvas. 19¹/₂ × 19¹/₂″. "∠K 29" l. l. SRG, New York, formerly collection Georg Muche, Krefeld. CC 312.

458 *Holding*. Oil on canvas. 15 × 21⁵/₈″. "∠K 29" l. l. Collection Prof. W. Löffler, Zurich. CC 313.

459 *Flat*. Oil on cardboard. 18¹/₄ × 13¹/₈″. "∠K 29" l. l. Galerie Maeght, Paris. CC 314.

460 *Green*. Oil on cardboard. 27⁵/₈ × 19¹/₄″. "∠K 29" l. l. Private collection, Paris. CC 315.

461 *For and Against*. Oil on canvas. 13³/₄ × 19¹/₄″. "∠K 29" l. l. SRG, New York (first Kandinsky acquired by S. R. Guggenheim). CC 316.

462 *Short*. Oil on canvas. 13¹/₂ × 9⁵/₈″. "∠K 29" l. l. Collection Charles Estienne, Paris.

463 *Fixed Points*. Oil on cardboard. 27¹/₂ × 13⁵/₈″. "∠K 29" l. l. SRG, New York. CC 317.

464 *Cold*. Oil on cardboard. 19¹/₄ × 19¹/₄″. "∠K 29" l. l. NK, Paris. CC 318.

465 *Point*. Oil on cardboard. 19¹/₄ × 19¹/₄″. "∠K 29" l. l. Formerly collection Otto Ralfs, Braunschweig.

466 *Fragment.* Oil on cardboard. 19$^1/_4$×13$^3/_4$''. "∠K 29" I. I. NK, Paris. CC 319.

467 *Picture within Picture.* Oil on canvas. 27$^5/_8$×19$^1/_4$''. "∠K 29" I. I. collection Mr. and Mrs. William de Vogel, Milwaukee, Wis., formerly collection H. Kirchhoff, Wiesbaden. p. 298.

468 *One – Two.* Oil on cardboard. 13$^1/_2$×9$^5/_8$''. "∠K 29" I. I. SRG, New York. CC 320.

469 *Light Counterpressure.* Oil on cardboard. 19$^1/_4$×19$^1/_4$''. "∠K 29" I. I. Private collection, Paris. CC 321.

470 *Upward.* Oil on cardboard. 27$^5/_8$×19$^1/_4$''. "∠K 29" I. I. Collection Mrs. Peggy Guggenheim, Venice. CC 323.

471 *Oppressed.* Oil on cardboard. 27$^1/_2$×19$^1/_8$''. "∠K 29" I. I. SRG, New York. CC 324.

472 *White-White.* Oil on cardboard. 19$^1/_4$×27$^5/_8$''. "∠K 29" I. I. CC 325.

473 *Angular Swing.* Oil on cardboard. 19$^1/_4$×27$^5/_8$''. "∠K 29" I. I. SRG, New York. CC 326.

474 *Stubborn.* Oil on cardboard. 27$^5/_8$×19$^1/_4$''. "∠K 29" I. I. SRG, New York. p. 299.

475 *Green Degrees.* Oil on cardboard. 19$^1/_4$×19$^1/_4$''. "∠K 29" I. I. Galerie Maeght, Paris. CC 327.

476 *Down.* Oil on cardboard. 19$^1/_4$×19$^1/_4$''. "∠K 29" I. I. Collection Gilda Fardel, Paris. CC 328.

477 *Circles in Brown.* Oil on cardboard. 19$^1/_4$×19$^1/_4$''. "∠K 29" I. I. SRG, New York, formerly collection A. von Jawlensky. CC 329.

478 *Two Crosses.* Oil on cardboard. 19$^1/_4$×27$^5/_8$''. "∠K 29" I. I. Private collection, Paris. CC 330.

479 *Blue.* Oil on cardboard. 9$^5/_8$×13$^1/_2$''. "∠K 29" I. I. Collection André Level, Paris. CC 331.

480 *Variegated but Quiet.* Oil on cardboard. 13$^5/_8$×19$^1/_4$''. "∠K 29" I. I. Collection Paule et Adrien Maeght, Paris. CC 332.

481 *Pink-Sweet.* Oil on cardboard. 27$^5/_8$×19$^1/_4$''. "∠K 29" I. I. Collection Mrs. Hilla Rebay, Greens Farms, Conn. CC 333.

482 *Sharp in Blunt.* Oil on cardboard. 19$^1/_4$×19$^1/_4$''. "∠K 29" I. I. NK, Paris. CC 334.

483 *Inflexible.* Oil on cardboard. 19$^1/_4$×13$^3/_4$''. "∠K 29" I. I. Collection Hans Stampfli, Basel. CC 335.

484 *Soft Interpretation.* Oil on cardboard. 21$^1/_2$×13$^3/_8$''. "∠K 29" I. I. Formerly Galerie J. Bucher, Paris.

485 *Jocular Sounds.* Oil on cardboard. 13$^3/_4$×19$^1/_4$''. "∠K 29" I. I. Busch-Reisinger Museum, Harvard University, Cambridge, Mass., formerly collection Ise Bienert, Munich. CC 336.

486 *Thrust in Violet.* Oil on cardboard. 19$^5/_8$×9$^7/_8$''. "∠K 29" I. I. CC 337.

487 *Co-operation.* Oil on cardboard. 10$^5/_8$×17$^1/_8$''. "∠K 29" I. I. Private collection, New York. CC 338.

488 *Pointed Yellow.* Oil on cardboard. 13$^3/_4$×19$^1/_4$''. "∠K 29" I. I. Formerly collection Prof. Schridde, Dortmund. CC 339.

489 *Eight Times.* Oil on cardboard. 9$^5/_8$×15$^3/_4$''. "∠K 29" I. I. CC 340.

1930

490 *Flat-Deep.* Oil on canvas. 19$^1/_4$×27$^5/_8$''. "∠K 30" I. I. Private collection, Paris. CC 341.

491 *Jolly.* Oil on cardboard. 13$^3/_4$×9''. "∠K 30" I. I. CC 342.

492 *Scarcely.* Tempera and plaster. 13$^3/_4$×6$^1/_4$''. "∠K 30" I. I. SRG, New York. CC 343.

493 *Upward through Blue.* Oil on cardboard. 19$^1/_4$×13$^3/_4$''. "∠K 30" I. I. NK, Paris. CC 344.

494 *Fluttering.* Oil on cardboard. 13$^1/_2$×9$^5/_8$''. "∠K 30" I. I. NK, Paris. CC 345.

495 *Central.* Oil on cardboard. 14×11''. "∠K 30" I. I. Collection Dr. Coller, Michigan University.

496 *Circle and Square.* Oil on cardboard. 27$^5/_8$×19$^1/_4$''. Formerly collection Gal. K. Nierendorf, New York.

497 *Yellow Border.* Oil on cardboard. 19$^1/_4$×19$^1/_4$''. "∠K 30" I. I. NK, Paris. CC 346.

498 *Arrow toward the Circle.* Oil on canvas. 31$^1/_2$×43$^1/_4$''. "∠K30" I. I. Formerly collection Aimé Maeght, Paris. CC 347.

499 *Unsteady Balance.* Oil on cardboard. 17$^3/_4$×13''. "∠K 30" I. I. Collection Bernard Maeght, Paris. CC 348.

500 *Stretched in the Corner.* Oil on cardboard. 19$^1/_4$×21$^1/_4$''. "∠K 30" I. I. Collection Dr. Othmar Huber, Glarus. CC 349.

501 *Round and Pointed.* Oil on cardboard. 19$^1/_4$×27$^5/_8$''. "∠K 30" I. I. Galerie W. Grosshennig, Düsseldorf. CC 350.

502 *Condensed Brown.* Oil on cardboard. 19$^1/_4$×19$^1/_4$''. "∠K 30" I. I. Collection Gilda Fardel, Paris. CC 351.

503 *Within Three Points.* Oil on cardboard. 19$^1/_4$×19$^1/_4$''. "∠K 30" I. I. Private collection, Paris. CC 352.

504 *Light.* Oil on cardboard. 27$^5/_8$×19$^1/_4$''. "∠K 30" I. I. NK, Paris. CC 353.

505 *Dark Point.* Oil on cardboard. 13$^3/_4$×19$^1/_4$''. "∠K 30" I. I. Collection André Bloc, Paris. CC 354.

506 *Dull Gray.* Oil on cardboard. 13$^3/_4$×10''. "∠K 30" I. I. Collection Georg Guggenheim, Zurich. CC 355.

507 *Disintegrated Tension.* Oil on cardboard. 19$^1/_4$×13$^3/_4$''. "∠K 30" I. I. Private collection, Paris. CC 356.

508 *Green-Empty.* Oil on cardboard. 13$^3/_4$×19$^1/_4$''. "∠K 30" I. I. NK, Paris. CC 357.

509 *From – To.* Oil on cardboard. 13$^3/_4$×19$^1/_4$''. "∠K 30" I. I. Collection Max Bill, Zurich. CC 358.

510 *Fixed-Loose.* Oil on cardboard. 15$^3/_4$×27$^5/_8$''. "∠K 30" I. I. Private collection, New York. CC 359.

511 *Diagonal.* Oil on cardboard. 19$^1/_4$×27$^5/_8$''. "∠K 30" I. I. Formerly Galerie Maeght, Paris. CC 360.

512 *White.* Oil on cardboard. 19$^1/_4$×13$^3/_4$''. "∠K 30" I. I. Collection Princess E. Zalstem-Zalessky, New York. CC 361.

513 *Erect.* Oil on canvas. 19$^1/_4$×27$^5/_8$''. "∠K 30" I. I. NK, Paris. CC 362.

514 *Serious-Joke.* Oil on cardboard. 19$^1/_4$×27$^5/_8$''. "∠K 30" I. I. CC 363.

515 *Yellow Arc.* Oil on canvas. 19$^1/_4$×27$^5/_8$''. "∠K 30" I. I. E. Weyhe Gallery, New York. CC 364.

516 *Great-Little.* Oil on cardboard. 14$^5/_8$×19$^1/_4$''. "∠K 30" I. I. Collection Mr. and Mrs. Edgar B. Miller, Chicago. CC 365.

517 *Stripes.* Oil on cardboard. 19$^1/_4$×6$^1/_4$''. "∠K 30" I. I. Collection Max Bill, Zurich. CC 366.

518 *Cool Condensation.* Oil on cardboard. 19$^1/_4$×14$^5/_8$''. "∠K 30" I. I. Collection Felix Klee, Bern. p. 300.

519 *Untitled.* Oil on cardboard. 10×13$^3/_4$''. "∠K 30" I. I. NK, Paris. CC 367.

520 *Dream-thing.* Oil on cardboard. 11$^3/_4$×19$^3/_8$''. "∠K 30" I. I. Formerly collection R. Drouin, Paris.

521 *Joyous-Bright.* Oil on cardboard. 27$^5/_8$×23$^5/_8$''. "∠K 30" I. I. Collection Aimé Maeght, Paris. CC 368.

522 *Surfaces and Lines.* Oil on cardboard. 19$^1/_4$×27$^5/_8$''. "∠K 30" I. I. Private collection, Paris. CC 369.

523 *Angular Structure.* Oil on cardboard. 23$^5/_8$×27$^5/_8$''. "∠K 30" I. I. NK, Paris. CC 370.

524 *Two Squares.* Tempera on cardboard. 13$^1/_8$×9$^1/_2$''. "∠K 30" I. I. NK, Paris. CC 371.

525 *Thirteen Rectangles.* Oil on cardboard. 27$^5/_8$×23$^5/_8$''. "∠K30" I. I. NK, Paris. CC 372.

526 *Ascended.* Oil on cardboard. 19$^1/_4$×14$^5/_8$''. "∠K 30" I. I. Collection Hans Arnhold, New York. CC 373.

527 *Cool Stripes.* Oil on cardboard. 19$^1/_4$×27$^5/_8$''. "∠K 30" I. I. Collection, Paris. CC 374.

528 *Definite.* Oil on cardboard. 27$^5/_8$×19$^1/_4$''. "∠K 30" I. I. Private collection, Paris. CC 375.

529 *Heavy and Light.* Oil on cardboard. 17$^5/_8$×23$^5/_8$''. "∠K 30" I. I. Collection Philippe Dotremont, Brussels, formerly collection Ida Bienert, Munich. CC 376.

530 *White Sharpness*. Oil on canvas. $27^5/_8 \times 19^1/_4''$. "∠K 30" l. l. SRG, New York. CC 377.

531 *White on Black*. Oil on canvas. $27^5/_8 \times 27^5/_8''$. "∠K 30" l. l. Collection Philippe Dotremont, Brussels. CC 378.

532 *Calmed*. Oil on cardboard. $19^1/_4 \times 19^1/_4''$. "∠K 30" l. l. Collection Louis Clayeux, Paris. CC 379.

533 *Far*. Oil on cardboard. $13^1/_2 \times 29^1/_2''$. – "∠K 30" l. l. SRG, New York. CC 380.

534 *Blue Set*. Oil on cardboard. $19^1/_4 \times 14^5/_8''$. "∠K 30" l. l. Collection Mrs. Julia Feininger, New York. CC 380.

535 *Figure in Red*. Oil on cardboard. $19^1/_4 \times 14^5/_8''$. "∠K 30" l. l. CC 381.

536 *Two*. Oil on cardboard. $27^5/_8 \times 23^5/_8''$. "∠K 30" l. l. Destroyed.

537 *Isolated*. Oil on cardboard. $27^5/_8 \times 19^1/_4''$. "∠K 30" l. l. CC 382.

538 *Moody*. Oil on cardboard. $15^3/_4 \times 19^5/_8''$. "∠K 30" l. l. SRG, New York. CC 383.

539 *Intimate Division*. Oil on cardboard. $27^5/_8 \times 19^1/_4''$. l. l. CC 384.

540 *Two Black Stripes*. Oil on cardboard. $19^1/_4 \times 27^5/_8''$. "∠K 30" l. l. Galerie Maeght, Paris. CC 385.

541 *Angular Line*. Oil on cardboard. $27^5/_8 \times 23^5/_8''$. "∠K 30" l. l. – CC 386.

542 *Liberated Bar*. Oil on cardboard. $19^1/_4 \times 19^1/_4''$. "∠K 30" l. l. Formerly collection F. Möller, Cologne.

543 *From the Little Arrow*. Oil on cardboard. $13^3/_8 \times 19^1/_4''$. l. l. Private collection, Paris. CC 387.

1931

544 *Stable*. Tempera and oil on cardboard. $19^1/_4 \times 27^5/_8''$. "∠K 31" l. l. Private collection, New York. CC 388.

545 *Pointed Black*. Oil on cardboard. $27^5/_8 \times 23^5/_8''$. "∠K 31" l. l. Collection Mme Marguerite Hagenbach, Basel. CC 389.

546 *Bridge*. Oil on cardboard. $27^5/_8 \times 23^5/_8''$. "∠K 31" l. l. Formerly Galerie Maeght, Paris. CC 390.

547 *Gray*. Oil on cardboard. $27^5/_8 \times 23^5/_8''$. "∠K 31" l. l. NK, Paris. CC 391.

548 *Flowing*. Tempera and oil on cardboard. $27^5/_8 \times 23^5/_8''$. "∠K 31" l. l. Collection Mr. and Mrs. E. L. Froelicher, New York. CC 392.

549 *Gentle Stress*. Oil on canvas. $39^3/_8 \times 39^3/_2''$. "∠K 31" l. l. Collection Princess Zalstem-Zalessky, New York. CC 393.

550 *Brownish*. Oil on cardboard. $19 \times 27^1/_2''$. "∠K 31" l. l. Collection San Francisco Museum of Art. CC 394.

551 *Below-Above*. Oil on cardboard. $27^5/_8 \times 27^5/_8''$. "∠K 31" l. l. Destroyed.

552 *Fragile*. Tempera on cardboard. $13^3/_4 \times 19^1/_4''$. "∠K 31" l. l. NK, Paris. CC 395.

553 *One in Two*. Oil on cardboard. $19^1/_4 \times 27^1/_2''$. "∠K 31" l. l. Formerly Museum of Lodz, Poland, lost.

554a *Sketch for Architectural Exhibition, Berlin* (actual size $116^1/_8 \times 196^1/_8''$). Oil on cardboard. $17^3/_4 \times 29^1/_2''$. NK, Paris. CC 396.

554b *Sketch for Architectural Exhibition, Berlin* (actual size $116^1/_8 \times 275^5/_8''$). Oil on cardboard. $17^3/_4 \times 39^3/_8''$. NK, Paris. CC 397.

554c *Sketch for Architectural Exhibition, Berlin* (actual size $116^1/_8 \times 275^5/_8''$). Oil on cardboard. $17^7/_8 \times 29^1/_2''$. NK, Paris. CC 398.

555 *Individual Forms*. Oil on cardboard. $27^5/_8 \times 23^5/_8''$. "∠K 31" l. l. Collection Aimé Maeght, Paris. CC 399.

556 *Hard Tension*. Tempera and oil on canvas. $27^5/_8 \times 27^5/_8''$. "∠K 31" l. l. Collection Aimé Maeght, Paris. CC 400.

557 *Green*. Oil on carboard. $23^5/_8 \times 27^5/_8''$. "∠K 31" l. l. Private collection, Paris. CC 401.

558 *Red Across*. Oil and tempera on cardboard. $27^5/_8 \times 31^1/_2''$. "∠K 31" l. l. Formerly collection J. B. Neumann, New York. CC 402.

559 *Between Bright*. Oil on cardboard. $27^5/_8 \times 31^1/_2''$. "∠K 31" l. l. Private collection, Brussels. CC 403.

560 *Black-White*. Oil on cardboard. $19^1/_4 \times 27^5/_8''$. "∠K 31" l. l. Collection Estorick, London, formerly collection Mrs. Ward, Hollywood, Cal. CC 404.

561 *Lightly touched*. Oil on cardboard. $27^5/_8 \times 19^1/_4''$. "∠K 31" l. l. Collection Sidney Janis, New York. CC 405.

562 (omitted in original manuscript)

563 *Hovering Pressure*. Oil and tempera on cardboard. $31^1/_2 \times 27^5/_8''$. "∠K 31" l. l. SRG, New York.

564 *Flutter-like*. Oil and tempera on cardboard. $19^1/_4 \times 27^5/_8''$. "∠K 31" l. l. NK, Paris. CC 406.

565 *Slowly out*. Tempera and oil on cardboard. $23^5/_8 \times 27^5/_8''$. "∠K 31" l. l. NK, Paris. CC 407.

566 *Gray Set*. Oil on cardboard. $23^5/_8 \times 27^5/_8''$. "∠K 31" l. l. NK, Paris. CC 408.

567 *Up from the Half-Circle*. Tempera on cardboard. $29^1/_2 \times 17^3/_4''$. "∠K 31" l. l. Private collection, Paris. CC 409.

568 *Inclination*. Tempera and oil on cardboard. $27^1/_2 \times 27^1/_2''$. "∠K 31" l. l. SRG, New York. CC 410.

1932

569 *Layers*. Tempera and oil on cardboard. $19^5/_8 \times 15^3/_4''$. "∠K 32" l. l. SRG, New York.

570 *To Four Corners*. Tempera, lacquer and oil on canvas. $27^5/_8 \times 27^5/_8''$. "∠K 32" l. l. Formerly collection Galka Scheyer, Los Angeles.

571 *Fixed Flight*. Oil on cardboard. $19^1/_4 \times 27^5/_8''$. "∠K 32" l. l. Galerie Maeght, Paris. CC 411.

572 *Secure Position*. Oil on canvas. $23^5/_8 \times 27^5/_8''$. "∠K 32" l. l. NK, Paris. CC 412.

573 *Decisive Pink*. Oil on canvas. $31^1/_2 \times 38^3/_8''$. "∠K 32" l. l. SRG, New York. CC 413.

574 *Rightward – Leftward*. Oil on canvas. $23^5/_8 \times 27^5/_8''$. "∠K 32" l. l. Galerie Maeght, Paris. CC 414.

575 *White - Soft and Hard*. Oil and tempera on cardboard. $31^1/_2 \times 39^3/_8''$. "∠K 32" l. l. Collection Mrs. L. M. Maitland, San Francisco. CC 415.

576 *Both Striped*. Oil and tempera on cardboard. $31^1/_2 \times 27^5/_8''$. "∠K 32" l. l. NK, Paris. CC 416.

577 *Uneven*. Oil and tempera on cardboard. $23^5/_8 \times 27^5/_8''$. "∠K 32" l. l. Formerly collection Galka Scheyer, Los Angeles.

578 *Drastic and Mild*. Oil on canvas. $39^5/_8 \times 47^1/_2''$. "∠K 32" l. l. SRG, New York. CC 417.

579 *Connection*. Oil on canvas. $27^5/_8 \times 23^5/_8''$. "∠K 32" l. l. Collection Aimé Maeght, Paris. CC 418.

580 *Cool Distance*. Oil and tempera on cardboard. $16^7/_8 \times 16^1/_2''$. "∠K 32" l. l. NK, Paris. CC 419.

581 *Thither*. Tempera on cardboard. $19^1/_4 \times 13''$. "∠K 32" l. l. NK, Paris. CC 420.

1933

582 *All the More*. Oil and tempera on canvas. $27^5/_8 \times 27^5/_8''$. "∠K 33" l. l. Collection Mrs. Kay Merill Hillman, New York, formerly collection Rose Fried, New York. CC 421.

583 *Balance-Pink*. Oil and tempera on canvas. $36^1/_4 \times 28^3/_4''$. "∠K 33" l. l. NK, Paris. CC 422.

584 *Light Formation*. Oil and lacquer on canvas. $39^1/_8 \times 47^1/_4''$. "∠K 33" l. l. Collection M. Doelemans, Brussels. CC 423.

585 *Succession*. Tempera and watercolor on cardboard. $16^1/_2 \times 22^1/_2''$. "∠K 33" l. l. NK, Paris. CC 424.

586 *Defiant*. Oil on canvas. $27^5/_8 \times 27^5/_8''$. "∠K 33" l. l. Collection Mr. and Mrs. Victor Kiam, New York. CC 425.

587 *Gray mood*. Tempera and oil on cardboard. $27^5/_8 \times 19^1/_4''$. "∠K 33" l. l. SRG, New York. CC 426.

588 *Soft Hardness*. Tempera on cardboard. 30¹/₄×16¹/₂″. I. I. "∠K 33" I. I. CC 427.

589 *Crowded Circles*. Tempera and oil on canvas. 39×24³/₄″. "∠K 33" I. I. Collection Aimé Maeght, Paris. CC 428.

590 *Green Texture*. Tempera on cardboard.16¹/₂×22¹/₂″. "∠K 33" I. I. Collection Mr. E. Lux, New York. CC 429.

591 *Stretched Bilaterally*. Tempera on cardboard. 16¹/₂×22¹/₂″. "∠K 33" I. I. Private collection, USA. CC 430.

592 *From Here to There*. Tempera on carboard. 16¹/₂×22¹/₂″. "∠K 33" I. I. CC 431.

593 *Lightly Together*. Tempera and watercolor on canvas. 13³/₈×24″. "∠K 33" I. I. Collection Paule and Adrien Maeght, Paris. CC 432.

594 *Development in Brown*. Oil on canvas. 39³/₈×47¹/₄″. "∠K 33" I. I. NK, Paris. (Jeu de Paume 1937). p. 301.

1934

595 *Start*. Watercolor on cardboard. 15³/₈×7⁷/₈″. "∠K 34" I. I. Formerly K. Nierendorf Gallery, New York.

596 *Graceful Ascent*. Oil on canvas. 31³/₄×31¹/₂″. "∠K 34" I. I. SRG, New York. CC 433.

597 *Yellow Center*. Oil and tempera on wood. 25¹/₄×31¹/₂″. "∠K 34" I. I. CC 434.

598 *Each for Itself*. Oil and tempera on canvas. 23⁵/₈×27⁵/₈″. "∠K 34" I. I. NK, Paris. p. 302.

599 *Ensemble*. Watercolor and oil on canvas. 23⁵/₈×27⁵/₈″. "∠K 34" I. I. Galerie Maeght, Paris. CC 435.

600 *Black Forms on White*. Oil on canvas. 27⁵/₈×27⁵/₈″. "∠K 34" I. I. Formerly collection Mme Yvonne Zervos, Paris. CC 436.

601 *In Between*. Oil, tempera and sand on canvas. 51¹/₈×30¹/₈″. "∠K 34" I. I. Collection Pierre Peissi, Paris. (Jeu de Paume, Paris 1937). p. 303.

602 *Blue World*. Oil and sand on canvas. 43¹/₂×47³/₈″. "∠K 34" I. I. SRG, New York. (Thesis, Antithesis, Synthesis, Lucerne 1935). CC 437.

603 *Dominant Violet*. Oil and sand on canvas. 51¹/₈×63³/₄″. "∠K 34" I. I. Collection Dr. F. Heer, Zurich. CC 438.

604 *Relations*. Oil and sand on canvas. 35×45⁵/₈″. "∠K 34" I. I. Collection Princess E. Zalstem-Zalessky, New York. Color plate, p. 223.

605 *Fragile-Fixed*. Watercolor and oil on canvas. 23⁵/₈×28³/₄″. "∠K 34" I. I. – CC 439.

606 *Division-Unity*. Oil and sand on canvas. 27¹/₄×27¹/₄″. "∠K 34" I. I. Kleemann Gallery, New York. CC 440.

607 *Animated White*. Oil on wood. 46×54″. "∠K 34" I. I. Collection Mrs. Hilla Rebay, Greens Farms, Conn. CC 441.

608 *Two Surroundings*. Oil and sand on canvas. 35×45⁵/₈″. "∠K 34" I. I. Collection P. A. Regnault, Laren, Loan to Stedelijk Museum, Amsterdam. p. 304.

609 *Striped*. Oil and sand on canvas. 31⁷/₈×39³/₈″. "∠K 34" I. I. SRG, New York. p. 305.

1935

610 *Fixed*. Oil on canvas. 28³/₄×23⁵/₈″. "∠K 35" I. I. Mrs. Hilla Rebay, Greens Farms, Conn.

611 *Raised Weight*. Oil and tempera on canvas. 23⁵/₈×29″. "∠K 35" I. I. Collection Emile Redon, Paris. CC 442.

612 *Balancing Act*. Oil and sand on canvas. 31⁷/₈×39³/₈″. "∠K 35" I. I. SRG, New York. p. 306.

613 *Contrast with Accompaniment*. Oil and sand on canvas. 38¹/₄×63³/₄″. "∠K 35" I. I. SRG, New York. CC 443.

614 *Two Circles*. Oil and tempera on canvas. 28³/₄×36¹/₄″. "∠K 35" I. I. SRG, New York. CC 452.

615 *Brown with Supplement*. Oil on canvas. 31⁷/₈×39³/₈″. "∠K 35" I. I. SRG, New York. CC 444.

616 *Two Green Points*. Oil and sand on canvas. 44⁷/₈×63³/₄″. "∠K 35" I. I. NK, Paris. Color plate, p. 225.

617 *Succession*. Oil on canvas. 31⁷/₈×39³/₈″. "∠K 35" I. I. The Phillipps Gallery, Washington. p. 307.

618 *Movement I*. Oil and tempera on canvas. 45⁵/₈×35″. "∠K 35" I. I. NK, Paris. p. 308.

619 *Light Tension*. Oil on canvas. 39³/₈×31⁷/₈″. "∠K 35" I. I. Collection Hermann Rupf, Bern. CC 445.

620 *Variegated Black*. Oil and lacquer on canvas. 45⁵/₈×35″. "∠K 35" I. I. Sidney Janis Gallery, New York. CC 447.

621 *Points*. Oil and lacquer on canvas. 31⁷/₈×39³/₈″. "∠K 35" I. I. Private collection, USA. CC 448.

622 *Violet-Orange*. Oil on canvas. 35×45⁵/₈″. "∠K 35" I. I. SRG, New York. CC 449.

623 *Green Accent*. Oil and tempera on canvas. 31⁷/₈×39³/₈″. "∠K 35" I. I. SRG, New York. p. 309.

624 *Delicate Accent*. Oil on canvas. 35×45⁵/₈″. "∠K 35" I. I. Collection Aimé Maeght, Paris. CC 450.

625 *Rigid and Bent*. Oil, tempera and sand on canvas.44⁷/₈×63³/₄″. "∠K 35" I. I. SRG, New York. CC 451.

1936

626 *Composition IX*. Oil on canvas. 44⁷/₈×76³/₄″. "∠K 36" I. I. Musée d'Art moderne, Paris. (Jeu de Paume, Paris 1937). Color plate, p. 229.

627 *Multiple Forms*. Oil on canvas. 38¹/₈×51¹/₄″. "∠K 36" I. I. Collection M and Mme Wormser, Paris. CC 453.

628 *Green Figure*. Oil on canvas. 45⁵/₈×35″. "∠K 36" I. I. NK, Paris. CC 454.

629 *Untitled*. Oil on canvas. 51¹/₈×31⁷/₈″. "∠K 36" I. I. Collection Mr. Higgins, Worchester, Mass. CC 455.

630 *Red Knot*. Oil on canvas. 35×45⁵/₈″. "∠K 36" I. I. CC 456.

631 *Dominant Curve*. Oil on canvas. 51¹/₈×76³/₄″. "∠K 36" I. I. SRG, New York. (Kunsthalle Bern 1937). Color plate, p. 231.

632 *Triangles*. Oil on canvas. 31⁷/₈×38³/₈″. "∠K 36" I. I. Collection Louis Clayeux, Paris. CC 457.

633 *Environment*. Oil on canvas. 39³/₈×31⁷/₈″. "∠K 36" I. I. SRG, New York. Color plate, p. 233.

634 *Tense Forms*. Oil on glass. 11³/₄×15³/₄″. "∠K 36" I. I. NK, Paris. CC 458.

635 *Stability*. Oil on glass. 11³/₄×15³/₄″. "∠K 36" I. I. Collection Heinz Rasch, Wuppertal. CC 459.

1937

636 *Thirty*. Oil on canvas. 31⁷/₈×39³/₈″. "∠K 37" I. I. NK, Paris. CC 460.

637 *Black Points*. Oil on canvas. 39³/₈×31⁷/₈″. "∠K 37" I. I. Collection Riccardo Jucker, Milan. p. 310.

638 *Calmed Tensions*. Oil on canvas. 35¹/₈×45⁷/₈″. "∠K 37" I. I. SRG, New York. CC 461.

639 *Sweet Trifles*. Watercolor and oil on canvas. 24⁵/₈×9⁷/₈″. "∠K 37" I. I. NK, Paris. Color plate, p. 235.

640 *Clear Tensions*. Oil on canvas. 35×45⁵/₈″. "∠K 37" I. I. – CC 462.

641 *Center with Accompaniment*. Oil on canvas. 44⁷/₈×57¹/₂″. "∠K 37" I. I. Collection Aimé Maeght, Paris. Color plate, p. 239.

642 *Two etc.* Oil on canvas. 35×45⁵/₈″. "∠K 37" I. I. Collection Aimé Maeght, Paris. p. 311.

643 *Capricious Forms*. Oil on canvas. 11³/₈×45⁵/₈″. "∠K 37" I. I. SRG, New York. CC 463.

644 *Grouping*. Oil on canvas. 57¹/₂×35″. "∠K 37" I. I. CC 464.

645 *Grids and others*. Oil on canvas. 18⁷/₈×14¹/₈″. "∠K 37" I. I. Collection Vittorio de Sica, Rome. CC 465.

646 *Animated Stability*. Oil and lacquer on canvas. 45⁵/₈×35″. "∠K 37" I. I. Collection Mr. and Mrs. Burton Tremaine, Meriden, Conn. p. 312.

1938

647 *An Arabesque.* Oil on canvas. 36¹/₄ × 25⁵/₈″. "∠K 38" I. I. CC 466.

648 *Touching Little Thing.* Oil and lacquer on canvas. 13³/₄ × 8⁵/₈″. "∠K 38" I. I. CC 467.

649 *The Good Contact.* Oil on canvas. 35 × 45⁵/₈″. "∠K 38" I. I. SRG, New York. CC 468.

650 *Many-Colored Ensemble (or Ordered Arrangement).* Oil and lacquer on canvas. 45⁵/₈ × 35″. "∠K 38" I. I. NK, Paris. CC 469.

651 *Penetrating Green.* Oil on canvas. 29¹/₂ × 49¹/₄″. "∠K 38" I. I. Baltimore Museum of Art, May Collection, USA. CC 470.

652 *Red Form.* Oil on canvas. 32¹/₄ × 23⁵/₈″. "∠K 38" I. I. CC 471.

653 *Yellow Canvas.* Oil and lacquer on canvas. 45⁷/₈ × 35″. "∠K 38" I. I. SRG, New York. CC 472.

654 *Serenity.* Oil on canvas. 57¹/₂ × 44⁷/₈″. "∠K 38" I. I. Collection Walter Stünzi, Horgen, Switzerland. CC 473.

1939

655 *Composition X.* Oil on canvas. 51¹/₈ × 76³/₄″. "∠K 39" I. I. NK, Paris. Color plate, p. 241.

656 *Toward Blue.* Oil and lacquer on canvas. 25⁵/₈ × 31⁷/₈″. "∠K 39" I. I. NK, Paris. CC 474.

657 *Warm Ensemble.* Oil and lacquer on canvas. 21¹/₄ × 31⁷/₈″. "∠K 39" I. I. Collection Walter Stünzi, Horgen, Switzerland. CC 475.

658 *The Red Square.* Oil and lacquer on canvas. 25¹/₂ × 32″. "∠K 39" I. I. Collection Mr. and Mrs. Morton G. Neumann, Chicago, Illinois. CC 476.

659 *Ambiguity (Complex-Simple).* Oil on canvas. 39³/₈ × 31⁷/₈″. "∠K 39" I. I. NK, Paris. CC 477.

660 *Elan.* Oil, gouache and lacquer. 25⁵/₈ × 31⁷/₈″. "∠K 39" I. I. Collection Aimé Maeght, Paris. CC 478.

661 *Red Circle.* Oil on canvas. 35 × 45⁵/₈″. "∠K 39" I. I. Collection Aimé Maeght, Paris. p. 313.

662 *Upward.* Oil on canvas. 45⁵/₈ × 35″. "∠K 39" I. I. Private collection, Paris. CC 479.

663 *Circuit.* Oil on canvas. 36¹/₄ × 28³/₄″. "∠K 39" I. I. NK, Paris. CC 480.

664 *Unanimity.* Oil on canvas. 28³/₄ × 36¹/₄″. "∠K 39" I. I. CC 481.

665 *One Figure among Others.* Oil and lacquer on canvas. 35 × 45⁵/₈″. "∠K 39" I. I. NK, Paris. p. 314.

666 *Neighborhood.* Oil on canvas. 23⁵/₈ × 36¹/₄″. "∠K 39" I. I. Collection Helmut Beck, Stuttgart. CC 482.

667 *Cheerfulness.* Oil and lacquer on wood. 12³/₈ × 16¹/₂″. "∠K 39" I. I. NK, Paris. CC 483.

668 *Overburdened.* Oil and lacquer on wood. 12⁵/₈ × 12⁵/₈″. "∠K 39" I. I. CC 484.

1940

669 *Green and Red.* Oil and lacquer on wood. 31¹/₂ × 20¹/₈″. "∠K 40" I. I. CC 485.

670 *Little Accents.* Oil on canvas on wood. 12³/₈ × 16¹/₂″. "∠K 40" I. I. Collection Mrs. Hilla Rebay, Greens Farms, Conn. CC 486.

671 *L'Ensemble.* Oil on canvas. 31⁷/₈ × 45⁵/₈″. "∠K 40" I. I. Collection Mrs. Eleanore Saidenberg, New York. p. 315.

672 *Various Parts.* Oil on canvas. 35 × 45⁵/₈″. "∠K 40" I. I. NK, Paris. p. 316.

673 *Sky Blue.* Oil on canvas. 39³/₈ × 28³/₄″. "∠K 40" I. I. NK, Paris. CC 487.

674 *Light Construction.* Oil on canvas. 28³/₄ × 19⁵/₈″. "∠K 40" I. I. Collection Hermann Rupf, Bern. CC 488.

675 *Around the Circle.* Sketch for 677. Oil on mahogany. 15³/₄ × 23⁵/₈″. "∠K 40" I. I. NK, Paris. CC 489.

676 *And more.* Oil and lacquer on canvas. 18¹/₈ × 15″. "∠K 40" I. I. Collection Hermann Rupf, Bern. CC 490.

677 *Around the Circle.* Oil and lacquer on canvas. 38¹/₈ × 57¹/₂″. "∠K 40" I. I. NK, Paris. p. 317.

678 *Moderation.* Oil on canvas. 39¹/₄ × 25¹/₂″. "∠K 40" I. I. SRG, New York. CC 491.

679 *Two Lines.* Oil and lacquer on cardboard. 23⁵/₈ × 27⁵/₈″. "∠K 40" I. I.

1941

680 *Two Blacks.* Oil and lacquer on canvas. 45⁵/₈ × 31⁷/₈″. "∠K 41" I. I. Collection Aimé Maeght, Paris. CC 492.

681 *Reduced Contrasts.* Oil and lacquer on canvas. 31⁷/₈ × 39³/₈″. "∠K 41" I. I. NK, Paris. p. 318.

682 *Coolness.* Oil and lacquer on cardboard. 19¹/₄ × 27⁵/₈″. "∠K 41" I. I. Galerie Maeght, Paris. CC 493.

683 *Various Actions.* Oil and lacquer on canvas. 35 × 45⁵/₈″. "∠K 41" I. I. SRG, New York. p. 319.

684 *The Fixed Square.* Oil on canvas. 23¹/₄ × 22⁷/₈″. "∠K 41" I. I. Private collection, USA. CC 494.

685 *Moderate Variation.* Oil on canvas. 27⁵/₈ × 27⁵/₈″. "∠K 41" I. I. Collection Aimé Maeght, Paris. CC 495.

1942

686 *Balancing.* Oil and lacquer on canvas. 35 × 45⁵/₈″. "∠K 42" I. I. CC 496.

687 *Reciprocal Accord.* Oil and lacquer on canvas. 44⁷/₈ × 57¹/₂″. "∠K 42" I. I. NK, Paris. Color plate, p. 243.

688 *Round Accent.* Oil on canvas. 28³/₄ × 36¹/₄″. "∠K 42" I. I. Museum de Arte Moderna, Sao Paulo. CC 497.

689 *Transparent.* Oil and lacquer on canvas. 28³/₄ × 36¹/₄″. "∠K 42" I. I. Aimé Maeght, Paris. CC 498.

690 *Delicate Tensions.* (Last painting on canvas). Oil on canvas. 31⁷/₈ × 39³/₄″. "∠K 42" I. I. NK, Paris. CC 499.

691 *A Fluttering Figure.* Oil on mahogany. 10¹/₄ × 7⁷/₈″. "∠K 42" I. I. CC 500.

692 *Vertical Accents.* Oil on wood. 12⁵/₈ × 16¹/₂″. "∠K 42" I. I. SRG, New York. CC 501.

693 *Support.* Oil on mahogany. 7⁷/₈ × 10¹/₄″. "∠K 42" I. I. Private collection, Paris. CC 502.

694 *Three Stars.* Oil on cardboard. 19¹/₄ × 13³/₄″. "∠K 42" I. I. Collection Philippe Dotremont, Brussels. CC 503.

695 *In the Middle.* Oil on cardboard. 19¹/₄ × 19¹/₄″. "∠K 42" I. I. NK, Paris. CC 504.

696 *Three Between Two.* Oil on cardboard. 19¹/₄ × 19¹/₄″. "∠K 42" I. I. NK, Paris. CC 505.

697 *Joyful Theme.* Oil on cardboard. 19¹/₄ × 19¹/₄″. "∠K 42" I. I. Collection Mme Lecoutoure, Paris. CC 506.

698 *Three Ovals.* Oil and tempera on cardboard. 19¹/₄ × 19¹/₄″. "∠K 42" I. I. Collection Aimé Maeght, Paris. CC 507.

699 *Community.* Oil on cardboard. 19¹/₄ × 19¹/₄″. "∠K 42" I. I. Formerly collection Jeanne Bucher, Paris.

700 *Junctions.* Oil on cardboard. 13³/₄ × 19¹/₄″. "∠K 42" I. I. Collection Alexandre Kojève, Paris. CC 508.

701 *An intimate Celebration.* Oil and tempera on cardboard. 19¹/₄ × 19¹/₄″. "∠K 42" I. I. NK, Paris. CC 509.

702 *Three Variegated Figures.* Oil on cardboard. 19¹/₄ × 19¹/₄″. "∠K 42" I. I. Collection Aimé Maeght, Paris. p. 320.

703 *Netting.* Tempera on cardboard. 16¹/₂ × 22⁷/₈″. "∠K 42" I. I. CC 510.

704 *Dark Center*. Tempera on cardboard. 16¹/₂×22⁷/₈″. "∠K 43" l. l. CC 511.

705 *White Figure*. Oil on cardboard. 22⁷/₈×16¹/₂″. "∠K 43" l. l. SRG, New York. p. 321.

706 *Light Ascent*. Tempera and oil on cardboard. 22⁷/₈×16¹/₂″. "∠K 43" l. l. CC 512.

707 *Fanlike*. Tempera and oil on cardboard. 22³/₄×16³/₈″. "∠K 43" l. l. SRG, New York, formerly private collection, USA. CC 513.

708 *Simplicity*. Tempera and oil on cardboard. 22⁷/₈×17¹/₂″. "∠K 43" l. l. CC 514.

709 *Division-Unity*. Tempera and oil on cardboard. 22⁷/₈×16¹/₂″. "∠K 43" l. l. NK, Paris. Color plate, p. 245.

710 *Around the Line*. Oil on cardboard. 16¹/₂×22⁷/₈″. "∠K 43" l. l. NK, Paris. CC 515.

711 *The Arrow*. Oil on cardboard. 16¹/₂×22⁷/₈″. "∠K 43" l. l. Kunstmuseum, Basel. p. 322.

712 *The Zigzag*. Oil on cardboard. 16¹/₂×22⁷/₈″. "∠K 43" l. l. Collection Prof. W. Löffler, Zurich. CC 516.

713 *Accord*. Oil on cardboard. 16¹/₂×22⁷/₈″. "∠K 43" l. l. p. 323.

714 *Seven*. Oil on cardboard. 22⁷/₈×16¹/₂″. "∠K 43" l. l. Collection Max Bill, Zurich. p. 324.

715 *Brown Impetus*. Tempera and oil on cardboard. 16¹/₂×22⁷/₈″. "∠K 43" l. l. NK, Paris. CC 517.

716 *Circle and Square*. Tempera and oil on cardboard. 16¹/₂×22⁷/₈″. "∠K 43" l. l. NK, Paris. Color plate, p. 247.

717 *Flowering*. Tempera and oil on cardboard. 16¹/₂×22⁷/₈″. "∠K 43" l. l. (Esquisse, Paris 1944). CC 518.

718 *Fragments*. Gouache and oil on cardboard. 16¹/₂×22⁷/₈″. "∠K 43" l. l. SRG, New York. p. 325.

719 *Three Columns*. Gouache and oil on cardboard. 16¹/₂×22⁷/₈″. "∠K 43" l. l. Collection Mr. Joubert, Montreal, Canada. CC 519.

720 *Dusk*. Oil on cardboard. 22⁷/₈×16¹/₂″. "∠K 43" l. l. SRG, New York. CC 520.

721 *Darkness*. Oil on cardboard. 22⁷/₈×16¹/₂″. "∠K 43" l. l. NK, Paris. p. 326.

722 *Red Accent*. Oil on cardboard. 16¹/₂×22⁷/₈″. "∠K 43" l. l. Collections Mrs. Hilla Rebay, Greens Farms, Conn. CC 521.

723 *Two Rays*. Oil on cardboard. 16¹/₂×22⁷/₈″. "∠K 43" l. l. Private collection, USA. CC 522.

724 *The Red Point*. Oil and tempera on cardboard. 16¹/₂×22⁷/₈″. "∠K 43" l. l. CC 523.

725 *4×5=20*. Oil and tempera on cardboard. 22⁷/₈×16¹/₂″. "∠K 43" l. l. Collection Mme Lecoutoure, Paris.

726 *Thin Threads*. Gouache and oil on card board. 22⁷/₈×16¹/₂″. "∠K 43" l. l. – CC 524.

727 *Three Rays*. Gouache and oil on cardboard. 16¹/₂×22⁷/₈″. "∠K 43" l. l. Collection Mrs. Carola Giedion-Welcker, Zurich. CC 525.

728 *A Conglomerate*. Gouache and oil on cardboard. 22⁷/₈×16¹/₂″. "∠K 43" l. l. NK, Paris. p. 327.

729 *4 Figures on 3 Squares*. Oil on cardboard. 16¹/₂×22⁷/₈″. "∠K 43" l. l. Formerly Galerie Raspail, Paris.

730 *Disquiet*. Oil on cardboard. 16¹/₂×22⁷/₈″. "∠K 43" l. l. NK, Paris. CC 526.

731 *Ribbon with Squares*. Gouache and oil cardboard. 16¹/₂×22⁷/₈″. "∠K 44" l. l. SRG, New York. p. 328.

732 *Five Parts*. Oil on cardboard. 22⁷/₈×16¹/₂″. "∠K 44" l. l. Private collection, Paris. CC 527.

733 *Isolation*. Gouache and oil on cardboard. 16¹/₂×22⁷/₈″. "∠K 44" l. l. Collection Aimé Maeght, Paris. CC 528.

734 *The Little Red Circle*. Gouache and oil on cardboard. 16¹/₂×22⁷/₈″. "∠K 44" l. l. NK, Paris. CC 529.

735 *White Balancing Act*. Gouache and oil on cardboard. 22⁷/₈×16¹/₂″. "∠K 44" l. l. Collection Prof. W. Löffler, Zurich. CC 530.

736 *Three Black Bands*. Oil on cardboard. 18¹/₈×21¹/₄″. "∠K 44" l. l. Collection Walter Stünzi, Horgen, Switzerland. CC 531.

737 *The Green Band*. Oil on cardboard. 18¹/₈×21¹/₄″. "∠K 44" l. l. NK, Paris. CC 532.

738 *Tempered Elan*. Oil on cardboard. 16¹/₂×22⁷/₈″. "∠K 44" l. l. NK, Paris. Color plate, p. 249.

– *Unfinished*. Oil on cardboard. 16³/₈×22⁵/₈″. NK, Paris. CC 533.

– *Unfinished*. Oil on cardboard. 16³/₈×22⁵/₈″. NK, Paris. CC 534.

Small Oil Studies

Kandinsky made a separate list of 108 oil studies, without further data. Only a few can be identified with certainty, since we do not know the dimensions. There are many Kochel and Kallmünz landscapes in the Gabriele Münter Foundation, Munich; a few of these were probably included in Kandinsky's list. The oil studies date from 1901 to 1907.

1.–2. *Siudy*.

3. *Park of Akhtyrka*. Oil on cardboard. 9¹/₂×13″. "Kandinsky" l. l. NK, Paris. CC 535.

4–8. *Kochel*. 9–10. *Kallmünz*. 11–18. *Studies*. 19. *Winter in Schwabing*. 20. *Nikolaiplatz*. 21. *Kochel at Nightfall*. 22. *Rothenburg*. 23. *Kochel*.

24. *Akhtyrka, Early Autumn*, probably the same as: *Autumn Study, Russia*. Oil on cardboard. 9¹/₂×13″. "Kandinsky" l. r. GMF, Munich.

25. *Study*. 26. *Russian Landscape*.

27. *English Garden*. Oil on cardboard. 9¹/₄×12⁵/₈″. GMF, Munich.

28–29. *Kochel*. 30. *Moscow (Winter)*. 31–34. *Study from Odessa*.

35. *English Garden*. 36. *Kochel*. 37. *Schwabing (The White House)*. 38. *Schwabing (Winter)*. 39. *Kochel (Lake)*.

40. *Kallmünz*. Oil on cardboard. 9¹/₄×12³/₄″. "Nr. 40" on back. Collection Karl Ströher, Darmstadt. CC 536.

41. *Kochel (with Lake)*, probably the same as: *Kochel on the Lake*. Oil on cardboard. 12⁵/₈×9¹/₂″. "Kandinsky" l. r. GMF, Munich.

42. *Vasilevskoie*.

43. *Nymphenburg*. Oil on cardboard. 9¹/₄×12³/₄″. "Kandinsky" l. r. Galerie Valentien, Stuttgart. CC 537.

44. *Starnberger See*. 45. *Vasilevskoie (Sergey with Horse)*. 46. *Vasilevskoie (Autumn)*. 47. *Kallmünz*. 48. *Schwabing*.

49. *Schliersee (Wendelstein)*, probably the same as: *Schliersee*. Oil on cardboard. 9¹/₂×12³/₄″. "Kandinsky" l. l. GMF, Munich.

50. *Nikolaistrasse (Winter)*.

51. *Scheveningen*, probably the same as: *Holland-Scheveningen*. 1904. Oil on cardboard. 9¹/₂×13″. "Kandinsky" l. r. GMF, Munich.

52. *Amsterdam (View from window)*. Oil on canvas. 9¹/₂×13³/₈″. "Kandinsky" l. r. SRG, New York. CC 538.

53. *Cloudy Landscape*. 54. *Near Kallmünz*.

55. *Upper Palatinate*. Oil on cardboard. 9¹/₂×12⁵/₈″. SRG, New York. CC 539.

56. *Kochel*. 57. *Akhtyrka*. 58. *Munich with Bridge*. 59. *Kallmünz, Rainy Day*. 60. *Kochel with Seehotel*. 61. *Kallmünz Rathaus-*

platz. 62. *Scheveningen*. 63. *Bidersteinpark in Winter*. 64. *Notburg (Palatinate)*. 65. *English Garden*. 66. *Schleedorf*. 67. *Binz auf Rügen*. 68–69. *Kochel*. 70–71. *Binz auf Rügen*.

72. *Spring (Surroundings of Augsburg)*. Oil on cardboard. 9¹/₂×13″. – NK, Paris. CC 540.

73. *Schliersee with Church*. 74. *Planegg near Munich*. 75. *Tunis, Sunny Park*. 76–77. *Studies*. 78. *Kochel (Mist)* 79. *Near Starnberg (Winter)*. 80. *Cemetery at Night*. 81. *Near Planegg* 82–83. *Kochel*. 84–99. *Studies*.

100. *St. Cloud, Park*, probably the same as: *In the Park of St. Cloud*. Oil on cardboard. 9¹/₂×13″. GMF, Munich.

101. *St. Cloud*. 102–107. *Murnau*. 108. *Munich (from My Window)*.

Color Drawings

Kandinsky used the term "color drawings" for tempera paintings. He lists 132 of them; some are reproduced in *Backward Glances*, others can be identified with a certain degree of probability. Beginning with No. 67 dimensions are added. The works date from 1901 to 1907.

1. *Rising Sun*. 2. *Nocturnal Rider*. 3. *In the Park*. 4. *Russian Knight*. 5. *Russian City*. 6. *Fairytale City*.

7. *Duel*. Tempera on cardboard. 12×16″. CC 648.

8. *Promenade*. 9. *Decorative Sketch*. 10. *Blue Lady* (sold to Grand Duke Vladimir). 11. *Excursion on Horseback*. 12. *Old Times*. 13. *Youth*. 14–16. *Three Church Windows*. 17. *Café*. 18. *The Shadow*. 19. *The Conqueror*. 20. *The Riding Knight*. 21. *In the Park*. 22. *Highway*. 23. *Village*. 24. *House*. 25. *Green Bird*. 26. *Promenade*.

27. *White Cloud* (reproduced in *Backward Glances*). CC 647.

28. *Trysting Place*. 29. *In the Garden*.

30. *The Bride*, probably the same as *Bridal Procession*. Tempera on cardboard. 16¹/₈×22¹/₂″. "Kandinsky" l. r. GMF, Munich. CC 646.

31. *Old Town*. 1903. Tempera on cardboard. 11³/₄×20⁷/₈″. "Kandinsky" l. l. GMF, Munich.

32. *Conversation at Table*. 33. *Flowers*. 34. *Young Couple*. 35. *Old Russian*.

36. *Once Upon a Time*. 1904. Tempera on cardboard. 13³/₄×7⁷/₈″. "Kandinsky" l. r. GMF, Munich.

37. *Farewell*. 38. *On the Beach*. 39. *The Warrior*. 40. *Summer Day*. 41. *Carnival*. 42. *Autumn*. 43. *Meeting*. 44. *A Saint*. 45. *Night Journey*. 46. *Recollection of Venice 1 (Reflection)*. 47. *Recollection of Venice 2 (Gondolas)*. 1906. Cf. reproduction in *Backward Glances*. 48. *Recollection of Venice 3 (Canal)*. 49. *Peacock*. 50. *Lady with Red Book*. 51. *Recollection of Venice 4 (Ponte Rialto)*. 52. *March*. 53. *Winter Journey (Russian)*. 54. *Recollection of Holland*. 55. *Dutch Woman*. 56. *Autumn, 1904*. 57. *Music*. 58. *The Conqueror*. 59. *Morning Hour (Dutch)*. 60. *Dialogue*. 61. *Nightfall (on the Beach)*. 62. *In the Königsgarten*. 63. *The Foreign City*. 64. *Painting*. 65. *Sketch for Painting on Glass*. 66. *Marseille (Vieux Port)*.

67. *Ships in Holland*. 1904. Tempera on cardboard. 15×22¹/₂″. "Kandinsky" l. r. NK, Paris. CC 649.

68. *Windmill (Holland)*. Tempera on cardboard. 13³/₄×19⁵/₈″. "Kandinsky" l. r. NK, Paris. CC 650.

69. *Spring (Laundry)*. 70. *Saturday Night (Holland)*.

71. *Mosque (Tunis, Twilight)*. 1905. Tempera on cardboard. – Cf. *Backward Glances*.

72. *Square in Tunis (Camels)*. 73. *Arab Café*. 74. *Interior*. 75. *Evening Promenade (Promenade at Tunis)*. 76. *Moon*. 77. *Bab Sonika (Moon, Tunis)*. 78. *Arab Riders*. 79. *Ammen (Nouneus)*. 80. *Russian Village*. 81. *Tamer of Snakes*. 82. *Vendor of oranges*.

83. *Café (Evening)*, probably the same as: *Moorish Café*. Tempera on cardboard. 13³/₄×19⁵/₈″. GMF, Munich.

84. *Riders (Arab Horses)*. 85. *Cavaliers (Russian)*. 86. *Mandoline-Player*. 87. *Street in Tunis*.

88. *Fête des moutons*. Tempera on cardboard. 16¹/₈×22¹/₂″. "Kandinsky" l. l. SRG, New York. p. 259.

89. *Working Negroes*.

90. *Carnival in Tunis*. 1905. Tempera on cardboard. 13×18⁷/₈″. "Kandinsky" l. l. Cf. *Backward Glances*.

91. *Old-Russian Knight*.

92. *Hammam (H. in Tunis)*.

93. *Ruin*. Tempera on cardboard. 12³/₈×18¹/₄″. "Kandinsky" l. l. Private collection, USA. CC 651.

94. *Parade (Carnival)*. 95. *Circus*.

96. *Arab Horsemen*. 1905. Tempera on cardboard. 11×16¹/₈″. – – Cf. *Backward Glances*.

97. *Walking Couple*. 98. *Nightfall*.

99. *The Spectators*. 1905. Tempera on cardboard. 22¹/₂×31¹/₈″. NK, Paris. CC 652.

100. *Roses*. 1905. Tempera on cardboard. 11³/₈×22¹/₂″. Cf. *Backward Glances*.

101. *Holidays*. 102. *Arab City*. 103. *Children*. 104. *Morning*. 105. *Fair*. 106. *Sketch for Mural*. 107. *Italian Fishing Village*. 108. *In the Sixties*. 109. *Washing Day*. 110. *Redoute*. 111. *Bal masqué*. 112. *Lady Friends*. 113. *Italian Port (Twilight)*.

114. *Winter (Skating)*. 1906. Tempera on cardboard. 19⁵/₈×26″. NK, Paris. CC 653.

115. *Caravan*. 116. *Mourning*. 117. *Song*. 118. *Province*. 119. *Venice*.

120. *Funeral*. 1907. Tempera on cardboard. F 17³/₄×25⁵/₈″. Cf. *Backward Glances*.

121. *The Bear*. 122. *Scene*, 1907. 123. *Night*. 124. *Don Quixote*. 125. *Noon*. 126. *Snake*. 127. *Color Drawing No. 1 (with Cat)*. 128. *Color Drawing No. 2 (with Green Tree)*. 129. *Color Drawing No. 3 (with Yellow)*. 130. *Color Drawing No. 4 (with Church)*. 131. *Yellow Cloud on White*. 132. *Landscape with Figures*.

Supplement

In addition to the works listed in his private catalogue, Kandinsky executed many others which he did not record. This is particularly true of the period prior to 1920. I have decided not to list all the studies, particularly the landscape studies of 1900–1908, to avoid placing too much emphasis on early works. Of these only a selection is given, but beginning with 1908, the list is complete.

1900

1. *Maria Krushchov*. Oil on canvas. 59×37³/₈″. "VK" (in Russian) l. r. SRG, New York. p. 257.

1901

1a. *Market Place*. Oil on cardboard. 5⁷/₈×13″. – NK Paris. Color plate, p. 49.
Cloudy Day. Oil on cardboard. 9¹/₂×13″. "Kandinsky" l. r. NK, Paris. CC 542.
Kochel. Oil on cardboard. 6×13″. Private collection, Paris. CC 541.

1902

Bridge at Kochel. Oil on canvas. 11³/₄×17³/₄″. "Kandinsky" l. l. Stedelijk Museum, Amsterdam. CC 543.
Winter in Schwabing. Oil on cardboard. 9¹/₂×13″. Collection Ragnar Moltzau, Oslo. CC 545.
Market Place. Oil on canvas. "Kandinsky" l. l. Formerly collection Alfred Hagelstange, Cologne. CC 544.
Lady in Landscape. Oil on canvas. 20¹/₂×14¹/₈″. Museum of Tel Aviv. CC 546.
Sluice. Study for KK 15a. Oil on cardboard. 12⁷/₈×9⁵/₈″. "Kandinsky" l. l. GMF, Munich.

1903

Landscape with Yellow Field. Oil on cardboard. 11³/₄×17³/₄″. GMF, Munich. CC 547.
Gabriele Münter Painting. Oil on cardboard. 9¹/₂×13″. – GMF, Munich. CC 548.

1904

Kallmünz. Oil on cardboard. 9¹/₂×13″. "Kandinsky" l. r. SRG, New York. CC 549.
Beach Baskets in Holland. Oil on cardboard. 9¹/₂×13″. "Kandinsky" l. r. GMF, Munich. CC 550.
Pond in the Park. Oil on canvas. 13×16″. "Kandinsky" l. l. Collection Mrs. Hilla Rebay, Greens Farms, Conn. CC 552.

1905

Carthage. Oil on cardboard. 9¹/₂×12⁵/₈″. GMF, Munich. CC 551.
Portrait of Gabriele Münter, Dresden. Oil on canvas. 18×18″. GMF, Munich. CC 553.
Port of Rapallo. Oil on cardboard. 9¹/₂×13″. "Kandinsky" l. r. Collection Erich Fahlbeck, Lund, Sweden. CC 554.

1906

Rapallo. Oil on cardboard. 9¹/₂×12³/₄″. NK, Paris. p. 260.
Fishing Boats in Rapallo. Oil on cardboard. 9¹/₂×12³/₄″. SRG, New York. CC 555.
Rapallo. Oil on cardboard. 9¹/₂×12³/₈″. SRG, New York. CC 556.
Park of St. Cloud (with Rider). Oil on cardboard. 9¹/₂×13″. "Kandinsky" l. r. NK, Paris. CC 557.
Park of St. Cloud (Among Trees). Oil on cardboard. 9¹/₂×13″. GMF, Munich. CC 559.
Basin in Park of St. Cloud. Oil on cardboard. 9¹/₂×13″. Saidenberg Gallery, New York. CC 558.
Bathing Women in Park. Oil on cardboard. 20¹/₈×26″. "Kandinsky 1906" l. r. Collection Ch. Henry Kleemann, New York. CC 560.
Street in St. Cloud. Oil on vardboard. 13×17³/₄″. NK, Paris.
Path. Oil on cardboard. 13×17³/₄″. NK, Paris. CC 562.
Back: Lancer in Landscape. CC 561.

1907

Waterfall near Lana in the Tyrol. Oil on cardboard. 9¹/₂×13″. GMF, Munich. CC 563.

1908

Street in Murnau with Women. Oil on canvas. 27⁵/₈×37³/₈″. "Kandinsky" l. l. NK, Paris. Color plate, p. 57.
Village Street. Oil on canvas. 18¹/₂×31⁷/₈″. "Kandinsky" l. r. Collection Mr. and Mrs. William H. Weintraub, New York, formerly collection A. J. Eddy, Chicago. CC 564.
Street in Murnau. Oil on cardboard. 13×17³/₈″. "Kandinsky" l. r. Collection Nils Wedel, Göteborg. CC 565.
Street in Murnau with Mountains. Oil on canvas. 19⁵/₈×25⁵/₈″. NK, Paris. CC 566.
Street in Murnau with Woman. Oil on cardboard. 13×17³/₄″. "Kandinsky" l. l. NK, Paris. CC 567.
Church of Murnau. Oil on cardboard. 13×17³/₄″. NK, Paris. CC 568.
Village Church. Oil on cardboard. 13×17³/₄″. "Kandinsky" l. r. Städt. Museum Wuppertal-Elberfeld, Gift of Baron v. d. Heydt. CC 571.
Bavarian Mountains with Church. Oil on cardboard. 13³/₄×17³/₄″. "Kandinsky" l. r. Private collection, USA. CC 572.
Bavarian Village with Tree. Oil on cardboard. 14³/₄×17³/₄″. "Kandinsky l. l. (?) Sidney Janis Gallery, New York. CC 570.
Bavarian Village with Field. Oil on cardboard. 15×18¹/₈″. "Kandinsky" l. l. (?) Collection Mr. and Mrs. Paul M. Hirschland, Great Neck, N. Y. CC 569.
Upper Bavarian Mountains with Village. Oil on cardboard. 27⁵/₈×37³/₄″. "Kandinsky" l. l. Collection Gustav Zumsteg, Zurich. CC 573.
Village with Mountains. Oil on cardboard. 13×16¹/₄″. GMF, Munich. CC 574.
Landscape near Murnau. Oil on cardboard. 15¹/₄×18″. "Kandinsky" l. r. Collection Helmut Beck, Stuttgart. CC 575.
Autumn Landscape near Murnau. Oil on cardboard. 13×16¹/₈″. "Kandinsky" l. l. Collection Baronesse Alix de Rothschild, Paris. CC 583.
Near Murnau. Oil on cardboard. 12⁵/₈×17³/₄″. Gal. Valentien, Stuttgart. CC 576.
Summer near Murnau. Oil on cardboard. 12³/₄×15⁷/₈″. Kleemann Gallery, New York, formerly collection Alexander Strakosch, Switzerland. CC 577.
Autumn near Murnau. Oil on cardboard. 12³/₄×15⁷/₈″. Kleemann Gallery, New York, formerly collection A. Strakosch, Switzerland. CC 578.
Stacks of Grain. Oil on cardboard. 12³/₄×17³/₈″. Kleemann Gallery, New York, formerly collection A. Strakosch, Switzerland. CC 579.
Church at Froschhausen. Oil on cardboard. 13×17³/₄″. Dalzell Hatfield Gallery, Los Angeles. CC 580.
Winter Study with Mountain. Oil on cardboard. 13×17³/₄″. "Kandinsky" l. r. Collection Vilem Feith, Sao Paolo. CC 581.
Gabriele Münter with Easel. Oil on cardboard. 13×17³/₄″. "Kandinsky" l. l. Galerie Änne Abels, Cologne, formerly collection Frau Helene v. Jawlensky, Ascona. CC 582.
Staffelsee. Oil on cardboard. 13×17³/₄″. GMF, Munich. CC 584.
Staffelsee. Oil on cardboard. 13×16¹/₈″. Kleemann Gallery, New York, formerly collection A. Strakosch, Switzerland. CC 586.
Staffelsee. Oil on cardboard. 13×17³/₄″. "Kandinsky" l. l. Collection Ed. Schmidt-Ott, Wuppertal-Elberfeld. CC 587.
Starnberger See (Tutzing). Oil on cardboard. 28×37³/₄″. "Kandinsky 1908" l. l. Collection Fritz Kaufmann, Scarsdale, New York. CC 585.
Starnberger See I. Oil on cardboard. 13×16¹/₈″. – NK, Paris. CC 588.
Starnberger See II. Oil on cardboard. 24³/₄×39″. Collection Fernand Graindorge, Liege. CC 590.

344

Ludwigskirche in Munich. Oil on cardboard. 27 × 39''. "Kandinsky 1908" l. l. Private collection, USA, formerly Collection A. J. Edda, Chicago. CC 590.

Houses in Munich. Oil on cardboard. 13 × 16¹/₈''. "Kandinsky" l. l. Museum of Wuppertal-Elberfeld, Gift of Baron E. v. d. Heydt. CC 591.

Before the City. Oil on cardboard. 13 × 16¹/₈''. "Kandinsky 1908" l. l. GMF, Munich. CC 592.

The Elephant. Oil on cardboard. 18¹/₈ × 27¹/₈''. "Kandinsky" l. r. NK, Paris. CC 593.

Ariel Scene from Faust II. Oil on cardboard. 15⁷/₈ × 13''. Collection Sylvester Labrot, Hope Sound, Florida, formerly collection A. Strakosch, Switzerland. CC 594.

1909

Bavarian Mountains with Village. Oil on canvas. 26³/₄ × 36⁵/₈''. "Kandinsky" l. l. Collection Dr. Zeissler, New York. Color plate, p. 63.

Dünaberg. Oil on cardboard. 12⁵/₈ × 17³/₄''. "Kandinsky 1909" l. r. Collection Verner Nielsen, Copenhagen. CC 595.

Houses at Murnau. Oil on cardboard. 19¹/₂ × 25¹/₂''. "Kandinsky 1909" l. r. Collection Mrs. Katharine Kuh, Chicago. CC 596.

Landscape with Tower. Oil on cardboard. 12¹/₂ × 17''. SRG, New York. CC 597.

Church in Murnau. Oil on cardboard. 19¹/₈ × 27¹/₂''. "Kandinsky" l. r. MMA, New York. CC 598.

Landscape near Murnau with Locomotive. Oil on cardboard. 19⁵/₈ × 25¹/₂''. "Kandinsky 1909" l. l. SRG, New York. CC 599.

Railroad near Murnau. Oil on cardboard. 14¹/₈ × 19¹/₄''. GMF, Munich. CC 600.

Murnau Street in the Snow. Oil on cardboard. 26⁷/₈ × 19¹/₄''. "Kandinsky" l. r. GMF, Munich. CC 601.

Bedroom (Murnau). Oil on cardboard. 19¹/₄ × 27¹/₈''. "Kandinsky" l. r. GMF, Munich. CC 602.

Graveyard in Kochel. Oil on cardboard. 13 × 17³/₄''. GMF, Munich. CC 603.

Mountain. Oil on cardboard. 43¹/₄ × 43¹/₄''. "Kandinsky 1909" l. l. GMF, Munich. CC 604.

On the Beach. Oil on cardboard. 20⁷/₈ × 29⁷/₈''. "Kandinsky 1909" l. l. Collection Louis Clayeux, Paris. CC 605.

Waterfall. Oil on cardboard. 27¹/₂ × 38³/₈''. "Kandinsky 1909" l. r. Yale University Art Gallery, Collection Société Anonyme. CC 606.

Horses. Oil on cardboard. 38¹/₈ × 42¹/₈''. "Kandinsky 1909" l. l. GMF, Munich. CC 607.

Oriental. Oil on cardboard. 27⁵/₈ × 38¹/₄''. – GMF, Munich. CC 608.

Study for Improvisation 2 (Funeral March). Oil on cardboard. 19⁵/₈ × 27⁵/₈''. GMF, Munich. CC 609.

1910

All Saints. Oil on cardboard. 23 × 26¹/₂''. " ⚠ " l. l. GMF, Munich, CC 610

Murnau in Winter with Church. Oil on cardboard. 12⁵/₈ × 17³/₈''. "Kandinsky" l. r. SRG, New York. CC 611.

Murnau with Church. Oil on cardboard. 12⁵/₈ × 17³/₈''. "Kandinsky" l. l. Collection Ferdinand Ziersch, Wuppertal-Barmen. CC 612.

View of Murnau with Church. Oil on canvas. 37⁷/₈ × 41¹/₂''. "Kandinsky 1910" l. r. Van Abbe Museum, Eindhoven, Holland. CC 613.

Church. Oil on cardboard. 25⁵/₈ × 19⁵/₈''. GMF, Munich. CC 614.

Garden. Oil on canvas. 26 × 32¹/₄''. "Kandinsky 1910" l. l. GMF, Munich. CC 615.

Mountain Landscape with Church. Oil on cardboard. 13 × 17³/₄''. "Kandinsky" l. l. GMF, Munich. CC 616.

Autumn Study. Oil on cardboard. 13 × 17³/₄''. "Kandinsky" l. r. GMF, Munich. CC 617.

Interior, Munich, Ainmillerstrasse 36. Oil on cardboard. 19⁵/₈ × 25⁵/₈''. "Kandinsky" l. r. GMF, Munich. CC 618.

Improvisation 3, Copy of 1909, 78. Oil on cardboard. 17³/₈ × 24³/₈''. "Kandinsky" l. r. Collection Ulrich Lange, Krefeld. CC 619.

Improvisation 7, Copy. Oil on cardboard. 26³/₄ × 18⁷/₈''. "Kandinsky 1910" l. r. Yale University Art Gallery, Société Anonyme. CC 620.

Study. Oil on cardboard. 22 × 30³/₄''. – Collection R. de M., Paris. CC 621.

Fragment for Composition II. Oil on cardboard. 22⁷/₈ × 18⁷/₈''. "Kandinsky 1910" l. r. NK, Paris. CC 622.

Sketch for Improvisation 5, 1910. Oil on cardboard. 28 × 28''. "Kandinsky" l. l. Collection Änne Abels, Cologne, formerly collection Frau Helene von Jawlensky, Ascona. CC 759.

1911

All Saints. Oil on cardboard. 22¹/₂ × 26''. ⚠ l. l. GMF, Munich. CC 623.

Study for Winter II. (1911, 122). Oil on cardboard. 13 × 17³/₄''. "Kandinsky" l. l. GMF, Munich. CC 624.

All Saints. Oil on canvas. 33⁷/₈ × 39³/₈''. GMF, Munich. p. 73.

Improvisation with Horses. Oil on canvas. 28 × 39''. Collection G. David Thompson, Pittsburgh. CC 625.

Landscape with Two Poplars, Study for 1912, 155. Oil on canvas. 13¹/₈ × 21¹/₈''. "Kandinsky 1911" l. r. Collection Hans Arnhold, New York. Color plate, p. 129.

The Last Judgment. Oil on canvas. 29¹/₂ × 50¹/₂''. "Kandinsky" l. r. Private collection, USA. p. 272.

1913

Improvisation, Deluge (Study for Comp. VI 1913, 172). Oil on canvas. 37³/₈ × 59''. GMF, Munich. CC 626.

1914

Improvisation. Oil on canvas. 43¹/₄ × 43¹/₄''. Collection Hugo Perls, New York, formerly collection Ferdinand Möller, Cologne. CC 627.

Improvisation. Oil on canvas. 29¹/₈ × 49¹/₄''. GMF, Munich. CC 631.

Untitled; called *Deluge*. Oil on canvas. 42⁵/₈ × 55¹/₈''. GMF, Munich. CC 629.

Study, called *Ravine*. Oil on canvas. 43¹/₄ × 43¹/₄''. GMF, Munich. CC 628.

Large Study. Oil on canvas. 39³/₈ × 30³/₄''. "∠K 14". SRG, New York. CC 630.

Studies for Panel (cf. KK 1914, 198-201):

Large Study for Summer. Oil on canvas. 39¹/₈ × 23³/₈''. GMF, Munich. CC 632.

Small Study for Summer. Oil on cardboard. 25⁵/₈ × 19⁷/₈''. GMF, Munich. CC 636.

Small Study for Autumn. Oil on cardboard. 25³/₄ × 19⁵/₈''. "∠K". GMF, Munich. CC 634.

Small Study for Winter. Oil on cardboard. 25⁵/₈ × 19⁷/₈''. GMF, Munich. CC 635.

1917-1922

Study, St. George. Oil on canvas. Probably executed in 1917. USSR. CC 636.

Painting with Archers. Probably executed in Moscow during the First World War. USSR. CC 637.

View from window of apartment in Moscow. 1919. Oil on canvas. USSR. CC 638.

View from window of apartment in Moscow. 1919. Oil on canvas. 15³/₈ × 14¹/₈''. – The Hague, Gemeente Museum. CC 639.

Peasant Houses. 1919. Oil on canvas. USSR. CC 640.

Sketches for Murals, Juryfreien Ausstellung Berlin 1922. Tempera on cardboard. Main wall, three lateral walls and four corners. NK, Paris. CC 641-645.
Not included in the list of Color Drawings:
Parade. 1903. Tempera on cardboard. 8¹/₄ × 39³/₈″. "Kandinsky" l. l. Busch-Reisinger Museum, Cambridge, Mass. Color plate, p. 49.
Crusader. 1903. Tempera on cardboard. 18¹/₈ × 20¹/₂″. "Kandinsky 1903" l. r. Private collection, USA. CC 655.
Russian Scene. 1904. Tempera on cardboard. 9 × 21₆/₈″. "Kandinsky" l. r. NK, Paris. CC 654.
Riding Couple. 1905. Tempera on canvas. 21⁵/₈ × 19⁵/₈″. "Kandinsky" l. r. GMF, Munich. CC 658.
Russian Beauty. 1905. Tempera on cardboard. 16¹/₂ × 11³/₈″. – GMF, Munich. CC 656.
Night. 1906. Tempera on cardboard. 12 × 19″. "Kandinsky" l. l. GMF, Munich. CC 659.
Song of the Volga. 1906. Tempera on canvas. 34⁵/₈ × 47¹/₄″. "Kandinsky 1906" l. l. CC 657.

Paintings on Glass

Kandinsky listed eighteen watercolors, which he entitled *Trifles*, and which he executed and sold in Stockholm. He also listed seventeen paintings on glass, which he executed in Moscow in 1917 and sold there. Twenty-three other glass paintings are in the Gabriele Münter Foundation, Munich. They date from 1909–1914. Most of them treat religious subjects. The selection given here includes items mentioned in the text.

Mythological Scene. 1908. Oil on glass. 6 × 6¹/₄″. Collection Helmut Beck, Stuttgart. CC 660.
With Sun. 1910. Oil on glass. 12³/₈ × 15⁷/₈″. GMF, Munich. CC 661.
Sancta Francisca. 1911. Tempera on glass. 6¹/₄ × 4⁵/₈″. " ⚠ "SRG, New York. CC 662.
The Last Judgment. 1911. Oil on glass. 13³/₈ × 17³/₄″. " ⚠ " NK, Paris. CC 663.
The Last Judgment. 1911. Oil on glass. 8¹/₄ × 4³/₄″. GMF, Munich. CC 664.
The Last Judgment. 1911. Oil on glass. 10¹/₄ × 6⁷/₈″. GMF, Munich.
Resurrection of the Dead. Oil and silver on glass. 9¹/₂ × 9¹/₂″. " ⚠ " GMF, Munich. CC 666.
All Saints. 1911. Oil on glass. 12³/₈ × 19″. " ⚠ " GMF, Munich.
All Saints. 1911. Oil on glass. 13¹/₂ × 15⁷/₈″. GMF, Munich. CC 667.
Horsemen. 1911. Tempera on glass. 11¹/₂ × 7⁷/₈″. GMF, Munich. CC 665.
St. George. 1911. Tempera on glass. 11³/₄ × 5⁷/₈″. GMF, Munich. CC 668.
Picture with Pince-nez. 1912. Oil on glass. 11³/₈ × 9″. NK, Paris. CC 670.
Cavalier. 1912. Oil on glass. 10³/₄ × 11″. " ⚠ " NK, Paris.
Cow in Moscow. 1912. Oil on glass. 11 × 12³/₄″. " ⚠ " NK, Paris.
With the Red Spot. 1913. Oil on glass. 10⁵/₈ × 9⁵/₈″. " ⚠ " GMF, Munich.
Apocalyptic Horsemen. 1914. Tempera on glass. 12 × 8³/₈″. GMF, Munich. CC 669.
Amazon. 1917. Oil, gold and silver on glass. "K" in circle. USSR.
With Sailboats. 1917. Oil on glass. "K" in circle. USSR.
With the Hobby Horse. 1917. Oil on glass. "K" in circle. USSR. CC 671.
In his list for 1902–1908 Kandinsky mentioned thirty-nine woodcuts, sometimes indicating the dimensions and places where exhibited. Sixty woodcuts were published in *Poems Without Words* (1904), *Xylographies* (1906), and the magazine *Tendances nouvelles* (1906–1907); ten in *On the Spiritual in Art* (1912), one color woodcut in *Blaue Reiter* (1912), and fifty-five black-and-white and

color woodcuts in *Klänge* (1913). For the Blaue Reiter period Kandinsky, in addition to a few individual prints, also noted "c. 1● etchings", which I have never seen, and for the Stockholm perioo (1916), he noted seven other etchings, calling them "the second series." *Kleine Welten* with ten prints appeared in 1922. After 1922 Kandinsky produced few lithographs, etchings, woodcuts, o● stencils, in all forty-five down to 1939, some of which were usec as supplements to books.
Kandinsky numbered his drawings separately by year.

Addenda

Watercolors

Oars, Study for Improvisation 26 (KK 148). 1910. Watercolor on parchment. 9³/₄ × 12⁷/₈″. " ⚠ " l. r. p. 40.
Improvisation. 1911. Watercolor. 11⁷/₈ × 18³/₄″. " ⚠ " l. l. Collection Bernhard Sprengel, Hannover. p. 40.
Sketch for Composition IV (KK 125). 1911. Watercolor on parchment. 7¹/₈ × 10³/₄″. " ⚠ " l. l. NK, Paris. p. 73.
Study for All Saints. 1911. Watercolor. 18³/₄ × 13¹/₄″. " ⚠ " l. l. (Photographed in Stockholm). p. 73.
Watercolor. 1911. 9¹/₄ × 11³/₈″. " ⚠ " l. l. Collection Karl Ströher, Darmstadt. p. 74.
Ten sketches for cover of Blaue Reiter Almanac. 1911. Städtische Galerie, Munich. CC 672–681.
Study for a composition. 1911. CC 682.
Study for Composition IV. 1911. 5¹⁵/₁₆ × 8⁷/₈″. " ⚠ " l. l. and "Kandinsky". Collection Mr. and Mrs. Emerson Woelffer, Colorado Springs, Colorado. CC 683.
With the Red Spot. 1911. 24³/₈ × 31″. "Kandinsky 1911" l. l. Collection Perelle, Paris. CC 684.
In the Circle. 1911. 19¹/₄ × 19¹/₄″. "Kandinsky 1911" l. l. NK, Paris. CC 685.
Study for Sketch KK 159. 1912. 15³/₈ × 16¹⁵/₁₆″. " ⚠ " l. r. CC 686.
With Three Riders. 1912. " ⚠ " l. r. Städtische Galerie, Munich. CC 687.
Announcement of the Blaue Reiter. 1912. 12⁵/₁₆ × 10⁵/₈″. "Kandinsky" l. l. CC 688.
To Mr. Alfred Meyer. 1912. "Kandinsky Munich 3.1.12" l. r. and dedication. Collection Mrs. Margit Winter Chanin, New York. CC 689.
Study for KK 160 b. 1912. 14³/₄ × 21⁵/₈″. " ⚠ " l. r. Collection Mrs. Hilla Rebay, Greens Farms, Conn. CC 690.
Study for Improvisation 25 (1912, 147). 1912. Watercolor. 12³/₈ × 18³/₈″. " ⚠ " l. r. SRG, New York. p. 75.
Study for a Last Judgment. 1912. Watercolor. 12¹/₈ × 9³/₈″. " ⚠ "
Rain Landscape. 1911/12. Watercolor. 9¹/₄ × 11⁷/₈″. "KK" l. r. Collection Mrs. M. Winter Chanin, New York. p. 76.
Study for a Last Judgment. 1913. Watercolor. 9³/₈ × 12¹/₄″. " ⚠ " l. r. MMA (Katherine S. Dreier Bequest), New York. p. 93.
Sketch for Bright Picture (KK 188). 1913. Watercolor and pen. 10 × 13¹/₂″. " ⚠ " l. l. Germanisches National-Museum, Nuremberg. p. 93.
Sketch for Painting with White Forms (KK 166). Watercolor. 10³/₄ × 14⁵/₈″. " ⚠ " l. r. MMA (Katherine S. Dreier Bequest), New York. p. 94.

Sketch for Small Pleasures (KK 174). 1913. Watercolor. 9³/₈ × 12¹/₈″. "△" l. r. NK, Paris. p. 94.

Study for Small Pleasures. 1913. Watercolor. 9³/₈ × 11³/₄″. "Kandinsky" l. r. Collection Jan W. E. Buijs, The Hague. p. 95.

Watercolor No. 6 for Composition VII. 1913. "△" l. r. Städtische Galerie, Munich. p. 96.

Watercolor No. 7 for Composition VII. 1913. "△" l. l. Städtische Galerie, Munich. p. 96.

Watercolor No. 5 for Composition VII. 1913. "△" l. r. Städtische Galerie, Munich. p. 153.

Untitled. 1913. 15³/₈ × 14″. "△" l. l. Germanisches National-Museum, Nuremberg. CC 691.

Watercolor. 1913, 13. 12³/₈ × 15¹⁵/₁₆″. "△" l. l. MMA, New York, Katherine S. Dreier Bequest. CC 692.

Red and Blue.1913. 14³/₁₆ × 15³/₄″. "△" l. r. NK, Paris. CC 693.

Sketch for Improvisation 31 (Sea Battle, KK 164). 1913. 11¹³/₁₆ × 9¹/₄″. "△" l. l. NK, Paris. CC 694.

Study for Painting with White Border (KK 162). 1913. "△" l. l. GMF, Munich. CC 695.

Untitled. 1913. 15³/₄ × 13³/₄″. "△ 1913" l. l. Collection Mr. and Mrs. John S. Schulte, New York. "△" CC 696.

Untitled. 1913. "△" l. l. CC 697.

Sketch for panel Spring. 1914. Watercolor. Städtische Galerie, Munich. p. 153.

Sketch for panel Summer. 1914. Watercolor. Städtische Galerie, Munich. p. 153.

Improvisation. 1915. 14³/₄ × 18⁵/₁₆″. "△" l.l. Collection Mrs. Louise Smith, New York. CC 698.

Untitled. 1915. "△ 15" l. l. and "Kandinsky" (in Russian) l. r. Tretiakov Gallery, Moscow. CC 699.

Untitled. 1916, 5. 8⁵/₈ × 11⁷/₈″. "△ 16" l. l. NK, Paris. CC 700.

Untitled. 1916. "△ 16" l. l. USSR. CC 701.

Untitled. 1916. "△ 16" l. r. USSR. CC 702.

Simple. 1916, 6. 8⁵/₈ × 11³/₁₆″. "△ 16" l. l. NK, Paris. CC 703.

Untitled. 1917. 11⁵/₁₆ × 7⁷/₈″. "∠K 17" l. l. Collection Russel Roberts, Cologne. CC 704.

Untitled. 1917. 9⁷/₈ × 11¹/₁₆″. "∠K 17" l. l. SRG, New York. CC 705.

Watercolor. 1917. 12¹/₈ × 8³/₄″. "∠K 17" l. l. Saidenberg Gallery, New York. p. 1. 154.

Watercolor. 1917. 9³/₄ × 10³/₄″. "∠K 17" l. l. SRG, New York. p. 154.

Untitled. 1918. 11³/₈ × 9¹/₁₆″. "∠K 18" l. l. Busch-Reisinger Museum, Harvard University, Cambridge, Mass. CC 706.

Untitled. 1919, 11. 9⁷/₈ × 13″. "∠K 19" l. l. SRG, New York CC 707.

Green Border. 1920. 10⁵/₈ × 14¹/₈″. "∠K 20" l. l. NK, Paris. CC 708.

Untitled. 1922. 15³/₄ × 14″. "∠K 22" l. l. Busch-Reisinger Museum, Harvard University, Cambridge, Mass. CC 709.

Untitled. 1922, 28. 13 × 19¹/₁₆″. "∠K 22" l. l. SRG, New York. CC 710.

Untitled. 1922, 37. 13³/₄ × 11¹³/₁₆″. "∠K 22" l. l. Collection Mrs. Rose Fried, New York. CC 711.

Untitled. 1923, 79. 14¹/₈ × 9⁷/₈″. "∠K 23" l. l. Private collection, Paris. CC 712.

Sketch for Black Accompaniment (KK 270). 1923, 109. 8⁵/₈ × 7¹/₁₆″. "∠K 23" l. l. NK, Paris. CC 713.

Sketch for Circles within the Circle (KK 261). 1923, 52. 18¹/₂ × 16¹/₂″. "∠K 23" l. l. NK, Paris. CC 714.

Calm Bend. 1924, 142. Watercolor. 12⁷/₈ × 9″. "∠K 24" l. l. Saidenberg Gallery, New York.

Black Relation. 1924, 158. Watercolor. 14¹/₄ × 13⁷/₈″. "∠K 24" l. l. MMA (Lillie P. Bliss Bequest), New York. p. 156.

Birthday gift for Gropius. 1924. Collection Walter Gropius, Lincoln, Mass. CC 715.

Untitled. 1924. 18⁷/₈ × 13″. "∠K 24" l. l. Collection William Landman, Toronto. CC 716.

In the Warm-Cool. 1924, 141. 13³/₄ × 9⁷/₈″. "∠K 24" l. l. Collection Hans Arnhold, New York. CC 717.

Dissolutions. 1924, 173. 19¹/₄ × 13³/₈″. "∠K 24" l. l. Collection Professor W. Löffler, Zurich. CC 718.

Sketch for Yellow-Red-Blue (KK 314). 1925. 12¹³/₁₆ × 18⁷/₈″. "∠K 25" l. l. NK, Paris. CC 719.

Black Tension. 1925, 187. 18⁷/₈ × 12¹³/₁₆″. "∠K 25" l. l. Collection G. David Thompson, Pittsburgh. CC 720.

Untitled. 1928. 21⁵/₈ × 15″. "∠K 28" l. l. Collection Mrs. Rose Fried, New York. CC 721.

Sketch for on Points (KK 433). 1928, 263. 18⁷/₈ × 12⁵/₈″. "∠K 28" l. l. Collection Rudolf Probst, Mannheim. CC 722.

Dull Depth. 1928, 291. 12⁵/₈ × 18⁷/₈″. "∠K 28" l. l. Collection Mrs. Marguerite Hagenbach, Basel. CC 723.

Scala. 1928, 297. 19¹¹/₁₆ × 18⁷/₈″. "∠K 28" l. l. Collection Mrs. Henry Cohen, New York. CC 724.

Untitled. 1928. 18¹/₂ × 12³/₁₆″. "∠K 28" l. l. Collection William Landmann, Toronto. CC 725.

Into. 1928, 299. 15¹/₈ × 10⁷/₁₆″. "∠K 28" l. l. Collection Bernhard Sprengel, Hannover. CC 726.

Glowing. 1928, 327. 17¹⁵/₁₆ × 19¹/₄″. "∠K 28" l. l. SRG, New York. CC 727.

Around the Corner. 1929, 355. 12⁵/₈ × 20¹/₂″. "∠K 29" l. l. NK, Paris. CC 728.

On Saturated Spots. 1929, 356. 12⁵/₈ × 20¹/₂″. "∠K 29" l. l. Collection Frau Ferdinand Möller, Cologne. CC 729.

Four Spots.1929,361. 15³/₄ × 18⁷/₈″. "∠K 29" l. l. Collection Hermann Rupf, Bern. CC 730.

Weak Support. 1930, 380. 12³/₈ × 9⁷/₁₆″. "∠K 30" l. l. Collection Felix Klee, Bern. CC 731.

Horizontal. 1931, 413. 19¹/₈ × 24″. "∠K 31" l. l. Private collection, Berlin. CC 732.

Light Structure. 1931, 427. 18¹/₂ × 12¹³/₁₆″. "∠K 31" l. l. Saidenberg Gallery, New York. CC 733.

Gradation. 1931, 428. 18¹¹/₁₆ × 13³/₄″. "∠K 31" l. l. Private collection, Paris. CC 734.

Sketch for Development in Brown (KK 594). 1933. 15³/₄ × 22⁷/₈″. "∠K 33" l. l. NK, Paris. CC 735.

Joined Surfaces, sketch for Two Green Points (KK 616). 1934, 535. 11 × 16¹/₂″. "∠K 34" l. l. NK, Paris. CC 736.

Above – Below. 1935, 553. 9⁷/₈ × 19¹/₈″. "∠K 35" l.l. Collection Felix Klee, Bern. CC 737.

The White Line. 1936, 571. 19¹¹/₁₆ × 15³/₈″. "∠K 36" l. l. Musée d'art moderne, Paris. CC 738.

Coincident. 1936, 573. 20¹/₂ × 19¹/₄″. "∠K 36" l. l. Gall. Apollinaire, Milan. CC 739.

Line with Accompaniment. 1937, 578. 25⁷/₁₆ × 19¹/₈″. "∠K 37" l. l. Niedersächsische Landesgalerie, Hannover. CC 740.

From the One to the Other. 1937, 584. 19¹/₈ × 9⁷/₁₆″. "∠K 37" l. l. Collection Frau Ferdinand Möller, Cologne. CC 741.

Fifteen. 1938, 589. 13⁹/₁₆ × 19¹¹/₁₆″. "∠K 38" l. l. NK, Paris. CC 742.

On the Green Line. 1938,592. 9⁷/₈ × 25⁷/₁₆″. "∠K 38" l. l. Art Institute, Chicago. CC 743.

Two. 1938, 593. 25¹/₄ × 9⁷/₈″. "∠K 38" l. l. Collection Luigi de Luca, Rome. CC 744.

Blue Arc. 1938, 610. 10⁵/₈ × 19¹/₂″. "∠K 38" l. l. Collection Emilio Jesi, Milan. CC 745.

In Height. 1939, 623. 19¹¹/₁₆ × 9⁷/₈″. "K 39" l. l. Gall. del Naviglio, Milan. CC 746.

Ascent of Grids. 1939, 632. 19¹/₄ × 13//₁₆″. "∠K 39" l. l. Galerie Maeght, Paris. CC 747.

Sketch for Ensemble (KK 671). 1940, 634. 11³/₈ × 15³/₈″. "∠K 40" l. l. NK, Paris. CC 748.

Untitled. 1940, 659. 8⁵/₈ × 6⁵/₁₆″. "∠K 40" l. l. Private collection, Cologne. CC 749.

Untitled. 1940, 663. 19¹¹/₁₆ × 12¹³/₁₆″. "∠K 40" l. l. Collection Arnold H. Maremont, Chicago. CC 750.

Sketch for Reduced Contrasts (KK 681). 1941, 721. 12⁹/₁₆ × 19¹¹/₁₆″. "∠K 41" l. l. NK, Paris. CC 751.

Last watercolor. 1944, 730. 10¹/₄ × 13³/₄″. "∠K 44" l. l. NK, Paris. CC 752.

Prints

Kandinsky's Poster for First Phalanx Exhibition. 1901. Color woodcut. 17⁵/₈ × 22⁵/₈". "Kandinsky 1901" c. r. MMA, New York (Gift of Nina Kandinsky). p. 37.
Night. 1903. Color woodcut. 12¹/₂ × 6⁵/₈". "△" l. l. p. 37.
Singer. 1903. Color woodcut. 7⁷/₈ × 5⁷/₈". p. 37.
On the Beach. 1902. Color woodcut. 12¹/₂ × 12¹/₄". "△" l. l. p. 38.
Farewell II. Color woodcut. 11⁷/₈ × 5¹/₈". p. 38.
Moonrise. Color woodcut. 9³/₄ × 5⁷/₈". p. 38.
Summer. Color woodcut. 12¹/₂ × 6⁵/₈". p. 38.
Title page of score of Glinka's opera Life for the Czar. 1906. CC 761.
Poster for Neue Künstlervereinigung, Munich. 1909. From color woodcut. "△" l. l. NK, Paris. p. 39.
Lyrical. 1911. Color woodcut. 5⁷/₈ × 8⁵/₈". "△" l. r. p. 74.
Poster for Gallery Maeght, from Klänge. CC 756.
From Klänge. 1913. CC 757.
Three color woodcuts from Klänge. 1913. p. 39.

Lithograph (proof). 1923. 18³/₄ × 17³/₈". "∠K 23" l. l. Felix Klee, Bern. p. 155.
Etching. 1926. Eleven prints; plate destroyed. 4⁵/₈ × 3⁵/₈". "∠K 26" l. l. Collection Felix Klee, Bern. p. 156.

Drawings

Outline of Composition VI (KK 172). 1913, 4. Drawing. 7³/₈ × 10¹/₂". p. 96.
Study for Composition VI. 1913. 6¹/₂ × 8⁷/₈". "△" l. l. NK, Paris CC. 753.
Pen drawing for Composition VII. 1913. "△" l. l. Städtische Galerie, Munich. p. 153.
Drawing for Composition VII. Städtische Galerie, Munich. p. 96.
Study for White, Soft, and Hard (KK 575) 1932, 8. 9¹/₁₆ × 11³/₈". NK, Paris. CC 754.
Study for Seven (KK 714). 1943, 1. 10⁵/₈ × 7⁷/₈". "K 43" l. l. NK, Paris. CC 755.

Classified Catalogue
Abbildungskatalog
Catalogue des Reproductions
Catalogo delle Jllustrazioni

1 Nos.   1–534   Paintings listed in KK
Gemälde verzeichnet im KK
Peintures inventoriées in KK
Quadri specificati in KK

2 Nos. 535–645   Supplement
Supplement
Supplément
Supplemento

3 Nos. 646–659   Tempera paintings
Temperabilder
Tableaux à tempera
Quadri a tempera

4 Nos. 660–671   Paintings on glass
Hinterglasbilder
Peintures sous verre
Pitture sotto vetro

5 Nos. 672–761   Watercolors, drawings, addenda
Aquarelle, Zeichnungen und Nachtrag
Aquarelles, dessins, complément
Acquerelli, disegni, appendice

1 Promenade, 1901, 3
Spaziergang, 1901, 3
Promenade, 1901, 3
Passeggiata, 1901, 3

2 Pond in the Woods, 1902, 10
Am Waldteich, 1902, 10
L'étang de la forêt, 1902, 10
Stagno nel bosco, 1902, 10

3 Old City, 1902, 12
Alte Stadt, 1902, 12
Vieille Ville, 1902, 12
Vecchia cittá, 1902, 12

4 Bright Air, 1902, 13
Helle Luft, 1902, 13
Air clair, 1902, 13
Aria chiara, 1902, 13

5 The Sluice, 1902, 15a
Die Schleuse, 1902, 15a
L'écluse, 1902, 15a
La cateratta, 1902, 15a

6 Trysting Place, 1903, 17
Stelldichein, 1903, 17
Rendez-vous, 1903, 17
Appuntamento, 1903, 17

7 Promenade Party, 1904, 24
Spazierende Gesellschaft, 1904, 24
Groupe en promenade, 1904, 24
A passeggio, 1904, 24

8 Sunday (Old Russia), 1904, 27
Sonntag (Altrussisch), 1904, 27
Dimanche (vieille Russie), 1904, 27
Domenica nella vecchia Russia, 1904, 27

9 Winter Twilight, 1904, 32
Winterdämmerung, 1904, 32
Crépuscule d'hiver, 1904, 32
Crepuscolo invernale, 1904, 32

10 Arrival of the Merchants, 1905, 40
Ankunft der Kaufleute, 1905, 40
L'arrivée des marchands, 1905, 40
Arrivo dei mercanti, 1905, 40

11 Rapallo, 1905, 43

12 Troika, 1906, 45

13 Panic, 1907, 49
Panik, 1907, 49
Panique, 1907, 49
Panico, 1907, 49

14 Storm Bell, 1907, 50
Sturmglocke, 1907, 50
Tocsin, 1907, 50
Campane a stormo, 1907, 50

15 White Sound, 1908, 59
Weißer Klang, 1908, 59
Sonorité blanche, 1908, 59
Suono bianco, 1908, 59

350

16 Autumn Landscape with Road, 1908, 61
Herbstlandschaft mit Landstraße, 1908, 61
Paysage d'automne avec route, 1908, 61
Paesaggio autunnale, 1908, 61

17 Winter I, 1909, 62
Winter I, 1909, 62
Hiver I, 1909, 62
Inverno I, 1909, 62

18 The Crinolines, 1909, 64
Die Krinolinen, 1909, 64
Les crinolines 1909, 64
Crinoline, 1909, 64

19 Domes (Red Wall), 1909, 66
Kuppeln (Rote Mauer), 1909, 66
Coupoles (Muraille rouge), 1909, 66
Cupole (Mura rosse), 1909, 66

20 Landscape with Tree, 1909, 67
Landschaft mit Baumstamm, 1909, 67
Paysage avec tronc d'arbre, 1909, 67
Paesaggio con tronco d'albero, 1909, 67

21 Painting with Boat, 1909, 71
Bild mit Kahn, 1909, 71
Tableau avec barque, 1909, 71
Quadro con barca, 1909, 71

22 Painting with Houses, 1909, 73
Bild mit Häusern, 1909, 73
Tableau avec maisons, 1909, 73
Quadro con case, 1909, 73

23 Improvisation 2 (Funeral March), 1909, 77
Improvisation 2 (Trauermarsch), 1909, 77
Improvisation 2 (Marche funèbre), 1909, 77
Improvvisazione 2 (Marcia funebre), 1909, 77

24 Improvisation 3, 1909, 78
Improvvisazione 3, 1909, 78

25 Landscape with Green House, 1909, 79
Landschaft mit grünem Haus, 1909, 79
Paysage avec maison verte, 1909, 79
Paesaggio con casa verde, 1909, 79

26 Landscape with Church, 1909, 80
Landschaft mit der Kirche, 1909, 80
Paysage avec l'église, 1909, 80
Paesaggio con chiesa, 1909, 80

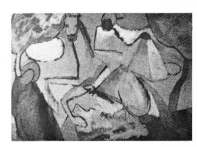

27 Sketch (Rider), 1909, 82
Skizze (Reiter), 1909, 82
Esquisse (Cavalier), 1909, 82
Schizzo (Cavaliere), 1909, 82

28 Improvisation 4, 1909, 83
Improvvisazione 4, 1909, 83

29 Landscape (Church in Murnau, large study),
1909, 87
Landschaft (Kirche in Murnau, große Studie),
1909, 87
Paysage (L'église à Murnau, grande étude), 1909, 87
Paesaggio (chiesa a Murnau, grande studio),
1909, 87

30 Group in Crinolines, 1909, 89
Gesellschaft in Krinolinen, 1909, 89
Dames en crinolines, 1909, 89
Riunione in crinolina, 1909, 89

31 Paradise, 1909, 91
Paradies, 1909, 91
Paradis, 1909, 91
Paradiso, 1909, 91

32 Improvisation 5 (Presto), 1910, 94
Improvvisazione 5 (Presto), 1910, 94

33 Study for Improvisation 8, 1910, 95
Studie zu ›Improvisation 8‹, 1910, 95
Etude pour ⟨Improvisation 8⟩, 1910, 95
Studio per ⟨Improvvisazione 8⟩, 1910, 95

34 Improvisation 7, 1910, 97
Improvvisazione 7, 1910, 97

35 Composition II, 1910, 98
Komposition II, 1910, 98
Composition II, 1910, 98
Composizione II, 1910, 98

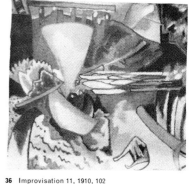

36 Improvisation 11, 1910, 102
Improvvisazione 11, 1910, 102

37 Garden, 1910, 103
Garten, 1910, 103
Jardin, 1910, 103
Giardino, 1910, 103

38 Landscape with Rain, 1910, 104
Landschaft mit Regen, 1910, 104
Paysage de pluie, 1910, 104
Paesaggio con pioggia, 1910, 104

39 Landscape with Wave-like Mountains, 1910, 104a
Landschaft mit wellenartigen Bergen, 1910, 104a
Paysage avec montagnes onduleuses, 1910, 104a
Paesaggio con montagne ondulatorie, 1910, 104a

40 Landscape with Factory Chimney, 1910, 105
Landschaft mit Fabrikschornstein, 1910, 105
Paysage avec cheminée d'usine, 1910, 105
Paesaggio con comignoli di fabbrica, 1910, 105

41 Lake (Boat Ride), 1910 106
See (Kahnfahrt), 1910, 106
Lac (Promenade en bateau), 1910, 106
Lago (Gita in barca), 1910, 106

42 Interior (with G. Münter and M. v. Werefkin),
1910, 107
Interieur (mit G. Münter und M. v. Werefkin),
1910, 107
Intérieur (avec G. Münter et M. v. Werefkin),
1910, 107
Interno (con G. Münter e M. v. Werefkin), 1910, 107

43 Improvisation 12 (Riders), 1910, 108
Improvisation 12 (Reiter), 1910, 108
Improvisation 12 (Cavaliers), 1910, 108
Improvvisazione 12 (Cavaliere), 1910, 108

44 Improvisation 13, 1910, 109
Improvvisazione 13, 1910, 109

45 Improvisation 14, 1910, 110
Improvvisazione 14, 1910, 110

46 Improvisation 16, 1910, 113
Improvvisazione 16, 1910, 113

47 The Last Judgment, 1910, 113a
Das Jüngste Gericht, 1910, 113a
Le Jugement Dernier, 1910, 113a
Giudizio Universale, 1910, 113a

48 Romantic Landscape, 1911, 115
Romantische Landschaft, 1911, 115
Paysage romantique, 1911, 115
Paesaggio romantico, 1911, 115

49 Impression III (Concert), 1911, 116
Impression III (Konzert), 1911, 116
Impression III (Concert), 1911, 116
Impressione III (Concerto), 1911, 116

50 Impression I (Fountain), 1911, 117
Impression I (Fontäne), 1911, 117
Impression I (Fontaine), 1911, 117
Impressione I (Fontana), 1911, 117

51 Lyrical, 1911, 118
Lyrisches, 1911, 118
Lyrique, 1911, 118
Lirica, 1911, 118

52 Fragment for Composition IV, 1911, 119
Fragment zu ›Komposition IV‹, 1911, 119
Fragment pour ‹Composition IV›, 1911, 119
Frammento per la ‹Composizione IV›, 1911, 119

53 Painting with Troika, 1911, 120
Bild mit Troika, 1911, 120
Tableau avec Troïka, 1911, 120
Quadro con Troika, 1911, 120

54 Arabs II, 1911, 121
Araber II, 1911, 121
Arabes II, 1911, 121
Arabi II, 1911, 121

55 Winter II, 1911, 122
    Winter II, 1911, 122
    Hiver II, 1911, 122
    Inverno II, 1911, 122

56 Improvisation 18 (with Tombstone), 1911, 126
    Improvisation 18 (mit Grabstein), 1911, 126
    Improvisation 18 (avec pierre tombale), 1911, 126
    Improvvisazione 18 (con pietra tombale), 1911, 126

57 Improvisation 19, 1911, 127
    Improvvisazione 19, 1911, 127

58 Improvisation 19a, 1911, 128a
    Improvvisazione 19a, 1911, 128a

59 The Cow, 1911, 131
    Die Kuh, 1911, 131
    La vache, 1911, 131
    La Mucca, 1911, 131

60 Arabs III (with Pitcher), 1911, 133
    Araber III (mit Krug), 1911, 133
    Arabes III (avec cruche), 1911, 133
    Arabi III (con anfora), 1911, 133

61 Nude, 1911, 134
    Akt, 1911, 134
    Nu, 1911, 134
    Nudo, 1911, 134

62 Sunday (Impression VI), 1911, 135
    Sonntag (Impression VI), 1911, 135
    Dimanche (Impression VI), 1911, 135
    Domenica (Impression VI), 1911, 135

63 Saint George III, 1911, 136
    Der heilige Georg III, 1911, 136
    Saint Georges III, 1911, 136
    S. Giorgio III, 1911, 136

354

64 Impression IV (Policeman), 1911, 137
    Impression IV (Gendarm), 1911, 137
    Impression IV (Gendarme), 1911, 137
    Impressione IV (Gendarme), 1911, 137

65 Improvisation 20, 1911, 138
    Improvvisazione 20, 1911, 138

66 Improvisation 21 (with Yellow Horse), 1911, 139
    Improvisation 21 (mit dem gelben Pferd), 1911, 139
    Improvisation 21 (avec cheval jaune), 1911, 139
    Improvvisazione 21 (con cavallo giallo), 1911, 139

67 Improvisation 22, 1911, 140
Improvvisazione 22, 1911, 140

68 Impression V (Park), 1911, 141
Impression V (Park), 1911, 141
Impression V (Parc), 1911, 141
Impressione V (Parco), 1911, 141

69 Improvisation 21 a, 1911, 143
Improvvisazione 21 a, 1911, 143

70 Improvisation 23, 1911, 145
Improvvisazione 23, 1911, 145

71 Improvisation 24 (Troika No. 2), 1912, 146
Improvvisazione 24 (Troika No 2), 1912, 146

72 Improvisation 25 (Garden of Love), 1912, 147
Improvisation 25 (Garten der Liebe), 1912, 147
Improvisation 25 (Jardin de l'amour), 1912, 147
Improvvisazione 25 (Giardino d'amore), 1912, 147

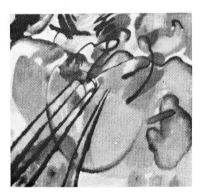

73 Improvisation 26 (Rowing), 1912, 148
Improvisation 26 (Rudern), 1912, 148
Improvisation 26 (Rame), 1912, 148
Improvvisazione 26 (Remi), 1912, 148

74 Improvisation 27 (Garden of Love), 1912, 149
Improvisation 27 (Garten der Liebe), 1912, 149
Improvisation 27 (Jardin de l'amour), 1912, 149
Improvvisazione 27 (Giardino d'amore), 1912, 149

75 Sketch for Deluge, 1912, 151 a
Skizze zu ⟩Sintflut⟨, 1912, 151 a
Esquisse pour ⟨Déluge⟩, 1912, 151 a
Schizzo per ⟨Diluvio⟩, 1912, 151 a

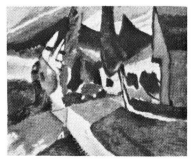

76 Moscow Lady, 1912, 152
Moskowitin (Dame in Moskau), 1912, 152
Moscovite (Dame à Moscou), 1912, 152
Moscovita (Dama a Mosca), 1912, 152

77 Black Spot I, 1912, 153
Schwarzer Fleck I, 1912, 153
Tache noire I, 1912, 153
Macchia nera I, 1912, 153

78 Landscape with Two Poplars, 1912, 155
Landschaft mit zwei Pappeln, 1912, 155
Paysage avec deux peupliers, 1912, 155
Paesaggio con due pioppi, 1912, 155

79 Autumn II, 1912, 156
Herbst II, 1912, 156
Automne II, 1912, 156
Autunno II, 1912, 156

80 Sketch, 1912, 159
Skizze, 1912, 159
Esquisse, 1912, 159
Schizzo, 1912, 159

81 Improvisation 29, 1912, 160
Improvvisazione 29, 1912, 160

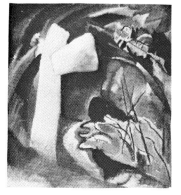

82 Second Sketch for Painting with White Border,
1913, 163
Zweite Skizze zu ⟩Bild mit weißem Rand⟨, 1913, 163
Deuxième esquisse pour le ⟨Tableau à bordure
blanche⟩, 1913, 163
Secondo schizzo per ⟨Quadro con bordo bianco⟩,
1913, 163

83 Improvisation 31 (Sea Battle), 1913, 164
Improvisation 31 (Seeschlacht), 1913, 164
Improvisation 31 (Bataille navale), 1913, 164
Improvvisazione 31 (Battaglia navale), 1913, 164

84 Sketch for Painting with White Forms, 1913, 165
Skizze zu ⟩Bild mit weißen Formen⟨, 1913, 165
Esquisse pour le ⟨Tableau avec formes blanches⟩,
1913, 165
Schizzo per ⟨Quadro con forme bianche⟩, 1913, 165

85 Landscape with Rain, 1913, 167
Landschaft mit Regen, 1913, 167
Paysage pluvieux, 1913, 167
Paesaggio con pioggia, 1913, 167

86 Landscape with Church II (with Red Spot),
1913, 169
Landschaft mit Kirche II (mit dem roten Fleck),
1913, 169
Paysage avec église II (à la tache rouge), 1913, 169
Paesaggio con chiesa II (con macchia rossa),
1913, 169

87 Improvisation 33 (Sketch for Orient), 1913, 170
Improvisation 33 (Entwurf für ⟩Orient⟨), 1913, 170
Improvisation 33 (Esquisse pour ⟨Orient⟩), 1913, 170
Improvvisazione 33 (Abbozzo per ⟨Oriente⟩),
1913, 170

88 Red Spot, 1913, 171
Roter Fleck, 1913, 171
Tache rouge, 1913, 171
Macchia rossa, 1913, 171

89 Composition VI, 1913, 172
Komposition VI, 1913, 172
Composition VI, 1913, 172
Composizione VI, 1913, 172

90 Painting with White Border, 1913, 173
Bild mit weißem Rand, 1913, 173
Tableau à bordure blanche, 1913, 173
Quadro con bordo bianco, 1913, 173

91 Landscape (Dünaberg in Murnau), 1913, 175
Landschaft (Dünaberg in Murnau), 1913, 175
Paysage (Dünaberg), 1913, 175
Paesaggio (Dünaberg a Murnau), 1913, 175

92 Painting with Green Center, 1913, 176
Bild mit grüner Mitte, 1913, 176
Tableau avec centre vert, 1913, 176
Quadro con centro verde, 1913, 176

93 Improvisation 34 (Motive from 170), 1913, 17/
Improvisation 34 (Motiv des Bildes 170), 1913, 177
Improvisation 34 (Motif du tableau 170), 1913, 177
Improvvisazione 34 (Motivo del Quadro 170),1913,177

94 Fragment 2 for Composition VII (Center and
Corners), 1913, 181
Fragment 2 zu ›Komposition VII‹ (Zentrum und
Ecken), 1913, 181
Fragment 2 pour ‹Composition VII› (Centre et
coins), 1913, 181
Frammento 2 per ‹Composizione VII› (Centro e
angoli), 1913, 181

95 Sketch 2 for Composition VII, 1913, 182
Skizze 2 zu ›Komposition VII‹, 1913, 182
Esquisse 2 pour ‹Composition VII›, 1913, 182
Schizzo 2 per ‹Composizione VII›, 1913, 182

96 Study for Composition VII, 1913, 183
Studie zu ›Komposition VII‹, 1913, 183
Etude pour ‹Composition VII›, 1913, 183
Schizzo per ‹Composizione VII›, 1913, 183

97 Improvisation with Red and Blue Ring, 1913, 184
Improvisation mit rot-blauem Ring, 1913, 184
Improvisation avec anneau rouge-bleu, 1913, 184
Improvvisazione con annello rosso-azzurro,1913,184

98 Sketch 3 for Composition VII, 1913, 185
Skizze 3 zu ›Komposition VII‹, 1913, 185
Esquisse 3 pour ‹Composition VII›, 1913, 185
Schizzo 3 per ‹Composizione VII›, 1913, 185

99 Dreamy Improvisation, 1913, 187
Träumerische Improvisation, 1913, 187
Improvisation rêveuse, 1913, 187
Improvvisazione fantastica, 1913, 187

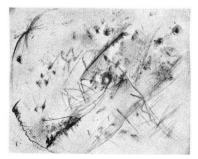
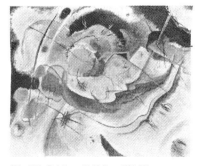

100 Bright Picture, 1913, 188
Helles Bild, 1913, 188
Tableau clair, 1913, 188
Quadro chiaro, 1913, 188

101 Little Painting with Yellow, 1914, 190
Kleines Bild mit Gelb, 1914, 190
Petit tableau avec jaune, 1914, 190
Piccolo quadro con giallo, 1914, 190

102 Improvisation with Cold Forms, 1914, 191
Improvisation mit kalten Formen, 1914, 191
Improvisation avec formes froides, 1914, 191
Improvvisazione con forme fredde, 1914, 191

103 Painting with Round Forms, 1914, 194
Bild mit runden Formen, 1914, 194
Tableau avec formes rondes, 1914, 194
Quadro con forme tonde, 1914, 194

104 Painting with Blue Border, 1914, 195
Bild mit blauem Rand, 1914, 195
Tableau à bordure bleue, 1914, 195
Quadro con bordo azzurro, 1914, 195

105 Painting with Three Spots, 1914, 196
Bild mit drei Flecken, 1914, 196
Tableau avec trois taches, 1914, 196
Quadro con tre macchie, 1914, 196

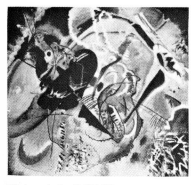

106 Improvisation 35, 1914, 197
Improvvisazione 35, 1914, 197

107 Painting with Two Red Spots, 1916, 202
Bild mit zwei roten Flecken, 1916, 202
Tableau avec deux taches rouges, 1916, 202
Quadro con due macchie rosse, 1916, 202

108 Painting on Light Ground, 1916, 203
Bild auf hellen Grund, 1916, 203
Tableau sur fond clair, 1916, 203
Quadro su fondo chiaro, 1916, 203

109 Painting with Orange Border, 1916, 204
Bild mit orange Rand, 1916, 204
Tableau à bordure orange, 1916, 204
Quadro con bordo arancione, 1916, 204

110 Blue Arch (Ridge), 1917, 210
Der blaue Bogen (Kamm), 1917, 210
L'arc bleu (Crête), 1917, 210
Arco azzurro (Cresta), 1917, 210

111 Entrance, 1917, 212
Eingang, 1917, 212
Entrée, 1917, 212
Entrata, 1917, 212

112 Twilight, 1917, 213
Dämmerung, 1917, 213
Crépuscule, 1917, 213
Crepuscolo, 1917, 213

113 Clarity, 1917, 215
Klarheit, 1917, 215
Clarté, 1917, 215
Chiarezza, 1917, 215

114 Gray Oval (Gray Border) 1917, 217
Graues Oval (Grauer Rand), 1917 217
Ovale gris (Bordure grise), 1917, 217
Ovale grigio (Bordo grigio), 1917 217

115 Red Border, 1919, 219
Rote Umrandung, 1919, 219
Encadrement rouge, 1919, 219
Cornice rossa, 1919, 219

116 White Oval (Black Border), 1919, 220
Weißes Oval (Schwarzer Rand), 1919, 220
Ovale blanc (Bordure noire), 1919, 220
Ovale bianco (Bordo nero), 1919, 220

117 In Gray, 1919, 222
Im Grau, 1919, 222
Dans le gris, 1919, 222
In grigio, 1919, 222

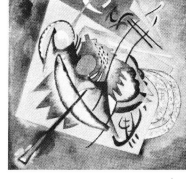

118 White Background, 1920, 224
Weißer Hintergrund, 1920, 224
Arrière-plan blanc, 1920, 224
Sfondo bianco, 1920, 224

119 Black Lines, 1920, 226
Schwarze Striche, 1920, 226
Traits noirs, 1920, 226
Strisce nere, 1920 226

120 Red Oval, 1920, 227
Rotes Oval, 1920, 227
Ovale rouge, 1920, 227
Ovale rosso, 1920, 227

121 Pointed Hovering, 1920, 228
Spitzes Schweben, 1920, 228
Flottement aigu, 1920, 228
Oszillazione a punte, 1920, 228

122 Sketch (Red with Black), 1920, 229
Skizze (Rot mit Schwarz), 1920, 229
Esquisse (Rouge et noir), 1920, 229
Schizzo (Rosso e nero), 1920, 229

123 The Green Border, 1920, 230
Der grüne Rand, 1920, 230
La bordure verte, 1920, 230
Bordo verde, 1920, 230

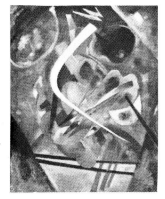

124 Points, 1920, 231
Spitzen, 1920, 231
Pointes, 1920, 231
Punte, 1920, 231

125 White Line, 1920, 232
Weißer Strich, 1920, 232
Trait blanc, 1920, 232
Tratto bianco, 1920, 232

126 On Yellow, 1920, 233
Auf Gelb, 1920, 233
Sur jaune, 1920, 233
Su giallo, 1920, 233

127 Red Spot II, 1921, 234
Roter Fleck II, 1921, 234
Tache rouge II, 1921, 234
Macchia rossa II, 1921, 234

128 Blue Segment, 1921, 235
Blaues Segment, 1921, 235
Segment bleu, 1921, 235
Segmento azzurro, 1921, 235

129 White Center, 1921, 236
Weißes Zentrum, 1921, 236
Centre blanc, 1921, 236
Centro bianco, 1921, 236

130 Chessboard, 1921, 237
Schachbrett, 1921, 237
Echiquier, 1921, 237
Scacchiera, 1921, 237

131 White Oval, 1921, 239
Weißes Oval, 1921, 239
Ovale blanc, 1921, 239
Ovale bianco, 1921, 239

132 Black Spot, 1921, 240
Schwarzer Fleck, 1921, 240
Tache noire, 1921, 240
Macchia nera, 1921, 240

 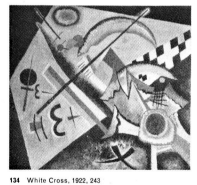 

133 Blue Circle, 1922, 242
Blauer Kreis, 1922, 242
Cercle bleu, 1922, 242
Cerchio azzurro, 1922, 242

134 White Cross, 1922, 243
Weißes Kreuz, 1922, 243
Croix blanche, 1922, 243
Croce bianca, 1922, 243

135 White Zigzags, 1922, 244
Weiße Zickzacks, 1922, 244
Zigzags blancs, 1922, 244
Zig-Zag bianchi, 1922, 244

360

136 Blue-Red, 1922, 245
Blau-Rot, 1922, 245
Bleu-rouge, 1922, 245
Azzurro-rosso, 1922, 245

137 Black Grid, 1922, 246
Schwarzer Raster, 1922, 246
Trame noire, 1922, 246
Retino nero, 1922, 246

138 Accented Corners, 1923, 247
Betonte Ecken, 1923, 247
Coins accentués, 1923, 247
Angoli accentuati, 1923, 247

139 Untitled, 1923, 248
Ohne Titel, 1923, 248
Sans titre, 1923, 248
Senza titolo, 1923, 248

140 In the Black Circle, 1923, 249
Im schwarzen Kreis, 1923, 249
Dans le cercle noir, 1923, 249
Nel cerchio nero, 1923, 249

141 Diagonal, 1923, 250
Diagonale, 1923, 250

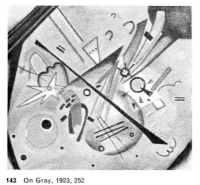

142 Black Form, 1923, 251
Schwarze Form, 1923, 251
Forme noire, 1923, 251
Forma nera, 1923, 251

143 On Gray, 1923, 252
Auf Grau, 1923 252
Sur gris, 1923, 252
Su grigio, 1923, 252

144 Through-going Line, 1923, 255
Durchgehender Strich, 1923, 255
Trait transversal, 1923, 255
Tratto trasversale, 1923, 255

145 Black and Violet, 1923, 257
Schwarz und Violett, 1923, 257
Noir et violet, 1923 257
Nero e viola, 1923, 257

146 The Arrow Form, 1923, 258
Die Pfeilform, 1923, 258
En forme de flèche, 1923, 258
La forma a freccia, 1923, 258

147 In the Black Square, 1923, 259
Im schwarzen Viereck, 1923, 259
Dans le carré noir, 1923, 259
Nel quadrato nero, 1923, 259

148 Circles within the Circle, 1923, 261
Kreise im Kreis, 1923, 261
Cercles dans cercle, 1923, 261
Cerchi nel cerchio, 1923, 261

149 Animated Repose, 1923, 262
Bewegte Ruhe, 1923, 262
Repos agité, 1923, 262
Quiete mossa, 1923, 262

150 Open Green, 1923, 263
Offenes Grün, 1923, 263
Vert ouvert, 1923, 263
Verde aperto, 1923, 263

151   Pink Square, 1923, 264
      Rosa Viereck, 1923, 264
      Carré rose, 1923, 264
      Quadrato rosa, 1923, 264

152   Without Support, 1923, 264a
      Ohne Stütze, 1923, 264a
      Sans appui, 1923, 264a
      Senza sostegni, 1923, 264a

153   Cheerful, 1924, 265
      Heiteres, 1924, 265
      Serein, 1924, 265
      Sereno, 1924, 265

154   Yellow Point, 1924, 266
      Gelbe Spitze, 1924, 266
      Pointe jaune, 1924, 266
      Punta gialla, 1924, 266

155   Blue Picture, 1924, 267
      Blaues Bild, 1924, 267
      Tableau bleu, 1924, 267
      Quadro azzurro, 1924, 267

156   In Red, 1924, 268
      Im Rot, 1924, 268
      En rouge, 1924, 268
      In rosso, 1924, 268

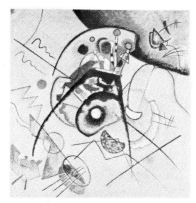

157   Backward Glance, 1924, 268a
      Rückblick, 1924, 268a
      Regard sur le passé, 1924, 268a
      Sguardo retrospettivo, 1924, 268a

158   Yellow Accompaniment, 1924, 269
      Gelbe Begleitung, 1924, 269
      Accompagnement jaune, 1924, 269
      Accompagnamento giallo, 1924, 269

159   Deep Brown, 1924, 271
      Tiefes Braun, 1924, 271
      Brun profond, 1924, 271
      Bruno profondo, 1924, 271

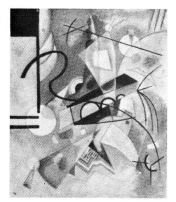

160   Self-Illuminating, 1924, 272
      Sich aufhellend, 1924, 272
      S'éclairant, 1924, 272
      Schiarita, 1924, 272

161   Sharp-Calm Pink, 1924, 273
      Das scharf-ruhige Rosa, 1924, 273
      Le rose aigu-paisible, 1924, 273
      Rosa forte e tranquillo, 1924, 273

162   Quiet Harmony, 1924, 274
      Stille Harmonie, 1924, 274
      Harmonie tranquille, 1924, 274
      Silenziosa armonia, 1924, 274

163 Horn Form, 1924, 275
Hornform, 1924, 275
Forme de corne, 1924, 275
Forma a corno, 1924, 275

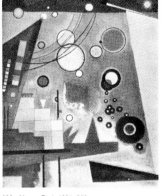

164 Heavy Red, 1924, 276
Schweres Rot, 1924, 276
Rouge lourd, 1924, 276
Rosso pesante, 1924, 276

165 Pink and Gray, 1924, 277
Rosa und Grau, 1924, 277
Rose et gris, 1924, 277
Rosa e grigio, 1924, 277

166 Silent, 1924, 278
Verstummen, 1924, 278
Mutisme, 1924, 278
Ammutolire, 1924, 278

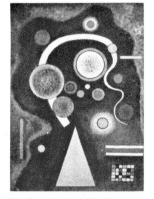

167 Capricious Line, 1924, 279
Launischer Strich, 1924, 279
Trait capricieux, 1924, 279
Tratto bizzarro, 1924, 279

168 Green Sound, 1924, 280
Grüner Klang, 1924, 280
Sonorité verte, 1924, 280
Suono verde, 1924, 280

169 Contrasting Sounds, 1924, 281
Gegenklänge, 1924, 281
Accords opposés, 1924, 281
Risonanze, 1924, 281

170 Red, 1924, 282
Rot, 1924, 282
Rouge, 1924, 282
Rosso, 1924, 282

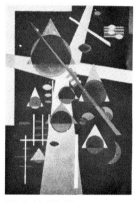

171 Quiet, 1924, 283
Ruhiges, 1924, 283
Paisible, 1924, 283
Tranquillo, 1924, 283

172 Contact, 1924, 284
Berührung, 1924, 284
Contact, 1924, 284
Contatto, 1924, 284

173 White Pentagon, 1924, 286
Weißes Fünfeck, 1924, 286
Pentagone blanc, 1924, 286
Pentagono bianco, 1924, 286

174 Calm Tension, 1924, 287
Ruhige Spannung, 1924, 287
Tension calme, 1924, 287
Tensione tranquilla, 1924, 287

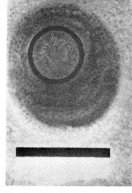

175 In Blue, 1925, 288
     Im Blau, 1925, 288
     En bleu, 1925, 288
     In azzurro, 1925, 288

176 Blue Circle No. 2, 1925, 289
     Blauer Kreis Nr. 2, 1925, 289
     Cercle bleu No. 2, 1925, 289
     Cerchio azzurro No. 2, 1925, 289

177 Sign, 1925, 290
     Zeichen, 1925, 290
     Signe, 1925, 290
     Segno, 1925, 290

178 Shaking, 1925, 291
     Schaukeln, 1925, 291
     Balancement, 1925, 291
     Dondolare, 1925, 291

179 Several Points, 1925, 292
     Einige Spitzen, 1925, 292
     Quelques pointes, 1925, 292
     Alcune punte, 1925, 292

180 Pointed and Round, 1925, 293
     Spitz und Rund, 1925, 293
     Pointu et rond, 1925, 293
     Punta e tondo, 1925, 293

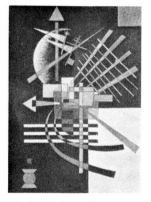

181 Above and Left, 1925, 294
     Oben und links, 1925, 294
     En haut et à gauche, 1925, 294
     In alto e a sinistra, 1925, 294

182 Three Elements, 1925, 295
     Drei Elemente, 1925, 295
     Trois éléments, 1925, 295
     Tre elementi, 1925, 295

183 Abstract Interpretation, 1925, 296
     Abstrakte Deutung, 1925, 296
     Interprétation abstraite, 1925, 296
     Senso astratto, 1925, 296

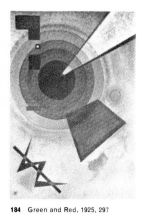

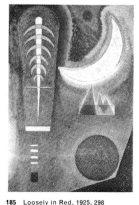

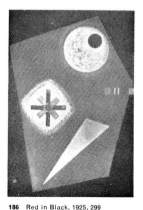

364

184 Green and Red, 1925, 297
     Grün und Rot, 1925, 297
     Vert et rouge, 1925, 297
     Verde e rosso, 1925, 297

185 Loosely in Red, 1925, 298
     Loses im Rot, 1925, 298
     Relâché en rouge, 1925, 298
     Libero in rosso, 1925, 298

186 Red in Black, 1925, 299
     Rot in Schwarz, 1925, 299
     Rouge en noir, 1925, 299
     Rosso nel nero, 1925, 299

187 White Point, 1925, 300
Weißer Punkt, 1925, 300
Point blanc, 1925, 300
Punto bianco, 1925, 300

188 Green Wedge, 1925, 302
Grüner Keil, 1925, 302
Coin vert, 1925, 302
Cuneo verde, 1925, 302

189 Small Signs, 1925, 303
Kleine Zeichen, 1925, 303
Petits signes, 1925, 303
Piccoli segni, 1925, 303

190 Steady Green, 1925, 304
Standhaftes Grün, 1925, 304
Vert permanent, 1925, 304
Verde costante, 1925, 304

191 Balanced, 1925, 305
Ausgewogen, 1925, 305
Equilibré, 1925, 305
Bilanciato, 1925, 305

192 Blue over Motley, 1925, 306
Blau über Bunt, 1925, 306
Bleu sur bigarré, 1925, 306
Azzurro su screziato, 1925, 306

193 Tempered, 1925, 307
Gemäßigt, 1925, 307
Mesuré, 1925, 307
Moderato, 1925, 307

194 Bright Unity, 1925, 308
Helle Einheit, 1925, 308
Unité claire, 1925, 308
Unità chiara, 1925, 308

195 Wavering, 1925, 309
Im Wackeln, 1925, 309
En vacillant, 1925, 309
Vacillando, 1925, 309

196 Intimate Communication, 1925, 310
Intime Mitteilung, 1925, 310
Message intime, 1925, 310
Comunicazione intima, 1925, 310

197 Untitled (Oval No. 2), 1925, 312
Ohne Titel (Oval Nr. 2), 1925, 312
Sans titre (Ovale No. 2), 1925, 312
Senza titolo (Ovale No. 2), 1925, 312

198 In the Bright Oval, 1925, 313
Im hellen Oval, 1925, 313
Dans un ovale clair, 1925, 313
Nell'ovale chiaro, 1925, 313

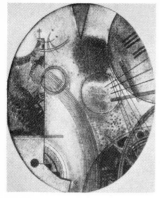

199 Whispered, 1925, 315
Geflüstert, 1925, 315
Chuchoté, 1925, 315
Sussurrato, 1925, 315

200 Red Depth, 1925, 316
Rote Tiefe, 1925, 316
Profondeur rouge, 1925, 316
Profondità rossa, 1925, 316

201 One Spot (Red on Brown), 1925, 317
Ein Fleck (Rot auf Braun), 1925, 317
Une tache (Rouge sur brun), 1925, 317
Una macchia (Rosso su bruno), 1925, 317

202 Becoming, 1925, 318
Werden, 1925, 318
Devenir, 1925, 318
Divenire, 1925, 318

203 Brown Silence, 1925, 319
Braunes Schweigen, 1925, 319
Silence brun, 1925, 319
Silenzio bruno, 1925, 319

204 Black Triangle, 1925, 320
Schwarzes Dreieck, 1925, 320
Triangle noir, 1925, 320
Triangolo nero, 1925, 320

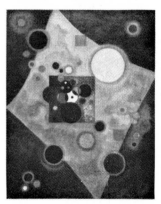

205 Pointed-Round, 1925, 321
Spitz-Rund, 1925, 321
Pointu-rond, 1925, 321
Punta e tondo, 1925, 321

206 Small Yellow, 1926, 324
Kleines Gelb, 1926, 324
Petit jaune, 1926, 324
Piccolo giallo, 1926, 324

207 Accent in Pink, 1926, 325
Akzent in Rosa, 1926, 325
Accent en rose, 1926, 325
Accento in rosa, 1926, 325

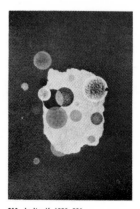

208 Tension in Red, 1926, 326
Spannung in Rot, 1926, 326
Tension en rouge, 1926, 326
Tensione in rosso, 1926, 326

209 Violet-Green, 1926, 329
Violett-Grün, 1926, 329
Violet-vert, 1926, 329
Verde-viola, 1926, 329

210 In Itself, 1926, 330
In sich, 1926, 330
En soi, 1926, 330
In sè, 1926, 330

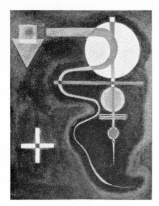

211 Cool Energy, 1926, 331
Kühle Energie, 1926, 331
Energie froide, 1926, 331
Energia fredda, 1926, 331

212 Connecting Green, 1926, 332
Verbindendes Grün, 1926, 332
Vert liant, 1926, 332
Collegemento verde, 1926, 332

213 Extended, 1926, 333
Ausgedehnt, 1926, 333
Distendu, 1926, 333
Disteso, 1926, 333

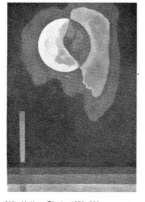

214 Counterweights, 1926, 334
Gegengewichte, 1926, 334
Contrepoids, 1926, 334
Contrappesi, 1926, 334

215 Yellow Circle, 1926, 335
Gelber Kreis, 1926, 335
Cercle jaune, 1926, 335
Cerchio giallo, 1926, 335

216 Small Values, 1926, 336
Kleine Werte, 1926, 336
Petites valeurs, 1926, 336
Piccoli valori, 1926, 336

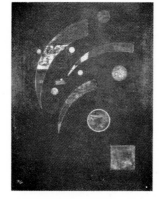

217 Blue Cross, 1926, 337
Blaues Kreuz, 1926, 337
Croix bleue, 1926, 337
Croce azzurra, 1926, 337

218 Discreet, 1926, 338
Diskret, 1926, 338
Discret, 1926, 338
Discreto, 1926, 338

219 Crescent, 1926, 339
Sichel, 1926, 339
Croissant, 1926, 339
Falce, 1926, 339

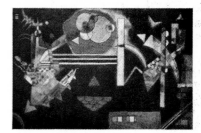

220 Wedge on Circle, 1926, 340
Keil auf Kreis, 1926, 340
Coin sur cercle, 1926, 340
Cuneo nel cerchio, 1926, 340

221 Sharp Hardness, 1926, 341
Scharfe Härte, 1926, 341
Dureté aiguë, 1926, 341
Estrema durezza, 1926, 341

222 Pointed Accents, 1926, 342
Spitze Akzente, 1926, 342
Accents pointus, 1926, 342
Accenti acuti, 1926, 342

223 Three Sounds, 1926, 343
    Drei Klänge, 1926, 343
    Trois sons, 1926, 343
    Tre suoni, 1926, 343

224 Dark Impulse, 1926, 345
    Dunkle Regung, 1926, 345
    Agitation sombre, 1926, 345
    Emozione scura, 1926, 345

225 Cool, 1926, 347
    Kühl, 1926, 347
    Frais, 1926, 347
    Freddo, 1926, 347

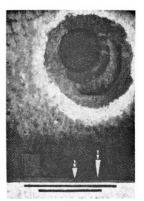

226 Toward Pink, 1926, 348
    Zum Rosa, 1926, 348
    Vers le rose, 1926, 348
    Verso il rosa, 1926, 348

227 Discreet Blue, 1926, 349
    Diskretes Blau, 1926, 349
    Bleu discret, 1926, 349
    Azzurro discreto, 1926, 349

228 Pressure, 1926, 351
    Druck, 1926, 351
    Pression, 1926, 351
    Pressione, 1926, 351

229 Rose in Gray, 1926, 352
    Rosa im Grau, 1926, 352
    Rose dans gris, 1926, 352
    Rosa in grigio, 1926, 352

230 Cross Form, 1926, 353
    Kreuzform, 1926, 353
    Forme de croix, 1926, 353
    Forma a croce, 1926, 353

231 Asserting, 1926, 355
    Behauptend, 1926, 355
    Affirmatif, 1926, 355
    Asserendo, 1926, 355

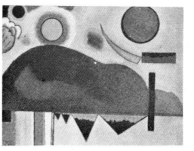

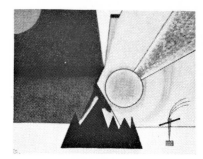

232 Thorny, 1926, 356
    Stachelig, 1926, 356
    Epineux, 1926, 356
    Spinoso, 1926, 356

233 Beginning, 1926, 358
    Anfang, 1926, 358
    Commencement, 1926, 358
    Inizio, 1926, 358

234 Development, 1926, 359
    Entwicklung, 1926, 359
    Développement, 1926, 359
    Sviluppo, 1926, 359

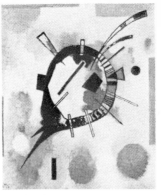

235 Conclusion, 1926, 360
Schluß, 1926, 360
Conclusion, 1926, 360
Conclusione, 1926, 360

236 Yellow Center, 1926, 361
Gelbe Mitte, 1926, 361
Milieu jaune, 1926, 361
Centro giallo, 1926, 361

237 Rift, 1926, 362
Riß, 1926, 362
Déchirure, 1926, 362
Squarcio, 1926, 362

238 Shifted, 1926, 367
Verschoben, 1926, 367
Déplacé, 1926, 367
Spostato, 1926, 367

239 Loose-Fast, 1926, 369
Locker-Fest, 1926, 369
Lâche-serré, 1926, 369
Lento-fisso, 1926, 369

240 Closely Surrounded, 1926, 370
Dicht umgeben, 1926, 370
Fermement entouré, 1926, 370
Circondato fisso, 1926, 370

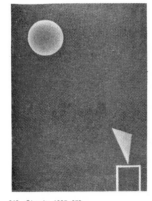

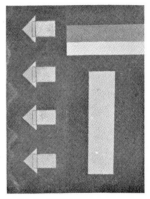

241 Free, 1927, 371
Frei, 1927, 371
Libre, 1927, 371
Libero, 1927, 371

242 Simple, 1927, 372
Einfach, 1927, 372
Simple, 1927, 372
Semplice, 1927, 372

243 Leftward, 1927, 374
Nach links, 1927, 374
Vers la gauche, 1927, 374
Verso sinistra, 1927, 374

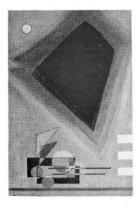

244 Supported, 1927, 375
Getragenes, 1927, 375
Soutenu, 1927, 375
Sostenuto, 1927, 375

245 Disturbance, 1927, 376
Trübung, 1927, 376
Obscurcissement, 1927, 376
Turbamento, 1927, 376

246 Square, 1927, 377
Quadrat, 1927, 377
Carré, 1927, 377
Quadrato, 1927, 377

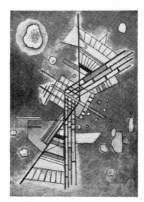

247 Red Cross, 1927, 378
Rotes Kreuz, 1927, 378
Croix rouge, 1927, 378
Croce rossa, 1927, 378

248 Dark Coolness, 1927, 380
Dunkle Kühle, 1927, 380
Fraîcheur sombre, 1927, 380
Freddezza scura, 1927, 380

249 Theme Point, 1927, 381
Thema Spitz, 1927, 381
Thème: pointu, 1927, 381
Tema-punta, 1927, 381

250 Sign with Accompaniment, 1927, 382
Zeichen mit Begleitung, 1927, 382
Signe avec accompagnement, 1927, 382
Segno con accompagnamento, 1927, 382

251 Sharp-Quiet, 1927, 384
Scharf-Ruhig, 1927, 384
Aigu-calme, 1927, 384
Forte-calmo, 1927, 384

252 Angular, 1927, 386
Winkelig, 1927, 386
Anguleux, 1927, 386
Angoloso, 1927, 386

253 Glow, 1927, 388
Aufleuchten, 1927, 388
Reluisant, 1927, 388
Splendore, 1927, 388

254 Arrows, 1927, 389
Pfeile, 1927, 389
Flèches, 1927, 389
Frecce, 1927, 389

255 Woven, 1927, 390
Geflecht, 1927, 390
Vannerie, 1927, 390
Intreccio, 1927, 390

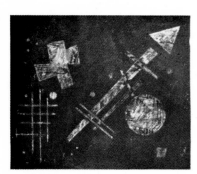

256 Several Sounds, 1927, 391
Einzelne Klänge, 1927, 391
Sons isolés, 1927, 391
Suoni singoli, 1927, 391

257 Hard in Soft, 1927, 392
Hart in Weich, 1927, 392
Dur dans mou, 1927, 392
Duro nel morbido, 1927, 392

258 Blue, 1927, 393
Blau, 1927, 393
Bleu, 1927, 393
Azzurro, 1927, 393

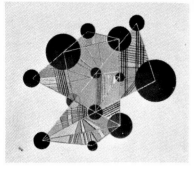

259 Hovering, 1927, 395
Schweben, 1927, 395
Flottement, 1927, 395
Sospeso, 1927, 395

260 Black Strip, 1927, 396
Schwarzer Streifen, 1927, 396
Raie noire, 1927, 396
Striscia nera, 1927, 396

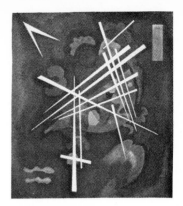

261 Netting, 1927, 397
Gitterform, 1927, 397
Forme de grille, 1927, 397
Graticcio, 1927, 397

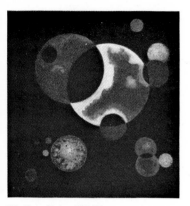

262 Heavy Circles, 1927, 398
Schwere Kreise, 1927, 398
Cercles lourds, 1927, 398
Cerchi neri, 1927, 398

263 Pointed Structure, 1927, 399
Spitzenbau, 1927, 399
Construction en pointes, 1927, 399
Costruzione a punte, 1927, 399

264 Dull Red, 1927, 400
Dumpfes Rot, 1927, 400
Rouge éteint, 1927, 400
Rosso spento, 1927, 400

265 Red Bar, 1927, 402
Roter Stab, 1927, 402
Bâton rouge, 1927, 402
Bastone rosso, 1927, 402

266 Red in the Net, 1927, 403
Rot im Netz, 1927, 403
Rouge dans le réseau, 1927, 403
Rosso nella rete, 1927, 403

267 Mild Hardness, 1927, 404
Milde Härte, 1927, 404
Dureté douce, 1927, 404
Mite durezza, 1927, 404

268 Black-Red, 1927, 405
Schwarz-Rot, 1927, 405
Rouge-noir, 1927, 405
Rosso-nero, 1927, 405

269 Warm-Cool, 1927, 406
Warm-Kühl, 1927, 406
Chaud-frais, 1927, 406
Caldo-freddo, 1927, 406

270 Sharp Heat, 1927, 408
Scharfes Heiß, 1927, 408
Chaud mordant, 1927, 408
Cocente, 1927, 408

271 Line-Spot, 1927, 409
Linie-Fleck, 1927, 409
Ligne-tache, 1927, 409
Linea-macchia, 1927, 409

272 Soft Hard, 1927, 410
Weiches Hart, 1927, 410
Mollesse dure, 1927, 410
Molle durezza, 1927, 410

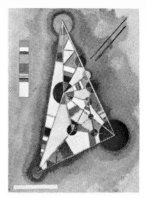

273 Variegation in the Triangle, 1927, 411
Bunt im Dreieck, 1927, 411
Bigarrure dans le triangle, 1927, 411
Multicolore in triangolo, 1927, 411

274 Several Cool, 1927, 412
Manches Kühl, 1927, 412
Mainte fraîcheur, 1927, 412
Un po' freddo, 1927, 412

275 Bipartite, 1928, 414
Zweiteilig, 1928, 414
En deux parties, 1928, 414
In due parti, 1928, 414

276 Little Black Bars, 1928, 415
Schwarze Stäbchen, 1928, 415
Bâtonnets noirs, 1928, 415
Bastoncini neri, 1928, 415

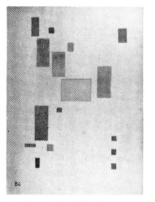

277 Square Lyrical, 1928, 416
Quadratlyrik, 1928, 416
Lyrisme au carré, 1928, 416
Lirica quadrata, 1928, 416

278 Repose, 1928, 417
Ruhe, 1928, 417
Repos, 1928, 417
Riposo, 1928, 417

279 Red-Cornered, 1928, 418
Roteckige, 1928, 418
Angles rouges, 1928, 418
Angoli rossi, 1928, 418

280 Mild Happening, 1928, 419
Milder Vorgang, 1928, 419
Evénement doux, 1928, 419
Scena dolce, 1928 419

281 A Circle A, 1928, 420
Ein Kreis A, 1928, 420
Un cercle A, 1928, 420
Un cerchio A, 1928, 420

282 Veiled Glow, 1928, 422
Verschleiertes Glühen, 1928, 422
Embrasement voilé, 1928, 422
Acceso velato, 1928, 422

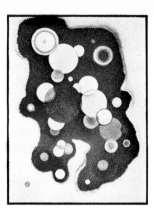

283 Variegated Signs, 1928, 423
   Bunte Zeichen, 1928, 423
   Signes multicolores, 1928, 423
   Segni colorati, 1928, 423

284 Deepened Impulse, 1928, 424
   Vertiefte Regung, 1928, 424
   Vibration approfondie, 1928, 424
   Profonda emozione, 1928, 424

285 Dull-Clear, 1928, 425
   Dumpf-Klar, 1928, 425
   Obscur-clair, 1928, 425
   Oscuro-chiaro, 1928, 425

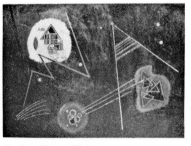

286 Three Places, 1928, 426
   Drei Stellen, 1928, 426
   Trois places, 1928, 426
   Tre punti, 1928, 426

287 To and Fro, 1928, 427
   Hin und Her, 1928, 427
   Par-ci par-là, 1928, 427
   Qua e là, 1928, 427

288 Variegated Accompaniment, 1928, 428
   Bunter Mitklang, 1928, 428
   Résonance multicolore, 1928, 428
   Consonanza multicolore, 1928, 428

289 Red Figure, 1928, 430
   Rote Figur, 1928, 430
   Figure en rouge, 1928, 430
   Figura rossa, 1928, 430

290 Powerful Red, 1928, 431
   Mächtiges Rot, 1928, 431
   Rouge puissant, 1928, 431
   Rosso potente, 1928, 431

291 A Circle B, 1928, 432
   Ein Kreis B, 1928, 432
   Un cercle B, 1928, 432
   Un cerchio B, 1928, 432

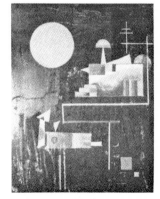

373

292 Mottled Bars, 1928, 434
   Bunte Stäbchen, 1928, 434
   Bâtonnets multicolores, 1928, 434
   Bastoncini colorati, 1928, 434

293 Red Repose, 1928, 435
   Rote Ruhe, 1928, 435
   Repos rouge, 1928, 435
   Calma rossa, 1928, 435

294 Two Sides Red, 1928, 437
   Zwei Seiten Rot, 1928, 437
   Deux faces rouges, 1928, 437
   Rosso da due lati, 1928, 437

295 Rigid, 1929, 438
Stramm, 1929, 438
Roide, 1929, 438
Vigoroso, 1929, 438

296 Loose Connection, 1929, 440
Lockere Bindung, 1929, 440
Liaison lâche, 1929, 440
Legame lento, 1929, 440

297 A Bit of Red, 1929, 441
Etwas Rot, 1929, 441
Un peu de rouge, 1929, 441
Un po' di rosso, 1929, 441

298 Circle and Spot, 1929, 442
Kreis und Fleck, 1929, 442
Cercle et tache, 1929, 442
Cerchio e macchia, 1929, 442

299 Light Blue, 1929, 443
Hellblau, 1929, 443
Bleu clair, 1929, 443
Azzurro chiaro, 1929, 443

300 Hovering above Firm, 1929, 444
Schwebend über Fest, 1929, 444
Flottement au-dessus du constant, 1929, 444
Sospeso su fisso, 1929, 444

301 Whitish, 1929, 445
Weißlich, 1929, 445
Blanchâtre, 1929, 445
Biancastro, 1929, 445

302 Round Accent, 1929, 446
Runder Akzent, 1929, 446
Accent rond, 1929, 446
Accento rotondo, 1929, 446

303 Inner Bond, 1929, 447
Innerer Bund, 1929, 447
Lien intérieur, 1929, 447
Legame interno, 1929, 447

304 Circle with Brown, 1929, 448
Kreis mit Braun, 1929, 448
Cercle avec brun, 1929, 448
Cerchio con bruno, 1929, 448

305 Ladder Form, 1929, 449
Leiterform, 1929, 449
Forme d'échelle, 1929, 449
Forma a scala, 1929, 449

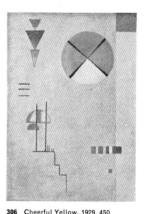

306 Cheerful Yellow, 1929, 450
Lustiges Gelb, 1929, 450
Jaune gai, 1929, 450
Giallo allegro, 1929, 450

307 Levels, 1929, 452
Etagen, 1929, 452
Etages, 1929, 452
Piani, 1929, 452

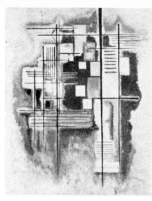

308 Condensation, 1929, 453
Verdichtung, 1929, 453
Condensation, 1929, 453
Condensazione, 1929, 453

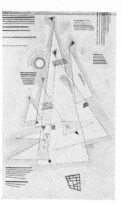

309 In the Clear Blue, 1929, 454
Im freien Blau, 1929, 454
Dans le bleu libre, 1929, 454
Nell'azzurro libero, 1929, 454

310 Dense, 1929, 455
Dicht, 1929, 455
Dense, 1929, 455
Denso, 1929, 455

311 Taciturn, 1929, 456
Schweigsam, 1929, 456
Silencieux, 1929, 456
Silenzioso, 1929, 456

312 Light in Heavy, 1929, 457
Leicht im Schwer, 1929, 457
Léger dans lourd, 1929, 457
Leggero in pesante, 1929, 457

313 Holding, 1929, 458
Haltend, 1929, 458
Tenant ferme, 1929, 458
Sostenendo, 1929, 458

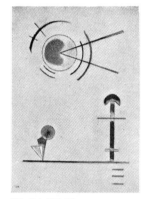

314 Flat, 1929, 459
Flach, 1929, 459
Plat, 1929, 459
Piano, 1929, 459

315 Green, 1929, 460
Grün, 1929, 460
Vert. 1929, 460
Verde, 1929, 460

316 For and Against, 1929, 461
Mit und Gegen, 1929, 461
Avec et contre, 1929, 461
Con e contro, 1929, 461

317 Fixed Points, 1929, 463
Fixierte Spitzen, 1929, 463
Pointes fixées, 1929, 463
Punte fissate, 1929, 463

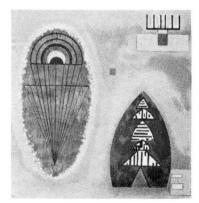

318 Cold, 1929, 464
Kalt, 1929, 464
Froid, 1929, 464
Freddo, 1929, 464

319 Fragment, 1929, 466
Ausschnitt, 1929, 466
Découpe, 1929, 466
Ritaglio, 1929, 466

320 One-Two, 1929, 468
Eins-Zwei, 1929, 468
Un-deux, 1929, 468
Uno-due, 1929, 468

321 Light Counterpressure, 1929, 469
Leichter Gegendruck, 1929, 469
Légère contre-pression, 1929, 469
Leggera contropressione, 1929, 469

322 Easter Egg, 1926, 327
Osterei, 1926, 327
Oeuf de Pâques, 1926, 327
Uovo di Pasqua, 1926, 327

323 Upward, 1929, 470
Empor, 1929, 470
En haut, 1929, 470
In alto, 1929, 470

324 Oppressed, 1929, 471
Gedrückt, 1929, 471
Oppressé, 1929, 471
Oppresso, 1929, 471

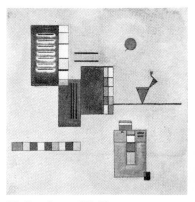

325 White-White, 1929, 472
Weiß-Weiß, 1929, 472
Blanc-blanc, 1929, 472
Bianco-bianco, 1929, 472

326 Angular Swing, 1929, 473
Winkelschwung, 1929, 473
Elan angulaire, 1929, 473
Slancio angolare, 1929, 473

327 Green Degrees 1929, 475
Grünstufen, 1929, 475
Degrés verts, 1929, 475
Gradazioni in verde, 1929, 475

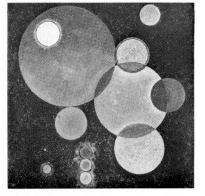

328 Down, 1929, 476
Herunter, 1929, 476
Vers le bas, 1929, 476
Verso il basso, 1929, 476

329 Circles in Brown, 1929, 477
Kreise im Braun, 1929, 477
Cercles dans le brun, 1929, 477
Cerchi in bruno, 1929, 477

330 Two Crosses, 1929, 478
Zwei Kreuze, 1929, 478
Deux croix, 1929, 478
Due croci, 1929, 478

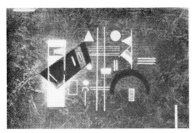

331 Blue, 1929, 479
Blau, 1929, 479
Bleu, 1929, 479
Azzurro, 1929, 479

332 Variegated but Quiet, 1929, 480
Bunt, aber still, 1929, 480
Bigarré mais calme, 1929, 480
Variopinto, ma calmo, 1929, 480

333 Pink Sweet, 1929, 481
Rosa-Süß, 1929, 481
Rose-doux, 1929, 481
Rosa-dolce, 1929, 481

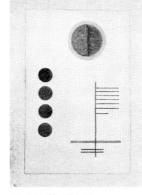

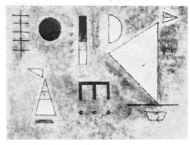

334 Sharp in Blunt, 1929, 482
Scharf im Dumpf, 1929, 482
Tranchant dans le mat, 1929, 482
Tagliente nel morbido, 1929, 482

335 Inflexible, 1929, 483
Unbiegsam, 1929, 483
Inflexible, 1929, 483
Inflessibile, 1929, 483

336 Jocular Sounds, 1929, 485
Scherzklänge, 1929, 485
Sonorités facétieuses, 1929, 485
Suoni scherzosi, 1929, 485

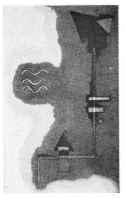

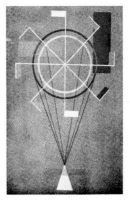

337 Thrust in Violet, 1929, 486
Stich in Violett, 1929, 486
Tirant sur le violet, 1929, 486
Punta nel viola, 1929, 486

338 Co-operation, 1929, 487
Mitwirken, 1929, 487
Collaboration, 1929, 487
Cooperazione, 1929, 487

339 Pointed Yellow, 1929, 488
Spitzes Gelb, 1929, 488
Jaune aigu, 1929, 488
Giallo a punte, 1929, 488

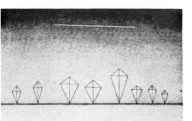

340 Eight Times, 1929, 489
8 Mal, 1929, 489
Huit fois, 1929, 489
Otto volte, 1929, 489

341 Flat-Deep, 1929, 490
Flach-Tief, 1929, 490
Plat-profond, 1929, 490
Piatto-profondo, 1929, 490

342 Jolly, 1929, 491
Fidel, 1929, 491
Joyeux, 1929, 491
Allegro, 1929, 491

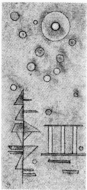

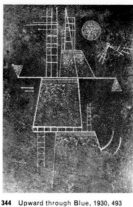

343 Scarcely, 1930, 492
Kaum, 1930, 492
A peine, 1930, 492
Appena, 1930, 492

344 Upward through Blue, 1930, 493
Zu oben durch Blau, 1930, 493
Vers le haut par le bleu, 1930, 493
Verso l'alto in azzurro, 1930, 493

345 Fluttering, 1930, 494
Flatternd, 1930, 494
Voletant, 1930, 494
Aleggiando, 1930, 494

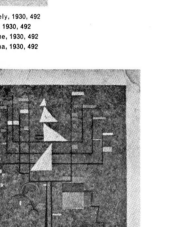

346 Yellow Border, 1930, 497
Gelber Rand, 1930, 497
Bordure jaune, 1930, 497
Bordo giallo, 1930, 497

347 Arrow toward the Circle, 1930, 498
Pfeil zum Kreis, 1930, 498
Flèche vers le cercle, 1930, 498
Freccia verso il cerchio, 1930, 498

348 Unsteady Balance, 1930, 499
Unfester Ausgleich, 1930, 499
Compensation instable, 1930, 499
Equilibrio instabile, 1930, 499

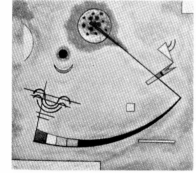

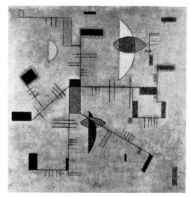

349 Stretched in the Corner, 1930, 500
Gespannt im Winkel, 1930, 500
Tendu dans l'angle, 1930, 500
Teso in angolo, 1930, 500

350 Round and Pointed, 1930, 501
Rund und Spitz, 1930, 501
Rond et pointu, 1930, 501
Tondo e punta, 1930, 501

351 Condensed Brown, 1930, 502
Dichtes Braun, 1930, 502
Brun dense, 1930, 502
Bruno intenso, 1930, 502

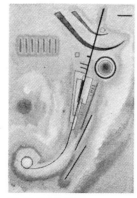

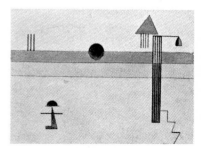

352 Within Three Points, 1930, 503
Zwischen drei Punkten, 1930, 503
Entre trois points, 1930, 503
Fra tre punti, 1930, 503

353 Light, 1930, 504
Leichtes, 1930, 504
Léger, 1930, 504
Leggero, 1930, 504

354 Dark Point, 1930, 505
Dunkler Punkt, 1930, 505
Point sombre, 1930, 505
Punto scuro, 1930, 505

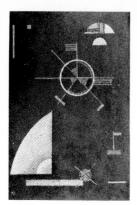

355 Dull Gray, 1930, 506
Stumpfes Grau, 1930, 506
Gris sourd, 1930, 506
Grigio ottuso, 1930, 506

356 Disintegrated Tension, 1930, 507
Zersetzte Spannung, 1930, 507
Tension décomposée, 1930, 507
Tensione decomposta, 1930, 507

357 Green-Empty, 1930 508
Grünleer, 1930, 508
Vide vert, 1930, 508
Vuoto verde, 1930, 508

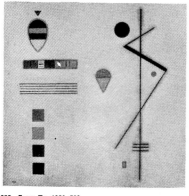

358 From-To, 1930, 509
Von-Zu, 1930, 509
De-vers, 1930, 509
Da-a, 1930, 509

359 Fixed-Loose, 1930, 510
Fixiert-Locker, 1930, 510
Fixé-lâche, 1930, 510
Fisso-libero, 1930, 510

360 Diagonal, 1930, 511
Diagonale, 1930, 511
Diagonale, 1930, 511
Diagonali, 1930, 511

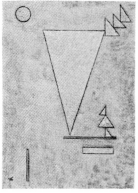

361 White, 1930, 512
Weiß, 1930, 512
Blanc, 1930, 512
Bianco, 1930, 512

362 Erect, 1930, 513
Aufrecht, 1930, 513
Debout, 1930, 513
Verticale, 1930, 513

363 Serious-Joke, 1930, 514
Ernst-Spaß, 1930, 514
Sérieux-plaisant, 1930, 514
Serio-giocoso, 1930, 514

364 Yellow Arc, 1930, 515
Gelber Bogen, 1930, 515
Arc jaune, 1930, 515
Arco giallo, 1930, 515

365 Great-Little, 1930, 516
Groß-Klein, 1930, 516
Grand-petit, 1930, 516
Grande-piccolo, 1930, 516

366 Stripes, 1930, 517
Streifen, 1930, 517
Raies, 1930, 517
Strisce, 1930, 517

367 Untitled, 1930, 519
     Ohne Titel, 1930, 519
     Sans titre, 1930, 519
     Senza titolo, 1930, 519

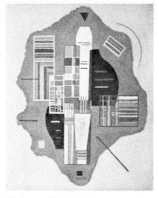

368 Joyous-Bright, 1930, 521
     Freudig-Hell, 1930, 521
     Joyeux-clair, 1930, 521
     Giocondo-chiaro, 1930, 521

369 Surfaces and Lines, 1930, 522
     Flächen und Linien, 1930, 522
     Surfaces et lignes, 1930, 522
     Piani e linee, 1930, 522

370 Angular Structure, 1930, 523
     Winkelbau, 1930, 523
     Structure angulaire, 1930, 523
     Costruzione ad angoli, 1930, 523

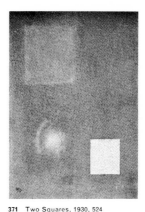

371 Two Squares, 1930, 524
     Zwei Quadrate, 1930, 524
     Deux carrés, 1930, 524
     Due quadrati, 1930, 524

372 Thirteen Rectangles, 1930, 525
     Dreizehn Rechtecke, 1930, 525
     Treize rectangles, 1930, 525
     Tredici rettangoli, 1930, 525

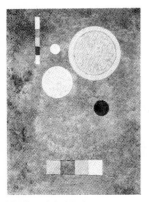

373 Ascended, 1930, 526
     Gestiegen, 1930, 526
     Monté, 1930, 526
     Ascesa, 1930, 526

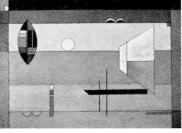

374 Cool Stripes, 1930, 527
     Kühle Streifen, 1930, 527
     Raies froides, 1930, 527
     Strisce fredde, 1930, 527

375 Definite, 1930, 528
     Bestimmt, 1930, 528
     Défini, 1930, 528
     Definito, 1930, 528

376 Heavy and Light, 1930, 529
     Schwer und leicht, 1930, 529
     Lourd et léger, 1930, 529
     Pesante e leggero, 1930, 529

377 White Sharpness, 1930, 530
     Weiße Schärfe, 1930, 530
     Rigueur blanche, 1930, 530
     Acuto bianco, 1930, 530

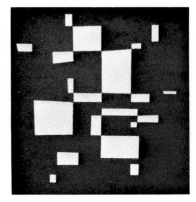

378 White on Black, 1930, 531
     Weiß auf Schwarz, 1930, 531
     Blanc sur noir, 1930, 531
     Bianco su nero, 1930, 531

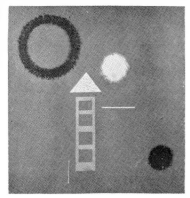

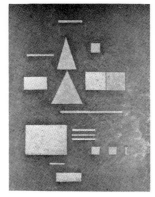

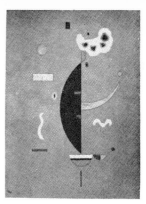

379 Calmed, 1930, 532
Beruhigt, 1930, 532
Apaisé, 1930, 532
Placato, 1930, 532

380 Blue Set, 1930, 534
Blaue Reihe, 1930, 534
Rangée bleue, 1930, 534
Fila azzurra, 1930, 534

381 Figure in Red, 1930, 535
Figur im Rot, 1930, 535
Figure dans le rouge, 1930, 535
Figura in rosso, 1930, 535

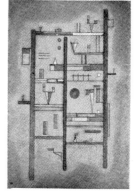

382 Isolated, 1930, 537
Vereinzelt, 1930, 537
Isoiément, 1930, 537
Isolati, 1930, 537

383 Moody, 1930, 538
Launisch, 1930, 538
Capricieux, 1930, 538
Lunatico, 1930, 538

384 Intimate Division, 1930, 539
Intime Teilung, 1930, 539
Partage intime, 1930, 539
Divisione intima, 1930, 539

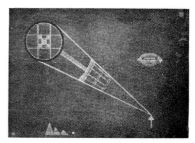

385 Two Black Stripes, 1930, 540
Zwei schwarze Streifen, 1930, 540
Deux raies noires, 1930, 540
Due strisce nere, 1930, 540

386 Angular Line, 1930, 541
Winkellinie, 1930, 541
Ligne angulaire, 1930, 541
Linea angolare, 1930, 541

387 From the Little Arrow, 1930, 543
Vom kleinen Pfeil, 1930, 543
Partant de la petite flèche, 1930, 543
Dalla piccola freccia, 1930, 543

381

388 Stable, 1931, 544
Stabil, 1931, 544
Stable, 1931, 544
Stabile, 1931, 544

389 Pointed Black, 1931, 545
Spitzes Schwarz, 1931, 545
Noir pointu, 1931, 545
Nero a punte, 1931, 545

390 Bridge, 1931, 546
Brücke, 1931, 546
Pont, 1931, 546
Ponte, 1931, 546

391 Gray, 1931, 547
Grau, 1931, 547
Gris, 1931, 547
Grigio, 1931, 547

392 Flowing, 1931, 548
Fließend, 1931, 548
Coulant, 1931, 548
Fluente, 1931, 548

393 Soft Pressure, 1931, 549
Sanfter Nachdruck, 1931, 549
Douce insistance, 1931, 549
Dolce pressione, 1931, 549

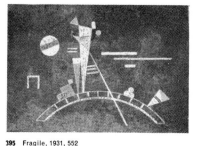

394 Brownish, 1931, 550
Bräunlich, 1931, 550
Brunâtre, 1931, 550
Brunastro, 1931, 550

395 Fragile, 1931, 552
Fragil, 1931, 552
Fragile, 1931, 552
Fragile, 1931, 552

396 Ceramics for Architectural Exhibition, Berlin, 1931, 554 a
Keramik für Bauausstellung Berlin, 1931, 554 a
Céramique pour l'exposition d'architecture, Berlin, 1931, 554 a
Ceramica per l'Esposizione di Architettura, Berlino, 1931, 554 a

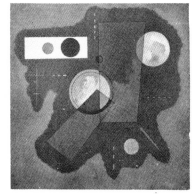

397 Ceramics for Architectural Exhibition, Berlin, 1931, 554 b
Keramik für Bauausstellung Berlin, 1931, 554 b
Céramique pour l'exposition d'architecture, Berlin, 1931, 554 b
Ceramica per l'Esposizione di Architettura, Berlino,1931, 554 b

398 Ceramics for Architectural Exhibition, Berlin, 1931, 554 c
Keramik für Bauausstellung Berlin, 1931, 554 c
Céramique pour l'exposition d'architecture, Berlin, 1931, 554 c
Ceramica per l'Esposizione di Architettura, Berlino, 1931, 554 c

399 Individual Forms, 1931, 555
Einzelformen, 1931, 555
Formes isolées, 1931, 555
Forme isolate, 1931, 555

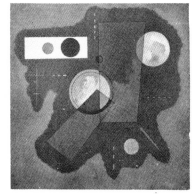

382

400 Hard Tension, 1931, 556
Harte Spannung, 1931, 556
Tension dure, 1931, 556
Dura tensione, 1931, 556

401 Green, 1931, 557
Grün, 1931, 557
Vert, 1931, 557
Verde, 1931, 557

402 Red Across, 1931, 558
Rotes Quer, 1931, 558
Rouge transversal, 1931, 558
Diagonale rossa, 1931, 558

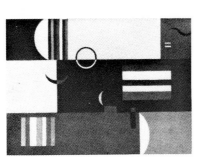

403 Between Bright, 1931, 559
Zwischen Hell, 1931, 559
Entre clair, 1931, 559
Tra chiaro, 1931, 559

404 Black-White, 1931, 560
Schwarz-Weiß, 1931, 560
Noir-blanc, 1931, 560
Nero-bianco, 1931, 560

405 Lightly touched, 1931, 561
Leichtberührt, 1931, 561
Effleuré, 1931, 561
Tocco leggero, 1931, 561

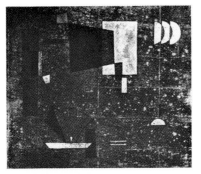

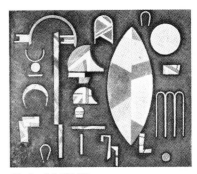

406 Flutter-like, 1931, 564
Flatterhaft, 1931, 564
Flottant, 1931, 564
Incostante, 1931, 564

407 Slowly out, 1931, 565
Langsam heraus, 1931, 565
Dégagement ralenti, 1931, 565
Lentamente fuori, 1931, 565

408 Gray Set, 1931, 566
Graue Reihe, 1931, 566
Rangée grise, 1931, 566
Fila grigia, 1931, 566

409 Up from the Half Circle, 1931, 567
Vom Halbkreis hinauf, 1931, 567
En montant du demi-cercle, 1931, 567
Dal semicerchio in alto, 1931, 567

410 Inclination, 1931, 568
Neigung, 1931, 568
Inclination, 1931, 568
Inclinazione, 1931, 568

411 Fixed Flight, 1932, 571
Fixierter Flug, 1932, 571
Vol fixé, 1932, 571
Volo fissato, 1932, 571

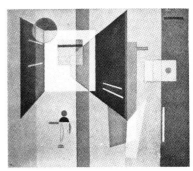

412 Secure Position, 1932, 572
Sichere Stellung, 1932, 572
Position sûre, 1932, 572
Posizione sicura, 1932, 572

413 Decisive Pink, 1932, 573
Entscheidendes Rosa, 1932, 573
Rose déterminant, 1932, 573
Rosa decisivo, 1932, 573

414 Rightward-Leftward, 1932, 574
Nach rechts-nach links, 1932, 574
Vers la droite-vers la gauche, 1932, 574
Verso destra-verso sinistra, 1932, 574

415 White-Soft and Hard, 1932, 575
Weiß-Weich und Hart, 1932, 575
Blanc-mou et dur, 1932, 575
Bianco-Morbido e duro, 1932, 575

416 Both striped, 1932, 576
Beide gestreift, 1932, 576
Tous deux rayés, 1932, 576
Entrambi striati, 1932, 576

417 Drastic and Mild, 1932, 578
Kraß und mild, 1932, 578
Abrupt et doux, 1932, 578
Forte e leggero, 1932, 578

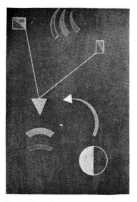

418 Connection, 1932, 579
Bindung, 1932, 579
Liaison, 1932, 579
Legame, 1932, 579

419 Cool Distance, 1932, 580
Kühle Entfernung, 1932, 580
Eloignement froid, 1932, 580
Fredda lontananza, 1932, 580

420 Thither, 1932, 581
Dahin, 1932, 581
Là-bas, 1932, 581
Laggiù, 1932, 581

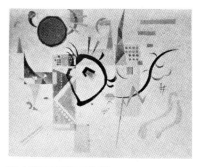

421 All the more, 1933, 582
Umsomehr, 1933, 582
D'autant plus, 1933, 582
Tanto più, 1933, 582

422 Balance-Pink, 1933, 583
Ausgleich-Rosa, 1933, 583
Compensation rose, 1933, 583
Equilibrio-rosa, 1933, 583

423 Light Formation, 1933, 584
Leichte Bildung, 1933, 584
Création légère, 1933, 584
Formazione leggera, 1933, 584

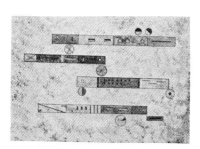

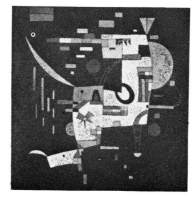

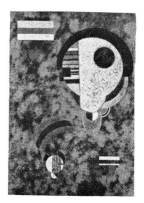

424 Succession, 1933, 585
Nacheinander, 1933, 585
L'un après l'autre, 1933, 585
Di seguito, 1933, 585

425 Defiant, 1933, 586
Trotzig, 1933, 586
Opiniâtre, 1933, 586
Ostinato, 1933, 586

426 Gray mood, 1933, 587
Graugestimmt, 1933, 587
Accordé sur le gris, 1933, 587
Intonazione grigia, 1933, 587

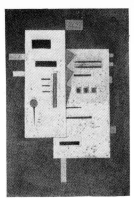

427 Soft Hardness, 1933, 588
Weiche Härte, 1933, 588
Molle rudesse, 1933, 588
Morbida durezza, 1933, 588

428 Crowded Circles, 1933, 589
Gedrängte Kreise, 1933, 589
Cercles serrés, 1933, 589
Cerchi serrati, 1933, 589

429 Green Texture, 1933, 590
Grüngewebe, 1933, 590
Tissu vert, 1933, 590
Tessuto verde, 1933, 590

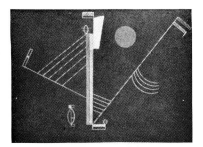

430 Stretched Bilaterally, 1933, 591
Zweiseitig gespannt, 1933, 591
Tendu dans les deux sens, 1933, 591
Tensione bilaterale, 1933, 591

431 From Here to There, 1933, 592
Von hier bis dort, 1933, 592
D'ici jusque là-bas, 1933, 592
Da qui a lì, 1933, 592

432 Lightly Together, 1933, 593
Leicht zusammen, 1933, 593
Légèrement associés, 1933, 593
Leggermente in sieme, 1933, 593

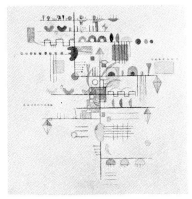

433 Graceful ascent, 934, 596
Zarter Aufstieg, 1934, 596
Montée gracieuse, 1934, 596
Salita graziosa, 1934, 596

434 Yellow Center, 1934, 597
Gelbe Mitte, 1934, 597
Milieu jaune, 1934, 597
Centro giallo, 1934, 597

435 Ensemble, 1934, 599
Ensemble, 1934, 599
Ensemble, 1934, 599
Insiene, 1934, 599

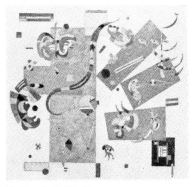

385

436 Black Forms on White, 1934, 600
Schwarze Formen auf Weiß, 1934, 600
Formes noires sur blanc, 1934, 600
Forme nere su bianco, 1934, 600

437 Blue World, 1934, 602
Blaue Welt, 1934, 602
Monde bleu, 1934, 602
Mondo azzurro, 1934, 602

438 Dominant Violet, 1934, 603
Herrschendes Violett, 1934, 603
Violet dominant, 1934, 603
Vi·la dominante, 1934, 603

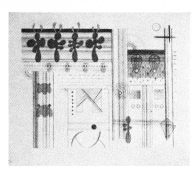

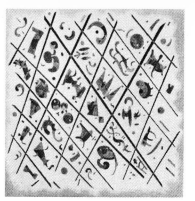

439 Fragile-Fixed, 1934, 605
Zartes befestigt, 1934, 605
Fragile-fixé, 1934, 605
Fragile-fisso, 1934, 605

440 Division-Unity, 1934, 606
Teilung-Einheit, 1934, 606
Division-Unité, 1934, 606
Divisione-Unità, 1934, 606

441 Animated White, 1934, 607
Bewegtes Weiß, 1934, 607
Blanc mouvementé, 1934, 607
Bianco movimentato, 1934, 607

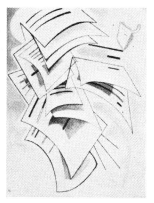

442 Raised Weight, 1935, 611
Erhöhtes Gewicht, 1935, 611
Poids monté, 1935, 611
Peso aumentato, 1935, 611

443 Contrast with Accompaniment, 1935, 613
Kontrast mit Begleitung, 1935, 613
Contraste accompagné, 1935, 613
Contrasto accompagnato, 1935, 613

444 Brown with Supplement, 1935, 615
Ergänztes Braun, 1935, 615
Brun supplémenté, 1935, 615
Bruno supplementato, 1935, 615

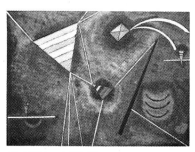

445 Light Tension, 1935, 619
Lockere Spannung, 1935, 619
Tension légère, 1935, 619
Tensione leggera, 1935, 619

446 Whitebound, 1929, 451
Weißgebunden, 1929, 451
Lié de blanc, 1929, 451
Legato in bianco, 1929, 451

447 Variegated Black, 1935, 620
Buntes Schwarz, 1935, 620
Noir bigarré, 1935, 620
Nero screziato, 1935, 620

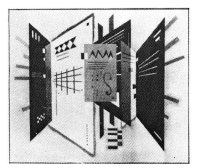

448 Points, 1935, 621
Spitzen, 1935, 621
Pointes, 1935, 621
Punte, 1935, 621

449 Violet-Orange, 1935, 622
Violett-Orange, 1935, 622
Violet-Orange, 1935, 622
Viola-arancione, 1935, 622

450 Delicate Accent, 1935, 624
Zarter Akzent, 1935, 624
Accent délicat, 1935, 624
Accento delicato, 1935, 624

451 Rigid and Bent, 1935, 625
Starr und Gebogen, 1935, 625
Rigide et courbé, 1935, 625
Rigido e curvo, 1935, 625

452 Two Circles, 1935, 614
Zwei Kreise, 1935, 614
Deux cercles, 1935, 614
Due cerchi, 1935, 614

453 Multiple Forms, 1936, 627
Vielfaltige Formen, 1936, 627
Formes multiples, 1936, 627
Forme multiple, 1936, 627

454 Green Figure, 1936, 628
Grüne Figur, 1936, 628
Figure verte, 1936, 628
Figura verde, 1936, 628

455 Untitled, 1936, 629
Ohne Titel, 1936, 629
Sans titre, 1936, 629
Senza titolo, 1936, 629

456 Red Knot, 1936, 630
Roter Knoten, 1936, 630
Noeud rouge, 1936, 630
Nodo rosso, 1936, 630

457 Triangles, 1936, 632
Dreiecke, 1936, 632
Triangles, 1936, 632
Triangoli, 1936, 632

458 Tense Forms, 1936, 634
Gespannte Formen, 1936, 634
Formes en tension, 1936, 634
Forme in tensione, 1936 634

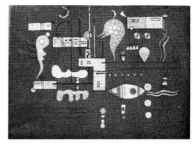

459 Stability, 1936, 635
Stabilität, 1936, 635
Stabilité, 1936, 635
Stabilità, 1936, 635

460 Thirty, 1937, 636
Dreißig, 1937, 636
Trente, 1937, 636
Trenta, 1937, 636

461 Calmed Tensions, 1937, 638
Beruhigte Spannungen, 1937, 638
Tensions calmées, 1937, 638
Tensioni placate, 1937, 638

462 Clear Tensions, 1937, 640
Helle Spannungen, 1937, 640
Tensions claires 1937, 640
Tensioni chiare, 1937, 640

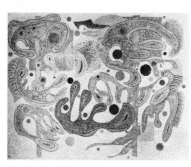

463 Capricious Forms, 1937, 643
Launische Formen, 1937, 643
Formes capricieuses, 1937, 643
Forme capricciose, 1937, 643

464 Grouping, 1937, 644
Gruppierung, 1937, 644
Groupement, 1937, 644
Raggruppamento, 1937, 644

465 Grids and others, 1937, 645
Gitter und anderes, 1937, 645
Grilles et autres, 1937, 645
Griglie e altro, 1937, 645

466 An Arabesque, 1938, 647
Eine Arabeske, 1938, 647
Une arabesque, 1938, 647
Un arabesco, 1938, 647

467 Touching Little Thing, 1938, 648
Kleine erregende Linie, 1938, 648
La petite émouvante, 1938, 648
La piccola linea commovente, 1938, 648

468 The Good Contact, 1938, 649
Der gute Kontakt, 1938, 649
Le bon contact, 1938, 649
Il buon contatto, 1938, 649

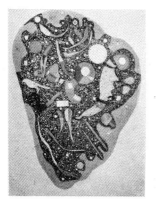

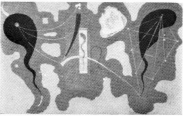

469 Many-colored Ensemble, 1938, 650
Buntes Ensemble, 1938, 650
Ensemble multicolore, 1938, 650
Assieme multicolore, 1938, 650

470 Penetrating Green, 1938, 651
Durchdringendes Grün, 1938, 651
Le vert pénétrant, 1938, 651
Il Verde penetrante, 1938, 651

471 Red Form, 1938, 652
Die rote Form, 1938, 652
La forme rouge, 1938, 652
La forma rossa, 1938, 652

472 Yellow Canvas, 1938, 653
Die gelbe Leinwand, 1938, 653
La toile jaune, 1938, 653
La tela gialla, 1938, 653

473 Serenity, 1938, 654
Heiterkeit, 1938, 654
Sérénité, 1938, 654
Serenità, 1938, 654

474 Toward Blue, 1939, 656
Zum Blau, 1939, 656
Vers le bleu, 1939, 656
Verso l'azzurro, 1939, 656

475 Warm Ensemble, 1939, 657
Heiße Einheit, 1939, 657
L'ensemble chaud, 1939, 657
L'insieme caldo, 1939, 657

476 The Red Square, 1939, 658
Das rote Viereck, 1939, 658
Le carré rouge, 1939, 658
Il quadrato rosso, 1939, 658

477 Ambiguïty (Complex-Simple), 1939, 659
Kompliziert-Einfach, 1939, 659
Ambiguïté (Complexité simple), 1939, 659
Ambiguità, 1939, 659

478 Elan, 1939, 660
Aufschwung, 1939, 660
L'Élan, 1939, 660
Lo slancio, 1939, 660

479 Upward, 1939, 662
Nach oben, 1939, 662
Vers le haut, 1939, 662
Verso l'alto, 1939, 662

480 Circuit, 1939, 663
Umkreis, 1939, 663
Circuit, 1939, 663
Circuito, 1939, 663

481 Unanimity, 1939, 664
Einhelligkeit, 1939, 664
Unanimité, 1939, 664
Unanimità, 1939, 664

482 Neighborhood, 1939, 666
Benachbart, 1939, 666
Voisinage, 1939, 666
Vicinanza, 1939, 666

483 Cheerfulness, 1939, 667
Frohsinn, 1939, 667
Allégresse, 1939, 667
Allegria, 1939, 667

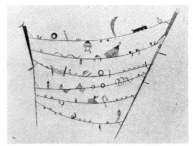

484 Overburdened, 1939, 668
Überladen, 1939, 668
Surchargé, 1939, 668
Sovraccaricco, 1939, 668

485 Green and Red, 1940, 669
Grün und Rot, 1940, 669
Vert et rouge, 1940, 669
Verde e rosso, 1940, 669

486 Little Accents, 1940, 670
Kleine Akzente, 1940, 670
Petits accents, 1940 670
Piccoli accenti, 1940, 670

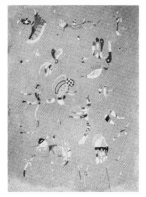

487 Sky Blue, 1940, 673
Himmelblau, 1940, 673
Bleu de ciel, 1940, 673
Azzurro cielo, 1940, 673

488 Light Construction, 1940, 674
Leichte Konstruktion, 1940, 674
Construction légère, 1940, 674
Costruzione leggera, 1940, 674

489 Around the Circle, 1940, 675
Um den Kreis, 1940, 675
Autour du cercle, 1940, 675
Attorno al circolo, 1940, 675

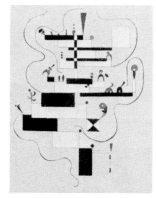

490 And More, 1940, 676
Überdies, 1940, 676
Et encore, 1940, 676
E ancora, 1940, 676

491 Moderation, 1940, 678
Mäßigung, 1940, 678
Modération, 1940, 678
Moderazione, 1940, 678

492 Two Blacks, 1941, 680
Zwei Schwarz, 1941, 680
Deux noirs, 1941, 680
Due neri, 1941, 680

493 Coolness, 1941, 682
Kühle, 1941, 682
Fraîcheur, 1941, 682
Freschezza, 1941, 682

494 The Fixed Square, 1941, 684
Das feste Viereck, 1941, 684
Le carré fixe, 1941, 684
Il quadrato fisso, 1941, 684

495 Moderate Variation, 1941, 685
Gemäßigte Variation, 1941, 685
Variation modérée, 1941, 685
Variazione moderata, 1941, 685

496 Balancing, 1942, 686
Balance, 1942, 686
Balancement, 1942, 686
In bilico, 1942, 686

497 Round Accent, 1942, 688
Runder Akzent, 1942, 688
Accent rond, 1942, 688
Accento tondo, 1942, 688

498 Transparent, 1942, 689
Trasparente, 1942, 689

499 Delicate Tensions, 1942, 690
Zarte Spannungen, 1942, 690
Tensions délicates, 1942, 690
Tensioni delicate, 1942, 690

500 A Fluttering Figure, 1942, 691
Eine flatternde Figur, 1942, 691
Une figure flottante, 1942, 691
Una figura fluttuante, 1942, 691

501 Vertical Accents, 1942, 692
Vertikale Akzente, 1942, 692
Accents verticaux, 1942, 692
Accenti verticali, 1942, 692

502 Support, 1942, 693
Stütze, 1942, 693
Appui, 1942, 693
Sostegno, 1942, 693

503 Three Stars, 1942, 694
Drei Sterne, 1942, 694
Trois étoiles, 1942, 694
Tre stelle, 1942, 694

504 In the Middle, 1942, 695
In der Mitte, 1942, 695
Au milieu, 1942, 695
Nel centro, 1942, 695

505 Three Between Two, 1942, 696
Drei zwischen Zwei, 1942, 696
Trois entre deux, 1942, 696
Tre fra due, 1942, 696

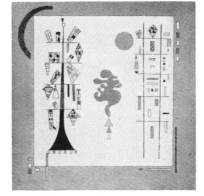

506 Joyful Theme, 1942, 697
Heiteres Thema, 1942, 697
Thème joyeux, 1942, 697
Tema gioioso, 1942, 697

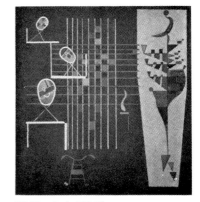

507 Three Ovals, 1942, 698
Drei Ovale, 1942, 698
Trois ovales, 1942, 698
Tre ovali, 1942, 698

508 Junctions, 1942, 700
Bindungen, 1942, 700
Jonctions, 1942, 700
Congiunzioni, 1942, 700

509 An Intimate Celebration, 1942, 701
Intimes Fest, 1942, 701
Une fête intime, 1942, 701
Una festa intima, 1942, 701

510 Netting, 1942, 703
Das Netz, 1942, 703
Le filet, 1942, 703
La rete, 1942, 703

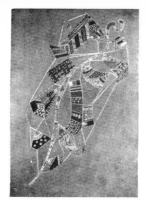

511 Dark Center, 1943, 704
Dunkle Mitte, 1943, 704
Le milieu sombre, 1943, 704
Centro scuro, 1943, 704

512 Light Ascent, 1943, 706
Leichter Aufstieg, 1943, 706
Ascension légère, 1943, 706
Ascensione leggera, 1943, 706

513 Fanlike, 1943, 707
Fächerförmig, 1943, 707
En éventail, 1943, 707
A ventaglio, 1943, 707

514 Simplicity, 1943, 708
Einfachheit, 1943, 708
Simplicité, 1943, 708
Semplicità, 1943, 708

515 Around the Line, 1943, 710
Um die Linie, 1943, 710
Autour de la ligne, 1943, 710
Attorno alla linea, 1943, 710

516 The Zigzag, 1943, 712
Das Zickzack, 1943, 712
Le zigzag, 1943, 712
Il Zigzag, 1943, 712

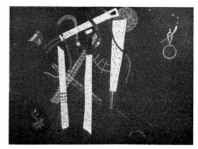

517 Brown Impetus, 1943, 715
Der braune Aufschwung, 1943, 715
L'Elan brun, 1943, 715
Slancio bruno, 1943, 715

518 Flowering, 1943, 717
Entfaltung, 1943, 717
Epanouissement, 1943, 717
Fioritura, 1943, 717

519 Three Columns, 1943, 719
Drei Säulen, 1943, 719
Trois colonnes, 1943, 719
Tre colonne, 1943, 719

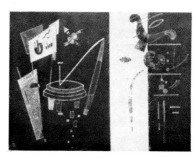

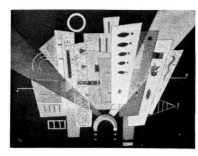

520 Dusk, 1943, 720
Dämmerung, 1943, 720
Crépuscule, 1943, 720
Crepuscolo, 1943, 720

521 Red Accent, 1943, 722
Roter Akzent, 1943, 722
Accent rouge, 1943, 722
Accento rosso, 1943, 722

522 Two Rays, 1943, 723
Zwei Strahlen, 1943, 723
Deux rayons, 1943, 723
Due raggi, 1943, 723

523 The Red Point, 1943, 724
Die rote Spitze, 1943, 724
La pointe rouge, 1943, 724
La punta rossa, 1943, 724

524 Thin Threads, 1943, 726
Dünne Fäden, 1943, 726
Fils fins, 1943, 726
Fili sottili, 1943, 726

525 Three Rays, 1943, 727
Drei Strahlen, 1943, 727
Trois rayons, 1943, 727
Tre raggi, 1943, 727

526 Disquiet, 1943, 730
Unruhe, 1943, 730
Inquiétude, 1943, 730
Inquietudine, 1943, 730

527 Five Parts, 1944, 732
Fünf Teile, 1944, 732
Cinq parties, 1944, 732
Cinque parti, 1944, 732

528 Isolation, 1944, 733
Isolierung, 1944, 733
Isolation, 1944, 733
Isolamento, 1944, 733

529 The Little Red Circle, 1944, 734
Der kleine rote Kreis, 1944, 734
Le petit rond rouge, 1944, 734
Il piccolo cerchio rosso, 1944, 734

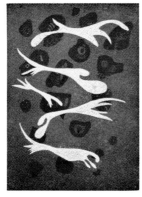

530 White Balancing Act, 1944, 735
Weißer Schwung, 1944, 735
Voltige blanche, 1944, 735
Volteggio bianco, 1944, 735

531 Three Black Bands, 1944, 736
Drei schwarze Streifen, 1944, 736
Trois bandes noires, 1944, 736
Tre strisce nere, 1944, 736

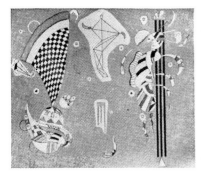

532 The Green Band, 1944, 737
Das grüne Band, 1944, 737
Le lien vert, 1944, 737
Legame verde, 1944, 737

533 Unfinished Painting, 1944
Unvollendetes Bild, 1944
Tableau inachevé, 1944
Quadro non finito, 1944

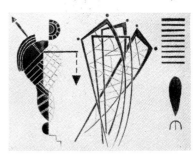

534 Unfinished Painting, 1944
Unvollendetes Bild, 1944
Tableau inachevé, 1944
Quadro non finito, 1944

393

2

535 Park of Akhtyrka, 1901 (3)
Park von Achtyrka, 1901 (3)
Le parc d'Achtyrka, 1901 (3)
Parco di Achtyrka, 1901 (3)

536 Kallmünz, 1903 (40)

537 Nymphenburg, 1904 (43)

538 Amsterdam, 1904 (52)

539 Upper Palatinate, 1904 (55)
Oberpfalz, 1904 (55)
Haut-Palatinat, 1904 (55)
Alto Palatinato, 1904 (55)

540 Spring, 1904 (72)
Frühling, 1904 (72)
Printemps, 1904 (72)
Primavera, 1904 (72)

541 Kochel, 1901

542 Cloudy Day, 1901
Trüber Tag, 1901
Jour sombre, 1901
Giorno tetro, 1901

543 Bridge at Kochel, 1902
Brücke in Kochel 1902
Pont à Kochel, 1902
Ponte a Kochel, 1902

544 Market-Place, 1902
Marktplatz, 1902
Place de marché, 1902
Piazza del mercato, 1902

545 Winter in Schwabing, 1902
Winter in Schwabing, 1902
Hiver à Schwabing, 1902
Inverno a Schwabing, 1902

546 Lady in Landscape, 1902
Bildnis einer promenierenden Dame, 1902
Portrait d'une dame en promenade, 1902
Ritratto di una signora a passeggio, 1902

547 Landscape with Yellow Field, 1903
Landschaft mit gelbem Feld, 1903
Paysage avec champ jaune, 1903
Paesaggio con campo giallo, 1903

548 Gabriele Münter at Work, 1903
Gabriele Münter beim Malen, 1903
Gabriele Münter peignant, 1903
Gabriele Münter mentre dipinge, 1903

549 Kallmünz, 1904

550 Beach Baskets in Holland, 1904
Strandkörbe in Holland, 1904
Cabines de plage en Hollande, 1904
Ceste-cabine in Olanda, 1904

551 Carthage, 1905
Karthago, 1905
Carthage, 1905
Cartagine, 1905

552 Pond in the Park, 1904
Parkteich, 1904
L'étang du parc, 1904
Stagno nel parco, 1904

553 Portrait of Gabriele Münter, 1905
Porträt von Gabriele Münter, 1905
Portrait de Gabriele Münter, 1905
Ritratto di Gabriele Münter, 1905

554 Port of Rapallo, 1906
Hafen von Rapallo, 1906
Le port de Rapallo, 1906
Il porto di Rapallo, 1906

555 Fishing-Boats, Rapallo, 1906
Fischerboote von Rapallo, 1906
Bateaux de pêche à Rapallo, 1906
Barche da pesca a Rapallo, 1906

556 Rapallo, 1906

557 Park of St. Cloud (Rider), 1906
Park von St. Cloud (Reiter), 1906
Parc de St-Cloud avec cavalier, 1906
Parco di St. Cloud (Cavaliere), 1906

558 Basin in the Park of St. Cloud, 1906
Bassin im Park von St. Cloud, 1906
Bassin dans le parc de St-Cloud, 1906
Laghetto nel parco di St. Cloud, 1906

559 Park of St. Cloud (Among Trees), 1906
Park von St. Cloud (Zwischen Bäumen), 1906
Au parc de St-Cloud (Entre des arbres), 1906
Parco di St. Cloud (Tra gli alberi), 1906

560 Bathing Women in Park, 1906
Badende Frauen im Park, 1906
Baigneuses dans le parc, 1906
Bagnanti nel parco, 1906

561 Lancer in Landscape, 1906
Lanzenreiter in Landschaft, 1906
Lancier dans paysage, 1906
Lanciere in paesaggio, 1906

562 Path, 1906
Allee, 1906
Allée, 1906
Viale, 1906

563 Waterfall near Lana, 1907
Wasserfall bei Lana, 1907
Cascade de Lana, 1907
Cascala di Lana, 1907

564 Village Street, 1908
Dorfstraße, 1908
Rue de village, 1908
Strada di paese, 1908

565 Street in Murnau, 1908
Straße in Murnau, 1908
Rue de Murnau, 1908
Strada a Murnau, 1908

566 Street in Murnau with Mountains, 1908
Straße in Murnau mit Bergen, 1908
Rue de Murnau avec montagnes, 1908
Strada a Murnau con montagne, 1908

537 Street in Murnau with Woman, 1908
Straße in Murnau mit Frau, 1908
Rue de Murnau avec une femme, 1908
Strada a Murnau con una donna, 1908

568 Church of Murnau, 1908
Kirche von Murnau, 1908
Eglise de Murnau, 1908
Chiesa a Murnau, 1908

569 Bavarian Village with Field, 1908
Bayrisches Dorf mit Feld, 1908
Village bavarois avec champ, 1908
Villagio bavarese con campo, 1908

570 Bavarian Village with Tree, 1908
Bayrisches Dorf mit Baumstamm, 1908
Village bavarois avec tronc d'arbre, 1908
Villagio bavarese con tronco d'albero, 1908

571 Village Church, 1908
Dorfkirche, 1908
Eglise de village, 1908
Chiesa di paese, 1908

572 Bavarian Mountains with Church, 1908
Bayerische Berge mit Kirche, 1908
Montagnes bavaroises avec église, 1908
Montagne bavaresi con chiesa, 1908

573 Upper Bavarian Mountains with Village, 1908
Oberbayerische Berge mit Dorf, 1908
Montagnes de Haute-Bavière avec village, 1908
Montagne dell'Alta Baviera con Villaggio, 1908

574 Village with Mountains, 1908
Dorf vor Gebirge, 1908
Village au bas de la montagne, 1908
Villaggio davanti alla montagna, 1908

575 Landscape near Murnau, 1908
Landschaft bei Murnau, 1908
Paysage près de Murnau, 1908
Paesaggio vicino a Murnau, 1908

576 Near Murnau, 1908
Bei Murnau, 1908
Près de Murnau, 1908
Vicino a Murnau, 1908

577 Summer near Murnau, 1908
Sommer bei Murnau, 1908
Eté à Murnau, 1908
Estate vicino a Murnau, 1908

578 Autumn near Murnau, 1908
Herbst bei Murnau, 1908
Automne à Murnau, 1908
Autunno vicino a Murnau, 1908

579 Stacks of grain, 1908
Kornhausten, 1908
Faisceaux de gerbes, 1908
Covoni in forma piramidale, 1908

580 Church at Froschhausen, 1908
Kirche in Froschhausen, 1908
Eglise à Froschhausen, 1908
Chiesa a Froschhausen, 1908

581 Winter Study with Mountain, 1908
Winterstudie mit Berg, 1908
Etude d'hiver avec montagne, 1908
Inverno con montagna (studio), 1908

582 Gabriele Münter with Easel, 1908
Gabriele Münter im Freien vor der Staffelei, 1908
Gabriele Münter, en plein air devant le chevalet, 1908
Gabriele Münter all'aperto davanti al cavalletto, 1908

583 Autumn Landscape near Murnau, 1908
Herbstlandschaft bei Murnau, 1908
Paysage d'automne près de Murnau, 1908
Paesaggio autunnale vicino a Murnau, 1908

584 Staffelsee, 1908

585 Lake of Starnberg (Tutzing), 1908
Starnberger See (Tutzing), 1908
Lac de Starnberg (Tutzing), 1908
Lago di Starnberg (Tutzing), 1908

586 Staffelsee, 1908

587 Staffelsee, 1908

588 Lake of Starnberg I, 1908
Starnberger See I, 1908
Lac de Starnberg I, 1908
Lago di Starnberg I, 1908

589 Lake of Starnberg II, 1908
Starnberger See II, 1908
Lac de Starnberg II, 1908
Lago di Starnberg II, 1908

590 Ludwigskirche in Munich, 1908
Ludwigskirche in München, 1908
Ludwigskirche à Munich, 1908
Ludwigskirche a Monaco, 1908

591 Houses in Munich, 1908
Häuser in München, 1908
Maisons à Munich, 1908
Case a Monaco, 1908

592 Before the City, 1908
Vor der Stadt, 1908
A l'entrée de la ville, 1908
Davanti alla città, 1908

593 The Elephant, 1908
Der Elefant, 1908
L'éléphant, 1908
L'elefante, 1908

594 Ariel Scene from Faust II, 1908
Arielszene aus Faust II, 1908
Scène d'Ariel du IIe Faust, 1908
Scena di Ariel dal Faust II, 1908

595 Dünaberg, 1909

596 Houses in Murnau, 1909
Häuser in Murnau, 1909
Maisons à Murnau, 1909
Case a Murnau, 1909

597 Landscape with Tower, 1909
Landschaft mit Turm, 1909
Paysage avec clocher, 1909
Paesaggio con torre, 1909

598 Church in Murnau, 1909
Kirche in Murnau, 1909
Eglise de Murnau, 1909
Chiesa a Murnau, 1909

599 Landscape near Murnau with Locomotive, 1909
Landschaft bei Murnau mit Lokomotive, 1909
Paysage près de Murnau avec locomotive, 1909
Paesaggio vicino a Murnau con locomotiva, 1909

600 Railroad near Murnau, 1909
Eisenbahn bei Murnau, 1909
Chemin de fer près de Murnau, 1909
Ferrovia vicino a Murnau, 1909

601 Murnau Street in the Snow, 1909
Murnauer Straße im Schnee, 1909
Rue de Murnau sous la neige, 1909
Strada a Murnau nella neve, 1909

602 Bedroom (Murnau), 1909
Schlafzimmer (Murnau), 1909
Chambre à coucher (Murnau), 1909
Camera da letto (Murnau), 1909

603 Graveyard in Kochel, 1909
Friedhof in Kochel, 1909
Cimetière de Kochel, 1909
Cimitero a Kochel, 1909

604 Mountain, 1909
Berg, 1909
Montagne, 1909
Monte, 1909

605 On the Beach, 1909
Auf dem Strand, 1909
Sur la plage, 1909
Sulla spiaggia, 1909

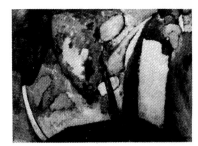

606 Waterfall, 1909
Der Wasserfall, 1909
La cascade, 1909
La cascata, 1909

607 Horses, 1909
Pferde, 1909
Chevaux, 1909
Cavalli, 1909

608 Oriental, 1909
Orientalisches, 1909
Oriental, 1909
Orientale, 1909

609 Study for Improvisation 2 (Funeral March), 1909
Studie zu >Improvisation 2< (Trauermarsch), 1909
Etude pour ‹Improvisation 2› (Marche funèbre), 1909
Studio per ‹Improvvisazione 2›(Marcia funebre),1909

610 All Saints, 1910
Allerheiligen, 1910
Toussaint, 1910
Ognissanti, 1910

611 Murnau in Winter with Church, 1910
Murnau im Winter mit Kirche, 1910
Etude d'hiver avec église (Murnau) 1910
Murnau in inverno con chiesa, 1910

612 Murnau with Church, 1910
Murnau mit Kirche, 1910
Murnau avec église, 1910
Murnau con chiesa, 1910

613 View of Murnau with Church, 1910
Blick auf Murnau mit Kirche, 1910
Vue de Murnau avec église, 1910
Panorama di Murnau con chiesa, 1910

614 Church, 1910
Kirche, 1910
Eglise, 1910
Chiesa, 1910

615 Garden, 1910
Garten, 1910
Jardin, 1910
Giardino, 1910

616 Mountain Landscape with Church, 1910
Berglandschaft mit Kirche, 1910
Paysage de montagne avec église, 1910
Paesaggio alpino con chiesa, 1910

617 Autumn Study, 1910
Herbststudie, 1910
Etude d'automne, 1910
Autunno (studio), 1910

618 Interior, Munich, Ainmillerstrasse 36, 1910
Interieur, München, Ainmillerstraße 36, 1910
Intérieur, Munich, Ainmillerstrasse, 36, 1910
Interno, Monaco, Ainmillerstrasse 36, 1910

619 Improvisation 3, copy, 1910
Improvisation 3, Replik, 1910
Réplique d'Improvisation 3, 1910
Improvvisazione 3, Replica, 1910

620 Improvisation 7, copy, 1910
Improvisation 7, Replik, 1910
Réplique, d'Improvisation 7, 1910
Improvvisazione 7, Replica, 1910

621 Study, 1910
Studie, 1910
Etude, 1910
Studio, 1910

622 Fragment for Composition II, 1910
Fragment zu ›Komposition II‹, 1910
Fragment pour ‹Composition II›, 1910
Frammento per ‹Composizione II›, 1910

623 All Saints, 1911
Allerheiligen, 1911
Toussaints, 1911
Ognissanti, 1911

624 Study for Winter II, 1911
Studie zu ›Winter II‹, 1911
Etude pour ‹Hiver II›, 1911
Studio per ‹Inverno II›, 1911

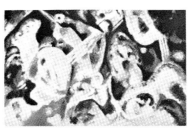

625 Improvisation with Horses, 1911
Improvisation mit Pferden, 1911
Improvisation avec chevaux, 1911
Improvvisazione con cavalli, 1911

626 Improvisation, Deluge, 1914
Improvisation, Sintflut, 1914
Improvisation, Déluge, 1914
Improvvisazione, Diluvio, 1914

627 Improvisation, 1914
Improvvisazione, 1914

401

628 Study, called Ravine, 1914
Studie, Klamm genannt, 1914
Etude (Gorge), 1914
Studio, detto ‹Burrone›, 1914

629 Untitled, called Deluge, 1914
Ohne Titel, ›Sintflut‹ genannt, 1914
Sans titre, nommé ‹ Déluge ›, 1914
Senza titolo, detto ‹Diluvio›, 1914

630 Large Study, 1914
Große Studie, 1914
Grande étude, 1914
Grande studio, 1914

631 Improvisation (Untitled), 1914
     Improvisation (ohne Titel), 1914
     Improvisation (sans titre), 1914
     Improvvisazione (senza titolo), 1914

632 Large Study for Panel Summer, 1914
     Große Studie zu Paneel ›Sommer‹, 1914
     Grande étude pour panneau ‹ Eté ›, 1914
     Grande studio per pannello ‹ Estate ›, 1914

633 Small Study for Panel Summer, 1914
     Kleine Studie zu Paneel ›Sommer‹, 1914
     Petite étude pour panneau ‹ Eté ›, 1914
     Piccolo studio per pannello ‹ Estate ›, 1914

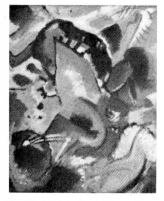

634 Small Study for Panel Autumn, 1914
     Kleine Studie zu Paneel ›Herbst‹, 1914
     Petite étude pour panneau ‹ Automne ›, 1914
     Piccolo studio per pannello ‹ Autunno ›, 1914

635 Small Study for Panel Winter, 1914
     Kleine Studie zu Paneel ›Winter‹, 1914
     Petite étude pour panneau ‹ Hiver ›, 1914
     Piccolo studio per pannello ‹ Inverno ›, 1914

636 Study for a Saint George, 1917
     Studie, Heiliger Georg, 1917
     Saint Georges étude, 1917
     Studio, San Giorgio, 1917

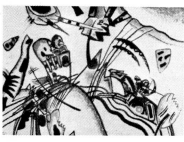

637 Picture with an Archer, 1917
     Bild mit Schützen, 1917
     Tableau avec archer, 1917
     Quadro con arciere, 1917

638 View from Window in Moscow, 1920
     Blick aus dem Fenster der Wohnung in Moskau
     A Moscou, vue de la fenêtre, 1920
     Mosca vista della finestra della sua casa, 1920

639 View from Window in Moscow, 1920
     Blick aus dem Fenster der Wohnung in Moskau
     A Moscou, vue de la fenêtre, 1920
     Mosca vista della finestra della sua casa, 1920

640 Farmhouses, 1920
     Bauernhäuser, 1920
     Maisons paysannes, 1920
     Case di contadini, 1920

641 Sketch for murals, Juryfreie-Exhibition, Berlin, 1922
     Entwürfe für die Wandbilder in der ›Juryfreien
     Ausstellung‹ Berlin 1922, Hauptwand
     Peinture murale pour la ‹Juryfreie› de Berlin, 1922.
     mur principal
     Progetto di pittura murale per l'espozione della
     ‹Juryfreie›, Berlin 1922

642 Side wall
     Seitenwand
     Mur latéral
     Parete laterale

643 Side wall
Seitenwand
Mur latéral
Parete laterale

644 Side wall
Seitenwand
Mur latéral
Parete laterale

645 Four corners
Vier Ecken
Quatre angles
Quattro angoli

646 Bridal Procession (Color Drawing 30), 1902, 1903
Brautzug (Farbige Zeichnung 30), 1902, 1903
Cortège de noce (Dessin en Couleur 30), 1902, 1903
Corteo nuziala (Disegno a colori 30), 1902, 1903

647 White Cloud (Color Drawing 27), 1903
Weiße Wolke (Farbige Zeichnung 27), 1903
Nuage blanc (Dessin en couleur 27), 1903
Nuvole bianche (Disegno a colori 27), 1903

648 Duel (Color Drawing 7), 1902
Zweikampf (Farbige Zeichnung 7), 1902
Duel (Dessin en couleur 7), 1902
Duello (Disegno a colori 7), 1902

649 Ships in Holland (Color Drawing 67), 1904
Die Schiffe (Holland) (Farbige Zeichnung 67), 1904
Des bateaux (Hollande) (Dessin en couleur 67)
Navi (Olanda) (Designo a colori 67), 1904

650 Windmill (Holland) (Color Drawing 68), 1904
Mühle (Holland) (Farbige Zeichnung 68), 1904
Moulin à vent (Hollande) (Dessin en couleur 68).
1904
Mulino (Olanda) (Disegno a colori 68), 1904

651 Ruin (Color Drawing 93). 1905
Ruine (Farbige Zeichnung 93), 1905
Ruine (Dessin en couleur 93), 1905
Rovina (Disegno a colori 93), 1905

652 Spectators (Color Drawing 99), 1905
Die Zuschauer (Farbige Zeichnung 99), 1905
Les spectateurs (Dessin en couleur 99), 1905
Gli spettatori (Disegno a colori 99), 1905

653 Winter (Skating) (Color Drawing 114), 1906
Winter (Eislauf) (Farbige Zeichnung 114), 1906
Hiver (Patinage) (Dessin en couleur 114), 1906
Inverno (Pattinaggio) (Disegno a colori 114), 1906

654 Russian Scene, 1904
Russische Szene, 1904
Scène russe, 1904
Scena russa, 1904

655 Crusader, 1903
Kreuzfahrer, 1903
Croisé, 1903
Crociato, 1903

656 Russian Beauty in a Landscape, 1905
Russische Schöne in Landschaft, 1905
Beauté russe dans un paysage, 1905
Bellezza russa in paesaggio, 1905

657 Song of the Volga, 1906
Wolgalied, 1906
Chant de la Volga, 1906
Canzone del Volga, 1906

658 Riding Couple, 1905
Reitendes Paar, 1905
Couple à cheval, 1905
Coppia a cavallo, 1905

659 Night, 1906
Die Nacht, 1906
La nuit, 1906
La notte, 1906

4

660 Mythological Scene, 1908
Mythologische Szene, 1908
Scène mythologique, 1908
Scena mitologica, 1908

661 With Sun, 1910
Mit Sonne, 1910
Avec soleil, 1910
Sole, 1910

662 Sancta Francisca, 1911
Sancta Franzisca, 1911
Sancta Francisca, 1911
Santa Francesca, 1911

663 The Last Judgment, 1911
Jüngstes Gericht, 1911
Jugement Dernier, 1911
Giudizio Universale, 1911

664 The Last Judgment, 1911
Jüngstes Gericht, 1911
Jugement Dernier, 1911
Giudizio Universale, 1911

665 Horsemen, 1911
Reiter, 1911
Cavaliers, 1911
Cavaliere, 1911

666 Resurrection of the Dead, 1911
Auferstehung, 1911
Résurrection, 1911
Resurrezione, 1911

667 All Saints, 1911
Allerheiligen, 1911
Toussaint, 1911
Ognissanti, 1911

668 Saint George, 1911
Heiliger Georg, 1911
Saint Georges, 1911
San Giorgio, 1911

669 Apocalyptic Horsemen, 1914,
Apokalyptische Reiter, 1914
Cavaliers de l'Apocalypse, 1914
Cavaliere dell'Apocalisse, 1914

670 Picture with Pince-nez, 1912
Bild mit Pincenez, 1912
Tableau avec pince-nez, 1912
Quadro con pince-nez, 1912

671 With the Hobby Horse, 1917
Mit dem Holzpferdchen, 1917
Avec le cheval de bois, 1917
Col cavallino di legno, 1917

5

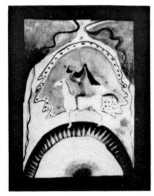

672–681 Ten Sketches for the cover of the Blaue Reiter almanac. 1911
Zehn Entwürfe für den Umschlag des Almanachs ›Der Blaue Reiter‹. 1911
Dix projets pour la couverture de l'Almanach ‹Der Blaue Reiter›. 1911
Dieci abbozzi per la copertina per l'Almanacco del ‹Cavaliere Azzurro›. 1911

674

675

676

677

405

678

679

680

681

682 Watercolor for a Composition, 1911
Aquarell zu einer ›Komposition‹, 1911
Aquarelle pour une ‹ Composition ›, 1911
Acquerello per una ‹ Composizione ›, 1911

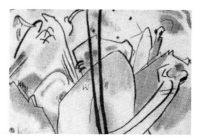

683 Watercolor for Composition IV, 1911
Aquarell zu ›Komposition IV‹, 1911
Aquarelle pour ‹ Composition IV ›, 1911
Acquerello per la ‹ Composizione IV ›, 1911

684 With the Red Spot, 1911
Mit rotem Fleck, 1911
Avec tache rouge, 1911
Con macchia rossa, 1911

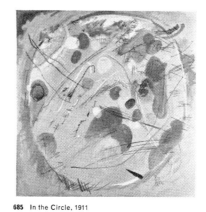

685 In the Circle, 1911
Im Kreis, 1911
Dans le cercle, 1911
Nel cerchio, 1911

686 Watercolor for Sketch, 1912
Aquarell zu ›Skizze‹, 1912
Aquarelle pour ‹ Esquisse ›, 1912
Acquerello per ‹ Schizzo ›, 1912

687 With Three Riders, 1912
Mit drei Reitern, 1912
Avec trois cavaliers, 1912
Con tre cavalieri, 1912

688 Announcement of the Blaue Reiter, 1912
Die Verkündigung des ›Blauen Reiter‹, 1912
L'annonce du ‹ Blaue Reiter ›, 1912
Annuncio ‹Cavaliere Azzurro›, 1912

689 To Mr. Alfred Meyer, 1912
Herrn Alfred Meyer zum Andenken, 1912
A M Alfred Meyer, en souvenir, 1912
Al Signor Alfred Meyer, in ricordo, 1912

690 Watercolor for KK 160b, 1912
Aquarell zu KK 160b, 1912
Aquarelle pour KC 160b, 1912
Acquerello per KC 160b, 1912

691 Untitled, 1913
Ohne Titel, 1913
Sans titre, 1913
Senza titolo, 1913

692 Watercolor, 1913
Aquarell, 1913
Aquarelle, 1913
Acquerello, 1913

693 Red and Blue, 1913
Rot und Blau, 1913
Rouge et bleu, 1913
Rosso e azzurro, 1913

694 Sketch for Improvisation 31 (Sea Battle), 1913
Skizze zu ›Improvisation 31‹ (Seeschlacht), 1913
Esquisse pour ‹ Improvisation 31 › (bataille navale)
Schizzo per ‹ Improvvisazione 31 › (Battaglia navale), 1913

695 Watercolor Study for Sketch for Painting with White Border, 1913
Aquarell zu ›Skizze des Bildes mit weißem Rand‹,
Aquarelle pour‹ Esquisse pour Tableau à bordure blanche ›, 1913
Acquerello per ‹ Schizzo per Quadro con bordo bianco ›, 1913

696 Untitled, 1913
Ohne Titel, 1913
Sans titre, 1913
Senza titolo, 1913

697 Untitled, 1913
Ohne Titel, 1913
Sans titre, 1913
Senza titolo, 1913

698 Improvisation, 1915
Improvvisazione, 1915

699 Untitled, 1915
Ohne Titel, 1915
Sans titre, 1915
Senza titolo, 1915

700 Untitled, 1916,5
Ohne Titel, 1916,5
Sans titre, 1916,5
Senza titolo, 1916,5

701 Untitled, 1916
Ohne Titel, 1916
Sans titre, 1916
Senza titolo, 1916

702 Untitled, 1916
Ohne Titel, 1916
Sans titre, 1916
Senza titolo, 1916

703 Simple, 1916,6
Einfach, 1916,6
Simple, 1916,6
Semplice, 1916,6

704 Untitled, 1917
Ohne Titel, 1917
Sans titre, 1917
Senza titolo, 1917

705 Untitled, 1917
Ohne Titel, 1917
Sans titre, 1917
Senza titolo, 1917

706 Untitled, 1918
Ohne Titel, 1918
Sans titre, 1918
Senza titolo, 1918

707 Untitled, 1919
Ohne Titel, 1919
Sans titre, 1919
Senza titolo, 1919

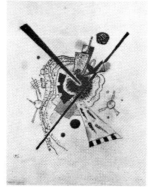

708 Watercolor Study for Green Border, 1920
Aquarell zu ›Grüner Rand‹, 1920
Aquarelle pour ‹ Bordure verte ›, 1920
Acquerello per ‹ Bordo verde ›, 1920

709 Watercolor, 1922
Aquarell, 1922
Aquarelle, 1922
Acquerello, 1922

710 Watercolor, 1922,28
Aquarell, 1922,28
Aquarelle, 1922,28
Acquerello, 1922,28

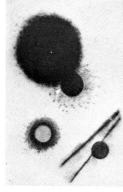

408

711 Watercolor, 1922,37
Aquarell, 1922,37
Aquarelle, 1922,37
Acquerello, 1922,37

712 Watercolor, 1923,79
Aquarell, 1923,79
Aquarelle, 1923,79
Acquerello, 1923,79

713 Sketch for Black Accompaniment, 1923,109
Entwurf zu ›Schwarze Begleitung‹, 1923,109
Projet pour ‹ Accompagnement noir ›, 1923,109
Abbozzo per ‹ Accompagnamento nero ›, 1923,109

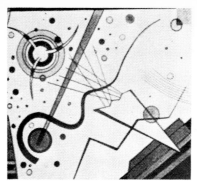

714 Sketch for Circles within a Circle, 1923,52
Entwurf zu ›Kreise im Kreis‹, 1923,52
Projet pour ‹Cercles dans cercle›, 1923,52
Abbozzo per ‹Cerchi nel cerchio›, 1932,52

715 Birthday gift for Gropius, 1924
Geburtstagsgeschenk für Gropius, 1924
Cadeau d'anniversaire pour Gropius, 1924
Regalo per il compleanno di Gropius, 1924

716 Watercolor, 1924
Aquarell, 1924
Aquarelle, 1924
Acquerello, 1924

717 In the Warm-Cool, 1924,141
Im Warm-Kühlen, 1924,141
Dans le chaud-frais, 1924, 141
Nel caldo-freddo, 1924, 141

718 Dissolutions, 1924,173
Auflösungen, 1924,173
Dissolutions, 1924,173
Decomposizione, 1924,173

719 Sketch for Yellow-Red-Blue, 1925
Entwurf zu ›Gelb-Rot-Blau‹, 1925
Projet pour ‹Jaune-rouge-bleu›, 1925
Abbozzo per ‹Giallo-rosso-azzurro›, 1925

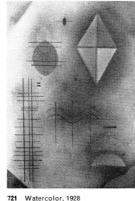

721 Watercolor, 1928
Aquarell, 1928
Aquarelle, 1928
Acquerello, 1928

722 Sketch for On Points, 1928
Entwurf zu ›Auf Spitzen‹, 1928
Projet pour ‹Sur pointes›, 1928
Abbozzo per ›Sulle punte›, 1928

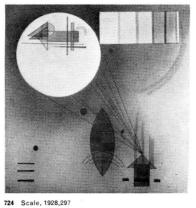

723 Dull Depth, 1928,291
Matte Tiefe, 1928,291
Profondeur mate, 1928,291
Debole profondità, 1928,291

724 Scale, 1928,297
Skala, 1928,297
Echelle, 1928,297
Scala, 1928,297

725 Watercolor, 1928
Aquarell, 1928
Aquarelle, 1928
Acquerello, 1928

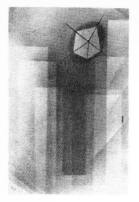

726 Into, 1928,299
     Hinein, 1928,299
     En dedans, 1928,299
     Dentro, 1928,299

727 Glowing, 1928,327
     Aufglühen, 1928,327
     Rougeoiement, 1928,327
     Infuocato, 1928,327

728 Around the Corner, 1929,355
     Um die Ecke, 1929,355
     Autour du coin, 1929,355
     Intorno all'angolo, 1929,355

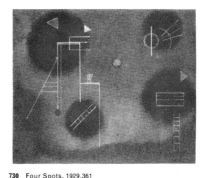

729 On Saturated Spots, 1929,356
     Auf satten Flecken, 1929,356
     Sur taches pleines, 1929,356
     Su macchie sature, 1929,356

730 Four Spots, 1929,361
     Vier Flecken, 1929,361
     Quatre taches, 1929,361
     Quattro macchie, 1929,361

731 Weak Support, 1930,380
     Schwache Stütze, 1930,380
     Faible appui, 1930,380
     Debole sostegno, 1930,380

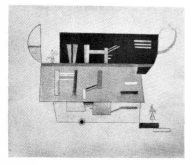

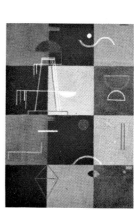

732 Horizontal, 1931,413
     Waagerecht, 1931,413
     Horizontal, 1931,413
     Orizzontale, 1931,413

733 Light Structure, 1931,427
     Leichter Bau, 1931,427
     Structure légère, 1931,427
     Construzione leggera, 1931,427

734 Gradation, 1931,428
     Stufung, 1931,428
     Par degrés, 1931,428
     Gradazione, 1931,428

410

735 Sketch for Development in Brown, 1933
     Entwurf zu ›Entwicklung in Braun‹ , 1933
     Projet pour ‹ Développement en brun ›, 1933
     Abbozzo per ‹ Sviluppo in bruno ›, 1933

736 Joined surfaces (Sketch for Two Green Points).
     1934,535
     Wiedervereinte Flächen (Entwurf zu ›Zwei grüne
     Punkte‹), 1934,535
     Surfaces réunies (Projet pour ‹ Deux points
     verts ›), 1934,535
     Superfici riunite (Abbozzo per ‹ Due punti verdi ›)
     1934,535

737 Above-Below, 1935,553
     Drunter und drüber, 1935,553
     Dessus-dessous, 1935,553
     Sopra-sotto, 1935,553

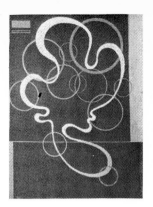

738 The White Line, 1936,571
Die weiße Linie, 1936,571
La ligne blanche, 1936,571
La linea bianca, 1936,571

739 Coincident, 1936,573
Übereinstimmend, 1936,573
Coïncidentes, 1936,573
Coincidenti, 1936,573

740 Line with Accompaniment, 1937,578
Linie mit Begleitung, 1937,578
La Ligne accompagnée, 1937,578
La linea accompagnata, 1937,578

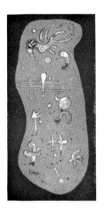

741 From One to the Other, 1937,584
Vom einen zum andern, 1937,584
De l'un à l'autre, 1937,584
Dall'uno all'altra, 1937,584

742 Fifteen, 1938.589
Fünfzehn, 1938,589
Quinze, 1938,589
Quindici, 1938,589

743 On the Green Line, 1938,592
Auf der grünen Linie, 1938,592
Sur la ligne verte, 1938,592
Sulla linea verde, 1938,592

744 Two, 1938,593
Zwei, 1938,593
Deux, 1938,593
Due, 1938,593

745 The Blue Arc. 1938.610
Der blaue Bogen, 1938,610
L'arc bleu, 1938,610
L'arco azzurro, 1938,610

746 In Height, 1939,623
In der Höhe, 1939,623
En hauteur, 1939,623
In altezza, 1939,623

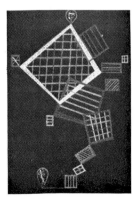
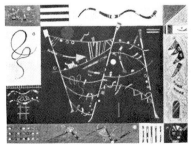
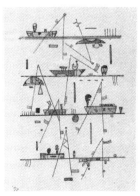

747 Rising Nets, 1939,632
Aufstieg der Gitter, 1939,632
Montée des grilles, 1939,632
Salita di grate, 1939,632

748 Sketch for L'Ensemble, 1940,634
Entwurf zu ›L'Ensemble‹, 1940,634
Projet pour ‹ L'Ensemble ›, 1940,634
Abbozzo per ‹ L'insieme ›, 1940,634

749 Watercolor, 1940,659
Aquarell, 1940,659
Aquarelle, 1940,659
Acquerello, 1940,659

411

750 Watercolor, 1940,663
Aquarell, 1940,663
Aquarelle, 1940,663
Acquarello, 1940,663

751 Sketch for Reduced Contrasts, 1940,721
Entwurf zu ›Reduzierter Kontrast‹, 1940,721
Projet pour ‹ Contraste réduit ›, 1940,721
Abbozzo per ‹ Contrasto ridotto ›, 1940,721

752 Last Watercolor, 1940,730
Letztes Aquarell, 1940,730
Dernière Aquarelle, 1940,730
Ultimo Acquerello, 1940,730

753 Drawing for Composizion VI, 1913,5
Zeichnung zu ›Komposition VI‹, 1913,5
Dessin pour ‹ Composition VI ›, 1913,5
Disegno per ‹ Composizione VI ›, 1913,5

754 Drawing for White, Soft and Hard, 1932,8
Zeichnung zu ›Weiß-Weich und Hart‹, 1932,8
Dessin pour ‹ Blanc-mou et dur ›, 1932,8
Disegno per ‹ Bianco-molle e duro ›, 1932,8

755 Drawing for Seven, 1943,1
Zeichnung zu ›Sieben‹, 1943,1
Dessin pour ‹ Sept ›, 1943,1
Disegno per ‹ Sette ›, 1943,1

756 Poster for Gallery Maeght, from Klänge (1913), 1951
Plakat für Galerie Maeght aus ›Klänge‹ (1913), 1951
Affiche pour Galerie Maeght, tirée de ‹ Sonorités › (1913), 1951
Cartellone per Galleria Maeght, da ‹ Suoni › (1913), 1951

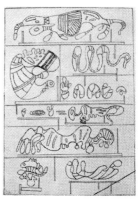

757 From Klänge (1913)
Aus ›Klänge‹ (1913)
De ‹ Sonorités › (1913)
Da ‹ Suoni › (1913)

758 From Small Worlds, 1922
Aus ›Kleine Welten‹, 1922
De ‹ Petits mondes ›, 1922
Da ‹ Piccoli Mondi ›, 1922

412

759 Sketch for Improvisation V, 1910
Skizze zu ›Improvisation V‹, 1910
Esquisse pour ‹ Improvisation V ›, 1910
Schizza per ‹ Improvisazione V ›, 1910

760 R. Delaunay: Night Cab (Oil on canvas), 1906
Nächtliche Droschke (Öl auf Leinwand), 1906
Fiacre nocturne (Huile sur toile), 1906
Carrozza di notte (Olio su tela), 1906

761 Title page of score of Glinka's opera Life for the Czar, 1906
Titelblatt der Partitur ›Leben für den Zaren‹ von M. I. Glinka, 1906
Page de titre de la partition de ‹La Vie pour le Tsar› de M. I. Glinka, 1906
Co partina per lo spartito di ‹La vita per lo Zar› di Glinka, 1906

Bibliography

Selection based on the comprehensive
Kandinsky Bibliography (unpublished)
by Bernard Karpel, Librarian
Museum of Modern Art, New York.

By Kandinsky

Classified references are arranged chronologically.

1. Major Works

Schwarz und Weiß. Grüner Klang. 1909.
2 stage-plays in Russian. Unpublished.
Violett. 1911.
Stage-play in German. Unpublished. A fragment in *Bauhaus* no. 3:6, 1927.

Über das Geistige in der Kunst

Über das Geistige in der Kunst. Insbesondere in der Malerei. 104 p. ill. München, Piper, 1912.
First edition. Printed December 1911; published January 1912.
8 plates, 10 original woodcuts; text and cuts composed 1910.
Second printing, enlarged, April 1912.
Third printing, Fall 1912. Same as »second edition«.
Russian reading. Read between Dec. 29–31, 1911, before the Congress of Russian Artists held in St. Petersburg. According to Dr. Lindsay, On the Spiritual in Art "was presented ... at the very time the German edition was going to press."

Extracts in *Der Sturm* no. 106: 11–13. April 1912 and in *Blast* I: 119–125, 1914.

The Art of Spiritual Harmony. 112 p. London, Constable; Boston, Houghton Mifflin, 1914. xxvi p, 112p, 9 plates, 3 diagrams.
Contents: Introduction. – About general aesthetic. – About painting. Translation by Michael T. Sadler.

The Art of Spiritual Harmony. [In Japanese.] Tokyo, Idea Shoin. 1924.
Translation from the German by Ohara Kuniyoshi.

Della Spiritualità nell'Arte. Particolamente nella Pittura. 110p. plus 12 plates. Roma, Edizioni di Religio, 1940. Translated by G. A. Colonna di Cesarò.

On the Spiritual in Art. 152p. New York, Museum of Non-Objective Painting 1946. Edited by Hilla Rebay. Includes a »Short Survey of Artistic Evolution ... 1904 to 1944«, p. 105, and »Public Comments«, p. 127–152.

Concerning the Spiritual in Art, and Painting in Particular, 1912. 93p. New York, Wittenborn, Schultz, 1947. No. 5 of the Documents of Modern Art. With notes of Motherwell, Nina Kandinsky, Julia and Lyonel Feininger and Stanley Hayter.

Du Spirituel dans l'Art, et dans la Peinture en Particulier. Paris, Drouin, 1949. Translated by M. Deman (Pierre Volboudt).

Du Spirituel dans l'Art. 109p. ill. Paris, de Beaune, 1951. Text by C. Estienne.

Über das Geistige in der Kunst. 4. Aufl. 144p. ill. Bern-Bümpliz, Benteli, 1952. Introd. Max Bill.

De lo Espiritual en el Arte, y la Pintura en Particular. Buenos Aires, Galatea & Nueva Visión, 1956. Translated from the French by Edgar Bayley.

Der Blaue Reiter. 131p. ill. München, Piper, 1912.
Edited by Kandinsky and Franz Marc. Edition of 300 copies. Second edition, 1914, added foreword by the artist and some additional material. Kandinsky's contributions include: Einband.– Eugen Kahler (p. 53–55). – Über Bühnenkomposition (p. 103–113).– Der gelbe Klang, Bühnenkomposition (p. 115–131). – Über die Formfrage (p. 74–100).

Klänge. 67p. ill. München, Piper, 1913.
»Gedichte in Prosa mit schwarz-weißen u. farb. Holzschnitten vom Stock gedruckt.«

Kandinsky Album: Rückblicke 1901-1913

Kandinsky, 1901–1913. 67p. ill. plus xxxxi p. text. Berlin, Der Sturm, 1913.

V. V. Kandinskii. Tekst Khudozhnika. 56p. 26 ill. Moskva, Izdanie Otdela Izobrazitelnikh Iskusstv Narodnago Kommissariata po Prosveshcheniiu, 1918.

Kandinsky. Edited by Hilla Rebay. 46p. ill. New York, Museum of Non-Objective Painting, 1945.

In Memory of Wassily Kandinsky. 117p. ill. New York, Museum of Non-Objective Painting, 1945. English translation of the second version of »Rückblicke« (Moscow, 1918).

Regard Sur le Passé. 36p. plus 15 plates. Paris, Drouin, 1946. Translation by Gabrielle Buffet-Picabia.

Regard Sur le Passé [Selection]. *Derrière le Miroir (Paris)* no. 42:2, 3, 5, 8 November-December 1951.

Rückblicke. 48p. 8 col. plates. Baden-Baden, Klein, 1955. Introd. Ludwig Grote.

Punkt und Linie zu Fläche

Punkt und Linie zu Fläche: Beitrag zur Analyse der malerischen Elemente. 198p. ill. München, Langen, 1926. Bauhausbücher 9; typography by Herbert Bayer. 102 fig. in text, 25 plates (1 colored). Second edition 1928.

Analyse des éléments premiers de la peinture. *Cahiers de Belgique* 4:126–132 May 1928. Translated by Hermann Closson.

Ekdhosi Pneumatikis Kalliergeis Kai Tekhins. (Athens, Edition of Fine Arts and Crafts, 1937). An outline of «Punkt und Linie zu Fläche».

Point and Line to Plane: Contribution to the Analysis of the Pictorial Elements. 196p. ill. (col. pl.) New York, Museum of Non-Objective Painting, 1947. Translated by Howard Dearstyne and Hilla Rebay.

Punkt und Linie zu Fläche: Beitrag zur Analyse der malerischen Elemente. 3. Aufl. 210p. ill. Bern-Bümpliz, Benteli, 1955. Introd. Max Bill.

Essays über Kunst und Künstler. 247p. ill. Stuttgart, Hatje, 1955. Herausgegeben und kommentiert von Max Bill. Writings from 1912–1943.

Bauhaus-Zeitschrift für Gestaltung. 1931. Edited by Kandinsky, Albers and Hilberseimer. This quarterly was edited from 1926–1931. Kandinsky illustrations passim.

2. Graphic Editions

Stikhi bez slov. [Poems without words.] Moscow, Stroganoff, 1904. The first album of woodcuts.
[Xylographies.] *Tendances Nouvelles* (Paris), no. 26, 27, 28, 29 1906–07.
Xylographies. Paris, Éditions Tendances Nouvelles, 1909. Introduction by Gérôme-Mäesse.

Der Sturm. Berlin, Verlag Der Sturm, 1910 ff. Illustrations passim

Der Blaue Reiter. München, Piper, 1912. Edition of 300 copies, also 10 copies in the de luxe museum edition containing the three-color print of 1908. Second edition, 1914.

Über das Geistige in der Kunst. München, Piper, 1912.

Klänge. München, Piper, 1913. With 55 black-and-white and color woodcuts.

Neue Europäische Graphik. Vierte Mappe: Italienische und Russische Künstler. Weimar, Staatliches Bauhaus, 1921. Including Kandinsky.

Kleine Welten. Zwölf Blatt Originalgraphik. Berlin, Propyläen 1922. Introduction by the artist. 4 etchings, 4 color lithographs, 2 color woodcuts, and 2 black-and-white woodcuts.

Meistermappe des Staatlichen Bauhauses 1923. Weimar, Staatliches Bauhaus, 1923. Including prints by Kandinsky.

Kandinsky, par Will Grohmann. Paris, Cahiers d'Art 1930. 500 copies ill. with engraving, 8 with gouache and engraving, and 8 with drawing and engraving.

Le Marteau sans Maître, par René Char. Paris, Éd. Surréalistes, 1934. Drypoint by Kandinsky.

Tzara, *Tristan*. La Main passe. Paris, G. L. M., 1935. With signed etching by Kandinsky.

Transition, no. 27. April–May 1938. Cover design by Kandinsky.

XXe Siècle. No. 5–6: 53 February-March 1939. Color woodcut.

10 Origin. Zürich, Allianz, 1942. Ten signed color-prints in folio, including one by Kandinsky.

Kandinsky (Album). Amsterdam, Duwäer, 1945.

Kandinsky: Oeuvre gravée. Paris, Berggruen, 1954.
Includes a reproductive facsimile, in miniature color plates, of »Kleine Welten«. Introduction by Will Grohmann.

3. Magazine References

Pismo iz München [Letter from Munich]. *Apollon (St. Petersburg)* II: 17–20, IV: 28–30, VI: 12–15, VIII: 4–7, XI: 13–17, 1909–1910. Five letters in the chronicle section, dated October 3, 1909; January 1910; April 1910; May–June 1910; October 1910. Reprinted *Zwiebelturm* 5: 24–44 Regensburg 1950.

Article in Bulletin of the All-Russian Congress of Artists. St. Petersburg, 1910.

[Answer to critics.] *Konst* no. 1–2 1912 (L.).

Über Kunstverstehen. *Der Sturm* 3 no. 129: 157–158 ill. October 1912. Dated March 1912. Reprinted in several catalogues.

Malerie als reine Kunst. *Der Sturm* no. 178–179: 98–99 September 1913. Reprinted in Walden's *Expressionismus* (1918). Several translations.

On stage composition.] *Iskustvo (St. Petersburg)* 1 : 39–49 1919.

Wassily Kandinsky: Selbstcharakteristik. *Das Kunstblatt* 3 no. 6: 172–174 1919.

Ein neuer Naturalismus. *Das Kunstblatt* 6 no. 9 : 384–387 September 1922. Response to a questionnaire.

Abstrakte Kunst. *Der Cicerone* 17 : 638–647 ill. 1925.

Tanzkurven: zu den Tänzen der Palucca. *Das Kunstblatt* 10: 117–120 March 1926.

Der Wert des theoretischen Unterrichts in der Malerei. *Bauhaus* 1 : 4 December 4, 1926.

Über die abstrakte Bühnensynthese. *Bauhaus* no. 3 : 6 1927.

»Und« Einiges über synthetische Kunst. *i 10 (Amsterdam)* 1 no. 1: 4–10 1927.

Analyse des éléments premiers de la peinture. *Cahiers de Belgique* 4 : 126–132 May 1928.

Kunstpädagogik. *Bauhaus* no. 2–3: 8–9 1928. Reprinted in »Die Maler am Bauhaus« 1950.

Unterricht Kandinsky, *Bauhaus* no. 2–3: 10–11 1928. English translation in »Bauhaus 1919–1928«.

Die kahle Wand. *Der Kunstnarr (Dessau)* 1: 20–22 April 19, 1929.

Der Blaue Reiter: Rückblick. *Das Kunstblatt* 14: 57–60 February 1930.

Bilder einer Ausstellung (Modeste Mussorgsky). *Das Kunstblatt* 14 no. 8: 246 August 1930.

Klee. *Bauhaus* no. 3: (not paged) December 1931.

Réflexions sur l'art abstrait. *Cahiers d'Art* 6 no. 7–8: 350–353 ill. 1931.

[Enquête.] *Cahiers d'Art* 10 no. 1–4: 53–54, 56 ill. 1935.

Toile vide, etc. *Cahiers d'Art* 10 no. 5–6: 117 ill. 1935.

Line and Fish. *Axis (London)* no. 2: 6 April 1935. Reprinted in Goldwater, p. 451.

Omaggio a Baumeister. *Il Milione (Milan)* no. 41: (5) May 25–June 11, 1935.

To retninger (det abstrakte rene malerei skåber). *Konkretion (Copenhagen)* September 15, 1935. Reprinted in *Essays* 1955.

Abstrakte Malerei. *Kronick von Hedendaagsche Kunst en Kultuur (Amsterdam)* 6: 167–172 April 1936.

Respuetas de Kandinsky [al cuestionario de Gaceta de Arte]. *Gaceta de Arte (Canarias)* no. 38: 85–87 June 1936.

Franz Marc. *Cahiers d'Art* 11 no. 8–10: 273–275 1936.

Tilegnelze af Kunst. *Linien (Copenhagen)* 1937. Reprinted in *Essays* 1955.

Salongespräch (June 1937). – Testimonium Pauperatia (1937). – Weiss-Horn. *Plastique (Paris)* no. 4: 14–16 1939. Reprinted in *Kandinsky Album. Amsterdam* 1945.

[Statement.] *Journal des Poètes* 10: 10 1938. Reprinted in *Art d'Aujourd'hui* 6: 5 January 1950.
L'art concret. *XXe Siècle* 1: 9–16 March 1938.

Blick und Blitz [etc.]. *Transition* no. 27: 104–109 April May 1938. Poems and texts.

Mes gravures sur bois. *XXe Siècle* no. 3: 19–31 ill. July-September 1938.

La valeur d'une oeuvre concrète. *XXe Siècle* 1 no. 1: 9–16 1938.

Préface. *London Bulletin* no. 14: 2 May 1939. French text written for Guggenheim Gallery catalogue.

Konkrete Kunst. *Abstrakt, Konkret (Zürich)* no. 8 1945. Bulletin der Galerie des Eaux-Vives.

Valore di un opera concreta. *Forma 2* 2 no. 1: 5–11 May 1950. Translation.

Un poème inédit de Kandinsky. *XXe Siècle* no. 3: 72 ill. June 1952.

Drei Briefe von Kandinsky [to Hans Hildebrandt.] *Werk* 42 no. 10: 327–331 ill. October 1955.

[Brief an Hermann Rupf.] *DU (Zürich)* 16 no. 3: 27–29, 57 March 1956. Letter on death of Klee.

4. Miscellaneous

[Arnold Schoenberg article on octaves and fifths.] Odessa. 1910–11. A translation by Kandinsky for the Odessa International Exhibition of Art: »Salon 2«.

[Kandinsky on synthetic art, a lecture.] Weimar, 1923.

[Bauhaus prospectus.] 44p. ill. Dessau, Bauhaus Verlag, 1929. Includes statement by Kandinsky.

Interview: Nierendorf-Kandinsky. 1937. Published in Essays 1955.

5. Books: Contributions and Extracts

Im Kampf um die Kunst. p. 73–75 Munich, Piper, 1911. »Die Antwort auf den ›Protest Deutscher Künstler‹« with an untitled statement by Kandinsky.

BERG, ALBAN [& OTHERS]. Arnold Schoenberg. With »Die Bilder« by Kandinsky, p. 59–64. Munich, Piper, 1912.

EDDY, ARTHUR J. Cubists and Post-Impressionists. p. 125–126, 130–135. Chicago, McClurg, 1914. »Letters to A. J. Eddy« by Kandinsky.

OM KONSTNÄREN. Stockholm, Förlag Gummeson Konsthandel, 1916.

BAUHAUS (Weimar). Staatliches Bauhaus in Weimar, 1919–1923. p. 26, 27, 28, 142–144, 186–187. 2 ill. (1 col. pl.). Bauhaus-Verlag, Weimar-München, 1923.
Includes »Die Grundelemente der Form«, »Farbkurs und Seminar«, »Über die abstrakte Bühnensynthese«.

EUROPA ALMANACH. p. 65 ill. Potsdam. Kiepenheuer, 1925. »Zwielicht« by Kandinsky.

WESTHEIM, PAUL. ed. Künstlerbekenntnisse. p. 164–165 Berlin, Propyläen Verlag [1925]. »Gestern-Heute-Morgen« by Kandinsky (Weimar, April 1923).

PLAUT, PAUL. Die Psychologie der produktiven Persönlichkeit. p. 306–308. Stuttgart, Enke, 1929. Answers, dated 1928, to three questions.

THOENE, PETER (pseud.). Modern German Art. Harmondsworth, England, Penguin, 1938. »Letter to Irmgard Burchard«, December 1, 1937.

10 ORIGIN. Zürich, Allianz, 1942. Folio of prints, with a Kandinsky statement, titled »Jede geistige Epoche«.

DOMELA, CESAR. Domela: Six Reproductions. 2p. plus plates, Paris, Galerie Jeanne Bucher, 1943.
»Préface de Vassily Kandinsky«, Paris, June 1943.

REBAY, HILLA, ed. Wassily Kandinsky Memorial. p. 93–99 New York, Museum of Non-Objective Painting, 1945.
Letters to Rebay, dated Paris, 1934–1938.

GIEDION-WELCKER, CAROLA. Poètes à l'Ecart; Anthologie der Abseitigen. p. 53–60, Bern-Bümpliz, Benteli, 1946. Biographical, bibliographical and poetic section.

SCHMIDT, GEORG, ed. Sophie Taeuber-Arp. p. 88 Basel, Holbein, 1948. »Les reliefs colorés de Sophie Taeuber-Arp«, dated Paris, June 1943.

SEUPHOR, MICHEL. L'Art Abstrait. p. 167–169, 180–184 Paris, Maeght, 1949. Poems, statements, fascimile mss.

PLATSCHEK, HANS, ed. Dichtung moderner Maler. p. 39–48 ill. Wiesbaden, Limes, 1956.

UHDE-BERNAYS, H., ed. Künstlerbriefe über Kunst. p. 934–938, 967 Munich, 1956.

Saarbrücken. Staatliches Museum. Erich Mendelsohn – Wass Kandinsky – Arno Breker. Saarbrücken, 1931.
Includes »From a Kandinsky letter«.

Möller, F. Galerie. Kandinsky Ausstellung. Berlin, 1932. With not

Luzern. Kunstmuseum. These, Antithese, Synthese. Lucern 1935. Statement, p. 15–16.

Bern Kunsthalle. Wassily Kandinsky. Bern, 1937. Statement b Kandinsky.

Liniens Sammenslutning. Efter-Expressionisme. Copenhage 1937. Includes »Zugang zur Kunst«.

Amsterdam. Stedelijk Museum. Tentoonstelling Abstracte Kuns April 1938. Includes »Abstrakt oder Konkret«, p. 8–10.

Guggenheim Jeune, Gallery. Abstract and concrete art. Londo 1939. Catalogue published in the London Bulletin, no. 14: 2– 21–22.

Milano. Palazzo Exreale. Arte astratta e concreta. 1947. »L'art concreta«, by Kandinsky.

München. Haus der Kunst. Der Blaue Reiter. September–Octobe 1949. Statements by Kandinsky.

Basel. Kunsthalle. Der Blaue Reiter, 1908–1914. Spring. 1950 Statements by Kandinsky.

München. Haus der Kunst. Die Maler am Bauhaus: Ausstel lung. München, Prestel, 1950. Introduction by Ludwig Grote Kandinsky's »Kunstpädagogik«, p. 27–28.

Valentin, Curt, Gallery. Der Blaue Reiter. New York, 1954. Include letter to Westheim in: Das Kunstblatt (1930).

6. Catalogues: Selected Texts

Neue Künstlervereinigung. Katalog – II. Ausstellung, Munich, 1910. September catalogue with article by Kandinsky, dated August 1910.

Salon 2. [Catalogue – International Exhibition of Art]. Odessa, 1910–11. »Content and form« by Kandinsky, p. 14–16, in Russian. Reprinted in Waldens »Expressionismus« 1918.

Thannhauser Galerie. Der Blaue Reiter I., Munich, 1911. Exhibited December 18–January 1; introduction by Kandinsky.

Der Sturm (Berlin). Kandinsky Kollektiv-Ausstellung, 1902–1912. Berlin 1912. Munich, Galerie Goltz, 1902–1912 (Fall 1912–January 1913). Two catalogues. Prefatory note by Kandinsky.

Arnold, Ernst, Galerie. Sonderausstellung Der Sturm. Dresden, 1919. »Über Kunstverstehen«, p. 4–6.

Billiet, Joseph, Galerie. Catalogue: Le Fauconnier. Paris, 1921. Statement by Kandinsky; reprinted in Fauconnier's 1927 monograph.

Internationale Kunstausstellung. Katalog. Düsseldorf, 1922. May 28–July 3. Preface by Kandinsky.

Gummesons Konsthandel. Kandinsky. Stockholm, 1922. September 1–October 15; statement.

Frankfurter Kunstverein. Kandinsky-Jubiläumsausstellung. Frankfurt-am-Main, 1928. Notes »Über die abstrakte Malerei«.

Möller, F. Galerie. Oktober-Ausstellung. Berlin, 1928. Statement.

II On Kandinsky

Classified references are arranged alphabetically

1. Monographs and Pamphlets

BERTRAM, H. Kandinsky. 30 ill. Copenhagen, Édition Wivels 1946.

BILL, MAX. Wassily Kandinsky: Zehn Farbenlichtdrucke nac Aquarellen und Gouachen. [10] p. plus 10 pl. in folio Basel Holbein, 1949.

BILL, MAX, ed. Wassily Kandinsky. 178 p. ill. Boston, Institute o Contemporary Art, in association with Maeght, Éditeur, Paris 1951. »Avec la participation de Jean Arp, Charles Estienne, Carol Giedion-Welcker, Will Grohmann, Ludwig Grote, Nina Kandinsky, Alberto Magnelli«. French texts with partial translations in German, English, Spanish.

BILLE, EJLER. Picasso, Surrealisme, Abstrakte Kunst. p. 113–12 ill. (port) Copenhagen, Helios, 1945.

BRISCH, KLAUS. Wassily Kandinsky. Bonn, University of Bonn 1955. Doctoral dissertation subtitled »Untersuchung zur Entstehung der gegenstandslosen Malerei«. Not printed, no available.

DEBRUNNER, HUGO, ed. Wir entdecken Kandinsky ... in Zusammenarbeit mit Laien, Künstlern, Psychologen. 64 p. Ill Zürich, Origo [1947].

EICHNER, JOHANNES. Wassily Kandinsky und Gabriele Münter. 221 p. plus 89 ill. (16 col.) München, Bruckmann, 1957.

ESTIENNE, CHARLES. Kandinsky. 15 p. plus 35 ill. Paris, de Beaune,
1950.

GROHMANN, WILL. Wassily Kandinsky. 33 ill. (1 col.) Leipzig,
Klinkhardt & Biermann, 1924. »Junge Kunst«, no. 42.

GROHMANN, WILL. Kandinsky. 36 p. plus 75 ill. (1 col.) Paris,
Cahiers d'Art, 1930.
»Les grands peintres d'aujourd'hui« series; »hommages de C.
Zervos, M. Raynal, E. Tériade, Th. Däubler, F. Halle, K. Dreier,
Clapp, Flouquet«. German edition issued privately by the Kan-
dinsky Society, Braunschweig.

GROHMANN, WILL. Kandinsky: Farben und Klänge – Erste Folge
(Aquarelle). [16] p. plus 15 col. ill. Baden-Baden, Klein, 1955.
– Zweite Folge (Gemälde). (16) p. plus 14 col. ill. 1956.

KANDINSKY, WASSILY. Kandinsky [Album: 11 Tableaux et 7
Poèmes]. Amsterdam, Duwaër. 1945. »Avant-propos« by the
artist. 1 color pochoir (1943).

LINDSAY, KENNETH C. E. An Examination of the Fundamental
Theories of Wassily Kandinsky. 244 p. 57 ill. (pt. col.) Madison,
Wis., University of Wisconsin, 1951.
Doctoral dissertation in typescript with mounted illustrations.
Contents: I. Bibliographical sketch of Kandinsky's writings. –
II. Content and form. – III. Reality and art. – IV. Colors and
forms. (»Chapter IV ... is essentially a critical rewriting of his
two books, Concerning the Spiritual in Art and Point and Line to
Plane«). – V. Space and time; movement. – Appendices: A. Trans-
lation of the program »Society of Painters, St. Petersburg, 10
December, 1912«. – B. List of exhibitions. – C. Announcement of
the Kandinsky school. – D. Graphic representation of Kandinsky's
works. – E. Color theories. – Bibliography.

SOLIER, RENÉ de. Kandinsky. Paris, Existences, 1946.

ZEHDER, HUGO. Wassily Kandinsky: Unter autorisierter Be-
nutzung der russischen Selbstbiographie. 53 p. 13 ill. (1 col.)
Dresden, Kaemmerer, 1920.

2 Selected Catalogues

Goltz, Hans, Galerie. Kandinsky, Kollektiv-Ausstellung, 1902-1912.
5 p. München.

Cabaret Voltaire. Recueil littéraire et artistique, édité par Hugo
Ball. 32 p. ill. Zürich, Meierei, 1916.

Diemen, Galerie van. Erste russische Kunstausstellung. p. 24, [56]
ill. Berlin, 1922. Preface by D. Sterenberg, Dr. Redslob, A. Holit-
scher.

Société anonyme. Kandinsky. 4 ill. New York. 1923. Text by K. S.
Dreier.

Oakland Art Gallery. The Blue Four: Feininger, Jawlensky, Kandinsky, Paul Klee ... May 2-May 31. [4] p. Oakland, Cal., 1926.
Nos. 1–13 by Kandinsky; foreword by W. H. Clapp. Addenda notes
three lectures delivered on »Art and the Blue Four« by Mme
G. E. Scheyer.

Arnold Galerie. Kandinsky: Katalog Jubiläums-Ausstellung zum
60. Geburtstag. 13 ill. Dresden, 1926. Held October 16–November
10. Contributions by Paul Klee, Will Grohmann, Fannina Halle
and Katherine Dreier.

Braxton Gallery. The Blue Four: Feininger, Jawlensky, Kandinsky,
Paul Klee. [18] p. ill. Hollywood, Cal., 1930.

France, Galerie de. Kandinsky, March 14–31. 6 ill. Paris, 1930. 32
paintings. »Hommages de E. Tériade, C. Zervos, F. Halle, M.
Raynal.«

Flechtheim, Alfred, Galerie. Kandinsky. 7 ill. Berlin, 1931. Held
February 1931; 70 works. Texts by A. I. Schardt; E. Tériade;
W. Grohmann.

Mexico. Biblioteca Nacional. Cuatro Azules–Feininger, Jawlensky,
Kandinsky, Paul Klee. [14] p. [Mexico, D. F.,] 1931. Exhibition of
the Oakland Gallery material. Homage by Diego Rivera. The full
text by Rivera on Kandinsky is translated in the catalogue issued
by the California Palace of the Legion of Honor (The Blue Four,
1931).

Chicago, Art Institute. Exhibition of the Arthur Jerome Eddy
Collection of modern paintings and sculpture. p. 14–19 3 ill. Chicago, 1931. Preface by D. C. Rich.

Milione, Galleria del. Kandinsky, April 24–May 9. ill. Milan, 1934.
45 watercolors, Statements by Grohmann, F. Morlion, G. Marlier,
C. Zervos, W. Baumeister, M. Seuphor, A. Sartoris, J. W. E. Buys.
D. Rivera, A. de Ridder.

New York. Museum of Non-Objective Painting. Homage to Kandinsky and other contemporary pioneers of non-objective painting. New York, S. R. Guggenheim Foundation. 1935–1939 five
editions. Second enlarged catalogue, 1937.–Third, 1938.–Fourth,
1939.–Fifth, 1939. Includes introduction by Hilla Rebay, biographical notes on the artists, numerous illustrations. Also issued as
»Loan Exhibition« catalogues, e. g. Third enlarged catalogue of the
Solomon R. Guggenheim Collection of Non-Objective Paintings,
March 7th until April 17, 1938.–Gibbes Memorial Art Gallery,
Charleston, S. C. 121 p. No. 103–150 by Kandinsky (all illustrated,
some in color).

Nierendorf, Karl, Gallery. Kandinsky. [8] p. New York, 1941. Preface
by Nina Kandinsky.

New York. Museum of Non-Objective Painting. Wassily Kandinsky,
1866–1944. [24] p. ill. New York, 1944. Includes letters to and notes
by Hilla Rebay.

Zurich. Kunsthaus. Georges Braque, Wassily Kandinsky, Pablo
Picasso. 22 p. ill. Zurich, 1946.
Kandinsky works, no. 27–134. »Quelques mots sur le développe-
ment de la peinture de Kandinsky«, p. 18–22, by Nina Kandinsky.

Amsterdam. Stedelijk Museum. Kandinsky. [8] p. plus 12 ill.
Amsterdam, 1947.
Lists 100 works »pour les expositions rétrospectives d'Amster-
dam, La Haye et Rotterdam, 1947–1948«. Also preface by Nina
Kandinsky.

Drouin, René, Galerie. Kandinsky: Gouaches, aquarelles, dessins,
14 p. 12 ill. Paris, 1947.
29 works; preface by Marcel Arland.

Drouin, René, Galerie. Kandinsky: Époque parisienne, 1934–1944.
[10] p. ill. Paris, 1949.
45 works. Texts by Charles Estienne: Actualité de Kandinsky, and
Henri-Pierre Roché: Souvenirs sur Kandinsky.

Venice. Biennale. Catalogo. Venezia, Alfieri, 1950. Special Kandinsky pavilion (30 works). Preface by Ch. Estienne. Also »Il Cavaliere azurro« (9 works); prefaces by E. Hanfstaengl and L.v.W.

Gimpel Fils. Kandinsky. [10] p. ill. London, 1950. Preface by D. Sutton.

Möller, Ferdinand, Galerie. Ausstellung Wassily Kandinsky: Arbeiten aus den Jahren 1912–1942. [12] p. ill. Cologne, 1953.

Gutekunst & Klipstein. Ausstellung: Von der »Brücke« zum »Bauhaus«. p. 14–15 ill. Berne, 1956.

Pasadena Art Museum. The Blue Four: Feininger, Jawlensky, Kandinsky, Paul Klee–Galka E. Scheyer Collection. [32] p. ill. Pasadena, Cal. [1956].

Addenda: Note that »Special Numbers« below frequently constitute the catalogue of a gallery exhibition, e. g. Galerie Maeght.

3. Special Numbers: Periodicals and Bulletins

Sélection. No. 14: Kandinsky. Antwerp, 1933.
Sélection, chronique de la vie artistique, July 1933; André de Ridder, directeur. Cahier XIV, 96 p., 67 ill. Contents: W. Grohmann. L'art de Kandinsky.–F. Morlion. Kandinsky, logicien.–G. Marlier. La revanche de Kandinsky.–Hommages de Ch. Zervos, W. Baumeister, M. Seuphor, A. Sartoris, J. W. E. Buys, Diego Rivera. A. de Ridder, E. L. Cary, G. E. Scheyer. Catalogue de l'œuvre gravé et dessiné de Kandinsky.–Plates, p. 33–96. The catalogue, compiled with the assistance of the artist, covers prints (1902–1932) and drawings (1910–1932).

Gaceta de Arte. no. 38. 1936.
Major portion devoted to Kandinsky (p. 51–76, 85–93). Includes Wassily Kandinsky by W. Grohmann, Notas biographicas, Respuetas de Kandinsky.

Art d'Aujourd'hui. No. 6: W. Kandinsky. Paris, 1950. Including »Situation de Kandinsky« (C. Estienne) etc.

Forma 2. No. 1: Omaggio à Kandinsky. Rome, 1950.
Published by Éditions »Age d'Or«, May 1950; 17 ill. (1 col.). Essays by Kandinsky: »Valore di un opera concreta«, »La pittura come arte pura«. Articles by M. Bill, E. Prampolini, K. Lindsay etc.

Derrière le Miroir. No. 42: Kandinsky, 1900–1910. Paris, 1951.
Bulletin of the Galerie Maeght, November–December 1951 issued for exhibition of same date. Lists 53 works, 16 ill. (4 col.). Text from Kandinsky's »Regard sur le Passé« (Drouin, 1946).

Derrière le Miroir. No. 60–61: Kandinsky. Paris, 1953.
October–November bulletin for exhibition of same date. Lists 45 works, 5 col. ill. Text by W. Grohmann.

Derrière le Miroir. No. 77–78: Kandinsky, période dramatique, 1910–1920. Paris, 1955. Essays by M. Brion and C. Giedion-Welcker.

4. Articles

ALVARD, JULIEN. Kandinsky. Cimaise no. 2:7 ill. Dec. 1953.

ARLAND, MARCEL. Rouault et Kandinsky. Hommes et Mondes no. 8: 582–586 May, 1947.

ASHMORE, JEROME. The old and the new in non-objective painting. Journal of Aesthetics and Art Criticism 9: 294–300 1951.

BEHNE, ADOLF. Wassily Kandinsky, 5–12–1886 – 5–12–1926. i 1 (Amsterdam) 1 no. 1: 11 ill. 1927.

BERENSON, RUTH. Kandinsky: first non-objectivist. Art News no.: 21, ill. April 1–14, 1945.

BILL, MAX. Die mathematische Denkweise in der Kunst unsere Zeit. Werk no. 3: 86–91 1949.

BRETON, ANDRÉ. Genèse et perspective artistique du surréalisme. Labyrinthe no. 5: 10–11; no. 6:4–5 ill. 1945.

BRETON, ANDRÉ & ELUARD, PAUL. Enquête. Minotaure no 4. 101–116 December 1933. Reply by Kandinsky, p. 110.

BRION, MARCEL. Le tournant spirituel. I 4 Soli 2 no. 6: 4–11 ill. 1955.

CHANIN, ABRAHAM. Storied pictures . . . New York Times X: 29 January 30, 1955. [On the Museum of Modern Art panels by Kandinsky].

COURTHION, PIERRE. Kandinsky et la peinture abstraite. Le Centaure (Brussels) 4 no. 9–10: 195–198 ill. 1930.

DAHLMANN-OLSEN, R. Kandinsky. Konstrevy (Stockholm) 28 no. 6: 268–271 ill. 1952.

D ÄUBLER, THEODOR. Kandinsky. Das Junge Deutschland (Berlin) 11–12: 340–341 1918.

DEGAND, LÉON. L'Abstraction dite géométrique. Quadrum (Brussels) no. 1: 27–28 ill. May 1956.

DEBRUNNER, HUGO. Der russische Maler-Pionier Kandinsky. Das Buch (Küssnacht-Zürich) 1 no. 1: 29–31 ill. December 1946.

DEKAY, CHARLES. Munich as an art center. The Cosmopolitan 13 no. 6: 643–653 October 1892.

DELAHAUT, JO. Kandinsky. Aujourd'hui no. 14: 14–17 ill. September 1957.

DORFLES, GILLO. Importanza storica dell' espressionismo tedesco. Arti Belle no. 2: 4–5 ill. 1947.

EINSTEIN, CARL. Kandinsky zum 60. Geburtstag. Kunstblatt 10 no. 10: 372–373 ill. 1926.

ESTIENNE, CHARLES. Deux éclairages: Kandinsky & Miró. XXe Siècle (n. s.) no. 1: 21–38 ill. 1951.

ESTIENNE, CHARLES. Kandinsky ou la liberté de l'esprit. Les Arts Plastiques 5 no. 4: 267–270 1952.

EVANS, E. P. Artists and art life in Munich The Cosmopolitan 9: 3–14 May 1890.

EVANS, E. P. Kandinsky's vision. Axis (London) no. 2: 7 April 1935.

FEININGER, JULIA & LYONEL. Wassily Kandinsky. Magazine of Art 38: 174–175 ill. May 1945.

FLEMMING, HANNS TH. Kandinsky's Entwicklungsstufen. Die Kunst und das Schöne Heim 54 no. 4: 128–131 ill. January 1956.

FRANCASTEL, PIERRE. L'expérience figurative et le temps. XXe Siècle no. 5: 41–48 ill. June 1955.

FRANCIS, H. S. A retrospective exhibition of Wassily Kandinsky. Bulletin of the Cleveland Museum of Art 39: 228 November 1952.

Für Kandinsky. Der Sturm 3 no. 150–151; 277–279 March 1913. Major section is a letter by W. Hausenstein and other protests o the Hamburger Fremdenblatt critique of February 15, 1913. Supplemented in no. 152–3: 288; no. 154–5: 3, 5–6.

ÜRST, HERBERT. Contrasts at Guggenheim Jeune's galleries: , Wassily Kandinsky. *Apollo* 27. no. 160:223 April 1938.

GEORGE, WALDEMAR. Les illuminations de Wassily Kandinsky. *Art et Industrie* (Paris) 28 no. 26: 21–24 ill. 1953.

GÉRÔME-MAËSSE. L'audition colorée. *Les Tendances Nouvelles* 27: 655–663 1907.

GÉRÔME-MAËSSE. Kandinsky: la gravure sur bois. *Les Tendances Nouvelles* 25: 436–438 1906.

GIEDION-WELCKER, CAROLA. Kandinskys Malerei als Ausdruck eines geistigen Universalismus. *Werk* 37 no. 4: 117–123 ill. April 1950.

GINDERTAEL, R. V. Kandinsky-Galerie Maeght. *Cimaise* (Paris) 2 no. 8: 10 ill. July 1955.

GINDERTAEL, R. V. Kandinsky jusqu'à l'abstraction. *Art d'Aujourd'hui* (Boulogne) 3 no. 1: 29–30 ill. December 1951.

GINDERTAEL, R. V. Quelques documents pour aider à mieux comprendre »Le passage de la ligne«. *Art d'Aujourd'hui* (Boulogne) 3 no. 5: 18–19 ill. June 1952.

GÖPEL, E. Brücke-Bauhaus-Blauer Reiter. *Die Weltkunst* 26 no.3: 7–8 ill. 1956.

GORDON, DONALD A. Experimental psychology and modern painting. *Journal of Aesthetics and Art Criticism* 9: 227–243 March 1951.

Great Armory Show of 1913: Kandinsky painting number one. *Life* (N. Y.) 28: 61 ill. (col.) January 2 1950.

GROHMANN, WILL. Wassily Kandinsky. *Cicerone* 16 no. 19: 887–898 ill. September 1924.
Also published in Jahrbuch der Jungen Kunst, 1924 (p. 256–265) and subsequently in the Junge Kunst series.

GROHMANN, WILL. Zehn Jahre Novembergruppe. *Kunst der Zeit* 3 no. 1–3: 1–9 ill. 1928.

GROHMANN, WILL. Wassily Kandinsky. *Cahiers d'Art* 4 no. 7: 322–329 ill. 1929. Biographical note and 16 illustrations.

GROHMANN, WILL. L'art non-figuratif en Allemagne. *Amour de l'Art* 15: 433–434, 438 April 1934.

GROHMANN, WILL. Wassily Kandinsky. *Gaceta de Arte* (Tenerife) no. 38: 51–76 ill. June 1936.

GROHMANN, WILL. L'art contemporain en Allemagne. *Cahiers d'Art* 13 no. 1–2: 7–8 1938.

GROHMANN, WILL. La grande retrospectiva de Kandinsky alla XXV Biennale. *La Biennale* (Venice). no. 3: 11 ill. January 1951.

GROHMANN, WILL. Le Cavalier Bleu. *L'Oeil* (Paris) no. 9: 4–13 ill. September 1955.

GROHMANN, WILL. Zu den Anfängen Wassily Kandinskys. *Quadrum* (Brussels) no. 1: 62–68 ill. May 1956.

GROHMANN, WILL. Bauhaus. *L'Oeil* (Paris) no. 28: 12–21 ill. Avril 1957.

GROTE, LUDWIG. Bühnenkompositionen von Kandinsky. *i 10* (Amsterdam) 2 no. 13: 4–5 July 1928.

GROTE, LUDWIG. Der Blaue Reiter. *Die Kunst* 48 no. 1: 4–11 ill. 1950.

HALLE, FANNINA. W. Kandinsky, Archipenko, Chagall. *Die Bildenden Künste* (Vienna) 4: 177–187 ill. 1921.

HALLE, FANNINA. Dessau: Burgkühnauer Allee 6-7 (Kandinsky und Klee). *Das Kunstblatt* 13: 203–210 ill. 1929.

HARTMANN, GEORG. Kandinskys Mussorgsky. *Querschnitt* 8: 666–667.

HAYTER, STANLEY W. The language of Kandinsky. *Magazine of Art* 38: 176–179 ill. May 1945.

HILBERSEIMER, LUDWIG. [Kandinsky review]. *Sozialistische Monatshefte* (Berlin) 59: 699 1922.

HOFMANN, WERNER. Studien zur Kunsttheorie des 20. Jahrhunderts. *Zeitschrift für Kunstgeschichte* (Vienna) p. 136–150 January 1956.

HOLTZMANN, HARRY. Liberating Kandinsky. *Art News* (New York) 51: 22–25 ill. May 1952.

JAFFÉ, MICHAEL. Een Schilderij uit Kandinsky's beginperiode. *Bulletin Museum Boymans* 7 no. 1: 2–5 26 ill. 1956.

JAMATI, PAUL. Kandinsky. *L'Arche* no. 15: 115–120 1946.

JEWELL, EDWARD A. Mondrian, Kandinsky memorials. *New York Times* March 25, 1945.

KALLAI, ERNST. Malerei und Photographie. *i 10* (Amsterdam) 1 no. 4: 148–157, no. 6: 227–236 ill. 1927.
Discussion by nine participants includes Kandinsky (no. 6).

KALLAI, ERNST. Vision und Formgesetz. *Blätter der Galerie Ferdinand Möller* no. 8: 1–10 September 1930.

Kandinsky. *Institute of Contemporary Art Bulletin* (Boston) 1 no. 3: 1–2 ill. April 1952. Includes catalogue of exhibition, nos. 1–52.

KANDINSKY, NINA [et al.]. Ciurlionis e Kandinsky. *La Biennale* (Venice) no. 12: 30–31 February 1953.
»Discussione sui rapport, d'inspirazione e di tecnica tra i due artista«. Texts by N. Kandinsky, W. Grohmann, Aleksis Rannit.

KANDINSKY, NINA. Kandinsky, mio marito. *La Biennale* (Venice) no. 3: 8–10 ill. January 1951.

KANDINSKY, NINA. [Some notes on the development of Kandinsky's painting]. 1946.
Originally published in Kunsthaus (Zurich) catalogue 1946.

Khronica. *Mir Iskusstva* 1: 11–13 ill. 1904.
Text in chronicle section; later reproduces Kandinsky's »An old town«, 2: 142.

KNOX, SANICA. 4 bargains in art make $ 150,000 set. *New York Times* May 23, 1956. On the Campbell panels, 2 in the Museum of Modern Art, 2 in the Guggenheim Museum (N. Y.).

KUHN, HERBERT. Kandinsky: 1. Für. *Das Kunstblatt* 3 no. 6: 178 1919. Followed by Wolfradt.

Künstlerclub »Phalanx«. *Die Kunst für Alle* 16: 488 1901.

LANKHEIT, KLAUS. Zur Geschichte des Blauen Reiters. *Der Cicerone* 3: 110–14 1949.

LARDERA, BERTO. Biennale 1950: notes sur la synthèse des arts plastiques. *Les Arts Plastiques.* 4: 185–198 ill. 1950.

LEONHARD, RUDOLF. Kandinsky. *Der Sturm* 3 no. 134–135: 204–205 November 1912.

LIBERMAN, ALEXANDER. Kandinsky. *Vogue* (New York) 126: 134–137, 172 ill. November 1, 1955.
Visit to his studio; summary of his views.

LINDSAY, KENNETH C. Om »Op og ned« paa et Abstrakt Billede. *Kunst* 1945 pp. 202–204 Copenhagen.

LINDSAY, KENNETH C. Kandinsky's method and contemporary criticism. *Magazine of art* 45: 355–361 ill. December 1952.

LINDSAY, KENNETH C. Mr. Pepper's defense of non-objective art. *Journal of Aesthetics and Art Criticism* 12 no. 2: 243–247 December 1953.

LINDSAY, KENNETH C. Genesis and meaning of the cover design for the first Blaue Reiter exhibition catalog. *Art Bulletin* 35: 47–52 ill. March 1953.

LINDSAY, KENNETH C. Kandinsky in 1914 New York. *Art News* 55: 32–33, ill. May 1956. On the Campbell panels.

Lithographies de Kandinsky. *Verve* no. 2: 93–96 Spring 1938.

LOUCHEIM, ALINE B. Time adds lustre to Kandinsky. *New York Times* April 13 1952.

LUNDHOLM, HELGE. Kandinsky. *Flammen* (Suede) no. 2 ill. 1917. »Analyse des théories de ce peintre«.

MARC, FRANZ. Kandinsky. *Der Sturm* 4 no. 186–187: 130 November 1913.

MARCHIORI, GIUSEPPE. Mondo di Kandinsky. *Ulisse* (Rome) 4 no. 12: June 1945.

McGREEVY, THOMAS. London show in short: Wassily Kandinsky. *London Studio* 15 no. 86: 278 May 1938.

MICHEL, WILHELM. Münchner Graphik: Holzschnitt und Lithographie. *Deutsche Kunst und Dekoration* 16: 437–457 1905.

MYERS, BERNARD. From abstract expressionism to new objectivity. *American Artist* 16: 26–28 April 1952.

Pionnier de l'art abstrait. *Arts* (Paris) no. 438: 6 ill. November 19, 1953. Includes »Neuf opinions sur Wassily Kandinsky«.

PLATSCHEK, HANS. Zweimal Kandinsky. *Baukunst und Werkform* 9 no. 10: 523–524 ill. 1956.

REBAY, HILLA. Pioneer in non-objective painting. *Carnegie Magazine* 20: 8–12 ill. May 1946.

READ, HERBERT. An art of internal necessity. *Quadrum* (Brussels) no. 1: 7–22 ill. May, 1956.

REED, JUDITH K. [Review of »Point and Line to Plane«]. *Art Digest* 22: 30 December 1, 1947.

RILEY, MAUDE. In memoriam: [Kandinsky.] *Art Digest* 19: 12 ill. January 1, 1945.

ROH, FRANZ. Zur gegenstandslosen Kunst. *Prisma* 1 no. 10: 26–28 ill. 1947.

ROUSSEAU, MADELEINE. De Cézanne et Seurat à l'art présent. *Musée Vivant* no. 34: 1, 13–18 ill. 1948.

SAN LAZZARO, GUALTIERI di. Kandinsky. *XXe Siècle* no. 3: 73–74 ill. June 1952.

SAN LAZZARO, GUALTIERI di. Lettera da Parigi. *Spazio* 6: 99–100 ill. 1951–1952.

SARTORIS, A. Circuito assolutista. *L'Arte* 51: 56–69 1950–51.

SCHNEIDER, THEO. Die Kunstlehre Kandinskys. *Kunstblatt* 11 no. 5: 198–200 1927.

SELZ, PETER. The aesthetic theories of Wassily Kandinsky. *The Art Bulletin* 39 no. 2: 127–136 ill. June 1957.

STEENHOF, W. De Expressionisten: Kandinsky. *De Amsterdammer* p. 6 ill. December 22, 1912.

STORA, R. SEIFFERT, P. Trois peintres en face de la vie. *Revue Esthétique* 2: 21–33 ill. 1949. »Turner, Kandinsky et Breughel«.

DER STURM. Wochenschrift für Kultur und die Künste. Berlin, H. Walden, 1910–1919.

SUTTON, DENYS. L'expressionisme à la XXXVe Biennale de Venise. *Les Arts Plastiques* 4: 171–178 ill. 1950.

TAILLANDIER, YVON. Kandinsky. *Amour de l'Art* 26 no. 5: 137 ill. 1946.

TIETZE, HANS. [Review of »Klänge«]. *Die Graphischen Künste* 37: 15–16 1913.

TÉRIADE, E. Kandinsky. *Le Centaure* (Brussels) 3 no. 8: 220–222 ill. May, 1929.

THWAITES, JOHN A. The Bauhaus painters in Munich. *Burlington Magazine* 92: 237 August 1950.

THWAITES, JOHN A. The Blaue Reiter, a milestone in Europe. *Art Quarterly* 13 no. 1: 12–20 Winter 1950.

LES TENDANCES NOUVELLES. (Paris) 1905–1909.

UMANSKIJ, KONSTANTIN. Russland IV: Kandinskij's Rolle im russischen Kunstleben. *Der Ararat* II. Sonderheft: 28–30 May-June 1920.

V., C. Kandinsky. *Elsevier's Geillustreerd Maandschrift* p. 197–199 ill. February 1913.

VALENTINER, WILHELM R. Expressionism and abstract painting. *Art Quarterly* 4 no. 3: 210–239 ill. 1941.

VAUXCELLES, LOUIS. Au Salon des Indépendants [review]. *Gil Blas* March 19 (p. 201), March 21 (p. 261) 1912.

VERONESI, G. Kandinsky verso l'astrazione: dal 1900 al 1910. *Emporium* 115: 84–88 ill. February 1952.

VERWEY, ALBERT. Der Maler: An Kandinsky. *Der Sturm* 3 no. 148–149: 269 February 1913. A poem, also published in *Rückblicke* 1913.

VOLBEHR, TH. Von Herder zu Kandinsky. *Die Kunst für Alle* 31: 297–298 July 10, 1926.

VOLBOUDT, PIERRE. L'humour formel de Kandinsky. *XXe Siècle* (n. s.) no. 8: 27–32 ill. January 1957. Additional plates (2) following p. 32.

VOLBOUDT, PIERRE. Wassily Kandinsky. *Cahiers d'art* 31–32: 177–215 ill. 1958.

VORDEMBERGE – GILDEWART, F. Bij het overlijden Kandinsky, *De Vrije Kunstenaar* (Amsterdam) 4 no. 4: 6–7 August 11, 1945.

WADSWORTH, EDWARD. »Inner necessity«: review of Kandinsky's book. *Blast* no. 1: 119–125 June 20, 1914.

WOLFRADT, WILLI. Kandinsky: II. Wider (Die Kunst und das Absolute). *Das Kunstblatt* 3 no. 6: 180–183 1919.

ZAHN, LEOPOLD. Bücher: Picasso und Kandinsky. *Der Ararat* 2: 171–173 1921. Comparative review of Raynal on »Picasso« and Zehder on »Kandinsky«.

ZERVOS, CHRISTIAN. Notes sur Kandinsky. *Cahiers d'Art* 9 no. 5–8: 149–157 ill. 1934.

ZERVOS, CHRISTIAN. Wassily Kandinsky, 1866–1944. *Cahiers d'Art* 20–21: 114–127 ill. 1945–46.

5. General References

ALPATOV, MIKHAIL. Russian Impact on Art. New York, Philosophical Library, 1950. Glossary includes references to absolute art, Blaue Reiter, etc.

APOLLONIO, UMBRO. »Die Brücke« e la Cultura dell'Espressionismo. p. 10, 21, 23, 27–28, 31–32, 37, 56 Venice, Alfieri, 1952.

ARLAND, MARCEL. Kandinsky. Paris, Drouin, 1947.

ARLAND, MARCEL. Chronique de la Peinture moderne. p. 109–116 Paris, Corréa, 1949.

ARNHEIM, RUDOLF. Art and Visual Perception. p. 108, 276, 279–281, 330, 336, 345 Berkeley & Los Angeles, Univ. of California Press, 1954.

ARP, HANS (JEAN). Onze Peintres Vus par Arp. p. 12–15 ill. Zürich, Girsberger, 1949.

DAS ATLANTISBUCH DER KUNST, p. 48, 131, 450, 829 Atlantis Verlag, 1952.

BAHR, HERMANN. Expressionismus. p. 54, 162, München, Delphin, 1916.

BARR, ALFRED H. Jr. Cubism and Abstract Art. p. 11–19, 64–70, 120–128, 153–160, 212 New York, Museum of Modern Art, 1936.

BARR, ALFRED H. Jr. ed. Fantastic Art, Dada, Surrealism. Essays by Georges Hugnet. ill. New York, Museum of Modern Art & Simon and Schuster, 1947.

BARR, ALFRED H. Jr. Masters of Modern Art. p. 120–121 ill. New York, Museum of Modern Art & Simon and Schuster, 1954.

BAZIN, GERMAIN, ed. History of Modern Painting, New York, Paris, London: Hyperion, 1951.

BAUHAUS. Staatliches Bauhaus, Weimar, 1919–1923, 226 p. ill. Weimar – München, Bauhaus-Verlag, 1923.

BAUMEISTER, WILLI. Das Unbekannte in der Kunst. Stuttgart, Schwab, 1947.

BAYER, HERBERT. Bauhaus 1919–1928, by Herbert Bayer, Walter Gropius, Ise Gropius. Boston, Branford, 1952.
Original edition: New York, Museum of Modern Art, 1938.

BAZAINE, JEAN. Notes sur la Peinture d'Aujourd'hui. Ed. du Seuil, 1953.

BEHNE, ADOLF. Zur neuen Kunst. 2. Aufl. 32 p. Berlin, Der Sturm, 1917. Sturm-Bücher VII.

BERKMAN, AARON. Art and Space. New York, Social Science Publishers, 1949.

BILL, MAX. Von der abstrakten zur konkreten Malerei im XX. Jahrhundert. *Pro Arte et Libris* (Geneva) July–August 1943.

BLANC, PETER. The artist and the atom. *Magazine of Art* 44: 145–152 ill. 1951.

BLANSHARD, FRANCES E. Retreat from likeness in the theory of Painting. Columbia University Press, 1949.

BLAVATSKY, H. B. The Key to Theosophy. London, Theosophical Society, 1898.

BÜNEMANN, HERMANN. Franz Marc. 2. Aufl. 111 p. Ill. München, Bruckmann, 1952.

BURGER, FRITZ. Cézanne und Hodler. 2 vol. München, Delphin, 1919.

BURGER, FRITZ. Einführung in die moderne Kunst. Berlin, Athenaion, 1917.

CHANIN, ABRAHAM L. The Metropolitan Museum of Art miniatures: Paintings from the Museum of Modern Art, series I. New York, Book of the Month Club, 1956.

CIRCLE – International Survey of Constructive Art. Edited by Martin, Gabo, Nickolson. ill. London, Faber & Faber, 1937.

DÄUBLER, THEODOR. Der Neue Standpunkt. p. 111,183 Dresden-Hellerau, Hellerauer Verlag, 1916.

DEGAND, LÉON. Langage et Signification de la Peinture en Figuration et en Abstraction. Boulogne (Seine), 1956.

DICKERMANN, PAUL. Die Entwicklung der Harmonik bei A. Skrjabin. [Dissertation]. Bern & Leipzig, 1935.

DOCUMENTS (Periodical). German Contemporary art. Offenburg in Baden, 1952. Articles by Roh, Grohmann, Grote, Haftmann and others.

DREIER, KATHERINE S. Modern Art. New York, Société Anonyme, 1926. Dedicated to Kandinsky.

DREIER, KATHERINE S. Western Art and the New Era. ill. New York, Brentano's, 1923.

DÜSSELDORF. SONDERBUND WESTDEUTSCHER KUNSTFREUNDE UND KÜNSTLER. ill. Düsseldorf, 1910.

EDDY, ARTHUR J. Cubists and Post-impressionism. rev. p. 110–139 et passim ill. (col. pl.) Chicago, McClurg, 1919. First edition 1914.

EINSTEIN, CARL. Die Kunst des 20. Jahrhunderts. Berlin, Propyläen, 1926, 1928, 1931.

FISCHER, OTTO. Das Neue Bild: Veröffentlichung der Neuen Künstlervereinigung. p. 21–23, München, Delphin, 1912.

[GALLATIN, ALBERT G.] A. E. Gallatin Collection. »Museum of Living Art«. p. 38, Philadelphia Museum of Art, 1954.

GIEDION-WELCKER, CAROLA. Poètes à l'Écart; Anthologie der Abseitigen. p. 53–60 ill. Bern-Bümpliz, Benteli, 1946.

GOLDWATER, ROBERT & TREVES, MARCO. Artists on Art. p. 449–451 New York, Pantheon, 1945.

GROHMANN, WILL. Wassily Kandinsky. *In*: René Huyghe. Histoire de l'Art contemporain: la Peinture. p. 438–439. Paris, Alcan, 1935.

GROHMANN, WILL. Bildende Kunst und Architektur. p. 132–143 et passim Berlin, Suhrkamp, 1953. »Zwischen den beiden Kriegen, dritter Band«.

GROHMANN, WILL. Paul Klee. New York, Abrams; Stuttgart, Kohlhammer 1954.

GROHMANN, WILL. Die Sammlung Ida Bienert. ill. Potsdam, Müller & Kiepenheuer, 1933.

GROTE, LUDWIG. Deutsche Kunst im Zwanzigsten Jahrhundert. 135 p. ill. München, Prestel, 1953.

GUGGENHEIM, PEGGY, ed. Art of This Century . . . 1910 ill. New York, Art of This Century, 1942.

GUTEKUNST & KLIPSTEIN, KUNSTHANDLUNG. Moderne Graphik: Die Sammlung Heinrich Stinnes. Bern, 1938.

HAFTMANN, WERNER. Malerei im 20. Jahrhundert. 2 vol. München, Prestel, 1954–1955.

HAFTMANN, WERNER. The Mind and Work of Paul Klee. New York, Praeger, 1954. München, Prestel, 1950.

HÄNDLER, GERHARD. Deutsche Maler der Gegenwart. 202 p. ill. Berlin, Rembrandt, 1956.

H[AUSENSTEIN], W[ILHELM]. Ausstellungen . . . Galerie Thannhauser, München: Arbeiten Kandinskys. Kunstchronik (n. f.) 25 no. 19: 293–295 January 30 1914.

HAUSENSTEIN, WILHELM. Die Bildende Kunst der Gegenwart, Stuttgart & Berlin, Deutscher Verlag, 1920.

HEATH, ADRIAN. Abstract Painting, its Origin and Meaning. p. 20–24 ill. London, Tiranti, 1953.

HENNIGER, GERD. Die Auflösung des Gegenständlichen und der Funktionswandel der malerischen Elemente im Werke Kandinskys 1908–1914. *In* Edwin Redslob zum 70. Geburtstag: eine Festgabe. p. 347–356 ill. Berlin, Blaschker, 1955.

HESS, WALTER. Das Problem der Farben in den Selbstzeugnissen moderner Maler. München, Prestel, 1953.

HESS, WALTER. Dokumente zum Verständnis der modernen Malerei. Hamburg, Rowohlt, 1956.

HILDEBRANDT, HANS. Die Kunst des 19. und 20. Jahrhunderts. Potsdam, Athenaion, 1924.

HITCHCOCK, HENRY – RUSSEL. Painting Towards Architecture: The Miller Company Collection of Abstract Art. New York, Duell, Sloan & Pearce, 1948.

HOFMANN, WERNER. Ein Beitrag zur »morphologischen Kunsttheorie« der Gegenwart. *Alte und Neue Kunst* (Vienna) 2 no. 2: 63–80 1953.

JAKOWSKI, ANATOLE. Essai sur 16 Peintures. Paris, Éditions Abstraction – Création, 1934.

JANIS, SIDNEY. Abstract & Surrealist Art in America. New York, Reynal & Hitchcock, 1944.

KANSAS. UNIVERSITY. MUSEUM OF ART. Albert Bloch [Exhibition]. 22 p. ill. Lawrence, Kansas, 1955.

KARPFEN, FRITZ. Gegenwartskunst, I: Russland. p. 25, 31–33 ill. Wien, Literaria.

KLEE, PAUL. Das bildnerische Denken. Hrsg. von Jürg Spiller. p. 521–522, Basel & Stuttgart, Schwabe, 1956.

KLEE, PAUL. Tagebücher von Paul Klee, 1898–1918. Cologne, DuMont Schauberg, 1957. Edited by Felix Klee.

KLUMPP, HERMANN, Abstraktion in der Malerei. 68. p. ill. Berlin 1932.

Das Kunstprogramm des Kommissariats für Volksaufklärung in Russland. *Das Kunstblatt* 3 no. 3: 91–93 1919.

KÜPPERS, PAUL E. Sammlung Herbert von Garvens – Garvensberg in Hannover. *Das Kunstblatt.* 1 no. 9: 260, 266 September 1917.

LAMM, ALBERT. Ultra-Malerei. p. 12 et passim München, Dürer-Bund, 1912. »99. Flugschrift zur Ausdrucks-Kultur«.

LARIONOV, MICHAEL & GONCHAROVA, NATHALIE. Luchism. Moscow, 1913. (Russian text on rayonism).

LEWIS, WYNDHAM. A review of contemporary art. *Blast* no. 2: 39–43 July 1915.

LOZOWICK, LOUIS. Modern Russian Art. New York, Société Anonyme, 1925.

MAEGHT, AIMÉ (PUBLISHER). 10 Ans d'Édition, 1946–1956. Paris, Maeght, Éditeur, 1956.

MALEWITSCH, KASIMIR. Die gegenstandslose Welt. München, Langen, 1927.

MARC, FRANZ. Briefe, Aufzeichnungen und Aphorismen. 2 vol. Berlin, Cassirer, 1920.

MARC, FRANZ. Die neue Malerei. *Pan* Berlin, 1912.

MARCHIORI, GIUSEPPE. Pittura moderna in Europa. Venezia, Pozza, 1950.

MÖLLER, FERDINAND, GALERIE. Blätter der Galerie. Köln. 1951–1954.

MICHEL, WILHELM. Münchner Graphik: Holzschnitt und Lithographie. *Deutsche Kunst und Dekoration* April–September 1905.

MOHOLY-NAGY, LÁSZLÓ. Vision in Motion. Chicago, Theobald, 1947.

MYERS, BERNARD. The Expressionist Generation. New York, Praeger; London, Thames & Hudson; Cologne, DuMont Schauberg, 1957.

MYERS, BERNARD. 50 Great Artists. New York, Bantam, 1953.

NEUE KÜNSTLERVEREINIGUNG. [Catalogue of the second exhibition.] Munich, 1910–1911. Includes article by Le Fauconnier.

PASSARGE, WALTER. Die Ausstellung des Staatlichen Bauhauses in Weimar. *Das Kunstblatt* 7 no. 10 1923.

PAULSEN, WOLFGANG. Expressionismus und Aktivismus. Strassburg, Heitz, 1934.

PHILADELPHIA. MUSEUM OF ART. The house and Walter Arensberg Collection: 20th Century Section. Philadelphia, 1954.

PHILLIPS, DUNCAN. The Phillips Collection – a Museum of Modern Art . . . Washington, D. C., 1952.

RAGON, MICHAEL. L'Aventure de l'Art abstrait. p. 16, 18, 22, 25–26, 29, 30. Paris, Laffont, 1956.

RAMSDEN, E. H. An Introduction to Modern Art. p. 31–37 ill. London, New York, Toronto, 1940.

RAPHAEL, MAX. Von Monet bis Picasso. 3. Aufl. München, Delphin, 1919.

RAVE, PAUL O. Kunstdiktatur im Dritten Reich. Hamburg, Mann, 1949.

RAYNAL, MAURICE (& others). History of Modern Painting. 3vol. ill. (col. pl.) Geneva, Skira, 1949–1950.

RAYNAL, MAURICE. Peintres du XXe Siècle. p. 20, 30 Genève, Skira, 1947.

READ, HERBERT. Art Now, rev. ed. London, Faber & Faber, 1948.

READ, HERBERT. The Philosophy of Modern Art. New York, Horizon, 1953.

RENÉ, DENISE, GALLERY. Prix Kandinsky, 1950. Paris, Galerie René, 1950. Preface by J. Cassou.

ROH, FRANZ. Expression und Konstruktion in der gegenstandslosen Malerei. Das Kunstwerk 9 no. 2 1955.

ROMAINS, JULES. Le Fauconnier. Paris, Seheur, 1927.

ROUSSEAU, MADELEINE. L'Art présent. Paris, La Hune, 1953.

SACHS, PAUL J. Modern Prints & Drawings. New York, Knopf, 1954.

SADLER, M. E. A Memoir by his son Michael Sadler, London, 1949.

SAMUEL, RICHARD & THOMAS, R. HINTON. Expressionism in German Life, Literature and the Theatre. Cambridge, Heffer, 1939.

SAN LAZZARO, G. di. Painting in France, 1895-1949. London, Harvill; New York, Philosophical Library, 1949.

SCHARDT, ALOIS J. Franz Marc. Berlin, Rembrandt, 1936.

SCHLITTGEN, HERMANN. Erinnerungen. München, 1926.

SCHMALENBACH, FRITZ. Jugendstil. Würzburg, Triltsch, 1935.

SCHMIDT, GEORG. Kleine Geschichte der modernen Malerei. Basel, Reinhardt, 1955.

SCHMIDT, GEORG. Sophie Taeuber-Arp. 152p. ill. Basel, Holbein, 1948.

SCHMIDT, PAUL F. Geschichte der modernen Malerei. 5. Aufl. Stuttgart, Kohlhammer, 1954.

SCHREYER, LOTHAR. Erinnerungen an Sturm und Bauhaus. p. 125–136 München, Langen & Müller, 1956.

SEDLMAYR, HANS. Die Revolution der modernen Kunst. p. 23–42 ill. Hamburg, Rowohlt, 1955.

SELZ, PETER H. German Expressionist Painting. 379 p. ill. University of California Press, 1957.

SEUPHOR, MICHEL, ed. L'Art Abstrait. Paris, Maeght, 1949.

SOCIÉTÉ ANONYME, INC. [Museum of Modern Art.] Report 1920–1921. [New York, The Association, 1921.]

SOCIETY OF PAINTERS. Program, December 10. St. Petersburg, 1912. Part I. Lecture by Kurnibovsky based on Kandinsky's art theories, especially Der Blaue Reiter.

STRAKOSCH, ALEXANDER von. Lebenswege mit Rudolf Steiner. Strassburg u. Zürich, 1947.

DER STURM. Berlin 1910–1919.
Numerous references to Kandinsky, e. g. no. 130 October 1912; no. 186 November 1913.

STUTTGARTER KUNSTKABINETT. 20. Kunst-Auktion: Sammlung Nell Walden (»Der Sturm«). Stuttgart, 1954.

SYDOW, ECKART VON. Die Deutsche Expressionistische Kultur und Malerei. Berlin, Furche, 1920.

TÉRIADE, E. Documentaire sur la jeune peinture: IV. Cahiers d'Art 5 no. 2 ill 1930.

THIEME, F. & BECKER, U. Allgemeines Lexikon der bildenden Künstler. Leipzig, Seemann, 1926.

THOENE, PETER (pseud. for MERIN). Modern German Art. Harmondsworth (England), Penguin, 1938.

TRIBÜNE DER KUNST UND ZEIT. Eine Schriftensammlung, hrsg. von K. Edschmid, Berlin, Reiss, 1919-1922.

UMANSKIJ, KONSTANTIN. Neue Kunst in Russland, 1914–1919. ill. Potsdam, Kiepenheuer, 1920.

UTITZ, EMIL. Über Kunst und Künstler. 102p. Leipzig, Haag-Drugulin, 1951. »Abraham ... bis ... Kandinsky«.

UTITZ, EMIL. Die Überwindung des Expressionismus. 190p. ill. Stuttgart, Enke, 1927. »Charakterologische Studien zur Kultur der Gegenwart«.

VENICE. ESPOSIZIONE BIENNALE INTERNAZIONALE DI ARTE. Catalogo, 25th. Venezia, Alfieri, 1950.
Charles Estienne: Wassily Kandinsky, p. 391–393.

VERKADE, WILLBROD. Le Tourment de Dieu. 283p. Paris, Rouart & Watelin, 1923.

VOLLMER, HANS. Künstlerlexikon des XX. Jahrhunderts. Leipzig, Seemann, 1957. Vol. III: K–P. Documentation extended from Thieme-Becker.

VSEROSSISKI S'EZD KHUDOZHNIKOV. Trudy Vserossiskago s'ezda Khudozhnikov ... Petrograd, P. Golika i A. Vil'borg 3 vols. 1912–1913. Includes On the Spiritual in Art, according to Lindsay.

WALDEN, HERWARTH. Einblick in Kunst: Expressionismus, Futurismus, Kubismus. Berlin, Der Sturm, 1917.

WALDEN, HERWARTH, ed. Expressionismus: Die Kunstwende. Berlin, Der Sturm, 1918.

WALDEN, NELL & SCHREYER, LOTHAR. Der Sturm: ein Erinnerungsbuch. passim ill. Baden-Baden, Klein, 1954.

WASHBURN, GORDON. Isms in Art since 1800. p. 45 Providence, R. I., The Author, 1949. Mimeographed.

WESTHEIM, PAUL. Gegenstandslose Kunst. Das Kunstblatt 5 no. 4 1921.

WESTHEIM, PAUL. Die Welt als Vorstellung. Potsdam-Berlin, Kiepenheuer, 1919.

WINKLER, WALTER. Psychologie der modernen Kunst. Tübingen, Alma Mater Verlag, 1949.

WOLF, GEORG J. Kunst und Künstler in München. Strassburg, Heitz, 1908.

WOLF, N. H. Derde jury vrye tentoonstelling der Onafhankellyke. De Kunst (Pays–Bas), 1915.

WRIGHT, WILLARD H. Modern Painting: its Tendency and Meaning. New York & London, Lane, 1915.

YALE UNIVERSITY ART GALLERY. Collection of the Société Anonyme. New Haven, Conn., Associates in Fine Arts, 1950.

ZAHN, LEOPOLD. Kleine Geschichte der modernen Kunst. III. Berlin, Ullstein, 1956.

ZERVOS, CHRISTIAN. Histoire de l'Art Contemporain. Paris' Cahiers d'Art, 1938.

ZERVOS, CHRISTIAN. Mathématiques et art abstrait. *Cahiers d'Art* 11 no. 1–2: 4–10 ill. 1936.

III. Exhibitions

1901 Munich, First Exh. of Phalanx.

1902 Munich, 2nd Exh. of Phalanx – Berlin, 5th Secession.

1903 Berlin, 8th Secession – Munich, 7th Exh. of Phalanx – Odessa.

1904 St. Petersburg – Munich, 9th Exh. of Phalanx – Rome, Intern. Exh. – Moscow – Dresden, Intern. Exh. – Munich, 11th Exh. of Phalanx – Warsaw – Odessa– Paris, Salon d'Automme – Berlin, 9th Secession.

1905 Rome, Intern. Exh. – Paris, Salon d'Automne – Paris, Union Intern. des Beaux Arts – Vienna, Secession – Moscow – Berlin, 2nd Exh. of the D. Künstlerbund.

1906 Prague – Paris, Salon d'Automne – Berlin, 11th Secession – Weimar, 3rd exh. of the D. Künstlerbund – Odessa, 17th Exh. of Russian Artists of the South.

1907 Dresden, Brücke – Rome, Intern. Exh. – Paris, 23rd Salon des Artistes Indépendants – Paris, Salon d'Automne – Odessa – Berlin, Secession.

1908 Paris, 24. Salon des Artistes Indép. – Salon d'Automne – Berlin, Secession.

1909 Paris, 25. Salon des Artistes Indép. – London – Paris, Salon d'Automne – Munich, First Exh. of the Neue Künstlervereinigung – Atelier-exh. – Odessa, Exh. Salon Izdebsky.

1910 Düsseldorf, Sonderbund – Munich 2nd Exh. of the N.K.V. – Paris, Salon d'Automne – Odessa, Intern. Exh. (54 numbers) – Moscow, Exh. (Karo Bube) – London.

1911 Paris, 27ième Salon des Artistes Indép. – Berlin, Neue Sezession – Munich, Der Blaue Reiter (Gal. Thannhauser).

1912 Moscow, Exh. (Karo Bube) – Munich, Der Blaue Reiter (Gal. Goltz) – Berlin, First Exh. of Der Sturm (Der Blaue Reiter etc.) – Paris, 28. Salon des Artistes Indép. – Cologne, Intern. Exh. of the Sonderbund – Zürich, Moderner Bund (Kunsthaus) – Berlin, 7th Exh. of Der Sturm (first K. collective exh. 1901 to 1912) – Munich, K. exh. 1902–1912 (Gal. Goltz).

1913 Hamburg, K. exh. – New York, Intern. Exh. of Modern Art, Armory Show – London – Berlin, Erster Deutscher Herbstsalon – Amsterdam.

1914 Köln (Kreis für Kunst). Munich, K. exh. (Gal. Thannhauser) – Odessa – Helsingfors, Der Blaue Reiter – Magdeburg, K. exh.

1915 Moscow.

1916 Stockholm, K. exh. (Gummesson) – Zürich, Galerie Dada – Oslo, K. and G. Münter exh.

1917 Zürich, Der Sturm – Helsingfors, K. exh. – St. Petersburg, K. exh.

1918 Berlin, Der Sturm.

1919 Moscow – St. Petersburg.

1920 New York, Société Anonyme – Moscow.

1921 Hannover, Gal. von Garvens – Moscow, K. exh. – Cologne, K. exh. (Nierendorf).

1922 New York, Soc. Anonyme – Berlin, K. exh. (Gal. Goldschmidt-Wallerstein) – Düsseldorf, Intern. Exh. – Munich, K. exh. (Gal. Thannhauser) – Stockholm, K. exh. (Gummesson) – Berlin, 1. Russische Kunstausstellung (v. Diemen).

1923 Hannover, K. exh. (Kestner-Gesellschaft) – New York, Soc. Anonyme – Weimar, Bauhaus Week (Museum) – Detroit – Berlin, K. exh. (Nierendorf).

1924 Dresden, K. exh. (Fides) – Vienna, K. Exh. – Belgrade – London – Zürich – Stockholm.

1925 Wiesbaden, K. exh. (Nassauischer Kunstverein) – Erfurt, K. exh. – Dresden, Seven Masters of the Bauhaus – New York, The Blue Four – Barmen, K. exh. (Museum) – Jena, K. exh. (Kunstverein) – Barmen, Bauhaus-Masters – Zürich, Intern. Exh. (Kunsthaus).

1926 Braunschweig, K. exh. – Oakland, The Blue Four – New York, Soc. Anonyme – Dresden, K. exh. (Gal. Arnold) – Dessau, K. exh. – Dresden, Intern. Exh.

1927 Mannheim, K. exh. (Museum) – Munich, K. exh. (Goltz) – Amsterdam, K. exh., and The Haag (Museum) – Zürich, K. exh. (Museum).

1928 Frankfurt/M., K. exh. (Kunstverein) – Brussels, K. exh. (Gal. L'Epoque) – Krefeld, K. exh. – Dresden, K. exh. (Fides) – Berlin, K. watercolors, (Gal. F. Möller) – Nuremberg, K. exh.

1929 Paris, K. exh. (Gal. Zak) – The Haag, K. exh. – Oakland, K. exh. (Art Gallery) – Antwerpen, K. exh. – Basel, Bauhaus Exh. – Brussels, K. exh. (Gal. Le Centaure) – Cologne, Deutscher Künstlerbund – Berlin, Juryfreie – Hamburg, Intern. Exh. – Berlin, The Blue Four (Gal. F. Möller) – Halle, K. exh. – Breslau, K. exh.

1930 Saarbrücken, K. exh. (Museum) – Essen, Bauhaus Masters (Museum) – Hollywood, The Blue Four – Paris, K. exh. (Gal. de France) – Krefeld, K. exh. (Museum) – Paris, Cercle et Carré – Düsseldorf, K. exh. (Gal. Flechtheim) – Kiel, K. exh.

1931 Berlin, K. exh. (Gal. Flechtheim) – Chicago, Eddy Coll. (Art Inst.) – Frankfurt/M., Vom Abbild zum Sinnbild – Zürich, K. exh. (Museum) – Mexico City, The Blue Four – San Francisco, The Blue Four – Brussels, L'Art vivant – Essen, Deutscher Künstlerbund.

1932 Berlin, K. exh. (Gal. F. Möller) – Santa Barbara, The Blue Four – Essen, K. exh. (Museum) – New York, K. exh. (Valentine Gall.) – Berlin, German Exh. (Gal. Flechtheim).

1933 London, Intern. Exh. – Beverly Hills, The Blue Four.

1934 Milan, K. exh. (Gall. del Milione) – Paris, K. exh. (Gal. Cahiers d'Art) – Hollywood, The Blue Four.

1935 Lucerne, These-Antithese-Synthese – San Francisco, K. exh. – Paris, K. exh. (Gal. Cahiers d'Art) – New York, Kandinsky, Weber, Klee (J. B. Neumann).

1936 New York, K. exh. (J. B. Neumann) – London, Intern. Exh. (Lefèvre Gall.) – Los Angeles, K. exh. – Paris, K. exh. (Gal. Bucher) – Cambridge, Mass., K. exh.

1937 Berne, K. and French Masters (Kunsthalle) – New York, K. exh. (Nierendorf) – Paris, Intern. Exh. (Museum Jeu de Paume) – Copenhagen, Exh. of Postexpress.

1938 New York, Three Masters of the Bauhaus (Nierendorf) – London, K. exh. (Guggenheim Jeune) – Exh. of 20th century German Art (New Burlington Gall.).

1939 New York, K. exh. (Nierendorf) – Paris, K. exh. (Gal. Bucher).

1940 Los Angeles, K. exh. (Stendahl Gall.).

1941 New York, K. exh. (Nierendorf).

1942 Paris, K. exh. (Gal. Bucher) – New York, K. exh. (Nierendorf).

1943 –

1944 Paris, K. exh. (Gal. Esquisse) – Basel, Konkrete Kunst (Kunsthalle) – New York, The Blue Four (Buchholz Gall.) – New York, K. exh. (Nierendorf).

1945 Basel, K. Memorial Exh. – New York, K. Mem. Exh. – Zürich, K. exh. (Gal. Eaux Vives) – Chicago, K. Mem. Exh.

1946 Paris, K. exh. – Pittsburgh, K. Mem. Exh. (Carnegie Inst.) – Paris, 1. Salon Réalités Nouvelles – Zürich, K. Mem. Exh.

1947 Paris, K. Retrospective (Gal. Drouin) – Liège, K. exh. – Amsterdam, K. exh. (Museum), also The Haag and Rotterdam.

1948 Basel, K. Retrospective – Munich, K. exh. (Gal. Stangl) – New York, K. exh. (Sidney Janis Gall.).

1949 Paris, Préliminaires á l'art abstrait (Gal. Maeght) – K. Epoque Parisienne (Gal. Drouin) – Munich, Der Blaue Reiter (Haus der Kunst) – New York, K. exh. (Sidney Janis Gall.).

1950 Basel, Der Blaue Reiter (Kunsthalle) – Paris, K. exh. (Gal. de Beaune) – Düsseldorf, K. exh. (Gal. Nebelung) – Munich, Die Maler am Bauhaus (Haus der Kunst) – London, K. exh. (Gimpel Fils) – Venice, 25th Biennale (special pavillon).

1951 Rome, K. exh. (Gall. dell'Obelisco) – Milan, K. exh. (Gall. del Naviglio – Paris, K. exh. 1900–1910 (Gal. Maeght).

1952 USA Traveling K. exh.: Boston (Inst. of Contemp. Art), New York (Knoedler), San Francisco (Museum of Art), Minneapolis (Walker Art Center), Cleveland (Museum), 1953: Miami (Lowe Gall.) – Paris, L'oeuvre du XXe siècle (Musée de l'art mod.).

1953 Lucerne, K. exh. (Gal. Rosengart) – Brussels, K. exh. (Ex Libris) – Cologne, K. exh. (Gal. F. Möller) – Paris, K. exh. (Gal. Maeght) – Lucerne, Deutsche Kunst (Museum) – Circulating K. exh. 1953/1954: Munich, Berlin, Hamburg, Cologne, Nuremberg, Stuttgart, Ulm, Wiesbaden, Mannheim.

1954 Munich, Kandinsky – Klee (Haus der Kunst) – Paris, Tapisseries (Gal. D. René) – K. Oeuvre gravé (Berggruen) – New York, Der Blaue Reiter (C. Valentin).

1955 Berne, K. exh. (Kunsthalle) – Kassel, Documenta (Fridericianum) – Cambridge, Mass., Der Blaue Reiter (Busch Reisinger-Mus.) – Munich, Kandinsky, Marc, Münter (Gal. Stangl).

1956 Stockholm, K. exh. (Samlaren) – Pasadena, The Blue Four – Berne, Von der »Brücke« zum Bauhaus (Gutekunst & Klipstein) – Coll. Rupf (Museum) – New York, K. Murals (Mus. of Mod. Art) – Seattle, The Blue Four (Museum).

1957 New York, K. exh. (Kleemann Gall.) – Munich, Kandinsky–Münter–Stiftung (Städt. Gal.) – Copenhagen, K. exh. (Statens Museum) – New York, German Art of the 20th Century (Mus. of Mod. Art – K. exh. (Chalette Gall.) – Paris, K. exh., aquarell. et gouaches (Gal. Maeght).

1957/58 Traveling K. exh. from Guggenheim Museum: London, Brussels, Paris, Lyon, Oslo, Rome.

Index of Names

Errata

p. 34 and p. 35 *for* H. Christ *read* H. Obrist

p. 62 *for* Rossi *read* Bossi

p. 88, 161, 191, 200, 203 *for* Point and Line
    to Surface *read* Point and Line to Plane

p. 172 *for* Pilonov *read* Filonov

p. 218 *for* Saw *read* saw